From Gluttony to Enlightenment

STUDIES IN SENSORY HISTORY

Series Editor
Mark M. Smith, University of South Carolina
Series Editorial Board
Martin A. Berger, University of California at Santa Cruz
Constance Classen, Concordia University
William A. Cohen, University of Maryland
Gabriella M. Petrick, New York University
Richard Cullen Rath, University of Hawai'i at Mānoa

A list of books in the series appears at the end of this book.

From Gluttony
to Enlightenment

*The World of Taste
in Early Modern Europe*

VIKTORIA VON HOFFMANN

UNIVERSITY OF
ILLINOIS PRESS
Urbana, Chicago, and Springfield

Expanded, revised, and translated edition of *Goûter
le monde: Une histoire culturelle du goût à l'époque
moderne*, published in French by PIE Peter Lang, 2013.
© 2016 by the Board of Trustees
of the University of Illinois
All rights reserved
1 2 3 4 5 C P 5 4 3 2 1
♾ This book is printed on acid-free paper.

Library of Congress Control Number: 2016953811
ISBN 978-0-252-04064-1 (hardcover)
ISBN 978-0-252-08214-6 (paperback)
ISBN 978-0-252-09908-3 (e-book)

Contents

Acknowledgments

The aim of this book was initially to provide an English translation of my first book, *Goûter le monde: Une histoire culturelle du goût à l'époque moderne* (2013), a history of taste in early modern Europe. However, writing on taste in another language made me think about related issues in a different way. This in turn was compounded by the experience I was gaining in the field while reading in other areas of scholarship, which helped me bring more details and texture to my inquiry, thus expanding upon some of the implications of my earlier work. I was also fortunate to receive insightful and encouraging reports from the two readers for the University of Illinois Press who commented on earlier versions of this book. These readers had been very carefully and wisely chosen, and provided many valuable comments and ideas that helped me reshape the manuscript and publish, in the end, a different book. The title *From Gluttony to Enlightenment: The World of Taste in Early Modern Europe* is only one among many suggestions provided by the first reviewer, who read the entire manuscript, for which I am particularly grateful.

Writing this book has been a long-term project during which I acquired numerous debts, the greatest of which is to Carl Havelange, who has been my supervisor, collaborator, and friend for many years now. With wit and enthusiasm, he introduced me to the wonderful research field of sensory history many years ago; the idea of this research on taste and eventually of this book stemmed from the many inspiring discussions I had with him. I am immensely grateful for his enlightening comments, kind critiques, invaluable guidance, and encouragement. I owe him more than I can say.

This book has also benefited enormously from the input of scholars who generously read and commented on part or all of its many drafts. For insightful observations, extensive commentaries, invigorating conversations, and tremendous support, I would like to thank especially Franz Bierlaire, Annick Delfosse, David Howes, Peter Scholliers, and Emma Spary. I would also like to extend particular thanks to David, who first suggested that I submit a book proposal to the Studies in Sensory History series. Moreover, all these years working on taste gave me numerous opportunities to discuss my work in progress with many scholars. At different times I greatly benefited from the advice and suggestions of Der-Liang Chiou, Ralph Dekoninck, Michel Delville, Frédérique Desbuissons, Alain Dierkens, Marie-Luce Gélard, David Gentilcore, Allen Grieco, Marie-Elisabeth Henneau, Pierre Leclercq, Isabelle Parmentier, Liliane Plouvier, Florent Quellier, David Szanto, Noëlie Vialles, Georges Vigarello, and Allen Weiss. My other debts are too numerous to list, but I am also grateful to the many departments, seminars, and colloquiums that gave me the opportunity to discuss my work in progress and helped me refine my work. To all go my warm and sincere thanks.

Writing a book in another language has been a challenge and a very rewarding experience. I would like to acknowledge the assistance I received from English native speakers who helped me improve the quality of my writing at different stages of this work. My sincere thanks go to Sara E. Wilson, who read and commented upon an earlier version of the entire manuscript, for which I am very grateful. I would also like to thank Scott A. Barton, who read the first draft of chapter 4. Portions of this book were edited in French in my book *Goûter le monde*; I thank Peter Lang for permission to use this material. I also wish to thank Mark Smith and Willis Goth Regier from the University of Illinois Press, who responded with such enthusiasm to the project of this book, and Laurie Matheson, Marika Christofides, and Julianne Rose Laut for their valuable contributions in finalizing the manuscript. Last and foremost, warm thanks to Ann Beardsley and Jennifer L. Comeau, who both displayed such a sharp eye in their thorough reading of the last draft of the manuscript.

Most of this research was funded by research fellowships from the Belgian National Fund of Scientific Research (F.R.S.-FNRS) and the University of Liège. I would like to express my gratitude for that support. I would also like to extend my thanks to the staff of the many libraries I have been working in during all these years, in particular from the University of Liège, Bibliothèque Nationale de France (Paris), Bibliotheca Hertziana (Rome), École Française de Rome, Concordia University (Montreal), and the University of Cambridge. For permission to reproduce pictorial material in their keeping, I thank the Master and Fellows of St John's College, Cambridge; the University of Glasgow Library; and the University of Liège, Bibliothèque Alpha.

In the end, I would like to mention the encouragement and warm friendship of my colleagues and friends. I owe special thanks to Pierre-François Pirlet,

Anneke Geyzen, Amandine Servais, Maïté Molina-Marmol, and Lucienne Strivay for their kindness, suggestions, support, and never-ending enthusiasm.

I would also like to thank my mother, Véronique de Lamalle; my father, Boris von Hoffmann; and my siblings, Astrid, Nikolai, and Harry. Food, taste, and cuisine have always been an important part of my family's life and culture, which is most likely the reason I ended up working on taste and the senses. This book is dedicated to them all, in memory of past and future lively discussions on taste and food.

Finally, I would like to express my utmost gratitude to Christophe Masson, my partner and best friend. I am immensely grateful for his help and support, as well as for his kindness and critical intelligence. I thank him for reading many drafts and engaging in challenging discussions, for his patience and encouragement, and for his wonderful sense of humor, which brings happiness and gourmandise to my life every day.

Introduction

De Gustibus Non Est Disputandum?

One must not dispute about tastes. Everybody has his own taste.
—*Dictionnaire de l'Académie françoise*, s.v. "Goût"

To each his own taste. . . . What a powerful commonplace. Why should we even bother discussing a topic such as taste? The sense of taste seems too personal to be generalized; it is so instantaneous that this sensation seems to precede thoughts and language; it may seem trivial to the point that such an insignificant matter should not deserve our interest. Associated with a form of animal instinct, the sensation of taste is deeply incommunicable, affective, utterly intimate, and idiosyncratic. Why then, and how, can we investigate the history of the sense of taste? What is more ephemeral than a flavor, more indefinable than pleasure? Taste, like any other form of sensory experience, always seems somehow to slip away. Yet although the ineffable aspects of sensation necessarily escape historical investigation, the elusiveness of the senses does not mean these cannot be addressed. Silences and impalpable objects are also part of history.[1]

What is, actually, the sense of taste? Defining such a complex phenomenon is definitely a challenge. Defined for centuries as the bodily sense ordered by nature to distinguish comestibles from poisons and to perceive flavors, *taste* also started to refer, from the seventeenth century onward, to that judgment discriminating the "good" from the "bad" in social behavior as much as in literature or in art.[2] The word then relates to the quality of the object perceived[3] as well as to the judgment of the person who perceives.[4] Taste, in a word, refers to pleasure and is used "figuratively in Morality about the judgments of the mind."[5] The use of a figurative sense of the word *taste*—meaning that it referred to something other than food—was innovative in the early modern era (c. 1500–1800), as *taste* had been used so far only to relate to the organ connected with food ingestion. As a result, in the late seventeenth and eighteenth centuries, a number of debates were held on the topic of taste in a variety of fields. New, suggestive metaphors started to circulate, sometimes remotely distant from the original bodily sense.

The first examples were found in the sixteenth century in mystical writings and related to the "Taste of God." Limited at first to specific theological realities, the uses of the concept of taste then spread to many other domains—for instance, to the *honnête homme* (honest man, or gentleman), who claimed to possess *bon goût* (good taste) in the seventeenth century. Finally, taste was used as the aesthetic judgment of beauty in the fine arts in the eighteenth century. As a result, this period witnessed an increasing interest in the topic of taste among scholars and the educated elite while revealing wider shifts in the meanings of taste.

The bodily taste of food and the spiritual taste of the mind are generally tackled by different research fields: food historians explore the former, while philosophers address taste within the field of aesthetics from the eighteenth century onward.[6] Hence there now is an extensive literature on the history of cuisine in early modern Europe, as well as on the rise of the aesthetic sense of beauty. Yet these two phenomena are most often considered as parts of different stories and have therefore rarely been examined together. But why should we consider these two forms of taste as parts of different histories? Metaphors of taste started to spread in the sixteenth century. What does this mean, exactly, regarding the history of taste as well as the history of early modern Europe? What is the connection between these different sorts of tastes, and how does this connection enlighten what we know of early modern cultures and, more generally, of modernity? One might argue that bodily and spiritual tastes refer to unrelated universes; indeed, there seems to be little in common between the pleasure in consuming food and an aesthetic appreciation of the fine arts. But why then was the same word chosen, in a specific historical context, to relate to both of these experiences? How did the people who started to use the word *taste* in a different context justify their decision to do so? What do the multiple uses of the word *taste* reveal regarding the meanings of this sense in early modern cultures?

The History of Taste: A History of Food?

There are two main research fields in which one may find information on the sense of taste, to which *From Gluttony to Enlightenment* is indebted: food and sensory history. First, food history has provided many valuable insights on the evolution of tastes over time and all over the world. The history of food, rooted in socioeconomic history and in historical approaches influenced by the École des Annales, really started to spread in the 1980s and especially from the 1990s onward.[7] In the context of these decades and especially since what Peter Scholliers has called the "cultural turn" in food history[8]—when cultural approaches to cuisine and food started to replace inquiries focused solely on food practices—a number of food historians have addressed the topic of taste, inscribed within the broader context of *food cultures*.[9] As a result, the history of taste seems to be well known today.[10] Yet since the development of food history and more broadly of *food studies*, the question of taste has systematically been reduced to a mere definition of food choices. The study of food practices is crucial, of course, to understanding food cultures of the past. But doesn't a history of the sense of taste limited to this sole aspect leave behind the very object (taste) one seeks to explore? If taste is merely a discussion of food choices, determining the content of these choices does not really tell us anything about what the sense of taste was or about the place it occupied in past cultures. Surprisingly, despite the wealth of titles listed in the bibliography of food studies, there are actually very few books genuinely related to the history of taste. Most works focus on cuisine instead of really embracing the question of taste as a sense.[11] For example, the introduction of Paul Freedman's *Food: The History of Taste* is significantly entitled "A New History of Cuisine," which is very revealing of the conceptions generally held about the sense of taste: a history of food and cuisine.[12]

Besides food studies, the second major historical development important for studies of taste is sensory history, or more generally, *sensory studies*. In the past few decades, an increasing number of works have been published that explore the multiple dimensions of the senses, notably in the field of history.[13] This research field has led to such a great deal of research that David Howes has called this transition toward the study of the senses a "sensual turn" or "sensual revolution."[14] However, not all five senses have been treated equally in these studies. Despite important research on diverse sensibilities, visual studies still prevail in the field, testifying, in a way, to the supremacy of sight, vision, and the image in contemporary Western societies.[15] Much research has also been done on the history of smell,[16] as well as on the history of the sense of hearing and especially of soundscapes.[17] Taste and touch, on the other hand, have been disregarded in comparison with extensive treatments of the other senses. More precisely, investigations of these two senses systematically focus on one specific domain: for the sense of taste, the focus is on food; for that of touch, the focus is on sexuality—and both foci have seen obvious success. Yet just as the history of sight is not limited to the study of painting, nor the history of smell to that of perfumes, the cultural significance of taste goes far beyond the topic of food and gastronomy; likewise, touch cannot simply be reduced to sensuality.[18] This epistemological reductionism consigns to obscurity broad swathes of early modern knowledge about the senses. Does one always necessarily need to apprehend the sensible by its objects or by sensory practices? Is it not possible to undertake a history of taste considered as a sensory experience of the world, released from the sole study of cuisine?

Although food and sensory history have provided fertile ground for historians interested in taste, crossovers between these two research fields are seldom, which is precisely what *From Gluttony to Enlightenment* wishes to do. Although the focus of this book is on a single sense, the relationship between taste and the other senses must also be addressed in order to determine the place and definition of taste in sensory cultures of the past. The research is thus inscribed within a larger perspective of sensory cultures, highlighting, for instance, associations between the senses in the past—taste often being connected to touch or smell. In the end, a multisensory approach is preferable, as it allows us to better grasp how taste was previously constructed.

A Lower Sense

To understand the position of taste among the five senses, one needs to consider at first the traditional "hierarchy of the senses," a very influential historical and cultural construction, elaborated in antiquity, within which each of the five senses, all endowed with a proper value, were classified in the following ascending order: touch, taste, smell, hearing, and sight. The higher senses—sight and hearing—were thought to be more spiritual, which made them useful for the development of the mind and of knowledge. The lower senses—taste and touch—were associated with the preservation of the body. They were perceived as more connected with matter and materiality and as revelatory of the physical proximity between humans and animals.[19] Between these two groups of senses, smell occupied a median position, divided between a spiritual dimension that linked it to the higher senses and a material foundation that connected it to the lower senses. As stressed by André du Laurens, court physician to King Henry IV and ordinary professor of medicine in Montpellier: "The human being consists of two parts, body and soul; sight and hearing are of use more to the soul than to the body, taste and touch are of use more to the body than to the soul; smell is of use to both."[20] The division between these two groups of senses (bodily senses vs. spiritual senses) was also founded on a distinction formulated in Aristotle's *De Anima* and assimilated and readjusted afterward. This distinction placed the "distance senses"—sight, hearing, and smell—in opposition with the "contact senses"—taste and touch.[21] In the first case, the sensory organ was understood to remain at a distance from its object during perception. This distance or gap conferred a higher reliability to sight and hearing, which were thought to be more objective and thus more valued. Thanks to this distance, the participation of reason and the mind was considered possible in the midst of sensory experience, which is why these "noble" senses were the only ones associated with spiritual activity; for a long time, they were the only senses admitted to the privileged realms of science, philosophy, and art, as emphasized by Carolyn Korsmeyer: "The sense of taste is among those subjects that have received only cursory theoretical attention on the part of philosophers. Even in earlier times when philosophy and science were indistinguishable, taste and its cousin smell were given short shrift in comparison with the 'higher' senses, especially vision. This relative neglect is especially noticeable in investigations of the abilities that represent the highest achievement of human effort: knowledge, morals, and art."[22] Taste was excluded from these noble realms because it belonged to the category of the "contact senses," which meant there was a greater proximity between the organ and the object of perception. Touch as well as taste—often considered a form of touch—enters into contact with its object. Because there is no possible sensation without this physical connection, taste and touch were thought to be more subjective; the intimacy that the "lower" senses have with material things partly explains their lower value.[23] For taste, the proximity is even deeper than for touch: the sensation occurs when food enters into contact with the tongue, melting in the mouth before penetrating the inner body where it will be digested, transforming the eater from the inside. Taste is the only sense that involves the assimilation and, in the end, the destruction of its object; it is also the only sense through which a part of the external world penetrates the body and changes it from the inside. The subject and object of perception mingle to the point of merging together.

According to ancient theories of perception, each sensation was admittedly considered a form of contact. Theories of vision, for instance, also involved an affective contact between visual rays and the material world; this theory prevailed for all of the senses.[24] But unlike the other senses, the qualification of taste as a contact sense remained throughout history despite evolutions in theories of perception. Regarding taste, there was a consistent emphasis on sensory contact characterized by a stronger intimacy between the person who perceives and what is perceived. This intimacy or lack of distance between perceiver and perceived would mean that taste was seen to resist all intellectualization. The sense of taste was therefore a mystery that left intact an enigma of sensibilities. Nevertheless, is it not possible to consider taste as a form of knowledge in experiencing the world? Which kinds of sensory knowledge can be revealed through this sense precisely because it *is* more intimate than the others?

Regarding the hierarchy of the senses, it is important to clarify that the intention of this book is to examine the construction and the meanings of this idea of a hierarchy of the senses, as it was elaborated in the past, and not to determine which sense was considered the most important in the early modern era, thus drawing an artificial, retrospective sensory hierarchy. Lucien Febvre and Robert Mandrou, for instance, have tried to establish such a chronological hierarchy, opposing a Renaissance that would have been more auditory and tactile to a seventeenth century allegedly more visually based.[25] As interesting as this idea was at the time, this theory is no longer considered relevant and historians have long known the importance of contextualising and historicising the meanings and uses of the senses in the past. Among others, Mark Smith argues that "a prevailing association characterizing the so-called proximate senses of smell, taste, and touch as 'premodern' is misleading and masks the ways in which non-visual senses proved central to the elaboration of modernity in a number of societies."[26] It is important to stress that if Febvre's model is invalid, in contrast, the theoretical concept of a "hierarchy of the senses"—that is, the intellectual idea of this construction, not the reality of sensory experience—was implied in early modern discourses related to the senses and sensory experience. Concurrently, there was a consistent suspicion regarding the nature of the bodily senses. During this period, there was a fascination with the alleged "nobility of sight," whereas taste was aligned to the degrading material dimension, causing it to be an unworthy subject of scholarly inquiry for centuries.

Obviously the lower value of taste in the past was also due to the moral implications of taste. All sensory delights were indeed very ambivalent during the Old Regime (i.e., prior to 1789). Food and taste were highly morally charged, as they were readily connected to the sin of gluttony. Taste, associated with a bodily need, naturally produced desire for food and intense bodily pleasure when fulfilled. The Church suspiciously considered these delights because abuses could lead to much harm, to the body and especially to the soul. As a result, pleasures of taste were not that easily and innocently enjoyed during the early modern era; discourses on taste would often include a warning against conspicuous consumptions and advise the readers to control their bodily senses—and, first of all, their sense of taste. Although the sin of gluttony and the sense of taste are two very different things, the dangers of the former would often corrupt the value of the latter, since without taste's delights there would be no food excesses and therefore no sin. Yet the early modern era also witnessed an increasing interest in the topic of taste, along with the rise of a new sensibility of taste, as people started to display new food preferences. A so-called modern or *nouvelle cuisine* was invented during the sixteenth and seventeenth centuries that strongly rejected medieval practices, while new rules of politeness and civility promoted new table manners and increasing culinary refinement.

In order to understand these tensions and contradictions, and to explain how the idea of a "hierarchy of the senses" was even thinkable, in which senses considered as more spiritual were opposed to others thought to be more corporeal, it is essential to explore the cultural framework that initiated and made these discourses conceivable. The idea of a sensory scale only makes sense insofar as the culture considered—European, in this case—is grounded in a dualistic conception of the world. Dualism is a heritage of antique philosophies (Platonic in particular) and monotheistic religions. It is deeply rooted in Western philosophy and is characterized by a system of oppositions between body and mind, senses and reason, the sensible and the intelligible, and later on, with the rise of naturalism, nature and culture.[27] The exploration of the historical meanings of the sense of taste brings us to address these questions and to expose how they evolved with the rise of the modern age. The work of anthropologist Philippe Descola constitutes here an important theoretical reference that will contribute to enlighten early modern gustatory culture in this historical investigation.[28] The theories he developed within his anthropology of nature partially explain the cultural upheaval that allowed for the invention of gastronomy at the end of the eighteenth and nineteenth centuries. His work also helps us to understand how a material sense, depreciated for its animality, rose to a level where it was claimed as an object of inquiry for art and science, as in the era of Brillat-Savarin.

The important insights provided by anthropology have persuaded me to engage in an intellectual history of taste and to focus not only on social and political considerations, and on questions of social standing, but moreover on the knowledge of taste and of senses that was produced, negotiated, and transformed between the sixteenth and the eighteenth centuries. Food studies and sensory studies have always been firmly rooted in interdisciplinary ap- proaches. Historians in these fields have for decades read inspiring works from anthropology, sociology, aesthetic and literary studies, philosophy, psychology, and many other related disciplinary areas, offering a variety of disciplinary approaches or theoretical frameworks. Seminal works such as Elias's *Civiliz ing Process*, Bourdieu's more socioeconomic model of taste developed in his well-known *La Distinction* (1979), and Habermas's *Structural Transformation of the Public Sphere* have opened up new and stimulating avenues of critical discussions on the history of taste.[29] Likewise, an extensive literature on the history of consumption and on material culture has developed in the past ten years, thanks to important contributions such as those of Maxine Berg. The early modern era was indeed a period that witnessed an incredible develop ment of commerce—notably an increasingly global food commerce—and of consumption—notably luxury food consumption. These important economic and social changes, along with an unprecedented development of print culture, naturally impacted the daily lives of people—rich or poor—in the seventeenth and eighteenth centuries. These socioeconomic transformations also certainly influenced the ways in which taste was conceived in the early modern era. However, although the cultural production of the sensory hierarchy is of course rooted in everyday economic experience with taste, the focus in this book will not be on food, consumption, and social and political conflicts, because there are already a number of remarkable works inspired by more socioeconomic approaches to food and taste. In contrast, because of the tendency of previous scholarship to reduce the question of taste to food, the sensory dimension of taste and the ways in which taste interacts with the other senses has received dis proportionately little attention in food and sensory history. I have thus decided to approach taste from a different angle and address taste from the perspective of an anthropological history of the senses. The major theoretical framework here is borrowed from cultural and historical anthropology, as *From Gluttony to Enlightenment*'s objective is to enlarge our perspective in order to address the cultural foundations of early modern European thinking about the sense of taste, and more broadly about sensory experience.

Moreover, I argue that a history of ideas is not necessarily disembodied, because discourses, as well as actions themselves, can be powerful actors in events.[30] Likewise, representations, defined by cultural history, are not to be considered as only mute vehicles or reflections of past events—within a rigid conception of a culture, thought of as a set of pictures constituting a preliminary program to experience the world, like with the older concepts of mentalities, structures, or *outillages mentaux*. Representations are also actors of change, as highlighted by recent research on the concepts of agency and performativity.[31] Likewise, the words chosen to relate to things are very revealing, as they display specific ways of thinking and being in the world.

A History of Sensory Cultures

Taste, as well as any other kind of sensibility, is partly indescribable, which makes it an especially complex historical object to address. Fragments of sources from the past can however provide some insights on early theories of perception as well as on the intellectual framework in which discussions on taste were held. Rather than focusing on one single kind of document—recipe books, for instance—I have chosen to address and confront a variety of different kinds of sources, which likely provides a broader and better understanding of the cultures of taste in the early modern era. More precisely, this research investigates four main registers: the culinary, medical, religious, and philosophical fields.

The culinary field is a classic one for inquiries on taste, where sources include cookbooks and treatises on civility. It is important to start from these texts, as cuisine was traditionally the privileged—if not unique—domain for investigations on the sense of taste. Food historians also frequently investigated the medical field, as medical systems such as humoral theory, influential up until the seventeenth century and beyond, are crucial to understanding medieval and early modern culinary practices and knowledge of food.[32] Since Galen and Hippocrates, it was admitted that diet depended on the eater's temperament. The products chosen, the ways of preparing and cooking them, and the seasonings were based on the humoral system, which aimed to create balanced dishes according to one's temperament. This temperament depended on the social position, age, and sex of the consumer, as well as on the seasons and movements of the stars.[33] Much of this history is already well known; thus, the aim here is not to repeat the system of the humors but to question the place of taste within this system, as taste also impacted how food related to individual temperaments.

Apart from dietetics and medicine, chemistry books are also useful sources to explore this "scientific" register.[34] Progressively, as we move away from the Renaissance, we see that practitioners started to distance themselves from the ideas of Galen and Hippocrates, who had dominated medicine for centuries. After centuries of medical research mainly centered on dietetics, the focus began to move away from temperaments toward the physiology of the organ of taste and the phenomenon of digestion. Starting in the sixteenth century, chemists became more influential and proposed a "chemistry of taste," elaborating new theories that would later be questioned and provoking controversies among specialists—for instance, between the iatrochemists and iatraphysicists, a debate that is addressed in chapter 5.[35] How did the evolution of medical and scientific theories influence the ways in which taste was conceptualized in the past? Other important sources on sensibilities include treatises of the senses and works on physics. Physics was indeed defined as "the science whose objects are the natural things," which was by then related to the study of nature and its manifestations.[36] This is the reason why works on physics often included chapters on the five senses.[37]

Furthermore, during early modern times, the religious dimension was obviously fundamental. The condemnation of gluttony as a sin by the Catholic Church reveals a negative value associated with taste, seen as directly linked to the carnal dimension of pleasure. From the codification of the seven deadly sins by Pope Gregory I until the success of gastronomy in the nineteenth century, the Church's tolerance of gluttony evolved and necessarily impacted representations of taste. Besides writings on gluttony and the seven deadly sins, broader spiritual considerations of the sense of taste can be found in a variety of documents. In addition to those customary sources—books of sermons, *artes moriendi*, moral works, and devotional literature—my investigation also includes more marginal sources, such as mystical and demonological writings. Historians have rarely considered these texts because of their emphasis on food instead of taste, which has brought them to address mainly the sin of gluttony, though the religious appropriation of taste was actually much more eclectic.

Finally, the philosophical field has probably been the most neglected by food historians who have investigated the history of taste. The early modern era is a particularly interesting context to consider in this regard, as it witnessed many important philosophical fractures likely to have contributed to the transformation of the representations of taste. If dualism and Cartesianism played an undeniable part in the depreciation of the bodily senses, in contrast, empiricism and sensualism, at the end of the seventeenth and throughout the eighteenth centuries, led to the celebration of sensory experience as the foundation of knowledge in the Enlightenment, as chapter 3 clarifies. Therefore, how did the conceptions of taste evolve in the eighteenth century, considering this was an era in which arose a new curiosity toward sensory worlds?

In the end, by addressing these four registers—the culinary, medical, religious, and philosophical fields—*From Gluttony to Enlightenment* aims to track early modern discourses on taste in many different cultural settings in order to explore the question of taste without reducing its discussion to food. This is not to say that food is not a constant reference point for taste at all—because, of course, it is, food being the object *par excellence* of the knowledge, practices, and emotions about taste—but that we should never lose sight of the intimate links between food practices and the wider cultural and anthropological contexts in which the former necessarily take their meaning. As such, food relates to many other and very different phenomena as the analysis proceeds, from morality, religion, and demonology to science, philosophy, and aesthetics. Rather than studying what was eaten, the aim of this research is thus to analyze the ways in which people thought about, discussed, constructed, and invented the concept of taste in early modern Europe, hence providing a better understanding of the broad social and cultural contexts in which "taste" arose. By embracing the question of taste from the perspective of a sensory history and highlighting the different uses of the word *taste*, this work provides a better understanding of the cultural and social values of taste as well as of the multiple meanings of the sense of taste in early modern Europe. Ultimately, the objective of this book is to understand how a lower sense, closely associated with the sin of gluttony and with the animal part of human beings, would eventually lead to the invention of gastronomy in the nineteenth century, promoting an art and a science of taste, during a period in which the social importance of taste became widely accepted and table manners linked to the idea of civilization.

The Example of Early Modern France

The chronological frame of my inquiry is the early modern era, with sources predominantly from the seventeenth and eighteenth centuries, during which a crucial transformation regarding the cultures of taste occurred. This period is a significant one for an investigation of taste, notably because in this moment, a figurative sense of taste really entered common usage in the French language. Moreover, at the same time, cuisine itself went through an important revolution when food practices inherited from the Middle Ages slowly transformed into a modern form of culinary art. France, whose cooks inspired every important table in Europe, would appear as a model in this respect.

Considering the large variety of primary sources addressed, an investigation of seventeenth- and eighteenth-century discourses on taste originating from all countries of Europe (addressing many different cultural traditions such as those of Britain, Italy, Germany, Spain, the Netherlands, Poland, and others) would have been an impossible enterprise on which to embark, as I did not wish to dilute the rich diversity of sources or the chronological frame. My objective is to highlight cultural evolutions that occurred through time and to enlarge the number of potential sources of a history of taste. For this reason, I decided to reduce the cultural and geographical area of the research and to focus on France, which in the period of interest appeared to be a particularly significant case study for analyzing the ways in which people invented the concept of *taste* in early modern Europe. In the seventeenth and eighteenth centuries, France was seen as a model of cuisine and of taste. French cooks, fashions, and recipe books inspired all the important tables in Europe, while their country was presented as a model of civility—a word that at the time meant "civilization," as evidenced by Norbert Elias—and as the center of the *bon goût*.[38] The French, in particular, were eager to underscore the preeminence of their cuisine, which allegedly reflected the supremacy of their culture, language, and politeness, all of which they considered to represent the most accomplished models in Europe. According to Antoine de Courtin, author of a civility treatise that was a true bestseller, it was believed that young people "would be civil in every country, if they are so in the French fashion,"[39] and that foreigners "only eat good food when they have French cooks."[40] Cuisine was especially connected with the *savoir-vivre à la française*—even bread was thought to be of a higher quality in Paris.[41] Both treatises of civility and cookery books used overly enthusiastic rhetoric celebrating the superiority of French manners and cuisine, as in François-Pierre de La Varenne's *Le Cuisinier françois* (The French Cook): "[O]ur France [being] higher in honor than any other nations of the world, regarding civility, courtesy and politeness in all sorts of conversations, is not less valued for her way of living, honest and delicate. And the city of Paris prevailing eminently over all the Provinces of the Kingdom, from which she is the metropolis, the capital and the seat of our Kings, it is without any doubts that her subordinates will follow her in this matter."[42]

According to Peter France, "similar views were being expressed all over Europe," which does not mean, of course, that "foreigners [did not] sometimes [resent] this superiority."[43] The French model—of cuisine, civility, culture, and even politics—was criticized and mocked as much as it was celebrated and appropriated all over Europe. Nevertheless, the cultural influence of France in seventeenth- and eighteenth-century Europe cannot be denied, although the hyperbolic conception presented above must obviously be nuanced and re-placed within a broader context. Regarding the domain of civility and politeness, for instance, France was largely influenced by the Italian models of the courtier as depicted by authors such as Baldassare Castiglione, Giovanni Della Casa, and Stefano Guazzo, whose works were translated into French and widely diffused in Europe.[44] Yet, though exaggerated, this rhetoric remains significant and re-vealing, as it was commonplace during the Old Regime. These ideas spread through a variety of sources and were used as a form of publicity to celebrate the superiority of the French art of living—therefore justifying the purchase of many books supposedly revealing its secrets. The same goes for all the books published on theories of taste in the context of the development of aesthetics in the late seventeenth and eighteenth centuries. Likewise, the focus on France here does not mean that there were no discourses on taste to be found in other countries. On the contrary, discussions on the various meanings of taste were in fact held all over Europe at the same time, especially in Britain and Germany, and some leading French formulations of taste actually stemmed from foreign authors such as David Hume.[45] Many influential English and German texts were rapidly translated into French and discussed by the philosophes and polite read-ers in France. France is thus considered here as a case study exemplifying wider discussions that were held elsewhere in Europe as well in the early modern era.

My research is based on an extensive corpus of printed primary sources, mostly in the French language. Apart from cooks, who often (though not al-ways) offered more practical considerations, the majority of the writers chosen for this study were members of the educated and cultivated elite of the time—scholars, doctors, philosophers, moralists, churchmen, writers, *mondains*, and polite readers. The major works—recognized as such by the members of the Republic of Letters, published within several editions, translations, or adapta-tions—have been privileged because they were influential and as such reveal commonly shared ideas, signs of a generality of knowledge related to taste that can be traced from philosophical, religious, medical, and culinary books of the early modern times. My objective, here, is clearly to be "comprehensive rather than exhaustive."[46] The aim is to confront a series of documentary fields rather than to try to exhaust the resources of any single one of them.

In conclusion, *From Gluttony to Enlightenment* intends to explore the trans-formations of learned discourse about taste as a sense, tracing its development from an empirical product of the senses to its metaphorical uses in religious, culinary, moral, and aesthetic treatises. The history of taste, whether celebrated or silenced, leads us to explore the margins of early modern society, revealing what seventeenth- and eighteenth-century polite readers and writers wished to place at the peripheries of knowledge. Studying what people of the past tried to repress or celebrate tells us much about their culture, as well as about our own. Today, taste has acquired such a huge importance in our experience of the world—without, however, completely ceasing to reflect its ambiguous heritage. The aim of my work is hence to discover how a lower and animal sense was gradually transformed into a higher form of judgment involving body and mind, an object of a human distinction.

1 The "Silences of Taste"

> It is bad-mannered to criticize the victuals or the sauces during the meal; constantly speaking of grub is an obvious mark of a sensual soul and of a lower education.
>
> —[Courtin], *Nouveau traité de la civilité*, 176

A "Revolution of Taste"?

The history of taste is deeply intertwined with that of cuisine, to the point that both often tend to be confused. Although taste cannot be reduced solely to the culinary universe, the latter is nevertheless the first and most obvious domain in which one might expect to find discourses on taste. Therefore, it is only natural to start this investigation of taste in the kitchen, with food and cooks, in order to see how taste, food, and the senses interact in the kitchen and in cookery books, and then more broadly in the polite world. How did cooks relate to the sense of taste, which plays such an obvious role in their daily practice? Are there discourses on taste to be found in cookery books? To what extent did the food people actually consume in early modern France influence the ways they thought about and discussed the sense of taste?

The early modern history of food is well known today, thanks to a range of historical research published from the 1980s onward.[1] This chapter does not again thoroughly investigate the transformations of food practices from the sixteenth to the eighteenth centuries; however, it is important to recall a few striking features of the social and cultural contexts impacting the evolution of attitudes toward food. Several scholars have demonstrated the major cultural turn that occurred during the sixteenth and seventeenth centuries, which represented a crucial transition between medieval cooking and modern forms of cuisine, so different from one another that many specialists consider this transition to have been a true "revolution."[2] The entire cookery process was transformed—the products, techniques, and seasonings, along with the presentation of dishes. If for centuries and up until the Renaissance people had enjoyed spicy and bittersweet dishes, they progressively started distinguishing the sugary from the salty flavors, while also diminishing the amounts of spices and combining them with local herbs like parsley. They also grew fond of vegetables, which had not been praised by medieval elites.[3] Furthermore, the whole foundation of cookery changed. The *fonds de cuisine*, so intimately linked to French haute cuisine, appeared at the time and were used as basic preparations for an array of delicate dishes and sauces.[4] Named "jus" (juice) or "coulis" (cullis), butter liaisons (white sauce) and flour liaisons (roux, also called "fried flour") naturally occupied an important place in early modern cookbooks.[5] These cuisine *fonds* favored the appearance of richer sauces with smoother textures, which replaced the acid or bittersweet dishes from the past.

The new culinary techniques and seasonings actually aimed to enhance the proper flavor of each ingredient, or, in the words of cooks, to valorize *le vray goust* (the real taste) of food.[6] The fracture with regard to ancient culinary habits is, then, obvious. The cultural and symbolic importance of spices had recently started to decline as the market grew significantly in the sixteenth century, making these luxury goods available to a much larger variety of consumers and thus losing their value as a distinctive feature of elite cuisine. Haute cuisine started to be defined less by the sole use of luxury products than by the delicacy of preparation, as it acknowledged the ephemeral and continually changing fashions of the moment. Every sign of earlier habits was perceived as vulgar and an index to membership in an inferior social rank.[7]

In the end, new products, techniques, and culinary principals provoked—or were stimulated by—a profound transformation of the sensibilities of taste in early modern France. Travel accounts are illuminating in this regard, since they contain several colorful examples of French repulsion toward foreign dishes, often considered too spicy.[8] Culinary habits had definitely changed in France. Indeed, the seventeenth century thus seems to have represented a "revolution of taste," as far as food practices and individual sensations are concerned. But what about discourse? What was written on food, taste, and the pleasures of eating at a time in which modernity transmuted food habits to engage the international triumph of French cuisine? How was this transformation translated from the ways one tasted the flavors of the world into the words of culinary narratives? More generally, what kinds of cultural representations of the sense of taste can be found within the culinary field?

First Discourses on Taste

Cooks are obviously very concerned with matters of taste. In order to prepare a successful dinner, they need to choose wisely the best products and ingredients required for each dish and decide how to prepare them. They use their senses to make these choices, observing, smelling, touching, and tasting the products at each stage of the cooking process, from raw ingredients to the final dish. The senses thus play an important part in cuisine, as cooking is an embodied and very sensory form of practice and knowledge, which required a lot of time and quite intense physical engagement. Taste was only one among many physical and sensory tools used by cooks in their daily work. But what did these practitioners have to say, precisely, on this particular sense?

Unfortunately, traces of earlier cooks' involvement with food are scarce, since for centuries cooks transmitted their knowledge through speech and practice, leaving very few written records behind, except for rare extracts in a few old recipe books. Culinary manuals were for long mainly designed for cooks and maîtres d'hôtel, or for the master of the household. They typically had a practical purpose, which explains why most of them were so concise. Manuals were habitually written in vulgar languages, not in Latin, which is an indication that they were likely written by cooks for cooks.[9] The author, addressing his peers, went straight to the point without annoying his readers with unnecessary details that were self-evident to the practitioner. This is the reason why many of these texts often seem confused and disorganized to contemporary readers, as they display no attention to techniques or proportions. Seldom were references to taste made within this kind of literature, except for some vague judgments on the "better" flavor of a special dish or ingredient. Furthermore, cookery books were originally devoid of prefaces and went directly into the heart of the matter, as, for instance, in *Le cuisinier Taillevent*: "Here starts the book of the cook Taillevent. Follows the Viandier to match all manners of meat that Taillevent, cook of the king our lord, made to realize boiled as well as roasted, marine as well as freshwater fish; sauces; spices and other things convenient and necessary as will be shown afterwards. And in the first place the first chapter. White wheelbarrow of capons."[10] The recipe of this dish immediately follows the reference to it on the first page. The only preliminary information in the book indicates that Taillevent was a royal cook.

But culinary writings would dramatically change during the early modern era. The invention of the printed book and its incredible development would favor the ever-increasing influence of cookery books.[11] It provoked a considerable extension of literacy, opening a new potential market for cookbooks as well. Recipe books were actually among the earliest printed books in Europe, although this did not necessarily lead to new forms of culinary writings. As stressed by Alain Girard, "the first century of printing did no more than increase the circulation of the manuscript texts of the previous age,"[12] a fact all the more true in France, where no new recipe book was published between 1550 and 1650. In this particular country, all culinary publications were actually reissues of previous works, such as the *Platine en françois*, known as *De l'Honneste volupté*, or *Le Viandier de Taillevent*, another great library success.[13] Food historians explain this absence of publication, which concerns only France, by pointing to troubles connected with the Wars of Religion (1562–1598) and the Thirty Years' War (1618–1648).

Evidently, the absence of literary novelty did not stop the evolution of culinary practices, but it is difficult to redraw its progression in a detailed way, for there are no records to testify to it. We can only note the outcome of the process, when the first recipe book came out in 1651 after a century without textual novelty.[14] The *Cuisinier françois*, attributed to François-Pierre de La Varenne, initiated a new generation of cookbooks, revealing the modern culinary principles that were slowly established during the previous century.[15] As the first book to disclose the new culinary practices, it saw incredible success and was often edited and translated (when not counterfeited, as soon as 1652).[16]

With his *Cuisinier françois*, not only did La Varenne offer a different form of cuisine, he also created an innovative cookery book. Like older manuals, still addressing his peers, he continued to present recipes in which the instructions were reduced to the essential. But the text had a much clearer structure as well as a true unity in style, as evidenced by the numerous references from one recipe to another. The work was also much easier to use, thanks to the presence of a table of contents. This clarification and simplification phenomenon of culinary writings would accelerate during the early modern era and would lead to food dictionaries in the eighteenth century, after several intermediate stages in which the ingredients were considered in alphabetic order. The aim was to extend the readership and reach a wider audience, though it is difficult to evaluate this tendency with any accuracy.[17] Librarians/publishers wished to increase their sales beyond the reduced circle of the maîtres d'hôtel from prestigious families, and sought to interest the members of low and medium nobility, as well as the rising bourgeoisie. The cookery books' many allusions to the moderation of expenses were clearly meant to address this potential new public.[18] Indeed, cooks such as La Varenne wished to expose "not only the most refined and delicate ways of dressing meats, pastries and other things served on the table of the *Grands* [great ones]" but also advice regarding "most common and ordinary things produced in the food of households that only make a regulated and moderate expense."[19] Nicolas de Bonnefons likewise insisted on this in his books. He was the first author in France to dedicate his work to women, which is another sign of the rise of a new audience.[20] His *Iardinier françois* (French Gardener) was furthermore meant not for professional gardeners but for amateurs concerned with improving the quality of their gardens.[21] He wished thus to address useful advice to masters and mistresses in a book whose format was precisely reduced so as to ease its consultation and transport.[22] The authors who would succeed the most in interesting the bourgeois readers would likewise become bestsellers of cookery literature: La Varenne, Massialot, and Menon.[23] The progressive emergence of a "bourgeois cuisine," when approaching the nineteenth century, also aimed toward culinary simplification, proposing delicious but unpretentious dishes.

However, if most cooks pretended to address more modest readers, the recipes proposed in these manuals were not always accessible to all fortunes. This is the case for L.S.R. in particular,[24] who clearly despised the bourgeois and their cuisine, as evidenced in his vigorous critiques of their bad taste, their outrageous expenses, or their ridiculous savings.[25] Despite its claims of opening toward a larger public, haute cuisine thus remained in the hands of the elite, as revealed by cooks' efforts to describe *une cuisine à la mode des grands* (cooking in the fashion of the great ones).[26] Moreover, many cookbooks related less the daily dishes than the exceptionally sumptuous meals, intending to delight the sense of taste and to stimulate the imagination of the reader, as disclosed by Nicolas de Bonnefons: "It [would not be] easy for me to titillate your taste by only treating you with the ordinary, which would only be to provide for your food."[27] It was especially by displaying fancy banquets that cooks could expect to intrigue their readers.

The Exquisite Discernment of the "True Taste" of Food

The multiplication of printed cookbooks is a sign of a slow rise of interest in matters of food and taste among the reading public. So is the content of this new generation of cookery books. The most significant invention of the time was to introduce the recipes with a preface, a creation probably linked to a desire to expand the readership. These preliminary pages are remarkably significant for this research, for they disclose an unprecedented discourse on taste and cuisine. They were written either by the cooks or by their librarians (the editors of the books). After centuries of silence, cooks expressed themselves in these introductions and revealed their personal conceptions of cuisine and taste—a very innovative development.

The first point highlighted in these prefaces was the pioneering nature of modern cuisine, which cooks were very much aware of and had already used for publicity purposes. This pretention appeared as soon as 1651 in the *Cuisinier françois*, presented as a book "whose matter and title seem new in Paris, for no such one was ever printed before."[28] The concept of "novelty" is, of course, commonplace in culinary writings, although the evolution of cuisine is inevitably gradual, if not conservative.[29] "Ancient" and "modern" elements were inevitably mixed with one another, yet the idea of innovation was highlighted in order to increase sales.[30] Most importantly, along with these expected pleas for novelty, a new form of rhetoric spread that celebrated the discernment of taste. Massialot also insisted: "One will thus find here many things unknown in the cookbooks printed before, things dressed with much more art and a better taste, and explained in a clearer and more understandable way."[31] The claim of culinary modernity can be traced in most introductions after the *Cuisinier françois* and would still be topical twenty years later when L.S.R. published *L'Art de bien traiter* (The Art to Treat/Dress Well), though in this case the cuisine stigmatized was La Varenne's.[32] Several recipe books had been published since the mid-seventeenth century, so each author had to distinguish himself from his predecessors.[33]

According to its defenders, modern cuisine was characterized by the order displayed on the table as well as on the plate, and by the exquisite refinement of dishes, capable of seducing the most distinguished society. Recent cookbooks stood against older practices considered as "confused mixtures of diverse species"[34] and costly "profusions that bring no delight to taste."[35] The main critique was the "prodigious overflowing of dishes" and the unnecessary "abundance of ragoûts and gallimaufries, the extraordinary piles of meats," supposedly constituting good food.[36] This "ancient . . . way of dressing and serving things" was, according to cooks, utterly "disgusting."[37] In contrast, the aim of modern cuisine was to respect and enhance the authentic flavor of each ingredient, sublimated and not hidden anymore behind spicy cookery. Proudly, L.S.R. explains that "it is not . . . these mountains of roasts, the successive services of *assiettes volantes*[38] and weirdly served entremets, in which it seems that artifice and nature have been entirely exhausted in the satisfaction of the senses, which is the most sensible object of our delicacy of taste." Rather, it is "the exquisite choice of meats [food], the refinement of their seasoning, the courtesy and the neatness of their service, their quantity well-proportioned to the number of people, and finally the general order of things which essentially contribute to the goodness and elegance of a meal." With this cuisine, "the mouth and the eyes equally find their charms by an ingenious diversity that satisfies the senses and that furnishes them with abundance and with everything that is capable of filling their desires and inclinations."[39]

Modern cuisine thus promoted the values of order and diversity, on the plate as much as on the table, and celebrated the delights of a refined sense of taste. The respect of the authentic flavor of foodstuffs was crucial in this culinary rhetoric. Some authors, like Nicolas de Bonnefons, deliver real pleas on the topic, insisting in respecting "*le vray goust* [the true taste] that must be given to each sort of meat and fish," in contrast with older practices when cooks used to "disguise and garnish their dishes in confusion," using the same kinds of spices all the time and hence giving "the same taste to all their dishes," which was definitely not a way to please and stimulate the taste of the audience.[40] In the past, they argued, the culinary habits seemingly led to the indistinctness of foodstuffs. This confusion was often perceived much like a disguise. Older culinary practices—such as mixing ingredients with such chaos that they be-came unrecognizable—were stigmatized by modern cooks for their disorder. These cooks argued that eaters greatly disliked that all dishes were monotonous and composed of similar flavors. According to cooks, with modern cuisine, the quality of the dish would not come from a mysterious and complicated prepara-tion but from the practitioner's ability to highlight the individual flavor of each ingredient. As Nicolas de Bonnefons declared in a famous passage:

> Let a *potage de santé* be a good domestic broth, well-enriched with good and care-fully chosen meats, and reduced into *bouillon*, with no *hachis* [chopped vegetables or meat], mushrooms, spices, nor any other ingredients, but let it be simple, since it bears the name *de santé* [healthy]; and let the cabbage soup taste entirely of cabbage, a leek soup of leeks, a turnip soup of turnips, and so on, leaving *bisques, hachis, pannades* [elaborate mixtures of chopped meat, diced vegetables, breadcrumbs] and other *déguisements* [disguises, deceptions]. . . . What I say about soup I mean to apply generally as a law for everything that is eaten.[41]

According to food historians, the quest for the "true taste" of food was not only rhetorical; it seems indeed that the new culinary principles did favor the authentic flavor of each ingredient, as did the butter-based cookery, fat-based sauces, and the increasing use of cuisine *fonds*, which allowed the creation of very diversified dishes.[42] Spices, used in moderation, were combined with local condiments and common herbs. Sometimes the seasoning was reduced to a minimum, "just with salt," in order to let the flavors fully express themselves.[43] In contrast, older practices would appear to have resulted in a series of identi-cal dishes, likely to become tedious, as they were always constituted with the same blend of spices.[44] The aim was to mix all the ingredients and transform them so as to make their components unrecognizable.[45] Modern culinary prin-ciples, added to the use of an increasing number of new products, were thus an opportunity to discover numerous new flavors, explored through a lighter cuisine and perceived as more natural. In opposition to a secular conception of culinary practices as a form of disguise—the word is everywhere—of food, cooks wanted the flavor of each element to be identified and enhanced, at a time when classical art and literature similarly celebrated the virtues of Nature.

Several techniques were used that favored order and simplicity within cuisine. First of all, it was crucial to choose products of a certain quality. Choosing only seasonal produce for menus was also essential for fruit and vegetables as well as for meat, if one wished to eat them "in their goodness."[46] At a time when gardeners developed greenhouse technologies, allowing the consumption of products at every moment of the year, a few voices rose against these artificial practices, pleading for a respect for the natural rhythms of nature.[47] Besides the quality of the products, it was essential to monitor the cooking time since an extended amount of time was likely to reduce taste (notably of meat, which was preferably cooked over high heat).[48] For each ingredient, "the perfect cooking" had to be reached.[49] So, according to L.S.R., for instance,

> to say the truth, the best and the healthiest way to eat roast that can be, is to devour it right out of the spit in its natural juice and not completely cooked, without bringing such inconvenient cautions that destroy in their weird way the true taste of things. Like those who, willing to make a good meal with a sirloin, after taking it out of the spit, cut it into pieces, add water, vinegar, stock, pepper and salt confusedly, garlic, shallots, lemon or orange peel, nutmeg, capers and an infinity of other hodgepodge that change the nature of this meat after a quarter of an hour boiling, which, by that way, stiffens itself and becomes harder and more insipid than wood. I maintain that this one, cooked conveniently according to its size and in the beginning gently simmered, considering its thickness, must be eaten first and all greedily in its juice with salt and a little white pepper only.[50]

Adding myriads of ingredients did not necessarily contribute to a better taste of food. In short, cooks would say, "each meat in its natural juice is always nicer."[51] Separate cooking processes were also very useful, because they preserved the individual flavor of all products, which could afterward be reunited in the same container for a joint preparation.[52] Moreover, a disagreeable element was likely to corrupt the whole dish, and this had to be avoided. For instance, the veal's skin and feet were better cooked "in a separate pot, because their broth that tastes like *tripes*, would spoil the others if cooked together in a big pot with the other butchery meat."[53] The "simple," "natural" taste was always considered better.[54] All these pleas reveal an increasing concern and a refined sensibility toward matters of taste on the part of cooks and the reading public, as evidenced by the cooks' attention to discerning and enhancing the delicate flavors of foods prepared in a "natural way."

A Sensory Experience of Cookery

Modern cookery books gave a voice to cooks who, after centuries of silence, began to share their experience with their fellow practitioners and soon with the reading public at large. They started by underlining their previous experience acquired within illustrious households, a guarantee of expertise and also a selling point for their books. Several mention prior positions on the front page, as did La Varenne, who presented himself as the "Escuyer de Cuisine de Monsieur le Marquis d'Uxelles," to whom the book was dedicated. This was a prestige tool, the dedication being the proof that the author was able to cook in the elite's fashion. More interestingly, experience was also a guarantee of the cooks' own taste, and especially as a proof they were able to satisfy the elite's delicate tastes. In the mid-seventeenth century, members of the court and of polite society were considered as the owners of good taste, which they defined and the cooks only sought to reproduce. By then, the cook most often attributed all the credit of the work to the talent of his master, considered as the sole owner of good taste. Reduced to the position of simple executioner, the cook did not yet present himself as the best culinary expert.[55] The fact that most cookbooks were published anonymously is another indication of this reduced position. Even an audacious and impertinent cook such as L.S.R. did not find it appropriate to sign *L'Art de bien traiter*. The presence of the name "La Varenne" on the title page of the *Cuisinier françois* is in this regard exceptional. It reveals the high self-esteem of a cook who considered his own work to be a "masterpiece,"[56] although he then attributed all the merit to the Marquis d'Uxelles; La Varenne was, moreover, not the real name but actually a pseudonym of François-Pierre.[57] For the moment, members of court society were still thought to be the exclusive representatives of delicate taste. But there would be a major cultural change in the eighteenth and even more in the nineteenth centuries that would lead to the appropriation of taste by cooks, as demonstrated by the increasing tendency of the chefs to sign their works with their own names.[58] This process eventually led to the rise of the cooks' status, which dramatically changed between the seventeenth and nineteenth centuries, as Sean Takats demonstrates in his book *The Expert Cook*, in which he investigates the process by which cooks attempted to take taste expertise into their own hands.[59]

The cooks' self-promotion was, however, gradual. It was still quite discreet in the middle of the seventeenth century. By then, a growing number of cooks started to use the first person singular in their recipe books, leaving many personal comments and value judgments. Cooks presented themselves as the ones who knew the ingredients and the best suitable seasoning for each of them, thanks to their long practical experience. For instance, when explaining the best recipes for "sugary rice pudding," La Varenne gladly emphasized his own ability: "As for me who have experienced it in all ways, I consider the most expedient to make it try in front of the fire after rinsing it neatly. When it is well dried, you should slowly cook it with very fresh milk, and be careful not to drown it; make it cook slowly and stir often, taking caution that it might burn; and, as you see fit, add milk."[60] Personal and professional experience guaranteed the practical efficacy of their advice, as Nicolas de Bonnefons notified his readers: "Please believe me that I would not have taken the chance to enlighten this little Work if I had not experienced everything that it contains."[61] Serving the public, cooks wanted to be considered as specialists devoted to instructing all "those who are not as advanced" as themselves "in this matter."[62] As Bonnefons explained to his fellow practitioners, the objective was to organize a meal "with such a caution that you would be able to receive not only the praise you expect from your Masters, but also a particular satisfaction in yourself, to see everything succeed remarkably."[63] The self-satisfaction of the specialist is striking in this extract, originating from a feeling of technical mastery.

For long considered an artisanal and mechanical art, cookery increasingly tended to appear as a form of "great knowledge" in its own right.[64] Cuisine is naturally first and foremost a physical form of knowledge, since the evaluation of quality originates from the senses. One must feel, see, touch, and especially taste before judging,[65] must verify the seasoning as well as the evolution of the cooking process.[66] L.S.R., especially, was keen to insist on the importance of tasting the dishes and seasonings, convinced that "one must never serve anything that one has not tasted before in order to remedy it if needed."[67] This physical nature of cuisine seems very obvious today, but to write these observations down in a recipe book was in this moment an inventive and modern gesture.

Cuisine was also progressively presented as a form of intellectual knowledge as well. One indication of this shift is the insistence on the planning required for every important dinner. The role of the cook and/or the maître d'hôtel became increasingly important. They became principally responsible for the organization of meals and were often true conductors leading the household staff. The preparation of a feast demanded lots of rigor, all the more since unexpected guests often showed up at mealtime. Several cookbooks therefore printed examples of preparatory drawings of the table and advised the maître d'hôtel to sketch diagrams before every important dinner. The distribution of tasks among the servants as well as the expected flavors had to be determined in advance. The cook was thus compared to an architect: "When an Architect wants to build a house, he makes a project or an estimate of it on paper; just as beautiful it must be, just as careful does he make the drawing; it is the same for everything; and in this matter also: if you are ordered to treat a company sumptuously, you must make a memorandum of what you want to serve, and even particularize the taste you want for each dish."[68] An important dinner requires planning, and the taste of the dishes was one among many items that needed to be thought through and written down in advance, just like an architect draws a plan of the house he wants to build. We shall find the metaphor of the cook-architect later, and in quite a different register, with Antonin Carême, who considered pastry as the main branch of architecture.[69] If in the nineteenth century the metaphor referred to aesthetically sophisticated desserts, in the seventeenth century we see that it meant something else, as it underscored the intellectual abilities of the maître d'hôtel. What is interesting here is that the metaphor reveals the importance, for matters of taste, not only of sensory but moreover of intellectual abilities, because in cuisine as much as "in all things, knowledge must precede action."[70] Good taste hence required a complex form of expertise on the part of the cook, although it was only discreetly suggested, the polite audience being the true judge of taste by then.

L.S.R is a unique example in his time, and it is precisely in his work in which one finds the most numerous allusions to taste and cuisine of all cookbooks of the century. Not only did he use the preface to deliver his thoughts, but every chapter of the work was also a pretext for personal comments. He presented his practice as a "real *science* to dress, disguise and neatly serve all sorts of meats and fishes, big and small soups, entrées [first courses], stews, entremets, pastries and vegetables."[71] His whole cookery was the object of "discernment" and "exquisite choice," from the initial choice of varied banquet dishes and service at the table to the preparation, cooking, and seasoning of the dishes.[72] These choices were dictated by the intellect, by technique, and by experience, but also by the sensibility of the palate. Both "pleasure and judgment" were important for the cook to determine what he "will best esteem to suit."[73] Cookery was thus not only a practical experience, but also a "discernment . . . a ray of his [the cook's] reason, and his spirit."[74] The notion of the culinary expert slowly appeared, emphasizing the worth and the technical control of the specialist, as much as his refined sense of taste: "There is certain trick to be given to things which often makes them pass from a mediocre state into a more considerable one, and which with a little application gives them a prestigious image."[75]

The cook was consequently an experienced connoisseur who, by his "art," was capable of "making things more delicious and richer."[76] He was presented not only as a specialist of cuisine but occasionally also as an expert of taste. The implications were much more discreet here, because officially, it was still the gourmets [*friands*] and delicate members of the elite who were considered the arbitrators of good taste. But in the heart of their work, the practitioners started being more assertive. Ceaselessly, they judged; they discerned the qualities of the various products by their flavors, distinguishing some varieties of fruits, vegetables, meats, or fish as unrefined and common compared to other "delicate," new, or rare varieties found on more "important" tables.[77] Regarding "the real sauce" of each product, the value judgments are numerous.[78]

Taste is a dialectic sense, opposed, by definition, to that of bad taste. The cook appears as a specialist, knowing the flavors that suit every product best. The words "most precious," "excellent," and "delicate" abound to qualify, on the one hand, the various ingredients and their possible preparations, and on the other hand, to refer to the eaters able to recognize them—the "vulgar" as opposed the "refined" and "illustrious friands."[79] Social and economic distinctions overlapped with differences in tastes, bringing into conflict those who had the "delicate" taste—as well as the financial means to satisfy it—and people with a more "common" taste who were generally more worried about savings. The food of the poor appeared as the antithesis of the food of people of rank, who were disgusted by the poor's food. The vocabulary used to qualify dishes is revealing. For instance, the opposite of the bread consumed by the poor is "the Bread of the Bourgeois or Bread of Masters."[80] There are numerous designations of products or recipes testifying to social differences: "Bread of the common," "bourgeois Bread," "Bread of the Chapter," "King's Biscuit," and so on.[81] The same goes for the various kinds and qualities of meats. Of "Sirloins," for instance, "there is a side of the bone softer than the other one, which is why one says the side of masters, and the [other the] side of the servants."[82] Good taste was thus readily defined by noting what it was *not*, and discernment came from the cook as much as—and even more, actually—from his audience.

In the end, although notations on taste are scarce and fragmented, early modern recipe books reveal the emergence of a new rhetoric on taste, intimately linked to the idea of expertise. Certain authors, such as Massialot, L.S.R., or Pierre de Lune, went as far as presenting their work as an "art" or a "science."[83] These were still marginal ideas in the mid-seventeenth century, but they would prove to be very popular in the next century, as we shall see in chapter 5. At the moment, we can already notice that a positive representation of cuisine emerged from those who practiced cookery on a daily basis. This favorable conception is definitely not a surprise, but the fact that these practitioners expressed themselves in their books is, on the other hand, powerfully new.

As evidenced by the number of quotations above, Nicolas de Bonnefons and L.S.R. were the most prolix authors on the subject. They were also the most singular. The former did not, strictly speaking, write a cookbook but rather a work on gardens—fruit and vegetable—in which he published recipes. As for the latter, he was, although a cook, completely unique in his kind, in his time, and even in all the history of cookery. Without being representative of all contemporary cooks, these two remarkable figures nevertheless reveal significant indications of new conceptions of taste that accompany the renewal of food practices. We shall see that these ideas, still peripheral in the seventeenth century, will really flourish in the eighteenth century.

The Discreet Pleasures of the Mouth: A Delicate Legitimization

Despite the slow rise of a new sensibility and of new discourses on taste and cuisine within the prefaces of mid-seventeenth-century cookery books, it was actually not that easy to publish a book for the sole purpose of delighting a sensual palate, even a culinary book. When explaining the intentions that led to their publications, the authors of culinary introductions seem eager to justify their enterprise by nobler motives than that of just pleasure. They insist that their work did not have the unique objective of satisfying the stomach but pursued higher goals. Doubtless they were particularly afraid, as they suggested, of being suspected by the Church of valorizing sensuality, encouraging readers-eaters to succumb to the sin of gluttony. This is the reason why several cooks tried hard to endow their works with a moral legitimacy by using a variety of discursive strategies. These strategies are particularly revealing of the ambiguous position of taste in the Old Regime, despite a rising interest in matters of food and cuisine at the time.

One of these strategies was to place food among the benefactions granted by God, like we see in Nicolas de Bonnefons's and Massialot's works. All the beauties of the world, including food, were pretexts to "admire the liberality" of the author of "such a fertile" nature, celebrating "the Providence" of the "liberal hand from which we received so many goods."[84] Nicolas de Bonnefons dedicated an epistle of the *Delices de la Campagne* "To the capuchins friars."[85] The monks were presented as the privileged readers of his work, due to their vegetarian diet and their concern for the garden, which allowed them to reach economic self-sufficiency.[86] Cooks, anxious to distinguish themselves from any practices of gluttony, especially insisted on moderation regarding food. They stressed the importance of avoiding useless "profusions that bring no enjoyment to taste, and in which God is offended rather than glorified, and thanked for his liberalities."[87] Hence it was not so much the gustatory pleasures as such that should be stigmatized, but their misuses and abuses. Moderation allowed one to supervise the intake of food and to endow it with a moral legitimacy; excesses were the opposites of devotion and good taste.

Other strategies were additionally implemented to legitimize culinary publications. The most popular emphasized the therapeutic contribution of modern cuisine, which was presented as healthier than older culinary practices.[88] Cookery has always been connected with medicine, with dietetics being one of the main branches of ancient medicine. Cuisine was traditionally supposed to correct the harmful qualities of food and facilitate digestion, while digestion itself was considered a form of cooking. Foodstuffs were then thought to be cooked twice: once in the kitchen and then again in the stomach. Culinary recipes and medical remedies were therefore often entangled in old *réceptaires*, and manuscript domestic recipe books in particular still carry these tracks.[89] The medical influence was more discreet in the case of printed collections, for only culinary recipes were supposed to be mentioned. Yet signs of this mutual history are still sometimes visible. For instance, Nicolas de Bonnefons took into account the medicinal virtues of garden vegetables, relying on medical arguments to favor or reject certain foodstuffs.[90] Like his contemporaries, he thought that flavorful dishes could have the effect of awakening the appetite of the sick—an effect that could, on the other hand, be thwarted by poorly prepared dishes.[91] The author proposed several recipes that could "serve to the recreation of taste, or to strengthen the stomach; also even Laxatives and Preservatives of all sorts that Medicine teaches."[92] Many other cooks, such as Massialot, would do the same.[93]

Insisting on the role of cookery in the preservation of health, as a complementary art to medicine, endowed the cookbook with a higher value, one less directly sensual. Of an antique origin, the idea of a therapeutic cooking allied to medicine is commonplace and regularly revisited. Rather than treating diseases with remedies, it was much better, according to the Hippocratic tradition, to prevent them with a healthier regime. La Varenne himself considers it "much more pleasant to make an honest and reasonable expense . . . in stews and other delicacies of meats, in order to keep life and health, than to use an immense sum on drugs, herbs, medicines, and other troublesome remedies to recover it."[94] Similar ideas were sometimes expressed in contemporary medical texts— for instance, in Gui Patin's *Traité de la conservation de santé* (Treatise on the Preservation of Health).[95] This is the reason why good cuisine was presented not only as "useful, but also . . . necessary."[96]

Moreover, modern cuisine was presented as better not only for the health of the body but also for that of the mind; a refined cookery was thought to stimulate intellectual activity: "All Books, old as modern, being mostly food for thought, it was very reasonable that the body, without the good arrangement of which it cannot act well, had its part, and mainly in a thing so necessary for its preservation."[97] Modern cuisine was thus presented as ideal for the health of the body as much as of the mind.

Nevertheless, the specialization of the medical and culinary domains was in progress. If Pierre de Lune mentioned once in a while a recipe meant to be therapeutic, such as the *restaurant*,[98] he trusted the doctor for the seasoning and prescription.[99] The medical part of cookbooks was generally limited to some introductory remarks. One still finds here and there a few occurrences of this tradition, but from the mid-seventeenth century onward, most of the books were concerned less with the actual therapeutic use of food than with methods of spicing up its taste by cuisine. The growth of a literary genre specifically dedicated to cooking is an indication of this progressive emancipation of cuisine from medicine. Culinary works tended toward a progressive specialization of the idea of cuisine itself—convenient, perhaps, to meditations on taste. The increasing separation of the medical and culinary spheres was bound in particular to the progressive questioning, from the sixteenth and seventeenth centuries onward, of the theory of the humors.

Hence, the declared objective of these modern culinary writings was not to induce gustatory pleasure or to sublimate the sense of taste but to contribute to the good health of the readers' body and mind, or to celebrate God's good graces. However, despite the many religious, medical, economic, and culinary justifications, a more sensual form of discourse would warily appear here and there in certain cookbooks, particularly in Nicolas de Bonnefons's and L.S.R.'s, which respectively legitimized their publications by the grace of God and by the therapeutic virtue of cookery before evoking more directly the pleasures of taste. In the foreword of the *Iardinier françois*, dedicated to women, Nicolas de Bonnefons celebrated the five senses' delights, glorified altogether by the garden that stimulates them all. He started by evoking the pleasures of the "domestic . . . Ladies . . . especially as each one has her quite particular taste": music, painting, poetry, theater, works of fiction, cabinets of curiosities, perfumes, cosmetics, and so on.[100] The passions of women, he writes, are numerous, "but as they only seek them to satisfy the senses, those whom I named only concern one of the senses; the garden has this prerogative over the others, that it gives of what to satisfy all five senses."[101] The perfumes of flowers and fruit delight the sense of smell. Sight is dazzled by a concert of colors "so lively as every most excellent Painters remain short by imitating their beauties, and the finest colors are tarnished by their brightness."[102] Concerning "taste, suffice it to say, that most friands and delicates, after having been more than enough filled with several sorts of good dishes, do not esteem to have eaten well, if they do not finish their feasts by fruit; whichever without being seasoned with anything else than Nature, are nevertheless so excellent, each in its sort, that it is necessary to admit that only fruit take the price in the satisfaction of taste."[103] As for the sense of hearing, it is enchanted by the praises of the visitors on the beauty of the garden, regarding especially "the thickness and diversity of your Fruit." Finally, the pleasure of touch comes from the contact with the fruit, "by handling, and peeling them; some have the skin so delicate, that it needs a subtle and light hand to remove it with more decency."[104] The garden thus provides a multisensory experience that completely gratifies the five senses altogether—taste, as well as hearing, sight, touch, and smell, making the orchard a place convenient to sensory pleasures, as suggested in the title of the work, *The Delights of the Countryside*.

The trope of the garden as a place of delights was common in the Old Regime. As Jean Delumeau stresses: "In former mentalities an almost structural link united happiness and the garden."[105] It is hence of little surprise that for contemporaries, the idea of a "Paradise on Earth" was pictured in the shape of a garden.[106] The central place of fruit in Bonnefons's extract on the pleasures of the senses is also significant. Fruit was traditionally used to symbolize the sense of taste, as well as *gourmandise*, in literature and in iconography.[107] Moreover, the author's praise of raw and not cooked fruit here reveals the high value of "natural" flavors at the time. It is also relevant to note that in this extract, fruits are connected to the other senses as well. Broadly speaking, pleasure gardens, as well as decorative flowers, were a luxury until the eighteenth century. As Sybille Ebert-Schifferer accurately emphasizes, "the texts of the time teach us that the garden was considered as a materialization of paradise on earth, in which all the senses of the man were solicited. It is only according to this context that we can understand why the representations of flowers carried in themselves a moral warning regarding the precariousness of sensory pleasures and an allusion to the fleetingness of any earthly thing."[108]

As for Nicolas de Bonnefons, he delivered rather unique conceptions for the time because he considered taste as the most important sense, which is very rare, even in cookbooks: "Of all the senses, there is not any one of them more delicious, nor more necessary for life than that of taste, and in which there are the most diversities."[109] Taste as a necessary sense is an old idea, but taste as the most pleasing and the most diversified of all the senses, on the other hand, is quite remarkable, for generally sight is considered the sense perceiving the largest number of objects.[110] Bonnefons was not the only one to mention the sensual delights of a sensory experience conjugating the pleasures of all five senses. L.S.R. also insisted in *L'Art de bien traiter* on the intrinsic legitimacy of cookery, "a subject where one shall meet nothing which feels reluctant to the common sense, and to the honesty of life."[111] Addressing the "most illustrious *friands* [gourmets]," he wished "to give the real means to eat with pleasure."[112] In order to prepare a successful banquet, he recommended delighting each of the senses in a pleasant atmosphere where nothing would be left at random. Colored flowers would charm sight, whereas perfumes would stimulate the sense of smell. In sum, he advises his readers: "You should spare nothing for the senses' delights and for the whole pleasure; decorate your buffet of small crystal flasks which you will fill with the most exquisite and most delicious drink of time."[113]

Multisensorial celebrations certainly existed in antiquity and in the Middle Ages, but they would become especially important to the festive aesthetic of the court in the second part of the seventeenth century, under Louis XIV. During the first part of his reign, the Sun King organized countless feasts in which all the senses were to be stimulated: taste was enchanted by the delicate *collations*, hearing with music, sight by the many spectacular shows, and even touch, when dancing. As Alain Viala stresses, "the senses were all the more strongly solicited that would intervene the fireworks' effects of surprise, the *trompe l'œil* of the decoration and of the 'machines.'" The aim of these political celebrations was the "enchantment of the senses," thanks to the use of an "aesthetic of joy."[114]

In the end, the discourses printed in the introductions of modern cookbooks reveal quite an ambiguous attitude toward the sense of taste and its pleasures.

On the one hand, some cooks—they are but a few—celebrated the discernment and refinement of the new culinary art while underlining the delicate sensory pleasures it offered. On the other hand, it seems this was not enough and that cuisine needed higher moral justifications for the publication of its secrets. The many reasons behind these justifications—the medical, religious, or public utility of the work—tend to indicate a certain uneasiness toward publishing a book solely for the pleasures of taste. There was obviously a tension between restraint and temptation toward food, leading to a paradoxical approach to this ambiguous sense.

Food Perceptions and Etiquette: The Invisibility of Taste

If there seems to be a discreet celebration of taste within some modern cookery books, the tone is quite different outside the culinary universe. When dealing with other kinds of closely related sources such as banquet reports or manner books, the cooks' apparent hesitancy to discuss taste is confirmed. The numerous reports of feasts in Versailles or Paris testify to this reserve of contemporaries toward the pleasures of taste, or at least, of the true difficulty of putting this sensation into words. Indeed, reports of banquets—sometimes very detailed—remain most of the time silent regarding the actual dishes consumed.[115] The chroniclers took particular care in enumerating the names of the people present, indicating the position occupied by each at the table, for it was a visible demonstration of the guests' social status.[116] Chroniclers remarked on the beautiful symmetry of the dishes displayed on the table, the wealth of utensils, the abundance of food, and the entertainments proposed—but the actual content of the meal was not stated. A successful dinner seemed to be related less to the taste of food than to the general order of the table and the impression of profusion and power displayed.

During the seventeenth century, the service evolved in parallel with cookery, both symbolizing the new French art of haute cuisine. The organization of the table had to respect strict rules of order and symmetry, highly valued by the aesthetics of classicism in fashion at the time. These rules applied both to the preparation, as mentioned before, and to the arrangement of the dishes on the table. The latter drew on geometrical structures; dishes were intended to impress dinner guests by communicating an impression of control. As L.S.R. explained to his readers, "to make the establishment with order," the culinary preparations must be carefully chosen, "by arranging them properly with one another and interlacing them in a way that they are neither pressed nor torn by their confusion, but on the contrary that in all their order one sees a certain equality which pleasantly satisfies the eyes and which gives some pleasure to the senses, even the most delicate and the most easily disgusted ones."[117] Everything had to be achieved "with a symmetry and a great decency," all the more reason to conceive the organization of the meal in advance.[118]

If the visual display of food on the table seemed to have mattered a lot, at the same time, no information is provided regarding the dishes chosen, and even less is recorded about the sensory effects provoked by their consumption. Gustation, it appears, was not the main interest of those preparing and attending the feast—or at least, of those who related them. The objective of the dishes served was to impress the eye of the dinner guests called to attend a prodigious banquet. It was thus the sense of sight that prevailed. If among the invitees a few took some pleasure in savoring the meal, they did not consider it appropriate to share their feelings and discuss this subject.

However, as Alain Corbin accurately noted, the historian should not "confuse the unspoken and the unfelt."[119] Specialists in food history have shown that there were at that time obvious indications of a higher form of sensibility toward the pleasures of the palate, yet most often this sensibility was not expressed and most definitely not written down. There were actually very few discourses on taste at that time, except perhaps in the context of comedy. Food was indeed omnipresent in grotesque literature or narratives of Cockaigne and was especially popular during the sixteenth century, as evidenced by the success of François Rabelais. Although the genre had started to decline, there were still several texts of this kind that circulated in the seventeenth century. However, this type of narrative is hardly comparable to a theoretical discourse written by a scholar or even to a personal report provided by a courtier. As Florent Quellier accurately asserts: "For a long time the West confined literary descriptions of the pleasures of good food only to registers of the comic, grotesque inversion, satire, and eroticism. Parodic works made possible the mention of *gourmandise*. . . . But is it possible to write seriously on the pleasures of the good food? Trivial, food remains widely absent in noble genres."[120] Der-Liang Chiou corroborates this absence when he writes that "the most talkative memorialists, the most loquacious journalists of the court have never tried to describe this intimate experience which relates to foodstuffs."[121] This is quite surprising when considering the seventeenth-century revolution of the art of French cookery. One might have expected the question of taste to be central during the classical period. However, a broad rhetorical and discursive celebration of the pleasure resulting from gustation does not inevitably accompany the period's development of a new sensibility of taste.

Manner books or treatises of civility are an interesting complementary source in this respect; although these must not be taken literally, since they reveal an ideal as much as a distorted reflection of reality, they likewise divulge the practical considerations of the place of taste in everyday life, particularly in high society. If the meal was an essential chapter in books of manners,[122] there was actually little room for taste within this kind of literature. The passages dedicated to food especially mentioned practical rules of behavior: What is it proper to do before, during, and after the meal? Do one's hands need to be washed? How should the table be arranged? What use should be made of the flatware? How must one behave when eating, and especially toward the other dinner guests? What about conversations? Normative prescriptions were multiple regarding the proper gestures and positions of the body, which had to be carefully monitored. These practices, of course, evolved throughout the early modern era, depending on the places and contexts under consideration. But it is striking to note that nothing, or very little, was said on taste—unless to instruct the reader to control his or her sensations or to highlight the despicable character of this particular sense, so inappropriate in polite conversations.

The growth of discourse insisting on the control of the body is salient during the early modern era. Wide-ranging studies have been published on the history of the body, notably drawing on the pioneering—and much discussed—work of Norbert Elias.[123] Manner books themselves make it very clear: internal sensations should not be displayed on the social stage.[124] Hunger, pleasures of eating, and feelings of disgust, as well as all signs likely to relate to them, had to be hidden from view. Bodily sounds, indiscreet glances, and clumsy gestures were so many revealing hints of the internal desires of the flesh or the "depth of the body."[125] The stomach had to be kept silent. Well-mannered people did their best to forget that eating was a physical need; they worked to hide everything that was connected with these corporeal necessities. The ideal civility was to exhibit a detached attitude toward food.

At table, *l'honnête homme* (the honest man) had to limit his meal to the dishes situated within a close environment. He was expected to consume the portion that he was given without trying to reach the better pieces. Choosing a particular morsel just for self-pleasure was considered a sin as well as the mark of a low education, for it broke the rules of decorum.[126] However, the most delicate parts of every meat had to be learned, for a well-educated person was supposed to be able to cut it neatly in order to give the most distinguished guest the finest portion. Meat carving was therefore an important technical skill in the polite world, a sign of distinction and of a good education, which is why several manner books along with cookbooks detailed the process.[127] The value of the morsel mattered more than the actual taste of the piece because it materially and visually translated the social hierarchy through food consumption.

If for the eater choosing a particular dish was inadmissible, refusing another was just as unacceptable because it was important to be able to eat everything. Nevertheless, during the Renaissance, Erasmus allowed some freedom here: he considered it acceptable to reject food that could not be tolerated for physical reasons, health being more important than decency.[128] But in the seventeenth century, disgust would gradually become unacceptable because, according to Antoine de Courtin, it was a matter of the imagination, an aversion that could be tamed.[129] However, de Courtin recognized that certain repulsions were too powerful to be overcome by will only; discretion was then required in order to keep one's disgust from the public. Later on, Jean-Baptiste de La Salle went even further, writing that in order to succeed one day in eating a variety of foods with indifference, one needed to mortify taste by forcing oneself to become accustomed to consuming unappreciated dishes: "Just as it is rude to ask for anything at table, it is also required by decorum that you accept whatever is presented, even if you feel some repugnance for it. Never allow it to be noticed that you have any distaste for eating anything served at table," because "such aversion is often purely imaginary" and could easily be corrected. He then advises his readers to "go hungry for a few days, for hunger makes everything seem appetizing. It often happens that things a person cannot force himself to eat when he is not hungry seem truly delicious to him when he is." Taste, as much as distaste, should not be cultivated, and everybody should accustom himself or herself "to eat any kind of food. To do this, have food you do not particularly like served often, especially when you have not eaten for some time."[130] According to de La Salle, these techniques would help to keep the sensations of taste under control, for individual food likes and dislikes were not to be publicly displayed.

The impatience with food aversions obviously increased between the eras of Erasmus and Jean-Baptiste de La Salle. First of all, this increasing intolerance toward food aversions is due to a factor linked to the general history of civility: conduct books became gradually more imperative and prescriptive concerning bodily control, the social construction of the self being linked to religious concerns as well as to public appearance within society. Rules of etiquette became more severe, limiting the space left for personal freedom and supervising each moment of everyday life. Every domain linked to the body or to intimacy was socially controlled and concealed. Eating was, of course, one of the most private actions there was, evidently connected with corporeality. Taste is a sense deeply connected with intimacy, for it has a unique character peculiar to each individual. In societies still largely dominated by the ideals of community and collective structures and identities, mitigating food preferences was one way among many to limit singularities in favor of collective norms of behaviors and thoughts.

Yet the erasure of tastes and disgusts may have been due to reasons less directly connected with the evolution of *savoir-vivre*. The progressive decline of dietetics could be one of the other reasons for this evolution. The theory of the humors traditionally held that tastes, bound to individual temperaments, should not be constrained, for they were justified by medical reasons. As stressed by

Jean-Louis Flandrin, "people believed that differences of appetite originated in nature. Taste was thought to be a matter of sympathy between the nature of the individual and the nature of certain food; similarly, distaste was believed to be a consequence of physiological antipathy."[131] Consequently, as stressed by L.S.R. and his contemporaries, "as the humors, also the tastes are different,"[132] which explains that personal preferences were not supposed to be impeded. The service *à la française* was linked to this principle; several dishes were simultaneously put at the disposal of the dinner guests, who were free to choose according to their physical constitution. In the introductions to their texts, cooks also insisted on the importance of diversity at the table, cautioning against forcing the tastes of any eater. The ideal was to give the impression of variety, offering several possible choices of sauces and alternating food so "that each can take what will suit his appetite," hence his temperament, or bodily constitution.[133]

The questioning of Galenic theories, from the sixteenth and seventeenth centuries onward, weakened this system of catering to the freedom of tastes, and created new habits that would lead to increasing the constraints toward individual preferences. Since likes or dislikes were no longer justified by a physical source independent from the eater's will, they had to be controlled and submitted to reason. From then on, treatises of civility sketched the portrait of the ideal *honnête homme* as capable of eating anything.

Paradoxically, the same cultural transformation simultaneously weakened liberty toward food and increased the value of the pleasures of taste. The ideal of variety at the table indeed remained, although it would later be justified not by temperament but by pleasure. Jean-Louis Flandrin demonstrated this progressive evolution from the emphasis on dietary principles to concerns with the pleasing sensuality of taste. This evolution explains the permanence of the *service à la française*, which lasted until the nineteenth century when the new fashionable *service à la russe* imposed the same menu for all eaters.[134] For cooks, food diversity was endowed with a positive value precisely because it "excite[d] the appetite."[135] The real delight of this sense was found in the variety of flavors and in the form and shape of food, thus also satisfying sight, for "there is nothing which pleases men more than diversity."[136] This explains why food diversity was so persistently criticized by the Church and by authors such as Jean-Baptiste de La Salle, promoter of a Christian civility. A large variety of dishes was indeed likely to provoke a consumption greater than that called for solely by need, since it entailed pleasure.

Yet if the evolution of dietetics and civility guidelines reveals the increasing control of the sensibilities of taste, it does not alone seem to explain the silences of polite society toward taste. Indeed, not only was it advisable to maintain distance toward food—mortifying the intimate sensations by consuming everything indifferently and controlling one's gestures so as to eat in the most profound silence—but it was also crucial to banish culinary tastes and aversions from formal and informal discourse, denying these idiosyncrasies access to words. Food was too trivial a topic to figure in "honest" conversations. Antoine de Courtin and Jean-Baptiste de La Salle were particularly explicit in this respect, clearly indicating their refusal to speak about these unworthy subjects:

> It is, however, no less an offense against decorum than against the laws of the Gospel for you to display great concern about eating and drinking. This, according to the words of Saint Paul,[137] would be to put your glory in what ought to be an embarrassment to you. For this reason, it is characteristic of people to speak little of these matters or of anything pertaining to them. When you are obliged to do so, you must do it soberly and with circumspection, so that you will appear totally unconcerned about it and not overeager to get the choicest pieces. It is neither courteous nor according to decorum for you to speak in rapturous terms of a meal or a banquet you attended or of one you have been invited to, nor to take pleasure in describing what was served or what you hope will be served.[138]

As this extract makes clear, religious concerns were intertwined with those of decorum. Judgments on the good or bad quality of the dishes served during a meal were banned from the register of civility, as they were thought to be very rude toward the host and the dinner guests, since a negative criticism might offend the person who received it.[139]

Generally speaking, any food-related subject was excluded from polite conversation, which could possibly indicate that people were actually talking about food at the table and that manner books only reflected a habit they wished to eradicate. But whether or not people respected the rule, these prescriptions reveal a cultural value of taste in classical France, where it was not yet the time for gastronomic discourses and refined analyses of the subtle delicacies of taste, as La Bruyère suggested in his ironic portrait of Clithon, the inappropriate gourmet who

> has never had in all his life but two affairs, which is to have dinner in the morning and to have supper in the evening; he seems born only for the digestion. He has only one concern: he says the starters that were served at the last meal where he was; he says how many soups there were, and which soups; he then places the roast and the entremets; he remembers exactly which dishes spiced up the first service; he does not forget the *hors d'œuvre*, the fruit and the plates; he names all the wines and all the liqueurs of which he drank; he possesses the language of kitchens as much as he can extend, and he makes me urge to eat at a good table where he is not.[140]

Discussing food and meals one attended in details was an obvious sign of a bad education. As a matter of fact, the analysis of manner books reveals the camouflage of tastes and disgusts within the beau monde. These had to be overcome, according to the elite ideal of physical control. Yet, as food historians have stressed, cookery art saw a considerable development in the seventeenth century, crystallizing in the new generation of cookbooks mentioned above. Food historians—such as Jean-Louis Flandrin and Florent Quellier—reveal the enhancement of cuisine that took place thanks to the rise of the rules of etiquette, which from the seventeenth century onward allowed the flourishing of a *honnête gourmandise*, accepted by good society and by the Church because it was strictly moderate.[141] In this context opened to the "reasonable" pleasures of the palate arose the notion of *bon goût* (good taste).[142] However, texts reveal besides that *friands*, *coteaux*, and *délicats*—in a word, gourmets—were not necessarily free to express publicly their sophisticated preferences, neither by their gestures nor with their words. The phenomenon of "silences of taste" in the polite world is strikingly similar to cooks' hesitation in publishing books that would only discuss the delights of taste.

Another likely reason for the "silences of taste" is that one did not talk about oneself; personal experience was not philosophically considered relevant because, according to Descartes, it did not generate truth. It is only in the eighteenth century onward that writers, inheriting from Montaigne's "quest of self," would seek moral truth inside the individual, hence confirming the relevance of disclosing personal inner thoughts and sensations.[143] As we will see in the following chapters, the history of taste is deeply intertwined with that of the modern subject, taste being a very idiosyncratic sense, connected with the individual and with individuality. Therefore, the ways in which the subject and personal experience were considered at a given place and time necessarily impact the uses of taste as well as the writings and discourses on the sense of taste. The early modern era is a crucial period with that regard. The whole genealogy of the rise of the modern subject, central to the understanding of early modern culture and, moreover, of modernity, is obviously beyond the scope of the present book and has besides already been tackled by a range of scholars. However, it is important to remember here that this question was at stake in a great variety of settings in early modern Europe. Early modern writers and philosophers ceaselessly questioned the extent of human knowledge and were deeply concerned with the question of truth, and especially with the part played by individual experience and subjectivity, as well as by the body, in the production of knowledge. We shall return to this question in the next chapters; suffice it for now to mention that the question of taste may have been one of the witnesses—if not one of the operators—of this new valorization and attention granted to individual thoughts and feelings, and hence also to the development of the self and of selfhood in the modern age.

Conclusion: A New Sensibility—The Ambiguous Celebration of Taste

The mid-seventeenth century was marked by a true revolution of taste, a profound transformation of sensibilities, and, though to a lesser extent, a transformation of discourses. From the 1651 edition of La Varenne's *French Cook*, the introductions to culinary textbooks became a discursive space where the cook (or his librarian) could freely express himself on cuisine and on taste. These comments were certainly positive but remained relatively brief in the first essays of this kind; later, they grew in length. The culinary introductions established the first forums permitting discourse on taste. Even in cookbooks, the presence of an introductory discourse on the question of taste was resolutely new and powerfully modern. Before this invention, taste had no appropriate or designated space; outside a certain literary register of comedy, no speech was specifically dedicated to this sense.

In these introductory pages, cooks revealed their ongoing concern with respecting the true flavor of each food, a concern indicating their attachment to the values of nature and simplicity, so important to classical aesthetics. The cook's practice appeared in their introductions as a professional knowledge of foodstuffs and their appropriate preparation. The senses—particularly sight, smell, and taste—allowed one to express a value judgment on the prepared dishes. But the organization of a meal also required an intellectual elaboration, which could take the shape of preparatory plans, requiring an architect of taste. Before actual preparation, a good dinner required much thought—while this may seem obvious, the written traces of this reflection collected in a book gave meal preparation a much higher value.

The rhetoric used in the introductory pages of the culinary collections was very evocative. At a time when René Descartes valued simple and distinct ideas, cooks rejected the older culinary practices with their disorderly preparations and variety of disguises. Cooks criticized the past as the domain of the vague, instead embracing Descartes's foundational emphasis on order in his *Discourse on the Method*.[144] In cuisine, as anywhere else, the reprehensible lexicon of error and confusion was in opposition to the new lexicon of order and discernment that was one of the major stakes of modernity. In art, literature, philosophy, and cookery, the ideas of simplicity and the natural dominated; the era thus displayed a passion for classical aesthetics. It is obvious for the universe of the visible, where beauty was embodied in order and symmetry, as exemplified in the aesthetics of gardens, which relied on diversity and discernment in their organization. The same logic made its way to the table. This logic was mainly visual, as suggested by the geometry of the dishes, but it was also more than visual: order also dominated the pallet of flavors, which had to be individually recognizable. While not literally expressed, a kind of cultural symmetry was displayed; the values, the lexicon, and the rhetoric of classicism were brought to bear on the table, in perfect harmony with some of the major cultural themes of modernity. Gradually, the sense of the taste was likewise anchored in the logic of discernment.

However, the above analysis of culinary literature also reveals the uneasiness of these authors to openly dedicate a book to the sensual pleasures of taste alone. Their prefaces insist on religious, medical, and social justifications; perceived as more valid morally, these variable excuses revealing a cultural difficulty of valuing the pleasures of the table, even in the proper culinary register. Tasting and talking—as, more broadly, sensations and words—are two different worlds. In spite of the transformation of the sensibilities, taste emerged in the social conversational scene with difficulty; at luxurious banquets, the visual impression of order and profusion mattered more than the gustatory quality of the dishes served. Obviously, sight occupied a place more important than taste, since it did not appear appropriate to describe what was eaten—at least, not yet. The cultural valuation of gustative pleasures had not emerged in its entirety.

Likes and dislikes were banished from the register of politeness, both in actions and in words. Rules of honesty aimed for an absolute control of the body, where every gesture, every glance, every noise was carefully monitored. The ideal was for physical and verbal silence to accompany the intake of food. It was necessary to remain unaware of the appeal of the stomach, to forget that eating was a need, and to adopt a detached attitude toward food. Food preferences and aversions—spontaneous effects derived from the inside of the body—were carefully hidden in this process of repressing intimate sensations, which could not be visible on the social stage. But the prohibition of taste went beyond this; not content with ordering the *honnête homme* to consume everything indifferently, the rules of good manners rejected all affairs of gustation from polite conversation. According to the prescriptions of the civility treatises discussed above, in a refined society it was not suitable to discuss these despicable subjects. No comment, positive or negative, could be made concerning the quality of the dishes presented. Further, the public reserve adopted toward personal preferences at the table seems to reveal indirectly the personal nature of taste. Taste's idiosyncratic nature, whatever the form of its manifestation, could not be valued in a culture still deeply influenced by the spirit of community. The history of taste also joined in the social and historical forces integral to the advent of the modern subject.

The "silences of taste" are striking, inasmuch as the word "silence" is not taken literally; it is undoubtedly less a silence per se than a hesitation to talk freely about the pleasures of eating or to openly record their taste-based impressions of food. In this era, taste seems to be relegated to the peripheries of discourse. Furthermore, the silences of the body and of speech were a normative prescription. We do not know whether this imperative was actually respected, but the rule itself conveys much and is moreover reinforced both by more implicit signs of a cultural uneasiness toward taste and a difficulty in relating to this ambiguous sense. Why this embarrassment in writing on the enjoyments of the table? The sole domain of cuisine and *savoir-vivre* obviously does not alone suffice to explain these tensions, which are rooted in much deeper concerns.

2 Pleasures, Disorders, and Dangers of an Animal Sense

> The pleasure of drinking and eating only lasts for a few moments;
> we only feel it while eating and drinking, and when what we drink
> or eat passes in the stomach. How such a pleasure is vile and
> despicable! We share it with beasts, and it only flatters some parts
> of the body—the tongue, the palate, the throat.
> —Lessius, *Conseils pour vivre longtemps*, 191

Discussing taste was obviously problematic in the seventeenth century, even in the culinary universe in which one would expect people to be eager to address the topic. In order to understand the reasons that might explain this uneasiness, it is worthwhile to consider sources less directly connected with the food domain, sources liable for establishing the broad moral value of the sense of taste in the early modern era. Religious and moral texts, emblem books, and ancient dictionaries—by then considered to be encyclopedic collections—are particularly enlightening in this respect. The two former are especially important, for the most evident explanation of the discomfort around taste lies in its association with the carnal sin of gluttony, as demonstrated by the emphasis on food moderation.[1] At this point, then, what were the actual connections drawn between the sense of taste and the sin of *gourmandise*? To what extent did the Church—and more generally, conventional morality—influence the ways in which taste was represented in early modern Europe?

Gula: A Mouthful of Disorders

Eating being a biological necessity, food comes along with pleasure, and there lies all the danger. There is a fine, easily crossed line between the satisfaction of a physiological need and the excesses of sensual delight leading to overindulgence. The theme of the essential *mediocritas* [moderation] at table is commonplace since antiquity and can be traced in various texts written by philosophers, theologians, moralists, and doctors. It is deeply rooted in modern Western culture and necessarily influenced the ways in which people related to food and taste.

In the seventeenth century, the word *gourmandise* was defined as "greediness, intemperance in eating and drinking."[2] It was not, as it is today, used to refer to the pleasure of eating, but to food excesses only—in a word, to gluttony. The *gourmand* "eats a lot";[3] he is a "glutton, greedy, who eats with greediness and with excess."[4] It was the *friand* who enjoyed "the delicate and well-seasoned pieces,"[5] also called the *délicat*, though the latter was sometimes endowed with a more pejorative connotation, for "one also says that a man plays the *delicat* to mean that he is very hard to please."[6] As for the *gourmet*, he was certainly recognized as a food judge, endowed with a refined palate, but his expertise was mostly about wines. He was the one "who knows how to try, taste wine, who knows if it is good and for aging."[7]

Gourmandise [gluttony] was codified within theology as one of the seven deadly sins.[8] As for all the other vices, theologians elaborated a complex and detailed system listing every possible form of *gourmandise*: eating overly refined food, eating too much, too often, outside mealtimes, and so on. Broadly speaking, however, the gourmand was the one who ate beyond necessity. Gluttony, it was thought, was produced through a bodily organ, which is why it was regarded as a carnal vice just like lust. It was certainly not the gravest sin, but it was considered as the "gate of vices,"[9] or "the mother of all vice."[10] Giving into greed would open the door to all the other sins, "because when the flesh is fed delicately, and pleasantly maintained, irregular love engenders from it, anger, arrogance, lust, bawdiness, which results from drinking and eating too much."[11] This is the reason theologians and churchmen insisted so much on food moderation. As recommended by Thomas à Kempis, author of *De Imitatione Christi* (The Imitation of Christ), one of the most esteemed and widely distributed devotional books: "Curb your appetite and you will more easily curb every inclination of the flesh."[12] The faithful had to be ceaselessly vigilant, for this was an especially insidious sin, and all the more so since it appeared to have been the first one committed in the Garden of Eden: Adam and Eve did indeed cause the Fall by biting into an apple. All the misfortunes entered the world after this initial greedy temptation—or so goes a literal interpretation of the book of Genesis (a view not widely shared by the whole Christian Church, then or now). The version most generally assumed as truth considered the fault of the first humans as a sin of pride. Nevertheless, the former reading existed as well, and likely contributed to the suspicion surrounding the delights of the table. The frequent choice in literature and art of the apple as a symbolic element to refer to taste and gluttony is relevant in this respect.[13]

The consequences of gluttony were markedly threatening. At first, succumbing to it on earth guaranteed an eternal life of misery. Since the Middle Ages, penitential texts, sermons, and works of art inspired by the seven deadly sins have contained multiple representations of divine punishment: gluttons punished with an eternal fast or filled up by force, obliged to eat disgusting objects like toads or excrements of the devil. The sinner could also be directly devoured by the mouth of the devil, cooked in smoking pots by nightmarish chefs, or—like in Dante's *Divine Comedy*—left to the mercy of Cerberus, a big worm endowed with claws and with three wild dogs' mouths.[14] The outcomes were terrible for such a small gustatory pleasure, which only lasted a short moment. According to Pascal and many other thinkers of the time, the gourmands exhibited a "completely unreasonable conduct," they "who live without thinking of this last end of life, driven by their inclinations and their pleasures, without reflection and without concern; and as if they could annihilate eternity by diverting their thought from it, they think of being happy in this moment only."[15] The position of the Church was clear: the afterlife mattered a lot more than these fleeting, earthly pleasures.

Narratives and images of the gluttons' punishments in Hell obviously aimed to impress the medieval people. However, after a while, it seems that these threats of eternal pain after death did not suffice anymore. The sin of gluttony gradually lost its gravity, as evidenced by the increasing number of exemptions for fasting from the seventeenth century onward.[16] The condemnation of *gourmandise* remained but took a different form, while the strategies of gluttony's repression became more diverse. Several theologians pointed out that the disastrous consequences of *gula* (gluttony) were not of a spiritual order only; the body of the sinner was also in danger. Churchmen allied with doctors to recall the risks that weighed on the health of the amateur of good food. The possible ailments were countless, indigestion being only a minor symptom of all diseases caused by gluttony, which "according to the proverb . . . kills more than the sword."[17] Food intemperance threatened the acuteness of the senses as well, even taste; whereas, as the Jesuit Leonardus Lessius underscored, "diet makes us find more taste and even more pleasure in common food and in dried bread, which the intemperate find in the most delicate and best-seasoned dishes. As soon as we get purged of these bad humors that caused disgust, the appetite returns and makes us find in food *the real taste and the real pleasure* that must be found there."[18]

The physical disorders of gluttony were, moreover, thought to affect intelligence, for heavy foods naturally darkened the brain; since Hippocrates, who had underlined the importance of a balanced diet, this notion had been prominent. Excessive feeding would corrupt the humors, thus polluting and thickening the *esprits* (spirits) surrounding the brain.[19] Aristotle and Plato likewise asserted that physical pleasures, like those of taste, were an obstacle to thought.[20] In the early modern era, it was still commonly admitted that one should eat with "measure according to nature and to the right reason" in order to "overcome the sensual appetite, and to increase the vigor of the mind, which is dulled by the quantity of food."[21]

Unsurprisingly, food moderation concerned both eating and drinking. Drunkenness, particularly prone to lead to excesses and debaucheries, was actually one of the most criticized forms of *gourmandise*. Erasmus, among many others, despised these "banquets or in other words these collective drinking bouts where everything is only hubbub and vague rumor; where the guests are forced to drink so much that is prescribed to them, and where each tries hard to attract his neighbor in sin."[22] Excessive drinking, moreover, loosened tongues, provoking a chaotic speech unworthy of propriety. The *péché de langue* (sin of the tongue) was never far away from an act of gluttony; there was a "dangerous physiological and temporal proximity of gluttony and loquacity,"[23] as we will see. Losing control of one's mouth when eating or speaking was not only a moral sin but also a social error. Theologians, moralists, and authors of conduct books severely condemned any public demonstrations of greed, which could be perceived in the polite world as an unacceptable rudeness.[24] "In this the rules of decorum [were] in accord with those of Christian Morality,"[25] so much so that they shared the same rhetoric: "Nothing is more contrary to decorum than to have your table at home always set, for this suggests that you have nothing more at heart or more in your dreams than filling your belly and making it your God, as Saint Paul observes.[26] In fact, a table that is always ready is like an altar constantly prepared to offer this deity choice meats that are the victims sacrificed to it."[27] Jean-Baptiste de La Salle implies, through the metaphors of the table as a sacrificial altar and of the *god-stomach*, traditionally used in holy writings to incriminate the sin of gluttony, that the Christian too attached to the pleasures of taste risks to exclude himself (or herself) from the realm of God.[28] These were common ideas, as evidenced by the work of Pierre Boaistuau, a moralist compiler, who repeatedly refers to the bad "gourmands who make a God of their belly."[29] Francis de Sales would approve, as we can see in his *Introduction to the Devout Life*, one of the most popular Catholic spiritual guides:

> It is a true mark of a beggarly, base, abject, and infamous spirit to think of the meats and dishes before meal-time, and still more so when we are interested after dinner in the pleasure we have had in eating, entertaining ourselves with it by words and thoughts, and allowing our spirit to wallow in the memory of the pleasure we have had in swallowing the morsels. When we do so, we are like those who before dinner turn their spirit to the spit and after dinner to the dishes, people worthy of being the scullions of the kitchen, who make, as St Paul says, a god of their belly. Men of honor do not think of the table except when they sit down, and after dinner wash their hands and their mouth so as no longer to have either the taste or the smell of those things which they have eaten.[30]

Therefore, it was not suitable to speak at table of these subjects that did not even deserve thought. La Bruyère drew a good example of a glutton in his story of Gnathon, who was stigmatized for breaking all the rules of propriety at table by his egocentric behavior, and is a figure who can be read as an antithesis of civility; he epitomized everything that should not be done and was a dreadful man who "live[d] only for himself."[31] Besides his total contempt for the rules of behavior at table, the main discourtesy of Gnathon was to think only of himself and his own pleasure, while the foundation of civility was to consider the other. In the caricature, the glutton, often represented by the shape of a fat person, "starves all the other" dinner guests by eating their portions.[32] At a time in which famines and scarcities were still frequent, the one who would consume an excessive amount of food was perceived as depriving the others of subsistence. This wasteful act was deeply condemned as a lack of Christian charity. In this respect, ecclesiastics as well as the laity did not escape the social penalty, as demonstrated by the popular figure of the gluttonous monk.[33]

The disapprobation was much more severe toward the glutton than the *friand*, because of the quantities of food ingested by the former. The latter's behavior was more easily acceptable because in his search for refined dishes, he did not risk consuming indispensable foodstuffs to the detriment of the rest of the community. Underscoring the refinement of their masters' taste, the cooks also more readily spoke of delicate *friands* than of gourmands. Certainly, it did not prevent the gourmet from reprehensible behavior—a love for delicacy remained a form of sin as well—but the Church more generally tolerated it, as far as it was under control.

In the end, gluttony promised a flood of disorders: disorders of the soul, of the body, of the senses, and of taste itself; of the mind, of social life, and even of politics.[34] It threatened the order of God, the order of the world, and that of men. In view of all the perilous consequences that weighed on the gourmand, succumbing to food temptation was a behavior unworthy of the reasonable man.[35] Only fools would fall for this, as shown by the expression *gastrimargia* (the madness or the fury of the stomach), which we can trace back to the *Ethics* of Aristotle and the Greek patristic.[36] This vice was one of weak beings, such as children, women, and old people.

The Threatening Margins of the World

The Witch: Refinements of Disgust

As a result of the numerous risks surrounding gluttony, taste was put under narrow surveillance in the early modern era, not only for the disorders and discomforts but also for the dangers it could convey. The mouth in particular had to be carefully monitored, for it was a border between inside and outside, between self and other; in a word, it was an opening toward the world, susceptible to penetration of the internal body. From there ensued all the fears of the disastrous consequences that could follow the consumption of a harmful dish, reminding the eater of the natural role of the senses in the protection of the body.[37]

Exploring the extensive literature written on witchcraft is enlightening in this regard, as it is especially revealing of the anxieties attached to food, taste, and the mouth in early modern Europe. Among the many consequences of gluttony already stated, one was indeed particularly dangerous, and it potentially favored the action of the devil, who constantly sought to trouble God's order. According to the authors of the many demonological writings, treatises on witchcraft, and witch-hunting manuals, most of which were published between the fifteenth and the seventeenth centuries, evil could easily get inside a victim not cautious enough to protect her mouth, conceived of as a door. One of the favorite strategies the devil displayed to reach his targets was actually to hide in food, which the innocent soul would consume without knowing that by doing so she was eating the demon. This was considered a frequent way of possessing people, where Satan, "assuming a body, appears as being something that he is not."[38] The *Malleus maleficarum* (The Hammer of Witches), one of the most famous treatises on sorcerers, divulged, for instance, the story "of a nun who ate a lettuce; this one however, the devil admitted it later, was not a lettuce but the devil in the shape of a lettuce or in the very lettuce itself."[39] Subsequently, the author clarified that the nun was possessed because she had not made the sign of the cross prior to eating.[40] Such examples were particularly frequent in the work of Henry Boguet, author of a successful treatise on witchcraft, who wrote the story of a girl, Loyse, who was obliged by a witch to eat "a crust of bread resembling dung . . . and on the next day the girl was found to be possessed" by five devils.[41] The author specified "the means usually employed by a witch to possess his victims with a devil is to offer them some sort of food; and I have remarked that he most often uses apples. In this Satan continually rehearses the means by which he tempted Adam and Eve in the earthly Paradise."[42] The stories of devils hidden in food were numerous and revealed the many dangers of food consumption, for gluttonous people, especially, were all the more easily targeted by Satan; in the same way, sorcerers as well were notoriously thought to be voraciously greedy.

Consequently, authors of witch-hunting guides encouraged the faithful to watch their mouths, which had to be integrated into God's order; the best way to keep the devils away was to ask for Christ's protection and to incorporate religion into food practices.[43] They insisted, for instance, in blessing the food before eating in moderation. It was in moving away from Christianity that the Christian took the risk of being attacked by Satan. The jurist Jean Bodin, who presided over several witch trials, testifies from his own experience: "I have noticed also that demoniacs for the most part confess that the evil attacks them when they eat something; and from this it may be supposed that there is gluttony on their part; a sin abominable to God, who does not wish us to abuse the good things which it pleases him to give us, or that instead of blessing and praising him for his mercies, we should take the food he sends us immoderately or without remembering him or thanking him for it."[44] Demonologues (i.e., experts in the study of witches and witchcraft) agreed on this point with many authors of manner books like J.-B. de La Salle, who were concerned with including religion within all aspects of everyday life, including the meals.[45]

Food was a dangerous area, for not only did it represent a temptation leading to gluttony and hence to evil, it was also one of the many weapons of sorcerers, who used edibles as vehicles for their poisons. However, according to demonologues, most ingredients used in malefic potions were inedible substances, disclosing a deviant and unnatural concoction of "matters which are contrary to God and Nature."[46] For example, Henry Boguet explains that sorcerers would cut a man's throat and give his blood "to the patient to drink while it [was] still warm."[47] Human blood was not the only repulsive substance mobilized; flesh, urine or excrements, dirt, organs—all of these organic matters were removed from humans, from animals, or from the devil himself. Countless ointments and potions consisted especially of human remains, particularly bodies of nonbaptized dead babies, which were classical references of the devilish action of the witch.[48] The sorcerer's concoctions, which revealed the horror of anthropophagy arising from a world upside down, exceeded the absolute taboo where children were killed and eaten by the women who were supposed to raise and feed them[49]: "going against the inclination of the nature of man and even animals, [wizards] are in the habit of dismembering and of devouring the children of their own species."[50] Constance Classen demonstrated how the logic of inversion of the domestic universe operated within the frame of witchcraft, as evidenced by the perversion of the cookery function displayed in this context. The cooking pot, reserved for the culinary domain of the household, allowing the woman to feed her family, was within the frame of witchcraft transformed into an evil spell instrument. Witches had "a diabolic sensorium in which each of the senses was perverted from its proper use and endowed with satanic powers. . . . The creation of magical potions . . . was a supernatural elaboration of the feminine art of cookery."[51]

The food consumed by the witches was also considered to be deviant. Henry Boguet writes, for example, that wizards used to take children born of "incestuous couplings" between witches and demons. "[T]hey cut them about all their bodies and collected their blood in phials, and afterwards burned the bodies. They mixed the blood with ashes and made a sauce, with which they seasoned their food and drink."[52] The rhetoric of disgust clearly prevailed.[53] The objects classically considered as disgust elicitors were all present in this universe: corpses, cannibalism, necrophagy, urine and other physical excrements, rotting carcasses, all of these soaking in an atmosphere of mortuary blackness.[54] This rhetoric was far from innocent, of course: all these revolting elements used in evil potions both manipulated the imagination of the reader and, more importantly, revealed the horror of a world situated outside of God's order.

Also noteworthy were banquets organized during the Sabbath, which gathered the most varied dishes. According to the authors of witch-hunting manuals, the quality of these meals was unpredictable. Some would feature the most delicious meats while others offered the most horrible dishes. It depended on the occasion, as explained by Pierre de Lancre, another demonologue:

> Sometimes there are many tables filled with good things to eat; at other times the food is very bad . . . the majority of witches who were heard most often confess that . . . only toads, the flesh of people who were hanged, carrion flesh that was dug up and torn from newly dug graves, the flesh of unbaptized children, or that of dead animals whom they had killed, were served. They [witches] said that no one ate anything that was not tasteless, given that nothing was ever salted. If anyone wanted to reach for the good meat, he touched nothing solid and found nothing but air, with the exception of these rotten meats, which could not be eaten without disgust. These are false meats, false cooks, and false servants.[55]

The Sabbath banquet was described as a feast of illusion. On that occasion, authors of witchcraft manuals include several reports of witnesses who stated that, at the end of the meal, all dishes would vanish and the wizards would feel an empty stomach. The "demonic" food did not succeed in satisfying the appetite of the participants, and this dissatisfaction revealed the void of a devilish universe opposed to God's fullness, the latter being the only provider of "true" food.

Another meaningful detail was salt, which was strictly forbidden in diabolical Sabbath feasts, for it was connected with the divine presence as "a symbol of immortality," eternity, and wisdom, and therefore was "held in bitter abhorrence by the Devil."[56] Salt had been highly valorized in the past, in many different ways. This substance was, of course, important for the preservation of food; the protection from physical rotting processes provided by salt was symbolically associated with protection from spiritual harm—hence from the devil: "Salt can prevent the spoilage that occurs in natural things. But those things which are blessed and thus part of God's grace can, when placed and kept in good hands, thwart the Devil's efforts and preserve things in their natural state."[57] Moreover, salt has always had an important symbolic value and was used in religious and cult practices, from Greek sacrifice to Christian baptism. An interesting example is found in earlier practices of baptism, which involved a series of catechumenate rituals, during which the priest put a pinch of salt into the mouth of the child or the future Christian; salt was here considered as the first food that would awaken in the Christian the taste of the true celestial food. Salt was therefore more holy than any other foodstuff. Just like salt stimulates bodily appetite, it opens the appetite to the true Christian food, the Eucharist.[58]

Furthermore, salt, as a symbol of incorruption, was held as a purification agent, and as such appeared to be "a sovereign antidote against the power of the Devil."[59] This substance was therefore commonly used in exorcism rituals, as it was believed to have the power to scare the enemy. More precisely, the main power attributed to salt was that of revealing the truth and thus disclosing all the illusions that might have been produced by the devil in disguise. The perception of salt, when added to food, escapes all the senses but taste. Likewise, the wise person reveals the true essence hidden under the appearance of things. Salt is therefore also "symbolical of wisdom," and "God in his hidden purpose does not allow it to be used at the Sabbath, so that the witches may know that all that they do is sheer folly."[60] Paradoxically, salt is also a substance that enhances the taste of food and furthered the likelihood of indulgence, which demonstrates how profoundly ambivalent salt as a substance and as a symbol could be.

As a result of this lack of salt in Sabbath feasts, witches would have frequently stressed the insipidity or the unpleasant flavor of the dishes served in devilish gatherings. According to the authors of treatises of demonology, this tasteless-ness was a divine precaution—let us remember that Satan, the devils, and the witches could act only with God's permission, as Pierre de Lancre states: "if God sometimes allows Satan to avoid salt at his abominable gatherings, he has added to this foresight and precaution, as he does in all his works, namely, that all the meats prepared by these demons will always be either fake or bland or taste bad. God does not want the demons to be able to use these meats, however fake or real they may be, to truly tempt the human race and throw it into the abyss of Hell."[61] Boguet's point here is to show that "the Devil is always a deceiver, since he feeds his own people with wind instead of solid meat, as if they were chameleons."[62] Actually, this caution also indirectly suggests the power of taste's seductions, a sense that could potentially truly tempt the human race—which could be one of the reasons this sense was apparently not mobilized within the witches' strate-gies. If sorcerers usually acted by the means of sight or of tactility, there was almost nothing written on taste that could be compared with the "bad eye"[63] or with the deadly touch of the sorcerer.[64] The witch used ointments, potions, and poisons, but if the components of these were sometimes stated, their taste was never explicitly described. We do not know either whether their administration was facilitated by a tasty temptation or by an illusion of good food—illusions being, as we know, one of the favorite means of action of witches and demons. Few demonologues suggest that God would never allow the devil to use such a powerful attraction as the one of taste; most of them do not talk about this at all. Taste was most definitely a multifaceted, dangerous sense, although it is difficult to know to what extent. Demonological literature, therefore, like many

other sources of the time, contains few references to this sense, despite the fact
that it provides a form of discourse in which references to the sensory worlds
abound, although they refer to worlds of the margins.

Witchcraft was gradually decriminalized in the seventeenth century and was
officially declared a superstition by the French royal edict of July 1682. However,
if the witches' powers were no longer believed to be real, a certain number of
commonly shared ideas connected with this universe remained influential, such
as the association between gluttony and sin or evil, the threatening mouth, or the
multiple disorders and dangers of overeating—hence, residue of the discourse
on witchcraft survived and contributed to the broad cultural mistrust of the
sense of taste.

The Saint: Fantasy of Immateriality

Considering all the dangers and disorders surrounding taste and its mortal
temptations, diverse authors—of devotional literature, for instance—prescribed
several strategies as a protection from *gula*. The most classic method of protection was, of course, moderation, and especially to avoid too-varied dishes in
order both to facilitate digestion and to prevent awakening desire. Nevertheless,
the best remedy against gluttony was most certainly fasting, which mortified
the body, elevated the spirit, and protected the Christian from the evil spells
of the devil.[65] The renunciation of food, especially meat, appeared moreover as
an effective way of fighting lust, which was deeply intertwined with gluttony.[66]
According to ancient medical theories, "an overly nourished body, especially
one fed with meat, was thought to produce a plethora of blood, which would
be subsequently converted into sperm (in both males and females), signaling
the libido and thus readying the body for procreation."[67] As Caroline Walker
Bynum stresses, "food was dangerous because it excited lust. . . . Controlling
eating and hunger" was thus an explicit way of "controlling sexuality."[68] This is
the reason why fasting consisted especially of renouncing meat, and why ascetic
nuns and monks often privileged a frugal, if not vegetarian, diet.

These misgivings toward food consumption were widespread in early modern
Europe, and Catholics were hardly the only ones to advise food abstinence. Protestants as well recommended the limitation of food, as demonstrated by Ken Albala,
who has thoroughly investigated the topics of food and Christianity, particularly
the role of fasting during the religious Reformation. He points out the remarkable
similarity between these two groups—Protestants and Catholics—regarding the
issue of food abstinence. Of course, there were major differences between the
members of these confessions, especially in the ways in which they considered
fasting in relation to salvation. But, broadly speaking, they "argue[d] in the end

the same essential point, that fasts [were] very beneficial for the body and soul and valuable for maintaining moral integrity."[69]

If the general position of the Church was to encourage moderation and regular periods of fasting, for some ascetics this was not enough. The advantages of fasting were such that they dreamed to extend this experience into a permanent one, meditating on the numerous exempla of lives freed from food constraints, such as Jesus's forty days in the desert or the incredible life of Saint Catherine of Siena. Heroic ascetics of the early Church—Christian fathers, for the most part—presented other inspiring examples to be followed. There were, moreover, many stories inspired from antiquity as well, such as the story of the "Astomes" reported by Pliny the Elder. The Astomes were a people coming from the "last extremities of India, from the East, around the fountain and the source of the Ganges . . . who live only from the smell and exhalation of certain roots, flowers, and fruits which they pull through the nose."[70] These perpetual fasters were allegedly deprived of a mouth, which explains why they were consuming smells.[71]

All these common exempla, found within the most diverse kinds of sources, were endlessly reproduced in early modern sources. They testify to an ideal of total deprivation of food, a fantasy that a few pious people, eager for a higher form of spirituality, endeavored to actualize in their everyday life. This was true for hermits, certain saints, and mystics, all of whom oppressed their bodies to pursue the impossible dream of becoming a disembodied spirit devoid of any materiality. Radical fasts were endowed with a spiritual value, if not with holiness. The most extreme example occurred in the late Middle Ages/early modernity—a phenomenon that specialists, since the work of Rudolph Bell, have called *holy anorexia*.[72] It concerned mainly women who were described in hagiographic texts as saints, capable of living without eating anything, except perhaps the sacred host.[73] Freed from human sensations and possessed by a supernatural grace that allowed her to communicate with God, the holy anorexic felt invested with a power, which explains why she was not afraid to face her family and the representatives of the Church.[74] The—male—clerical hierarchy felt challenged by these singular women who claimed to be able to access God directly and by themselves, which the former perceived as a possible threat of insubordination. The Church leaders traditionally called to decide whether the anorexia was of holy origin or not thus took measures to reduce these fasts. The cases of holy anorexia gradually lessened as these women were more often accused of heresy, witchcraft, and mental disease in the sixteenth century. These women exhibiting holy anorexia moreover displayed a dangerous example of singularity, perceived as a dangerous example for the order of the Church.

Further, the risk of starvation was high, as evidenced by Saint Catherine of Sienna, who died from repeated fasts. Consequently, many pious people chose other alternatives, which consisted less in eliminating all food than in removing the pleasure taken from it. The objective was simply to annihilate the sense of taste. Since it was impossible to give up feeding entirely, several saints chose to feed themselves through suffering, voluntarily torturing their palate by mixing their meals with ashes or dirt to make it lose all flavor.

The deprivations of these anorexic saints constitute a unique example of an *extra*-ordinary feeding that led to a kind of devotion and holiness accessible only to a minority of exceptional souls. Marginal as they were, they nevertheless indicate certain ways in which taste was apprehended; because of their peculiarity, they indirectly reveal certain common representations of gustation. Thus, these examples highlight the profound religious guilt affecting the sense of taste, which had to be repressed, even annihilated, for higher spiritual goals. At stake here is an opposition between common culinary practices and extreme forms of food-related spirituality—a dialectic between the periphery and the center that confirms the vital importance of *mediocritas* in the cultural system of taste and, more broadly, in the whole culture of early modern Europe.[75] The extreme recurring fasts practiced by the adepts of holy anorexia constituted somehow the antithetical side of gluttony, the opposite of the gourmands and of the gluttonous witch. The saint and the sorcerer hence draw two symmetric poles of excess ordered around *mediocritas*, the ideal food system defined by the Church and by the whole of early modern society.

The Animality of Taste

Voracious Beasts

Until the eighteenth century, *gourmandise* was broadly criticized by diverse authorities, contributing to an understanding of taste as a sense of disorders and dangers threatening body and soul. The gustatory sense was not, strictly speaking, sinful, but the mouth generated the vice, and the pleasure that came along with its delightful sensations encouraged intemperance. That is why countless authors, using powerful images to condemn gustation, often seemed to confuse taste and gluttony, dooming the former when condemning the latter; the moral disgust surrounding gluttony led to the moral disgust of taste.

The dissemination of this understanding of taste spread through several rhetorical strategies that leaned on symbolic associations, contributing to a cultural system of representations organized around taste. A real catalog of references to taste and gluttony takes shape when addressing more general kinds of sources, such as dictionary entries, emblem books, and conference proceedings organized by learned societies like the Bureau d'Adresse, founded by Théophraste Renaudot in the seventeenth century.[76] If not directly addressing the question of taste, these documents are bursting with discussions linked to this universe. For instance, we find record of a talk held on the five senses, on pleasure, and on the relations between body and mind; we find emblems related to the seven deadly sins and to the moral prejudices of *gula*; dictionary notes include terms located within the conceptual and semantic field of taste, gluttony, the five senses, food, and pleasure. Regularly repeated examples and clichés linked to taste, then, emerge from these texts, perhaps primarily because in the past the multiplication of learned references was a way for scholars to establish their erudition.

The first evidence that comes out when analyzing these texts is the profusion of animal references. The senses were traditionally attached to bestial imagery that can be traced in written texts as well as in early modern visual culture, which developed an already rich medieval tradition of bestiaries.[77] The senses represented the animal part of human beings, which explains why the senses were sometimes literally transformed into beasts.[78] It was the case for all the senses and thus also of taste, the archetypal iconographic and literary symbol of which was the monkey, held as the zoological emblem of the sense of taste. Thomas of Cantimpré likely introduced the symbol of the monkey in the thirteenth century. The ape was accompanied by an apple, supposedly referencing the Fall of the first humans.[79] Specialists suggest that this animal might have been chosen to be associated with taste because it enjoys eating fruit, and thus would remind the association of taste with the sin of gluttony. At any rate, the symbol was adopted without discussion, and it gradually became recognizable to everybody; the monkey had a sensory expertise, filling for the gustatory sense the role assumed by the dog for smell or by the eagle for sight. As stated by the fourth speaker of the Bureau d'Adresse's conference held on the senses: with the exception of touch, "animals overcome us in all the other senses. The dog excels us in smell, the monkey in taste, the deer in hearing, and the eagle in sight."[80] Besides the connection with the apple and the sin of gluttony, the physical similarity of monkeys and humans could also explain why this particular animal was chosen to refer to the taste sense. Especially as, since Aristotle, "man" was often himself appointed as the expert of touch, and therefore of taste, which Aristotle himself considered a form of touch.[81] The monkey symbol could also have a less positive dimension, the ape being "a traditional epitome of ugliness and low morality,"[82] embodying the unreasonable nature of man, who easily forgets where his honor and salvation lie. The monkey was moreover considered as a ridiculous animal, laughed at in numerous proverbs, as shown by Erasmus's proverb "Not pluris quam simias" [is not worth more than monkeys].[83]

Besides the traditional figure of the monkey, there were countless other animals symbolically associated with taste and gluttony. The list of references is inexhaustible: pig, wolf, duck, crane, pike,[84] cat, bear,[85] fox,[86] lion,[87] and many others. All associated with food, these animals were literary topoi and part of a common cultural heritage.[88] Diverse and fragmented symbols of gustation, these animals had one feature in common: voracity, by then a synonym of gluttony.[89] Is the wolf not "the most greedy, the most carnivorous, and the finest of animals"?[90] Birds, such as the duck,[91] the crane, the swan, and the cock of India (turkey),[92] were all conceived as "real symbols of a greedy and completely disturbed appetite."[93] The cat was gluttonous as much as devilish, as evidenced by the fact that witches and devils readily adopted its shape in their bestial transformations.[94] Additionally, there was also a fantastical animal combining the features of several animals of the gustatory bestiary; in French, it was called the *glouton*, which can be translated as "glutton" or "gluttonous." The dictionary of Richelet proposes this definition:

> [A] very black and very gleaming wild animal we find in Lapland, and Muscovy, which lives in the water and on the ground. It is big as a dog. It has the teeth of a wolf, the snout of a cat, the body and the tail of a fox. The feet are short and the head round. It lives only on rotting carcasses, and eats so much of this that it becomes as fat as a drum. It then presses itself between two trees to bring up what it ate, but as soon as it brings it up, it fills up again with it. To catch the glutton, the Laplanders kill it with arrows when it presses itself between two trees to bring up what it ate.[95]

Dog, wolf, cat, and fox—all animals associated with gluttonous eating habits—compose the various parts of this particular being. Combined together, they represent a metaphor of bulimia and the embodiment of gluttony, revealed even in the animal's name.

All these greedy beasts are associated with a selfish hunger, suggesting the obsessive anxiety of contemporaries toward famine and undernourishment, which were realities experienced on a daily basis, at least until the eighteenth century. They also underscore the contiguity between gluttony and avarice, two vices particularly close to one another.[96] In emblem books, representations of avarice and gluttony therefore often followed one another. Dante also highlighted the connections between these entangled vices, which were symbolically and geographically translated within the succession of circles in Hell: the second circle concerned the lustful; the third the gourmands; and the fourth the misers.

The pig was another famous symbolic illustration of taste and gluttony.[97] As Cesare Ripa, author of an *iconologia*—an emblem book that would become extremely influential in the seventeenth and eighteenth centuries—explains: "The swine tastes everything, even mud and the nastiest garbage."[98] The pig was presented as a disgusting and gluttonous animal. Of the pig, Buffon writes that "all its tastes are revolting, all its sensations are reduced to a furious lust and to a brutal gluttony, which makes it devour indistinctly all it sees, and even its progeny at the moment it was just born. Its voracity apparently depends on the continual need that it has to fill the big capacity of its stomach and the rudeness of its appetites, the lethargy of the senses of taste and touch."[99] The pig symbolized gluttony more than just taste; the gourmand, insatiable, "only thinks of growing fat, in the imitation of the Swine which accompanies him."[100] This is notably evidenced by Ripa, who chose the swine to embody Gluttony (figure 1).[101] Gluttons were, moreover, often called *pourceaux* (swines), a particularly deprecating adjective suggesting that an unrestrained sense of taste was a potential opening for the devil and also for the animal that slumbers in every man.[102] As Jean Bodin regrets,

> there are many men who never devote to contemplating intellectual things, and never raise the spirit higher than their mouth, living as swines and savage animals, of which the holy writing says: they are not men anymore, but look like beasts, from whom dies the soul and the body together. And as for those, it seems that they cannot have company with the spirits, good or bad, for the vast difference between these swines and the spirits, which by nature are immaterial and spiritual essences. But the one who devotes his thoughts to any evil and meanness, then his soul degenerates into this devilish nature.[103]

The bestial and the demonic were hence inseparable. Pigs, as well as gluttons or witches, "never raise the spirit higher than their mouth"; contemporaries believed that they all turned away from heaven, from God, and from the

Figure 1. "Gloutonnie" (Gluttony). From Cesare Ripa, *Iconologie, ou, Explication nouvelle de plusieurs images*, 156. By permission of the Master and Fellows of St John's College, Cambridge.

civilized world.[104] Although considered a disgusting animal, the pig—a food taboo in numerous cultures—was nevertheless consumed in the early modern era, at least by Christians. There were indeed no specific food restrictions in Christianity, since the main issue here was immoderation. The problem with food consumption, Saint Augustine explains, "is not the impurity of food" but the "uncontrolled desire."[105] Hence, as highlighted by Shapin, "the Jews feared certain foods, while to Christian all foods were equally clean or unclean."[106] The solution was thus to adopt a "routine consumption of *the same* foods."[107]

Besides the pig and the other animals mentioned above, let us finally note that there were also examples of beasts "that have no taste, nor any feeling of flavors": the crocodile that "has no tongue, which is the organ of it"; the ostrich, "when it eats the iron"; the wolf, when it eats dirt, "the one [iron] and the other [dirt] insipid." As pointed out during a conference on taste held at the Bureau d'Adresse, there were taste disorders to be found among humans as well: "Such was this Lazare, who mentions Colombe, who swallowed glass, pitch, soot, and all other things without disgust; and this girl domestic of the King of Persia, who ate any kind of poisons, so acrid they were, and fed on it."[108] Images of the tongueless crocodile and the starved wolf that eats dirt, also common in texts from this era, were borrowed from Pliny the Elder.[109] It was, furthermore, commonly known that "the ostrich, by a secret virtue, digests the iron and converts it into food."[110] Consuming iron was perceived as a lack of taste and as a form of gluttony, since it was in some sense excessive in its indifference to the things gulped down, even if they were inedible objects. This indifference was considered not unlike the attitude of the swine or the disgusting feast of the Sabbath. The figure of the crocodile demonstrates well the idea that an extreme lack of taste could be associated with gluttony, the obsessive compulsion to eat being indifferent to the nature of the objects consumed; this animal was frequently chosen as an icon of gluttony, as we see in Cesare Ripa's *Iconologia*, in which the personification of fasting is represented "up on a Crocodile, to show that it tramples Greed, from which this Animal was an hieroglyphic figure by the Egyptians."[111]

The crocodile and the ostrich were, however, less frequent cultural references than those that illustrated the damaged senses, such as the blind mole. Most of the time, the examples of sensory handicap referenced the sick, pregnant women, and the elderly.[112] But it was not uncommon in passages discussing the lack of one sense to simply "forget" to mention taste in the list, either that ageusia—a term that was invented in the nineteenth century to mean the loss of the ability to taste different flavors was too rare to be stated, or that it appeared to be less significant than deafness or blindness, indirectly confirming the marginal position of taste among the five senses.

Figure 2. "Ieusne" (Fasting). From Cesare Ripa, *Iconologie, ou, Explication nouvelle de plusieurs images*, 130. By permission of the Master and Fellows of St John's College, Cambridge.

A Powerful Bestiary: The Civilization of Taste

With the exception of the monkey, which may appear as an expert on taste, all the animals that were associated with taste and with *gourmandise* in this bestiary of gluttonous animals displayed an unbridled feeding. The figure of a disorder obviously dominated the shared conceptions of taste. The list of animals mentioned in the bestiary above is not meant to be exhaustive. Besides the duck, the crane, and the turkey, there were numerous other species of gluttonous birds—for instance, the vulture or the crow—which are not enumerated here. The examples emphasized above were, however, the most common. They were constantly repeated and mentioned in different sources and cultural settings, and they were so representative that they appeared in dictionary's entries associated with food immoderation. What I want to highlight here is that if the bestiaries built around the other senses could often express sensory expertise—the sight of the vulture or the power of the basilisk's glaze, the dog's smell or the delicate touch of the spider—the bestiary of taste was commonly a deviant one, expressing a physical loss of control through food immoderation. However, this is not to say that all animals were necessarily gluttons or that animality was systemically linked to gluttony. Although it is perhaps difficult to see what animal would not pursue a selfish hunger, the aim of these texts—emblems, iconologies—was not to examine real animals in the perspective of a natural history or a philosophy of nature but to use exemplary animal references as symbols, illustrations, and signs to be interpreted that represented vices and qualities of humans. There are thus many nuances in the ways in which animals and humans were intertwined in these texts. What the profusion of animal references demonstrates, on the other hand, is that the sense of taste was indisputably associated with animality.

Gustation was disturbing because—more than the other senses and parts of the body—it revealed the animalistic dimension of humanity, and therefore questioned the idea of a frontier between humans and animals. The relation between humans and animals, and moreover the limit between animality and bestiality, is one of the most debated issues in the history of Western thinking.[113] There were countless theoretical, religious, and political debates that have been held since antiquity to question the differences between humans and animals, and the frontier between these two realms. The development of Christianity was a decisive moment in this regard: the Old Testament established man as the most divine being, to which all the rest of the natural world—animals, plants, and so forth—was to be subordinated. The existence of the latter was thought of as in relation to the human order: the aim of all living creatures was to satisfy human needs. Humans, elected by God, had to protect themselves against any potential risk of corruption from bestiality, which led to an intense and long-lasting anxiety toward any forms of behaviors likely to threaten the frontiers separating men from animals, and an obsession to track down all which in men could possibly evoke the animal. Gluttonous acts were one of these, which is why they had to be repressed.

In the early modern era, suppressing any potential sign of animality became even more important with the rise of modern court society, marked by the development of good manners and the establishment of new standards of behavior, a phenomenon notably theorized in Norbert Elias's civilization process. Elias has highlighted the part played by civility in this process: the *honnête homme*, shaped by the rules of etiquette, built his self by learning to domesticate his internal drives. Gustation, again, was disturbing; its association with a bodily need reminded one of the despicable proximity of human and animal physicality—a proximity that members of polite society were trying very hard to repress and forget, by distinguishing themselves not only from other men but also from the boorish, the foreign, and the common people. But the distinction between human and animal spheres was porous. The bestial behavior of certain gourmands revealed the power of the stomach. This is why the ambiguous sense of taste, along with its ominous mouth, was to be socially excluded in behavior as well as in speech. Taste and feeding were indeed likely to lead to the loss of control, by which the man could become again, if only for a moment, an animal. In the introduction to *The Anatomy of Melancholy*, where Robert Burton stigmatizes the animalistic madness and vices of men, he leans on Jean Chrysostom, who "pleads farther yet, that they [men] are more than mad, very Beasts, stupified and void of common sense: *For how* (saith he) *shall I know thee to be a man, when thou kickest like an Asse, neyghest like an [sic] Horse after women, rauest in lust like a Bull, rauenest like a Beare, stingest like a Scorpion, rakest like a Woolfe . . . shall I say thou art a man, that hast all the symptoms of a Beast?*"[114] The treatises of civility seized this rhetoric to slander deviant behaviors, as illustrated, for instance, in the writing of Erasmus, which was particularly rich in metaphors inspired by the bestiary:

> Certain people descend upon dishes while they are barely installed. They behave like wolves. . . . It is storks and pigs that gulp down enormous pieces at one time . . . do not nibble bones with your teeth, as a dog. . . . It is cats, not men, that lick with their tongue a plate or a dish at the bottom of which remains stuck some sugar or some other sweetness . . . others open a mouth so big when chewing that they emit sounds close to the growl of a pig.[115]

Wolf, stork, cat, pig: Erasmus drew from traditional bestiary symbols when condemning gluttony. We find similar considerations in other books of manners, as in Antoine de Courtin's, who specified that it "is necessary to cut small pieces, not to make pockets for cheeks, as monkeys."[116] Moderation and order at the table distinguished the man from the animal, gluttony being perceived here as a bestial characteristic: "When one eats, one should not eat fast nor greedily, however much hunger one has . . . it is necessary when eating to join the lips, in order not to lapper as animals."[117] Consequently, Furetière would write that the sin of gluttony is "not a vice of the honest people."[118] Elite cuisine was convenient in this respect, because it "humanized" eating due to a bodily need; the civilization process transformed a biological necessity into an increasingly refined social activity.

As we move away from the Renaissance, references to the bestiary gradually disappear from dictionaries and books of manners. One finds fewer cases in Antoine de Courtin than in Erasmus, and none in Jean-Baptiste de La Salle. As for dictionaries, the article "Gourmandise" of the 1757 French *Encyclopédie* mentions no animal figure.[119] These references were no longer useful because the dismissal of animality had been internalized by the culture generally. The definitions of the gourmet, the *friand*, and the *delicate* already moved away from this animality toward a proper human imagery: the entries to these words in early modern dictionaries (of the seventeenth and eighteenth centuries) make no reference to the bestiary. This is a significant nuance because delicate taste began to be presented as strictly human, in contrast to the voracious bestiality of the glutton.

The collective rites supervising the intake of food—increasingly refined by the development of table manners and *l'art de la cuisine*—distinguished human gustation from the way the rest of nature consumed food. The best way to separate humanity from beasts consisted in the integration of God into food practices, just like when protecting the soul from demonic attacks. The prayer over the meal was fundamental, a sign of a Christianized humanity superior to bestiality.[120] The rejection of animality and a respect for God were intertwined, Christian rules being an opportunity to distinguish men from animals, as in the traditional order of Creation where man was situated in the center of the world between God and superior spiritual creatures on the one hand, and the lower animals on the other hand. The ideal was always to distance oneself from the earth and aspire toward heaven. Blaise Pascal states an old and traditional fact, referring in particular to Pseudo-Dionysius's hierarchy of beings, when he writes that "it is dangerous to show too much to the man how he equals animals, without showing him his greatness. And it is still dangerous to show him too much his greatness without his lowness. It is even more dangerous to let him ignore both, but it is very advantageous to represent both to him. . . . The man should not believe that he is equal to animals neither to angels, nor ignore both, but know both."[121] Following this ideal, taste had to be controlled by the Christian, as part of the low animal nature of men.

Crazy Gluttons in History

Besides the bestiary, there were other recurring cultural references summoned when taste and greed were mentioned. Here, also, the major historical greedy figures were systematically examples of food excesses. They were used in diverse contexts and sources: in medical, moral, and religious books; in treatises of the senses or in physics; in cookbooks; in conduct books; and in modern dictionaries. These works were pursuing a long-lasting tradition mocking the gourmand's lack of body control, which were already present in a number of antique satyrs, extended and Christianized in the late antiquity and in the early Middle Ages.[122]

Since the fourth century, Marcus Gavius Apicius, contemporary of the Roman emperors Augustus and Tiberius, has been considered the attributed author of the first preserved antique recipe book (*De re coquinaria*), although there is a lack of evidence to support this claim. Apicius—already considered as the representation of the gourmand, if not the cook[123]—appeared in the early modern era most of the time as a glutton driven crazy by the pleasures of the mouth. After wasting his fortune on food delicacies, this famous and extravagant gourmet was rumored to have supposedly decided to commit suicide; acknowledging that he did not have enough money left to satisfy all his desires, he considered death a sweeter outcome than limiting his delights, which would be just as terrible as hunger itself.[124] Apicius was sometimes praised for the delicacy of his palate, but this praise was often (as for the speakers of the Bureau d'Adresse) followed by a moral judgment that limited its impact: "Because to speak well about something it is necessary to know the differences, it seems that a treatise on taste would be more a matter for an Apicius than for a Philosopher; *in whom* [Apicius] *one could turn in disapproval the too exact knowledge of sauces.*"[125] Hence, if the delicacy of Apicius's taste was recognized, it was, however, not valorized. Dionysus II, tyrant of Syracuse (fourth century BCE), was another "crazy" glutton of history who was assumed to have died of obesity.

The most famous glutton, though, was Philoxenus, a comedic figure who apparently desired to have a crane's neck in order to eat more. With its excessive dimension leading to ridicule, Philoxenus's desire constitutes another topos of the history of taste. The crane's very long neck was thought to help it consume huge quantities of food, which made the gourmands fantasize, dreaming to be able to increase their eating capacity. It was commonly believed that "those who exercise one of their senses more than the others, who benefit from it or delight themselves in it. . . . Philoxenus who wished for a crane's neck, and those who live only to drink and to eat, instead of we who drink and eat to live, will give the advantage to taste."[126] The idea of developing the capacities of the neck was understandable, given the fact that in the Roman world, it was not the tongue but the *gula* [the gullet or the throat] that was considered the locus of pleasure, while the stomach was fed and strengthened by food.[127] According to Aristotle, the sensory delight in this case was one resulting from touch: it occurred when food crossed the esophagus, coming down from the mouth toward the stomach.[128] The Greek philosopher actually used the example of Philoxenus to demonstrate the tactile character of taste, which for him led to intemperance only when working as a form of touch, not in its role of discriminating flavors.[129]

The story of Philoxenus was extremely popular and overly repeated in the most diverse sources. One traces it, for instance, in emblem books to illustrate gluttony.[130] The engraving represented here (figure 3) comes from a widely circulated book of emblems published in the sixteenth century by Andrea Alciato.[131]

We see a man with a long neck and a wide stomach; birds are in the background, as well as in both hands of the central character. The long necks of the man and of the birds are an obvious reference to Philoxenus, easily recognized by contemporaries who were familiar with his story. The birds—particularly the crane, the gull, and the pelican—were traditionally held to be gluttonous creatures. The episode of Philoxenus was thus situated between the traditional references to animals of the bestiary and the greedy figures of history, and composed a commonplace so usual of gluttony in the culture of the Old Regime that one traces it as late as the eighteenth century in Diderot and D'Alembert's *Encyclopédie.*[132] By then, scholars studying the physiology of taste would certainly

Gourmandie.

APODEIXE.

A col de Grue,& grand ventre de Tor
Vng homme tient,vng Loir,& vng Butor.
Telleforme eſt des Denys,& Apices,
Et tous gourmans par friandes delices.

Les friandz deſirent long col,pour plus lon-
guement ſentir la ſaueur des bons morſeaulx,& les Gourmans hont grand ventre,
& graſſe panſe.

Figure 3. "Gourmandie" (Gluttony).
From Andrea Alciato, *Emblemes*,
112. By permission of University of
Glasgow Library, Special Collections.

question the absurd idea of extending the neck in order to savor more—for,
they argued, pleasure did not come from that region of the body but from the
tongue.[133] Yet it is fascinating to note that even those who emphasized the inco-
herence of Philoxenus still felt necessary to make a reference to the anecdote.[134]

The engraving reproduced here was published in a section entitled "Gueule"
(mouth), which included six emblems relative to gluttony. The same image
was printed to open and close the series, accompanied with a specific title and
epigram. If the first emblem was related to *Gueule, Gourmandie* [sic] (mouth.
gluttony), the second bore the name *Contre ung bavard Glouton* (Against a
greedy chatterbox).[135] In the latter, food intemperance was directly linked to
verbal disorder, as evidenced by its epigram:

> With a gaping throat and a harsh cry, which pierces the air:
> A beak like a nose or a many-holed trumpet,
> The pelican paints [displays] a huge ranting figure,
> Which thinks of nothing except its mouth and its belly.

This emblem is self-explanatory, the pelican bird with big, long, gaping beak
and thick wide throat, and a cry like a donkey
braying, signifying a ranting glutton, thinking
only of his arse and his belly.[136]

Speaking and eating, two functions coming from the same organ, the mouth, is
the theme of this section. Excesses in one domain were naturally supposed to
lead to an overflow in the other one. Birds were another allusion to this association, because they were renowned as greedy and noisy creatures. This emblem
denounced the double sin of the tongue, which, fed by greedy pleasures, loosens
itself, with all the aggravating consequences that this loosening entails for one's
morality.[137] Gluttons tend to talk more, to speak more loudly, and to discuss inappropriate subjects when they eat or drink excessively, as also suggested by the
emblem of the *escornifleurs*, gluttons who "sting others with a malicious mouth."[138]

Similar representations of *gula* appeared in most books of emblems. The image sometimes slightly differed, but the symbolic elements—the long neck, the
prominent stomach, the birds—and the cultural references in the epigrams—
Philoxenus, Apicius, Dionysus, and so forth—remained. The emblems relative
to food systematically highlighted excess, presenting the mouth as a dangerous
door open to disorders. This is certainly the case in "The captive for his greed"
(figure 4), where a gluttonous rat is tempted by an oyster that closed itself on
him, depicting the disastrous consequences of the sin of gluttony:

Several make themselves slavish, captive in the good
houses: only for the good pieces, Sev-
eral also make their pit with the teeth, getting themselves
killed before the age, by excess of greed.[139]

A host of other emblems found in the era's texts are situated in the same critical tone.

In the end, religious, medical, moral, cultural, social, and symbolic texts and
signifiers devaluated taste and *gourmandise*, often associated with one another
and just as often negatively represented in the early modern era. As a result, there
was a deep collective guilt and uneasiness toward the pleasures of eating and
consequently of discussing taste. Most of the time, when taste was considered,
the intemperance, the disorders, and the dangers accompanying taste were highlighted; rarely were discernment and judgment of flavors considered. Taste itself
was not a vice, but its intimacy with carnal sin entailed a devaluation of the very
sense itself. This devaluation explains why authors of conduct books insisted so
much on concealing any indication of greed; it also clarifies why cooks chose to
publish their works under the seal of more honorable justifications.

Le Rat regnant au cellier, rongeant tout,
Des huyſtres vit baïllantes par vng bout:
Sa barbe y mit:& faulx os il atrappe,
Leſquelz touchéz feirent tomber la trappe,
Et le larron en priſon hont tenu,
Qui par ſoy meſme en ſa foſſe eſt venu.

Pluſieurs ſe rendent ſerfz,& captifz aulx bonnes
maiſons:ſeullement pour les bons morſeaulx, Plu_
ſieurs auſsi font leur foſſe auec les dens,ſe procurãs
mort auant eage,par exces de gourmandiſe.

Figure 4. "Le captif pour sa
gourmandise" (The Captive for
His Greed). From Andrea Alciat,
Emblemes, 116. By permission of
University of Glasgow Library, Special
Collections.

In the Shadows of the Body

Inescapable Duality

There are many reasons explaining the historical depreciation of taste, but the
two main causes of the cultural construction of taste as a lower sense are its
systematic association with the body and with animality, both closely linked to
one another. The uneasiness toward taste is symptomatic of a wider discomfort
of early modern cultures toward bodily pleasures, in particular—evidently—
for religious reasons. The Christian Church severely criticized sensory delights
and promoted bodily control through mortification, for what really mattered
to the faithful was the afterlife, although a closer look at religious discourse
and practices discloses a much more nuanced picture. The Church has often
had a paradoxical discourse on the body. On the one hand, it tried to restrain
it as the place of all drives, uncontrollable desires, and of sin. On the other
hand, it excited it and troubled it to cause a "sacred shiver" to the believers,
as we can see in the efforts displayed by the Jesuits regarding the display
of impressive paintings in churches and music within religious ceremonies

and processions, all these sensory stimuli being meant to inspire and thrill the bodies and souls of the faithful. It was in particular the case in the areas of baroque culture that adopted an extremely sensory form of Tridentine Catholicism—Spain and Southern Netherlands, for instance—as opposed to regions like France, which practiced classical education and a more rational Tridentine Catholicism.[140] Yet, despite this intriguing ambiguity, the official discourse in early modern times generally encouraged the mortification of the sinner's body.

The Renaissance was a period more amenable to the valuation of physical pleasures, especially in Italy. The humanists rediscovered countless antique texts like those of Epicurus. Inspired by the Ancients, several Renaissance writers tried to rehabilitate the pleasures of the senses, pleading for *l'honnête volupté* (fair sensual delight). The most significant example of this rehabilitation with regard to taste is the work *De honesta voluptate et valetudine* (On honorable pleasure and health) of Bartolomeo Sacchi (named Platina), printed in Rome by 1473–1475.[141] Platina, a humanist who was neither a cook nor a doctor, proposed an ethics of reasonable pleasure in a "hybrid body of work"; being at the same time a treatise on cookery and on dietetics, it mixed medical and culinary advice, and promoted a healthy lifestyle by including descriptions of products, recipes, and considerations on the pleasures of the table.[142] A French version of this text appeared in 1505 in Paris under the title *Le Platine en François*, published by Desdier Christol, who translated and adapted the original text.[143] This book became a bestseller and would largely impact further writings on taste and cuisine. According to Florent Quellier, it notably contributed to the implementation in France of the Italian cultural model, more open to sensory delights.[144] The work thus affirmed the emergence of a culture more favorable to the pleasures of taste, although the dominant dietary tone of the text indicates that this emergence was still quite hesitant.

Despite these cultural evolutions favoring the senses and their delights, even in the Renaissance, intellectual gratifications were still considered superior to the short-lived pleasures of the senses. The gustatory enjoyment was especially fleeting, for it was connected to a biological need; as soon it was satisfied, it disappeared. Thus, for some, there was no point in enjoying these momentary enchantments: "If at least this pleasure of taste was long-lasting, one might take its defense, but one hardly experiences it and it is already gone; whereas the infirmities it gives birth to are quite prolonged."[145] In the sixteenth century, many were those who, like Erasmus, would dream to be exempted from the necessity of food. Hence, people of the Renaissance obviously did not lack uncertainty and vacillated between the valuation of sensory experience and the condemnation of fleeting, "imaginary" pleasures of the senses.

In early modern France, the religious, political, and cultural context was not very favorable to sensory pleasures, especially from the second half of the

sixteenth century onward, notably because of all the troubles connected with
the Wars of Religion. The context was also more problematic for the senses in
the seventeenth century, when a stronger religious power initiated a period of
increased severity toward sensual enjoyments and strengthened the repression of
the body of the sinner. Due to the chaos resulting from religious wars, the Roman
Catholic Church strove to regain control over bodies and souls, undertaking a
vast program of edification, preaching, and education. "The Counter-Reforma-
tion strengthened the suspicion toward the body which the magisterium had
already demonstrated in the middle Ages. The body, as an 'abominable garment
of the soul,' was denigrated, as the sinner ceaselessly heard saying that it was
by the body that he risk[ed] losing himself."[146] The power of the Church in the
seventeenth century contributed to the period's general distrust of everything
related to the body, and consequently to taste as well, as this is a particularly
corporeal sense.

Religious concerns explain part of the reasons why taste was depreciated in the
past, yet they cannot explain it all. Long before the appearance of Christianity,
the appreciation of taste was already highly ambivalent.[147] From its foundation,
the Roman Catholic Church inherited ideas spread both by Judaism and Greco-
Roman thought; it was notably influenced by antique ascetic philosophies such
as Stoicism or Platonism, which already condemned sensory pleasures. Hence it
seems that there was something more fundamental regarding the sense of taste
and its systematic displacement to the peripheries. Antiquity is traditionally
recognized as a period more favorable to pleasure, in particular to pleasures
of the body, and the Renaissance is likewise understood to have inherited, to a
certain extent, this more positive valuation. But writers of these periods were
indeed wary of the disorders of taste and considered the delights of the body
as lower than those of the spirit.

Plato, whose writings had an enormous impact on medieval and early modern
thinkers, contributed the most to this rejection of taste, which he considered
useless to philosophy. The *Banquet* demonstrates the Platonic contempt for the
matters of the table: in spite of the title, nothing in the work concerns food. The
dishes eaten on this occasion are not mentioned at all. The main part of the narrative takes place after the meal, for only the discussions that follow gustation
deserve the attention of the reader.[148] In *The Republic*—as in *Phaedrus* and most
of his other works—Plato asserts the superiority of the mind over the body, and
the importance, for the philosopher, to distance himself from the body, because
there is much "less of truth and reality in the things which serve the needs of the
body than in those which feed the soul." Hence "those who have no experience of
wisdom and virtue and spend their whole time in feasting and self-indulgence are
all their lives, as it were, fluctuating downwards from the central point and back
to it again, but never rise beyond it into the true upper region, to which they have

not lifted their eyes." As a result, these people—actually, "most people" according to the Greek philosopher—are "[n]ever really satisfied with real nourishment, the pleasure they taste is uncertain and impure." Most importantly, they behave like beasts: "Bent over their tables, they feed like cattle with stooping heads and eyes fixed upon the ground; so they grow fat and breed, and in their greedy struggle kick and butt one another to death with horns and hoofs of steel, because they can never satisfy with unreal nourishment that part of themselves which is itself unreal and incapable of lasting satisfaction."[149] People looking down to the earth and its pleasures behave like beasts, only concerned with their belly. The position of the body, especially, was thought to impact their thoughts, as we see in Plato's insistence on these people whose eyes are "fixed upon the ground." We have already encountered similar remarks when dealing with *gourmandise*, gluttons being presented as pigs which "never raise the spirit higher than their mouth." This is a distinctive feature of animality as opposed to humanity, the upright position being considered unique to humans and thought to have permitted the development of the human touch and especially of the human brain.[150]

Obviously, the cultural depreciation of the body cannot be explained solely by religious reasons; these were ideas profoundly anchored in Western cultures. Closely associated with the physical dimension of humanity, taste sends us back to the wide issue of the relationship between the sensible and the intelligible, a major philosophical problem. The system of dualism dominated the intellectual landscape from Plato to Descartes, establishing a clear division between the soul—immortal, immaterial, and peculiar to humans only—and the body—corruptible, material, and common to all living beings; the superior value of the former confirmed the latter's finiteness. The dualistic background manifested itself in multiple ways over the centuries, whether of philosophic or religious nature, but dualism was always implicitly present. This notably explains the construction of a "hierarchy of the senses," distinguishing senses perceived as more spiritual from others considered more physical. We shall return to this hierarchy in the following chapter, but let us for now acknowledge that the history of dualism considerably influenced that of taste, especially in the early modern era, a period of profound cultural, social, political, religious, and economical changes, which had important repercussions on the way contemporaries made sense of the world and how they related to their senses. The seventeenth century, especially, was a turning point in the history of dualism—hence also of taste. A real epistemological shift took place during this period, marked notably by the highly influential works of René Descartes.

Descartes, of course, did not invent mind–body dualism, but his works represented a decisive step that contributed to make of dualism an acute problem in his time. Descartes and his contemporaries developed a keen interest—if not a true fascination—toward machines, mechanical clocks, and autonomous devices, to the point that clockwork became an emblem of political authority and cosmology, an image of the divine design of the universe as well as of the new experimental and mechanical philosophy.[151] During his life, Descartes had been put into contact with a variety of automata. He had previously been a part of Prince Maurice of Nassau's army, which, Peter Dear explains, would have seemed so disciplined to him that soldiers could appear as "human automata." Moreover, before settling in Holland in 1628, he had had the opportunity to travel throughout Europe, going to Germany, France, and Italy, during which he discovered, especially by German princes, many forms of "literal automata," such as "artificial people, animals, and ships run by clockwork," which had become "a commonplace of expensive courtly frivolity." This wide interest in machines and automata had an enormous impact on his works and partially explains why Descartes decided to offer a "mechanistic picture of the physical world."[152]

"Descartes's understanding of the essence of human being was inseparable from his perception of machines" and *automates*, which were used as "models of intelligibility."[153] He considered the human body and the senses, as much as the animals and the entire material universe, to be governed by mechanical laws.[154] These all composed what he called the *res extensa* (the material/corporeal substance), which he opposed to the *res cogita* (the mental substance), the latter belonging exclusively to man, whose nature was to be a thinking subject. These two substances were thought to be of different natures and were the core of the radical form of dualism, splitting body and soul, that Descartes argued for in his writings. The mental and corporeal substances, however, Descartes explains, could mutually influence one another, for they were somehow juxtaposed in the brain's pineal gland. The *automate* model actually facilitated the distinction between the soul and the body, between the man (thought of as a union of the soul and the body) and the animal (which had feelings, sensations, and life, but, according to Descartes, no thoughts).[155]

Moreover, the French philosopher wanted to raise human knowledge to the certainty of sciences and mathematics, thanks to the assistance of Reason, which he defined as the faculty to distinguish truth from falsehood. In this system, the senses, useful for the preservation of the body, were not considered as particularly reliable. As Descartes explains: "All that I received until now for the most true and assured, I learned it from the senses, or by the senses; yet I *sometimes* felt that these senses were misleading, and it is of the caution to never completely trust those who once deceived us."[156] To reach clear and distinct truths, this methodical doubt demands that one gives up all prior knowledge and distrust the illusions of sensory experience. The philosopher insisted: to reach the truth, "I shall now close my eyes, I shall block my ears, I shall divert all my senses, I shall erase even of my thought all the physical images, or at least, because it can hardly be done, I shall consider them as vain and false; and so, discussing only with myself, and considering my inside, I shall try to make me little by little more known and more familiar to myself."[157] The senses, since they can sometimes be misleading, are not to be trusted blindly; which is not to say that they are always deceiving. In some cases, Descartes admits, their judgment makes no doubt: "For instance, that I am here, sitting near the fire, dressed in a robe, with this paper in my hands, and other things of this nature. And how could I deny that these hands and this body are mine?"[158] But in others, like when perceiving very remote objects, they can be utterly deceitful. Consequently, the most extreme precaution is required toward the judgment of the senses. Descartes's writings, however, have often been misinterpreted, and the passage mentioned above could read-ily be taken as a general Cartesian mistrust toward the senses, thus leading to the depreciation of the senses, particularly of taste, which was one of the senses most closely connected with the body.

Nonetheless, if Descartes's writings on the senses would often be transformed and presented without the original nuances and hesitations of their author, it remains that the sense of taste was neglected and held in little esteem by Des-cartes, who barely mentions this sense at all in his books. He was much more fascinated by the eye—vision, optics, and light—to which he devoted many of his works.

The Loss of the Human Sense of Taste

The Cartesian influence would be very strong in seventeenth-century France and beyond. The books of Descartes were repeatedly edited and translated, while his theories were taught in colleges and popularized by his partisans in salons and in other learned academies. His influence was all the more remarkable that his works, along with Galileo and the rise of mechanistic physics, contributed to the emergence of a new form of dualism, which represented, more profoundly, a new epistemology: naturalism. The rise of naturalism has generated an incred-ible body of literature, and it is impossible here to explore each aspect of this profound cultural transformation, which actually engages the entire history of modernity. However, since naturalism had such an important impact on the history of the senses and thus of taste, a brief discussion about some of the fundamental changes brought by this philosophical revolution, which changed the way in which the relations between humans and their environment were conceived, is therefore useful.

Among the numerous authors who have offered analyses of this intellec-tual transition, the anthropological insights of Philippe Descola are especially suggestive. In his book *Beyond Nature and Culture*, he developed a general theoretical framework particularly enlightening for the history of taste. In this work Descola offers a wide-ranging theory in which he identifies four major ontologies existing all over the world and throughout history. Each ontology (animism, naturalism, totemism, and analogism) is defined by a specific primary mode of identification and of relations between humans and their environment (animals and what we would call the natural world). Differences and continuities are established between a self and some other existing being, producing a variety of distributions of "interiority" (that is, a soul, a mind, a spirit, or any other concept related to an internal world of subjectivity and intention) and "exteriority" or "physicality" (a physical constitution).[159]

Descola situated the early modern period in between two epistemologies: analogism and naturalism. Before the seventeenth century, the meaning of life and the world was established according to an analogic mode, as already evidenced, for instance, by Foucault in Les Mots et les Choses (The Order of Things). The world was interpreted as unified yet extremely diversified, where everything referred to something else in a complex universe of signs. This system was characterized, according to the terminology of Descola, by a discontinuity between the interiorities and physicalities of human and nonhuman beings. The system of sympathies and antipathies, just like the chain of beings, organized knowledge and made sense of this universe where void did not exist, where visible and invisible were intertwined, and where analogies between the microcosm and the macrocosm—between celestial and human bodies, between the senses and the four elements, between minerals, plants, animals, and human beings—wove together networks of correspondences that gave meaning to the world.[160] Taste as well was inscribed within this complex network of correspondences. Perceived as a necessary sense, it was meant to allow men and animals to distinguish edible elements from poisons. Likes and dislikes were traditionally conceived as physiological sympathies or antipathies between the nature or temperament of a person and specific types of food. The flavors of things, the sensations felt through their consumption, were considered as reliable indications of their effect on the body. According to the theory of the humors, each temperament naturally provoked desire and taste for its suitable food. What was tasty in the mouth was therefore also profitable for the body, because "the pleasure we take in one thing is the most certain indication of the good or the harm that it brings us."[161] In this analogical context, taste's judgment was decisive; individual food preferences were respected for natural and medical reasons. Moreover, taste was endowed with a therapeutic value. Indeed, when observing the sick body, the doctor used all his senses to develop a diagnosis. Taste, for instance, was used to evaluate the quality of urine, considered as a sign (among others) of the ailments affecting the body.

But this cosmology, so deeply interwoven with Renaissance cultures, would be challenged in the seventeenth century by decisive events such as the development of a new science of anatomy and medicine and the discovery of blood circulation by Harvey, both leading to the decline of Galenic humoral theory; the "scientific revolution," and the advent of empirical philosophy, but also of humanism and the many religious reforms that established a new relation between the individual and the divine; the many travels and explorations of other continents, which shifted the existing representation of the geography of the world; the internationalization of trade and exchanges that led to major economic and monetary transformations. All the changes mentioned here (and many others) utterly transformed early modern perceptions of self and the world; some of these changes represented concrete experiences in the material world of a naturalist ontology and of philosophical dualisms of which the texts are not the only loci of expression. It is, of course, impossible to mention here all the people, events, causes, and consequences that led to these important cultural, social, religious, political, and economical transformations. But all of these many changes contributed to deeply alter people's perception of their environment and encouraged scholars, philosophers, and scientists to think of other ways of explaining the human body and the natural universe, thus making these deep transformations of thought possible.

Building from the traditional split between mind and body, based on both philosophical and religious influences, a new dualism arose that Descola has called the "dualism of the individual and of the world."[162] Until the seventeenth century, human beings, in spite of the transcendence Christianity granted them, had never been considered as distinct from their environment. But from now on, they would "become *like* foreign and superior to nature," of which they intended to become "*like* masters and possessors."[163] A great distance—or *grand partage*—severed humanity and their environment: Nature was born. In this system, humans were considered as the only species endowed with an interiority, for they were the unique beings thought to have a mind and a soul. With the rest of the world, they shared the same physicality, a physical constitution that answered to similar laws and constraints. As stressed by Philippe Descola, the "mechanistic revolution of the seventeenth century . . . [represented] the world just like a machine, the machinery of which [could] be dismantled by scholars, and not anymore like a composite whole of humans and non-humans endowed with an intrinsic meaning by the divine creation."[164]

Both systems, analogism and naturalism, cohabited during this pivotal period. This intellectual and cultural transformation is of particular interest here, for it also altered the values granted to taste and its judgments. Since sensory experience itself was uncertain, flavors started to be considered deceptive as well. As a result, a suitable diet could only be established by Reason. Sixteenth- and seventeenth-century medical authorities consequently established a regimen much too complicated for the nonspecialist.[165] Doctors took control of dietetics, to the detriment of the cooks, whose preparations had for centuries been inspired by forebears' dietary prescriptions. Jean-Louis Flandrin attributes this loss of faith in taste to the disintegration of Galenic theory, which was gradually questioned as chemistry and physiology developed. But it seems that this upheaval was also due to the advent of naturalism, a major early modern cultural transformation that indicates, moreover, why the senses were slowly removed from medical diagnosis.

Taste, in this context, lost its value as a sign. This loss is noticeable in the multiple works on self-medication, such as Luigi Cornaro's *La vita sobria*, a particularly popular book celebrating dietary tolerance.[166] Cornaro, who presented himself as a centenarian, recommended that his readers observe and examine themselves, at a time when the rise of individualism was first discernible. Attentive to his personal sensations, he tried to analyze the physical reactions following the intake of food, in order to determine which dishes suited and which harmed him. An appropriate diet appeared the best way to live a long and healthy life without fear of either death or disease, for "with sobriety all the causes of the harm disappear. There would thus be no need of doctors nor of medicine."[167] But taste was a misleading clue, as testified by Cornaro, who recognized that the food that pleased him the most was the food that did the most harm:

> I thus studied at first the nature of the food that suited it [my temperament], and first of all I tried the effect of those [foods] whose taste was pleasant to me. I wanted to verify a proverb which I had formerly considered true, which is universally thought of as valid, and which is of use as rule to the gourmands: "That what one finds good is nourishing and profitable." The examination demonstrated to me the falseness of the proverb. So I liked over all the bitter and very cold wine, melons and other fruits, raw salad, fishes, pork, pies, vegetable soup, pastries, and other similar dishes, and nevertheless all these foods were harmful to me.[168]

The dishes most pleasant to the taste organs were thus not necessarily the best ones for the body. Why, in this case, follow these deceptive sensations? Formerly a reliable witness, taste had become a deficient arbitrator. It was therefore important to ignore gustatory temptation and to observe instead the physical effects, to determine the value of food by reason and experience, and not anymore by the palate.[169] A healthy diet would, in return, sublimate the sense of taste. Pleasure was then more intense because the stomach received only the food that suited it best, at the time when it needed it. As Cornaro confessed: "I indeed find more flavor today in the simple food which is my food at any moment, than I formerly found, in the time of my disorders, in the most delicate dishes."[170]

Taste, finally, lost much of its value, since it did not have the same utility anymore. Some authors, such as Malebranche—a French Oratorian priest and rationalist philosopher inspired by Descartes—therefore recommended repressing this sense and eating without pleasure—a choice that would, moreover, favor devotion and social life: "It is reason and not instinct which must lead it [the soul]. That the spirit likes or dislikes bread, it is indifferent to the body. If one eats it without enjoying it, the body will feed on it anyway; and if one likes it without eating it, the body will not become stronger from it."[171] So for Malebranche it would be advisable to consume everything with indifference, without granting dishes any attention. This was also the ideal prescribed by Francis de Sales, who recommended that devout souls renounce food choices in their everyday life, for in the "indifference as to what we ought to eat and what we ought to drink lies the perfection of the practice of this sacred saying: 'Eat what is set before you.'"[172]

Taste, which was not the sign of anything anymore, was dismissed from then on as defective, unreliable, and useless. The loss of taste's meaning was, moreover, justified by history, beginning with the doctrine of Original Sin. Many authors celebrated the myth of the origins of taste, which was an effective judge for humans and animals in the Garden of Eden. The first people were naturally sober before the Fall, which disrupted everything and introduced concupiscence into the world. Human taste had been, since then, totally disordered:

> Hunger warns of need, and settles more or less the quantity of food. Formerly it settled it right; and it would still settle it well enough, if we ate fruit such as God makes them grow. Taste is a short and indisputable proof, whether certain bodies are or are not appropriate to eat. Without knowing the texture of a stone or an unknown fruit, it suffice to present it to the tongue, the faithful doorman, *at least before the sin*, of all which has to enter the house, to make sure it will not bring any disorders there. . . . *It was formerly so*. But the sin of the first man changed this admirable order; and the union of mind and body remaining the same, the mind was unfortunately scolded by the senses, because of the loss which it made of the power to command them.[173]

Man was believed to have lost his sense of taste when corrupted by the refined art of cookery, an art that signified the moral degradation of society. Animals, on the contrary, had acute senses and were still capable of instinctually finding their food in the environment because they were able to remain moderate: "Their total abstinence and continence [of animals] is displayed by the fact that they content themselves with licit and necessary pleasures, far from the muddled appetites of men, which, not content with a single food . . . depopulate the air, the earth, and the water to irritate rather than quench their greed."[174] The orderly taste of animals opposed the unbridled greed of men, who traveled the entire

universe to satisfy their insatiable gluttony.[175] Animals "limit so well their appetites . . . that they only take what is necessary for them for the preservation
of their health, so that they are not hurt by an infinity of diseases as we are."[176]
Yet we previously saw the inverse idea in the analysis of the bestiary of greedy
animals. The references to animals did not lack paradox: beasts could just as
easily appear as models of sobriety as of food disorders. However, we can perhaps
see that, most often, the characteristics of gluttony were attributed to specific
creatures—the bird, the pig, the wolf—whereas the animal realm as a whole
was more generally considered naturally temperate.

Within the framework of this cultural transformation, the place of the animal
was also altered. Accepted within an analogic culture for all that the visible animals told us about ourselves and the invisible elements composing the universe,
beasts were reduced, via naturalism, to the status of machines. The advent of
a new system of cultural representations also explains why references to the
bestiary—plentiful in the sixteenth and early seventeenth centuries, especially
in manner books and dictionaries' entries—gradually declined, as we get closer
to the eighteenth century. In their own way, these fading references seem to
indicate the progressive detachment of humans from other creatures in nature.
Gustation, from then on, was left in the peripheries because it epitomized the
proximity of human and animal physicality, which polite society was trying
hard to conceal. Taste, being part of the body, of the senses, and thus of the
animal nature of human beings, was relegated to the margins of discourse as
insignificant, despicable, and useless for the development of philosophy and
elevated thought. Taste did not at all channel this unique interiority of a humanity superior to the rest of nature, but revealed, on the contrary, the inmost
community between all beings in the world.

3 The Lowest Sense of All

The external . . . senses are five. Five organs were assigned to them,
arranged so that the highest were also the purest. So the eyes, placed
at the very top of the body are the purest, they perceive fire and
natural light. Ears come secondly as they are second also in order
of decreasing purity: they correspond to air. In the third place come
the nostrils that hold an intermediate place between air and water.
Finally, the most unrefined organs of taste, which have the same
nature as water, and lastly of touch, more or less distributed in all the
body and which holds its materiality from the earth.
—Agrippa, *La magie naturelle*, 177

Like the four elements, the four seasons, the four temperaments, the seven deadly
sins, and many other serial concepts, the five senses are a literary and iconographic
topos. They join a long tradition dating from antiquity that was developed in
the Middle Ages and renewed in the early modern era. These serial concepts are
particularly enlightening, for they convey stereotypes so deep that they sometimes appear to be self-evident truths that do not require critical scrutiny. These
commonplaces thus reveal meaningful values that highlight some of the many
conventional beliefs attached to the gustatory sense. Taste, furthermore, cannot
strictly be investigated alone. To fully grasp the cultural value of taste, it is essential
to consider the place this sense occupied in relation to the four other senses. How
was taste portrayed when considered alongside vision, hearing, smell, and touch?

The senses are a rich theme of inspiration. One can track information in a
range of varied sources: in studies of human perception, such as treatises of the
senses; in the natural sciences; in works of physics; in medical and philosophical
texts; and in religious, moral, and literary works. Meditations on the senses may
thus be found in diverse domains—especially considering that early modern
knowledge was not subdivided into clearly distinct disciplinary areas.

The Hierarchy of the Senses

The number of senses was set at five from antiquity, but the debate was never firmly
closed. Even in the early modern era, scholars continued to discuss this number,
examining the possibility of additional senses peculiar to men or animals. The

conference given at the Bureau d'Adresse that examined "if there are more than five external senses" is a testimony of this secular hesitation.[1] On that occasion, the invited speakers proposed various solutions: four, eight, nine, or even an indefinite number of senses. Countless authors wondered about the same problem in early modern France. Guillaume Lamy, doctor of medicine of the Faculty of Paris, considered, for example, that there were eight senses, because to the five classical senses should be added those of hunger, thirst, and the pleasures of love, which have different organs and specific perceptions.[2] However, the former two, Lamy explains, whose organs are respectively situated in the upper opening of the stomach and in the esophagus, are limited because they are only capable of feeling "these two perceptions [hunger and thirst], and the pleasures opposed to them," and such is not the case for taste, which is capable of experiencing several kinds of flavors.[3] These examples reveal the conventional nature of the number five for the senses, a number discussed throughout history by many scholars interested in theories of perception, most of whom generally believed that "perfect animals have five senses."[4]

The five external senses, conceived as gates, were meant to protect the body and to give the mind information about the world. All five of them, however, were not equal in achieving these purposes, which is the reason why they were not granted the same value. It was commonly admitted that "knowledge, which is the only good of the soul, is acquired by . . . [the] eyes and ears. The good smells recreate and restore the spirits. Touch and tasting are the bodyguards; the former by protecting it from hostile qualities attacking from the outside, and the latter, from those entering inside which are taken by the mouth."[5] If all the senses were considered as sentinels and "messengers of the soul," allowing the animal "to avoid all which can damage, and follow all which can benefit," taste and touch were granted an especially crucial role in the protection of the body, defending it against internal and external threats.[6] The studies of gluttony and demonology addressed earlier have shown the strategic position of the mouth as a border between inside and outside, self and world, with all the fears ensuing from this situation. As for sight and hearing, they were thought to be less directly essential in the physical defense of a person. Instead, they were endowed with a nobler design, for they presided over the development of knowledge and all the other "goods of the soul," including knowledge of God, which was seen as the highest form of knowledge of all.

This distribution of functions was the origin of an imbalance in value between two groups of senses destined to fulfill divergent purposes. Taste and touch were considered to be more closely associated with the body and with matter, and thus depreciated—notably because of the everlasting influence of dualism—whereas sight and hearing were conceived as senses connected with the mind and the spirit, hence as higher and nobler senses. The sense of smell was a median sensibility belonging to both orders, depending on the context. This particular cultural system of opposing spiritual and bodily senses was commonplace in early modern Europe. As explained by French physician André du Laurens (1558–1609), "the man consists of two parts, body and soul: sight and hearing are more of use to the soul than to the body, taste and touch are more of use to the body than to the soul: smell is of use to both also, recreating and purifying the *spirits*, which are the main instruments of the soul."[7] The higher senses, directed outward to the world, were thus conceived as "cognitive" or "intellectual" senses, whereas the lower senses, directed inward to the body of the perceiver, were regarded as "bodily" senses.[8] The body's degree of involvement in sensory perception was, moreover, at the origin of a hierarchy supported by a value system classifying all the senses from the noblest to the inferior ones. The most traditional order was the following: sight, hearing, smell, taste, and touch. This order was not decided arbitrarily. There was a tremendous body of work written on theories of perception that justified the idea of a hierarchy. Of antique origin—some attribute it to Plato—the hierarchy of the senses was an enduring stereotype still current in the early modern era.[9] It is a cultural construction particularly revelatory of the depreciation of taste, situated in the penultimate position of the sensory ranking.

The hierarchy of the senses was also theoretically justified by the place each sensory organ physically occupied on the body, relying on ancient analogical ways of thinking addressed in chapter 2. Most senses were "located" on the head, considered as the seat of reason and of the soul, the "most divine part of the body, reigning over the other parts," according to Plato.[10] The eyes were the highest organs situated on the head, and the closest to the brain; they were thus considered the noblest. The ears as well were higher than the other sensory organs—the nose, the mouth, and the hands. Although experienced in the mouth, taste was fully felt when the food descended from the mouth into the stomach, a much less noble part than the head.

The hierarchy of the senses was not only a philosophical concern; its influence was much wider than solely the world of scholars, as evidenced by the numerous representations of this hierarchy in visual art. Allegories of the five senses were particularly popular in the sixteenth and seventeenth centuries, in France as well as in Northern Europe.[11] The topic was also investigated within a specific literary genre particularly popular in the Renaissance, during which several texts appeared on the theme of the fight for ascendancy between the five senses. The text entitled *Lingua, or The Combat of the Tongue and the Five Senses for Superiority*, a very successful work attributed to Thomas Tomkis, is a well-known example of this literary genre.[12] Unsurprisingly, sight won most of these battles between the senses, even when the title of the work referred to another sense, testifying to the obvious superiority of vision in the thinking of people of the Old Regime. This literary genre staging the combat between the senses gradually disappeared as we move away from the Renaissance. But if the hierarchy of the senses was not the object of a specific literature any longer, it remained no less profoundly rooted in common early modern representations. Most of the treatises of the senses repeated this hierarchy, even if it was only present in the order of succession chosen to present the senses, which systematically respected the classical order.

The conceptual framework ranking the senses was built upon a division of the senses between two groups. The first distinction posited an opposition between the senses conceived as more intellectual and the supposedly more bodily senses. The justification of this sensory duality additionally leaned on a second division connected with the ways in which sensory objects were apprehended, distinguishing the "contact senses" from the "distance senses." It rested in particular on Aristotle's theories, extremely influential on all studies of human perception. The treatises *De Anima* (On the Soul) and *De Sensu* (On the Senses) were mainly dedicated to the question of the senses, but one also finds information in other works, such as the *Historia Animalium* and the *Nicomachean Ethics*. Aristotelian theories were still very influential in early modern Europe—Thomas Aquinas had notably disseminated them throughout the medieval Christian world.

Among the most important of these ancient theories is Aristotle's division between the five senses according to the presence (or not) of a medium of sensation between the sensory organ and its object: this medium would transmit the object's stimuli to the sense organ. It is the case for the senses of sight and hearing, which respectively require light and air. This form of perception is thus an indirect contact; the sensory object gets in touch with the medium, which then affects the sense organ. Thus, the sensory object does not directly meet the sensory organ. Due to this indirect contact between object and organ, sight and hearing were therefore qualified as "distance senses," as they perceived at a certain distance from their object. This distance, according to Aristotle and his many followers, allows a higher objectification of the information transmitted, which is why sight and hearing were considered to be cognitive or intellectual senses. Alternately, touch and taste—which is a form of touch—were seen as "contact senses" because they require an immediate meeting with their object, and thus work without any medium. In order to experience taste, food necessarily needs to be in direct contact with the tongue, which is not the case for sight, where an object on the eye would be an obstacle to vision. The great proximity between the organ and its object makes taste a more subjective sense, hence an unreliable one useless to the development of knowledge. The sense of smell is, for Aristotle, in a median position between these two sensory groups, kind of a "*sens mixte*" (mixed sense).[13] Like sight and hearing, smell is remote and also requires a medium of sensation, but it is considered as a lower sense for its closeness to taste, notably in the context of the search for food, as evidenced, for instance, in a debate held at the Bureau d'Adresse in which Aristotle's theories were discussed: "As the nose, the instrument of smell, is situated in the middle of all the others: so is this sense of average nature between the other senses, because it is more material than hearing and sight, but more subtle than touch and taste; although it has a big rapport with the latter."[14] Later on, actually, Aristotle clarified his thought and showed that taste and touch needed a medium of sensation just like the other senses—respectively, the tongue and the flesh themselves. The only difference is that, for these two senses, the medium was so close that it went unnoticed and the sensation seemed immediate, because the perception happened at the very moment the medium was affected. In essence, the distance between the sense organ and the sensory object at the moment of perception distinguished the higher and the lower senses: the objects of sight, hearing, and smell were "perceived from a distance," whereas those of touch and taste were more closely felt.[15] In the end, the Greek philosopher, wishing to offer a unified theory of the senses, stated that all the senses are perceived in a similar way, by means of a medium of sensation between the organ and the object of sense.[16] But followers of the philosopher often forgot these nuances, and it is easy to track early modern references to the absence of a medium for the lower senses.[17]

Following Aristotle, new theories obviously appeared that explained the functioning of the senses' organs. But the opposition between the distance senses and the contact senses remained, elaborated under multiple forms in time. Traces of this opposition persisted even when Aristotelian ideas began to be questioned in the seventeenth century. The former sensory theories were then the object of a specific appropriation. The "medium" concept was replaced by the theory of the *espèces sensibles* (sensible species). François Bernier, a doctor in Montpellier, summarizing Gassendi, a notorious author among the Moderns (in the famous *Quarrel* against the Ancients) thus explains that "Aristotle says that taste is a sort of touch . . . for the organs of the other senses being only touched by their objects from far away, and by the species that these objects transmit to them, the organ of taste demands the contact of the object itself, that is of the tasty thing."[18] By the seventeenth century, the vocabulary had certainly changed, and the theory of perception as well, but the idea of a division between the two groups of senses remained, as evidenced by the very successful work of Cureau de La Chambre, a contemporary of René Descartes and ordinary doctor of King Louis XIV. This French physician and philosopher stressed that the sensory objects of sight and hearing were too remote to be apprehended directly. Consequently, sight and hearing could only get knowledge of the sensible species (images, representations of the objects) that were detached from the sensory objects—in other words, through the light and the sound rays that sent the image of the sensory object to the eyes and to the ears. But taste and touch—and, in this case, the sense of smell[19]—did not need any sensible species because they were immediately united with their object.[20] Consequently, these sensory objects were also likely to alter the percipient's sense itself—a likelihood particularly true of taste because a flavorful object had to enter inside the body to modify it. The closeness of taste with its object influenced the reliability of the gustatory sense; subject and object of sensation get involved to the point of being confused, a perception altering body and mind.

The first sensory division—spiritual senses/bodily senses—was thus reinforced by a second opposition—contact senses/distance senses—which itself gave rise then to another common categorization confronting the necessary senses and the senses of well-being. Often despised for their allegedly minimal participation in knowledge, taste and touch were, however, the only senses really essential to life, since they fulfill two vital bodily needs.[21] Taste is deeply interwoven with feeding, necessary for the survival of the individual as it restores and preserves the body. It is this sense that determines the edible food and distinguishes it from poisons. Consequently, although "taste is not the noblest of all the senses, yet it is the most necessary."[22] The same may be said of touch, linked to reproduction and essential to the durability of species. There is no possible existence without these two senses, shared by all life forms in the world, from plants to humans and animals, which is also the reason why taste and touch are always accompanied by pleasure or pain, which is not necessarily the case for the other senses. The sensual pleasures they cause are, furthermore, much more intense than the others, and consequently more likely to provoke overindulgence, which was deeply stigmatized for religious, moral, and medical reasons. Taste and touch were also, as demonstrated earlier, the senses most likely to reveal the animality of humans.[23] Touch and taste are two senses without which there is no possible existence, but the loss of sight or hearing is not an obstacle to life, as indicated by the many living beings lacking theses senses. These two superior senses simply bring an increased pleasure to the existence; they are the senses of well-being, of enjoyment, or of convenience, and thus oppose the essential senses.[24] As André du Laurens explains:

> I would say that of the five senses, there are two that are quite necessary for the being and simply for life, the three others are for the well-being and for the good living only. Those that are necessary for the being are touch and taste. Touch (if we believe the naturalists) is like the foundation of animality (I shall use this word, because it expresses very well the thing). Taste serves for the preservation of life. Sight, hearing, and smell are only for the well living: because the animal can be and remain without them. Both first ones because they were necessary had their medium inside and so close to the organ that it is almost inseparable: because to

taste and to touch, the Doctors confuse the means and the instrument. The three others had their medium outside and separated from the organ, as sight has air, water and any translucent [*diaphane*] body for medium.[25]

The various divisions of the five senses into two groups (bodily senses/spiritual senses, contact senses/distance senses, necessary senses/senses of well-being) were actually closely linked: taste and touch are so essential to the preservation of the body that these senses require a direct contact with their object.

What is more, the categorization of the vital and the well-being as opposing ends of a spectrum was also sometimes used to qualify the various functions of the tongue. This organ is indeed endowed with a double function, being used at the same time for taste and for speech. The first purpose is connected with survival, whereas speech impacts the well-being of people, as Aristotle explains: "[N]ature . . . uses the tongue for both tasting and articulation, and of these tasting is essential (and so is found in a greater number of creatures), while expression is for the sake of well-being."[26] Although the gustative function is shared with animals, the double functionality of the tongue is, for Aristotle and his contemporaries, peculiar to human beings only.

In this way, the same groups of senses were constantly rearranged—sight and hearing on the one hand, taste and touch on the other hand, smell being connected sometimes with the first group, sometimes with the second. The multiple fragmentations of the sense hierarchy contributed to the construction of well-established categories that were largely influenced by the dualistic theories, bringing into conflict the higher and the lower senses. These oppositions crossed time and gradually declined but ultimately contributed to the construction of taste as a lower sense, the "foundation of animality."[27]

The Sense of Taste: A Sense Neglected by Scholars

"Between all the senses, sight was judged by all philosophers as the noblest, the most perfect, and the most admirable."[28] This statement, expressed by André du Laurens, author of a *Discours de la conservation de la veüe* (Discourse on the Preservation of Sight), was collectively shared. Sight was unquestionably the greatest of all the senses, for it was traditionally likened to reason and to the mind.[29] Numerous early modern books, chapters, and extracts magnify the subject, celebrating the superiority and the marvelous beauty of the eye, the internal view being the symbol of knowledge. The preeminence of sight was already deeply rooted in early Greek philosophy. In Plato's work, there were countless "visual metaphors and images to explain knowledge of the disembodied world of intellect," and these later inspired many Neo-Platonists during the Renaissance.[30] The idea that sight was the greatest of all the senses remained throughout history and was well established in the early modern era, as evidenced in Carl Havelange's remarkable study on the history of sight.[31]

The reasons highlighted to justify sight's supremacy were numerous. Writing in the late sixteenth century, André du Laurens underscores four essential features: "[T]he diversity of the objects which it [sight] represents to the soul . . . the means of its operation which is almost quite spiritual . . . the excellence of its particular object which is light, the noblest and the most perfect quality which God ever created, and has the certainty of its action."[32] Furthermore, he adds, sight allows the perception of a much greater diversity of objects because "all the natural bodies are visible, but they are not all touchable, from all of them does not come out a smell, a taste, a sound."[33] The study of sight is also especially stimulating for scholars because this sense is considered "the most difficult to explain."[34] Finally, du Laurens concludes, "how much nobler is thus sight, since by representing us so many wonders and so many diversities of objects, it leads us to the knowledge of God," the highest form of knowledge.[35]

According to early modern scholars, the eye, like the mind itself, was capable of judging two opposites at the same time, which was not the case of the other senses, specially of taste, "because having enjoyed the bitter, one could not at the same time judge well and discern the sweet."[36] Consequently, stated Bernier, "there is nobody who does not recognize the excellence of sight, or because it reaches its object from a greater distance than any of the other senses, or because it reaches it in a moment, or in an imperceptible time, in a purer way, and as one usually says, more immaterial, with much more diversity . . . and with a more ample, purer, more long-lasting pleasure."[37]

Sight also appeared as the most autonomous sense: "The intellect is free of its nature, and has a will to talk or not. Sight in its operation has like a sort of freedom that nature has denied the other senses. The ears are always opened and the nose also, the skin is exposed to cold, warmth, and to all insults of the air; but the eyes have eyelids which open and close when we want, to see or not when it pleases us."[38] This liberty to feel is always first and foremost granted to sight, which can choose when to exercise its action, while the nose, the ear, and the skin cannot oppose the external stimuli. According to the representation of a providential Nature, which makes nothing in vain, it is because sight is endowed with a higher end that it is the most protected of all the five senses, thanks to an especially remarkable organic defense of the eye, as stressed by Claude Perrault: "As every sense has more perfection, its organ is also preserved with more care."[39] One can however wonder about the fact that the tongue was never granted this freedom: it is protected by the mouth and, just like the eye, can choose whether or not to taste. Early modern scholars never made any reference to this, while the topoi of the admirable defense of the eye and the freedom to see were ceaselessly repeated. The choice involved in tasting was obviously not part of the usual and traditional references—another sign, among many others, of taste's cultural depreciation.

Hearing was also an object of much concern. Not only was it thought to be the privileged instrument of language and education, it was also considered as the best way by which people could communicate with God. The functioning of the ear and of sound also fascinated scholars, who dedicated a lot of research to this faculty. Diverse metaphors enthusiastically celebrated the wonders of hearing and sight, while countless academic studies were devoted to sound as well as sight. As for taste, often reduced to a form of touch that deserved only minor attention in the analysis of five senses, it is conspicuously absent in many sources, demonstrating a kind of silence about taste.

Despite the abundance of theories related to the study of the five senses, however, the works did not grant all the senses the same attention. Many books were dedicated to the study of optics, light, and sound, but not all senses received special treatment in a longer chapter or an extensive investigation. Taste was rarely considered independently from the other senses; there was, frankly, no treatise to be found that was entirely dedicated to the study of the sense of the taste, at least not before the late eighteenth century. Medical works were more concerned with the study of food, dietetics, appetite, and digestion than with taste itself. As for the treatises of taste that appeared in the eighteenth century within the framework of aesthetic debates, they were more concerned with the judgment of beauty than with that of gustation.

The imbalance between the senses was even more accentuated when the five of them were addressed within the same inquiry, such as in the treatises of the senses. The order of presentation of the senses, the words chosen to evoke them, and the material space that was reserved for each of them—the number of words, lines, or pages—constitute significant material indications of the values individually conferred to each. The study of sight, hearing, and—especially in the eighteenth century and onward—of touch obviously composed the main part of these works. Taste was systematically neglected under these broad treatises, followed closely by the sense of smell, which was also readily neglected. In his *Abrégé de la philosophie de Gassendi* (Summary of Gassendi's Philosophy), Bernier examines each of the senses, from touch to sight, in the traditional order.[40] Vision obviously received the first place in this work, since it was studied in five chapters, composing a total of a hundred pages, while each of the other senses was the object of only a brief chapter.[41] The same proportion is found within the works of two contemporaries of Bernier, French physicists Claude Perrault and Jacques Rohault. The former dedicates one page to the other senses but twelve to sight, while the latter reserves a thirteen-page chapter to flavors but eight chapters for a total of one hundred pages to light and vision.[42] Claude-Nicolas Le Cat, an eighteenth-century surgeon, begins his *Traité des Sens* (Treatise on the Senses) by studying touch, the most unrefined yet the surest and the most general sense, to which he dedicates fifteen pages. He then studies taste and smell, according ten pages to each of these lower senses. Finally, he grants all his attention and more than half his work to the "higher" senses: hearing (forty pages) and especially sight (224 pages)![43] For Le Cat, hearing would later be the object of a separate treatise.[44]

These proportions speak for themselves. When the five senses were considered together within the framework of a general discussion on perception, the passages dedicated to taste were always less developed than the chapters related to the other senses. The little room left to taste within the treatises of the senses could additionally be explained by ignorance of this function; the physiology of taste was indeed neglected for a long time. This lack of knowledge is in itself significant of the value granted to this sense, which did not really interest scholars. Lorenzo Bellini and Marcello Malpighi gave an important boost to the study of the anatomy of the taste sense in the second half of the seventeenth century, particularly thanks to the use of the microscope. Malpighi notably underscored the illiteracy about the functioning of the tongue in his time, but the first large-scale research on the subject only appeared in the nineteenth and the twentieth centuries.[45] In the end, as Étienne Bonnot de Condillac admitted, "the eye is of all the senses the one from which we know best the mechanism."[46]

Although next to last on the traditional hierarchy, taste appeared de facto as the lowest of all the senses. Touch, located at the bottom of the hierarchy, in fact benefited from a particular status that granted it a certain importance: it was the only sense possessed by all forms of life. Some scholars used particularly eloquent metaphors to communicate this central position of touch:

> That what is center in earth, earth between the elements, star in the sky, sovereignty in the state, faith in religion, movement of nature in medicine, equity in law, reason in philosophy, body in man, sense in the animal; touch is this in all the other senses: that is to say it is their foundation and the condition without which none of them can remain. Because there are many animals that do not see, like moles; which do not hear, like the deaf and most insects; which have no sense of smell, like those who have a cold; which have no taste, like the ill. But if someone has no feeling of touch, at the same time he stops being an animal, because he is considered an animal as he has a sensory life.[47]

Touch is subsequently the "first one of the senses," because it is the one that defines the animal. It is also, Bernier explains, "the most necessary of all. . . . The other senses being like a kind of touch more exquisite and more perfect . . . an animal cannot be without this sense, though he can nevertheless be without that of sight and the others, and even without taste, at least for some time."[48]

Touch is, moreover, the unique sense of certain animals, in particular of "zoophytes, as are the sponge and the coral, and all the species of oysters."[49]

Aristotle had already emphasized the superiority of touch (even if he also placed taste in this category of the necessary senses, a categorization with which the speaker of the Bureau d'Adresse would disagree). Moreover, if a visual, hearing, or olfactory excess only affects the sensory organ concerned, the excesses of touch—and sometimes, according to the authors of the time, of taste—threaten the whole body, possibly leading to its destruction. Indeed, while sight, hearing, smell, and taste have a particular and located sense organ, touch is perceived across the entirety of the body.[50]

The tactile sense was also, since Aristotle, the only one through which humans revealed their superiority to animals, for they were the ones with the most refined sense of touch, thanks to their hands and their "smooth and polished skin."[51] Since Aristotle, the quality of touch thus appeared as closely connected to the value of intelligence.[52] Moreover, the tactile sense was also traditionally presented as the most reliable sense, particularly in religious contexts:

> The fifth [speaker] said, that the nobility of touch appears mainly in that is the most infallible of all the senses; as the most honorable people are considered the most reliable. That is why having to deal with S. Thomas by then incredulous, Our Lord made him touch his side; and the obvious things are said tangible; for the fact that our touch is the last one of the senses who makes a mistake. That is why those who dream do not often recognize their error until putting their hand on the ghost they begin to make sure that it is only wind.[53]

In conclusion, although situated at the bottom of the hierarchy of the senses, touch was presented as central, the most grounded sense, which was not the case for taste, the lowest sense of all at the time. The fundamental position of touch was even more reinforced in the eighteenth century when Condillac's work enhanced its prestige to the point of challenging sight's place in the sense hierarchy. It was especially the crucial role touch played in the development of knowledge that would be highlighted. For Buffon, as for many others in the eighteenth century, touch is an "important sense, on which all our knowledge depends. . . . It is by touch alone that we can acquire complete and real knowledge; it is this sense which rectifies all the other senses, the effects of which would be only illusions and would produce only errors in our spirit, if touch did not teach us to judge."[54] Touch, although traditionally the lowest sense, became in the Enlightenment one of the most important senses of all.

Sense Associations

Another meaningful side effect of the traditionally lower position of taste within the sense hierarchies is that most of the time this sense, unlike others, was rarely considered in isolation. Explanation of its functioning almost systematically relied on connections with another sense—sometimes with touch, sometimes with smell. There were, of course, many and frequent sensory associations emphasized by scholars that concerned the other senses as well—notably, sight and touch, which were often considered as deeply intertwined (all the more so in light of Molyneux's debate-inspiring question).[55] The bond between the senses inspired popular works related to theories of perception, especially in the eighteenth century. But while investigations of the other senses could also be considered alone—and their analyses did not necessarily rely on a comparison drawn with another sense—for taste, on the contrary, the analyses systematically referred to other senses.

Taste had been considered, since Aristotle, as a particular form of touch: both are bodily senses that require contact with a sensory object. Scholars frequently highlighted their similar function and organic constitution. Certain doctors therefore considered these two senses to have a common physiology, taste being a more refined or more specific form of touch that allowed a feeling of flavors. If, in the end, Aristotle conceded that taste was a specific sense in its own right, scores of his followers—notably early modern—would refuse this status to the gustatory sense. Some even felt that there were only four senses; in a series of debates on the number of sense organs, one scholar argued: "[T]aste being included under touch by the definition of the Philosopher [Aristotle], it must be a specie of it; and therefore there are only four senses like four elements."[56] But others reflected that "taste, however it may be included under touch . . . constitutes well a distinct sense,"[57] a sentiment akin to Aristotelian thought, which specified that even if taste was intimately likened to touch, it was nevertheless a specific sense, for the tongue could feel flavors inaccessible to the rest of the body.[58]

Touch's absent medium of sensation and the proximity of taste with touch caused some authors to accentuate the delicacy of the human palate in the discernment of flavors.[59] "Aristotle considers that taste is more exquisite in the man than in any other animal, because it is, he says, a sort of touch, and that the touch of the man surpasses the one of all other Animals."[60] Yet we also saw, in the previous chapter with the figure of Philoxenus, that the same association would also be criticized; it was when taste worked as a form of touch that it most easily led to overindulgence and debauchery, and hence to sin, because of the intense pleasures these basic and deeply intertwined senses provided. Taste and touch were thus perceived as particularly dangerous and as stimulating one another; they had to be kept under control, especially since these were the senses that most plainly revealed the animal nature of men.

When they did not connect taste with touch, scholars linked it to the sense of smell, both functioning in a similar way. The close union of these two senses was most often mentioned in the register of bestiality, especially in the context of feeding. The fact that eating is a natural need, satisfied thanks to both taste and smell, became an argument for the physiological closeness of two senses served by common organs, as in Cureau de la Chambre's works: "Smells are mainly intended to discern the good and the bad food. That is why the nasal organ is quite close to the mouth; and before an animal eats something, it does not feel it nor taste it as we do to know if it is good, it just smells it and judges of its goodness by its smell."[61] Several physicians suggested that taste and smell constituted two parts of one unique sense used to determine the edible character of food, the nose being the guide of taste in the search of foodstuffs. This was the position adopted by Claude-Nicolas Le Cat, surgeon of Rouen, in his *Traité des Sens* (Treatise on the Senses), a significant work for the time as the Chevalier de Jaucourt in the *Encyclopédie*'s article on taste copied it. The "particular connection which reigns between taste and smell," he explains, is a

> greater connection than between taste and the other senses.... Because, although sight and hearing produce on the organs of taste effects similar to those which causes the sense of smell—as exciting the appetite or provoking the vomiting when one sees or hears mentioning things the taste of which pleases or displeases enough to revolt—it is nevertheless certain that smell acts more powerfully. One finds the reason in the immediate and close relationship smells and flavors have together; they both consist in the *spirits* developed by fragrant and delicious matters; besides that the membrane which covers the nose nasal organ is a continuation of the same membrane which covers the mouth, the throat, the esophagus and the stomach, organs of taste generally. It is by virtue of the same causes that one savors coffee beforehand with sensual delight by its aromatic smell, and that one is revolted against some dish, or against a medicine, the smell of which is unpleasant.[62]

The comparison leads once again to the problem of the acuity of the senses. If the association with touch was a way to point to the refinement of human taste, taste's connection with smell revealed, on the contrary, the weakness of the human's organs of senses, especially of the nose. It was commonly argued that smell was "the weakest sense in men"[63]; seen as ill-developed, the human nose was limited to giving vaguely pleasant or unpleasant impressions. Words lacked competence in qualifying scents perceived merely as pleasant or not. The smell of animals, on the other hand, was seen as much more refined. According to early modern physicians like Claude Perrault, the organic disparity between the noses of men and of animals explained their differing sensibilities.[64] But the physical difference justified itself by a different end; indeed, the organs of animals allow them to have a more developed sense of smell because they need it in order to feed themselves, to hunt. A man, on the other hand, has a weaker smell because he does not need his nose to find food. In comparison to animals, "the man between them all had the least perfect smell: so much because it was mainly given by nature to the animals which live on prey, as the dog and the vulture, (and the man had to hunt differently than with the nose) that for the situation of the mammillary *procez* near the brain, colder and wetter, and more ample in the man than in any other animal: that is also why men do not know the differences of smells like those of the other objects of the senses."[65] Aristotle already noticed this olfactory weakness in men (as opposed to humans' nuanced ability to taste)—which is why, according to him, smell would have borrowed most of its vocabulary from the gustatory lexical field.[66] He explained this more acute sensibility by asserting that taste was a sort of touch, a sense exceptionally developed by human beings.

When associated with taste, smell appeared as a lower sense. Whereas taste and smell "only perceive their proper objects; instead, touch and sight, besides their own objects, still discern size, figure, motion, and rest."[67] All these qualities perceived by more than one sense at once (size, figure, motion, etc.) constitute the *common sensibles*, a concept that, with that of common sense, comes once again from Aristotle. As Sophia Rosenfeld stresses, common sense is a "kind of central . . . sense . . . at the point of intersection of all the rest, that has the primary function of comparing and coordinating the impressions received by each of them. . . . [T]his faculty . . . made humans aware that they were engaged in the act of perception itself." It is common sense that allows one to understand that "what is simultaneously sweet and white is sugar but also that sweet and white are different kinds of sensible qualities and sugar is ultimately different from salt."[68] This sense is thus, as David Howes explains, "the relational sense *par excellence*."[69] In the Middle Ages, the evolution of this theory would lead to the development of the doctrine of the internal senses, of which common sense is part.[70] Sight and touch are thus the senses thought to provide the most complex ideas.

On the other hand, when an object being smelled was immaterial, it became associated with sight and hearing, and smell was transformed into a "higher" sense, as displayed in the religious context—for instance, with "the odor of sanctity" or in religious ceremonies, where perfumes and incense occupy an important place.[71]

In conclusion, the associations of taste with touch and/or smell could thus take a wide variety of forms according to the author and the context in which it was considered. But what is significant for this inquiry are the authors' habits toward taste; writers would dodge writing a chapter on taste by referring to it only in a comparative mode. Authors spoke of taste only in a relative or contrastive sense, instead of truly dealing with the topic of taste. Nevertheless, all authors recognized the necessity of taste for the preservation of the body. But often, the scholars contented themselves with these preliminary considerations and did not investigate taste—obviously a minor, uninteresting sense—more thoroughly. A bodily, material, and animalistic sense, taste was the lowest of all the senses for early modern scholars.

Philosophy and Gustation

Taste was represented in the early modern era in ways that were largely influenced by traditions and domains poles apart from the culinary register, especially by philosophical theories. The above analysis of the hierarchy of the senses stressed the power of analogism and dualism in shaping the common representations of taste. Descartes, as we already saw, strengthened the dualism and confirmed the lower position of taste within the rankings of the senses. But what would happen when Cartesian ideas would begin to be questioned in the late seventeenth and eighteenth centuries? This period is indeed a particularly significant period for the investigation of the senses, for it is marked by the rise of a culture that valued sensory experience, which from now on would be considered the foundation of all knowledge. Without intending to offer a detailed study of the movement of influential thought arising from empiricism and sensualism, I shall favor here the study of some key texts that marked the intellectual debates of this time, such as those of John Locke and the Abbot of Condillac, intensely read and commented upon in eighteenth-century France. How were the references to taste articulated in this new era favorable to sensory experience? I shall then consider the authors—doubtless among the most controversial of their time—who would promote materialism, a philosophical movement that flourished in the eighteenth century. The radical reexamination of the duality of man, which had been scholarly and religious truth for centuries, recalled in a disturbing way the porosity of the borders between humans and animals, both conceived as machines. Did authors such as La Mettrie, Helvétius, and the Baron of Holbach grant a new attention to the sense of taste?

From Empiricism to Sensualism

Late seventeenth- and eighteenth-century philosophes were fascinated by the genesis of the human mind. They thought that by determining the origin of knowledge they would be able to define its nature.[72] After Cartesian thought dominated for several decades in France, the rationalist beliefs declined when John Locke's highly influential *Essay Concerning Human Understanding* appeared. Published in English in 1690, the work was quickly translated into French by Pierre Coste—with Locke's supervision—and appeared in 1700 in France under the title *Essai philosophique concernant l'entendement humain.*[73] This text was quite successful and gave rise to crucial debates on knowledge and the senses among the members of the educated community in eighteenth-century France. By way of empiricism, John Locke proposed a drastically new theory of knowledge and perception. Questioning the thesis of innate ideas defended by the Church and by scholars for ages, he considered sensory experience as the foundation of all knowledge. Salvaging Aristotle's intuition that *nothing is in the mind that was not first in the senses,* we find that in his *Essay,* Locke believes the spirit to be, at birth, a tabula rasa, or "white paper, void of all characters, without any *ideas.*" According to the English philosopher, "all the materials of reason and knowledge" come from experience only: "Our observation, employed either about *external sensible objects, or about the internal operations of our minds perceived and reflected on by ourselves, is that which supplies our understandings with all the materials of thinking.* These two are the fountains of knowledge, from whence all *ideas* we have, can naturally have, do spring."[74] Locke thus distinguished sensation and reflection. As he explains, the "ideas of things [are] discovered to us only by the senses from without or by the mind reflecting on what it experiments in itself within."[75] Locke then still relied on dualism, since he kept the idea of innate faculties while rejecting the notion of innate ideas.

With experience as the foundation of knowledge, Locke granted the sensory world much wider attention. In this respect, taste appeared to be a good way of showing that it was necessary to feel in order to know. Locke notes that it is impossible to imagine the flavors of a pineapple or an oyster without having tried these beforehand:[76] "I would have anyone try to fancy any taste which had never affected his palate, or frame the *idea* of a scent he had never smelt; and when he can do this, I will also conclude that a blind man hath *ideas* of colors and a deaf man true distinct notions of sounds."[77] The pineapple was by then a little-known fruit, a fact that strengthens the power of his argument. Coste, Locke's translator, specifies on this matter that it is "one of the best fruits of India, rather similar to a pine cone by its figure."[78] Among others, the abbot Noël-Antoine Pluche—French priest and author of *Le Spectacle de la nature,* a best-selling work on natural history—would use Locke's recurring example of the pineapple in order to demonstrate the senses' fundamental role in the development of knowledge.[79] In *Le Spectacle,* he derides Descartes, who would have never been able to determine the flavor of this fruit by reason alone:

A reason which goes alone, and which only works metaphysically, is a reason which wanders or is about to wander. . . . Present to Descartes a pineapple recently cut on the foot, and perfectly ripe. Ask him to examine the inside of this fruit which has just been cultivated in Europe for the first time, and to tell you which taste it must have. We are entitled to ask everything to a reason such as his, which embraces everything, and which explains everything. . . . No, Descartes will never discover this flavor in his reason . . . having made the dissection and the analysis of it: only his palate can inform him on this matter. But if reason is absolutely powerless when from the structure of a body that he sees and freely dissects it is necessary to deduct the necessity of such a flavor; which enterprise is his to dare to tell us about the generation of the sun . . . ? He knows it much less than our pineapple. . . . Here are Physicists who act otherwise to reach all at once what can be discovered of the real value of the pineapple. They begin by carrying the fruit to their mouth, which is immediately flooded with a delicate syrup, and spotted, still long later, by a flavor which embalms it: they become bolder to the point of suspecting that this fruit will be salutary, and the experience justifies the prediction. It is thus our taste, together with experience, that has to teach us first of all if a fruit which was unknown to us, will be or not a pleasant and useful food. That is the real philosophy.[80]

According to Locke, flavors, conceived as secondary qualities, are clear and distinct ideas, even if, in contrast to Descartes, they come from the senses. Although the experience of flavors can sometimes vary with the context of consumption—a person with a fever could feel bitterness when eating sugar— yet "the *idea* of bitter in that man's mind would be as clear and distinct from the *idea* of sweet as if he had tasted only gall." There is no possible confusion between the two ideas of sweetness and bitterness, no more than between the "two *ideas* of white and sweet or white and round."[81]

In the *Essay*, the example of taste seems, furthermore, particularly illustrative of the profusion of possible sensations that language inevitably fails to describe. Like the vocabulary for smells, the vocabulary of flavors is much poorer than that of the other senses. As Locke acknowledges, "sweet, bitter, sour, harsh, and salt are almost all the epithets we have to denominate that numberless variety of relishes which are to be found distinct, not only in almost every sort of creatures, but in the different parts of the same plant, fruit, or animal."[82] He explains that the lack of words related to flavors is due to the fact that "men, in framing different complex *ideas* and giving them names, have been much governed by the end of speech in general. . . . Thus we see that there are great varieties of simple *ideas*, as of tastes and smells, which have no names . . . which either not having been generally enough observed, or else not being of any great use to be taken notice of in the affairs and converse of men, they have not had names given to them, and so pass not for species."[83] For Locke, the poverty of language about taste is thus not really a problem, since such a vocabulary would not be of much utility. Conversely, the philosopher admits, the absence of appropriate names could have somehow led to a certain inattention toward flavors. Most tastes and smells "being such as generally we have no names for, are less taken notice of and cannot be set down in writing, and therefore must be left without enumeration to the thoughts and experience of my reader."[84] Taste, then, seems to be a sense that mostly resists the grip of language; we shall see in the next chapter that Locke was far from being the only one to highlight the indefinable character of this sense.

Taste is, moreover, says Locke, among the first sensations felt by the human who wakes up to the world. The gustatory sensation is indeed closely connected to hunger, one of the first simple functions developed by the newborn child

before he is conscious that he thinks.[85] Without knowing why, the child is immediately capable of distinguishing differences between basic flavors: "[L]ong
before it has the use of words, or comes to that which we commonly call the
use of reason. . . . a child knows as certainly, before it can speak, the difference
between the *ideas* of sweet and bitter (i.e. that sweet is not bitter) as it knows
afterwards (when it comes to speak) that wormwood and sugar-plums are not
the same thing."[86] The figure of the child reveals how knowledge generated by
taste was thought to be utterly instinctive and immediate. This form of knowledge was linked to taste's status as a necessary sense and even more to the idea
that it is a contact sense, felt immediately when food touches the tongue. There
is no need to think or to articulate this sensation to know how one feels about
a particular taste. The immediacy of the gustatory sensation was often underscored in early modern sources and related to the intimate and idiosyncratic
nature of this sense.

The primacy of flavors in the genesis of knowledge did not make taste a
valued sense though—quite the opposite, actually—for infantile knowledge
was perceived as lower, just like knowledge observed by "*idiots, savages,* and
the grossly *illiterate.*"[87] All these examples allowed Locke to demonstrate that
innate ideas don't exist: these people, who are "the least corrupted by custom or
borrowed opinions," show none of the principles of knowledge considered to be
innate.[88] From birth, the child is conscious of differences in taste because flavors
are among the first sensory objects with which they are frequently in contact.
"The child certainly knows that . . . the *wormseed* or *mustard* it refuses is not
the *apple* or *sugar* it cries for: this it is certainly and undoubtedly assured of; but
will anyone say it is by virtue of this principle, that *it is impossible for the same
thing to be and not to be,* that it so firmly assents to these and other parts of its
knowledge?"[89] There are thus no innate ideas; moreover, knowledge is acquired
through the senses. Experience and education would make the greatest difference in the child's life, and the thoughts of some among the young people will
"enlarge themselves, only as they come to be acquainted with a greater variety
of sensible objects, to retain the *ideas* of them in their memories, and to get the
skill to compound and enlarge them, and several ways put them together."[90]
There is thus nothing in the mind at birth; the development of human thought
and intelligence depends on the number of experiences a person has while
growing up, as well as on personal abilities to deal with complex ideas.

Broadly speaking, however, except for the few examples stated above, taste was
barely present in Locke's *Essay.* Sight remained "the most comprehensive of all
our senses,"[91] and numerous visual metaphors made the traditional comparison
of the function of the eye and cognitive understanding.[92] Locke, just like his
predecessors, considers the mind as "the eye of the soul," its sensations like "the
windows by which light is let into [the] . . . *dark room.*"[93] Moreover, according

to the English thinker, "[t]he perception of the mind" is "most aptly explained by words relating to sight."[94] Light is, finally, "the most pleasant of all sensible objects."[95] Touch, too, is an essential sense that, when allied with sight, develops the most complex ideas, notably the traditional *common sensibles* mentioned above: the concepts of space, extent, figure, movement, and rest.[96] As a matter of fact, "the eyes and touch" are "the busiest of all our senses."[97] Taste, on the other hand, is not considered that relevant and does not deserve to be the object of an appropriate discourse; it preexists language and reason.

John Locke's ideas inspired numerous philosophers, particularly those in France who generated the theories of sensualism (also called sensationalism or sensism), starting with Étienne Bonnot de Condillac, who exercised a huge influence over his contemporaries. He met frequently with encyclopedists such as Diderot and Rousseau, and his work occupies an important place in the French *Encyclopédie*. Condillac was highly inspired by Locke's ideas, which he widely spread in France, while adding his own new theories on sensory experience. If Locke distinguished the ideas resulting from sensation from those stemming from reflection, Condillac felt that everything was sensation, including thought itself. At the origin of everything, sensations constituted the raw material of all the mind's knowledge as well as its faculties, which were also particular ways of feeling: "judgment, reflection, desires, passions, etc., are only sensations in differing forms."[98]

In his *Traité des sensations* (Treatise on the Sensations, 1754), Condillac used a fictional narrative in order to expound his theory. He imagined a statue constituted like a human being, enlivened by a soul that had never had any thoughts and a body that had experienced no sensation. He then gave her [the statue] back all her senses, one after the other, beginning with the sense of smell, followed by hearing, taste, sight, and finally by touch; the senses are treated separately in order to highlight the different ideas and faculties coming from each sense. Let us note that the order in which Condillac considered the senses was not the classic order: he begins with the sense of smell because he considers that "it is of all the senses the one who seems to contribute least to the knowledge of the human mind."[99] Limited to the perceptions of one sense at a time, the statue does not make the distinction between herself and the world. She is all smell or all taste, and is endowed with a weak memory. "She thus does not suspect that she owes her ways of being to foreign causes; she ignores that they come to her by four senses. She sees, she feels, she tastes, she hears, without knowing that she has eyes, a nose, a mouth, or ears: she does not know that she has a body."[100] When limited to the gustatory sense, the statue is not capable of distinguishing the various flavors in a mouthful, but only one flavor at a time because she is not conscious that different flavors come from different elements.[101] It is only at the end of Condillac's narrative, when the statue receives touch in combination with all the other senses, that she becomes aware that she is endowed with a body, that there is a reality outside of her, and that the sensations she feels come from objects distinct from herself. Condillac finishes his story by insisting on the fundamental character of touch, the true master sense because it is the only one capable of revealing the exteriority of the world.

If touch was the impetus for new attention to sensualism in eighteenth-century Europe, one cannot say the same for taste, to which Condillac only granted two pages in his whole treatise, composing the shortest chapter of the entire work.[102] For more information on the sense of taste, he referred to the parts regarding smell, which had such a strong analogy with taste "that their sensations must sometimes become confused."[103] Many times in his book, the French philosopher enumerates a few senses as examples in order to make his point; unlike the four other senses, in these lists the sense of taste does often not even come in for mention.[104] Also, having separately envisaged each of the senses in the early part of his work, Condillac decides in several chapters of the third part to discuss the senses as a group. He studies, for instance, touch and smell combined, or hearing, smell, and touch together. Yet he reserves no place for a section that would have been dedicated to the combination of hearing, smell, touch, and taste together; indeed, taste seems systematically forgotten within the lists of the senses, as well as within his work as a whole.

In the two pages he wrote on taste, Condillac nevertheless recognized the fundamental character of gustation for animal economy, because it satisfies hunger. Just like Locke who considered "delight or uneasiness" as the driving force in the discovery of self and the world,[105] Condillac considers that "pleasure and pain are the unique principles, which determining all the operations of her [the statue's] soul, has to raise her gradually to all the knowledge of which she is capable."[106] He continues: "The principle which determines the development of her faculties is simple; the sensations contain it: because all of them being inevitably pleasant or unpleasant, the statue is interested in enjoying some and escaping the others."[107] She thus naturally tries to avoid the pains of hunger, one of the most powerful of all drives. Bound to a need, gustatory pleasures consequently appear among the most vivacious sensations: "Taste can usually contribute more than smell to her happiness and her misfortune [of the statue]: because flavors usually affect with more strength than smells. It contributes to it even more than harmonious sounds; because the need for food makes flavors more necessary, and consequently make her taste them with more vivacity. Hunger can make her unfortunate, but as soon as she would have noticed the sensations appropriate to appease it, she would grant her attention more to it, would desire them with more violence, and would enjoy them with more delight."[108] The power of food, taste, and hunger is such that taste dissatisfied can lead to forgetting all about the other senses: "As . . . flavors must interest her more than any other sensation, she [the statue] will take care of it all the more, as her hunger will be greater. Taste can thus be prejudicial to the other senses, to the point of making her insensible to smells and to harmony."[109] One hence finds here again the old idea of taste as a necessary sense, now transformed into sensual delight, the satisfaction of a bodily need that naturally brings an intense form of pleasure that was in the eighteenth century not as morally condemned as in the previous centuries.

Condillac further writes that taste is a sense that demands no education because its essential nature makes it instinctive. "The sense of taste educates itself so quickly that one barely notices that it needs learning. It had to be, since it was necessary for our preservation, from the first moments of our birth."[110] Tastes are not necessarily the object of language or of a particularly developed thought; that reason in particular would lead to the depreciation of this sense, considering the importance Condillac granted language within the elaboration of the ideas. Despite the decisive transformations in theories of knowledge and perception, taste retained its long-established status as a necessary sense, a sense of immediacy and of ineffability—just like with Locke and in all the tradition that preceded them. Yet if these ideas about taste were deeply rooted in the past, empiricists and sensualists gave a more positive value to it, as pleasure was considered a powerful drive leading to knowledge of the world.

The statue's increasing awareness of her environment and her discovery of flavors evoke the awakening of the first man, as illustrated in Buffon's "philosophical narrative":

> I thus imagine a man such as one can believe that was the first man at the time of creation, that is a man whose body and organs would be perfectly formed, but who would wake up all new for himself and for all which surrounds him. . . . I was sitting in the shade of a beautiful tree; fruits of a ruby color came down in the shape of bunch within the reach of the hand. . . . I had seized one of these fruits. . . . I had approached this fruit of my eyes, I considered its shape and colors, a delicious smell made me approach it more; it was near my lips; I smelled the perfume in long inspirations, and enjoyed the pleasures of smell for a long time. I was filled inside with this embalmed air; my mouth opened to exhale it, it reopened to take some back: I felt that I possessed an even finer, more delicate internal sense of smell than the first one; finally I tasted. What a flavor! What a novelty of sensation! Until then I had had only pleasures; taste gave me the feeling of sensual delight. The intimacy of the enjoyment [*jouissance*] created the idea of *possession*; I believed that the substance of this fruit had become mine, and that I was able to transform beings. Flattered by this idea of power, incited by the pleasure I had felt, I picked a second and a third fruit, and I could not keep from exercising my hand to satisfy my tastes.[111]

In the case of Condillac's statue as well as in Buffon's discovery of the first man, taste is awakened by hunger, which pulls the man to carry things to his mouth—at first, variable objects, including nonedible stuff, and then food, which provides him the pleasure of satisfying a bodily need. It is, in every case, by tasting fruit that true delight is experienced. The closeness between subject and object—real "possession," which formerly caused the condemnation of this sense of contact—was in the eighteenth century celebrated as leading to a higher form of sensual delight.

However, the traditional valuing of taste as a lower sense remained as well. While prized for its utility and for the pleasure it provided, in comparison with all the other senses, taste was always less interesting for scholars, even in the eighteenth century when people were so passionate about the question of sensations. Another indication of this lower esteem granted to taste is its minor presence within the large number of texts on synesthesia, multisensory connections, collaborations, and interactions between the senses. The figure of the blind person was central; Molyneux's question was only one reference among many others of a general movement of thought. Authors underscored the close collaboration of sight and touch in a situation of blindness, the importance of hearing in a world deprived of light, and the heightened sense of smell for one who cannot make use of his eyes. The taste of the blind, on the other hand, was rarely mentioned. There is not a single line on this sense in Diderot's *Lettre sur les aveugles à l'usage de ceux qui voient* (Letter on the Blind for Those Who Can See). The example of taste was, however, used by Condillac in his study of the blind who recovered sight after birth; the latter realized that the visual aspects and flavors of food do not always match. He was "surprised that . . . the dishes that he enjoyed more, were not the most pleasant to the eye."[112] But this is only a minor example; the majority of his discussion rested on the essential nature of touch.

Also, in the numerous narratives of inhabited fictional worlds depicting people with alternative senses—found in Locke, Condillac, Malebranche, Diderot, and many others—taste was rarely stated as an example of alternative senses. The authors imagined peoples endowed with higher visual acuteness and amplified hearing but rarely with a nuanced palate capable of refined discernment of flavors. A possible explanation of this absence could be that taste was considered useful only to enjoy and not to know the world. Fontenelle testifies to this; describing a dialogue between Galileo and Apicius, he declares that, unlike the tools available for improving the acuteness of sight or hearing, there is no instrument that can perfect taste—though not for lack of wishing this were so. Indeed, the famous gourmand of antiquity writes: "But you invented the glasses of long sight; afterward, you made for the ears what you had made for the eyes, and I hear that another invented trumpets that double and enlarge the voice.

Finally, you perfected and you taught others to perfect the senses. I would have asked you to work for the sense of taste, and to imagine some instrument that would enhance the pleasure of eating."[113] Galileo answers that taste has "naturally all its perfection":[114] "Glasses are the eyes of the Philosophers. . . . *If you only want to enjoy things, nothing lacks you to enjoy them; but everything lacks you to know them.* Men need nothing, and Philosophers need everything. Art has no new instruments to give to the former, and never would it give it enough of these to the latter."[115]

Ultimately, the new theories proposed by empiricism and sensualism in the late-seventeenth and eighteenth centuries fundamentally modified sensory notions and granted, from then on, a positive value to the five senses, which were perceived as necessary for the preservation of the body and for the development of knowledge, useful for the pleasure of living, and crucial for communication between beings and the world. The Age of Enlightenment was a period during which the educated elites were fascinated by sensory experience, to the point of making it the central theme of the *Discours préliminaire* [Preliminary Speech] of the *Encyclopédie*: "All our direct knowledge is reduced to what we receive by the senses; from which it follows that it is to our sensations that we owe all our ideas. . . . Of all the objects affecting us by their presence, our own body is the one whose existence strikes us most, because it belongs more intimately to us. . . . Subject to a thousand needs, and intensely sensitive to the action of external bodies, if would be soon destroyed, if the care of its preservation did not preoccupy us."[116] One could have supposed a priori that such valuation of the senses would have led to new representations of taste. Yet, the rehabilitation of the senses apparently did not really benefit the gustatory sense, always left at the periphery of discourses, as usual. Taste was, of course, mentioned alongside the five senses, but the philosophers did not grant it much attention. It was touch that benefited, in particular with Condillac, from a fundamentally new appreciation, because it was associated with sight in the discovery of the world. It became, then, the most important sense, the one that corrects the faulty impressions of all the others. But taste, in Condillac's estimation (and indeed in a majority of texts) did not necessarily receive a more favorable treatment.

The idea of the hierarchy was itself replaced by the idea of a collaboration between the senses. But sight remained the noblest sense for Locke, whereas touch dominated for Condillac and Buffon.

Sensory associations, however, evolved in this new context. Touch was from now on connected with sight, a connection that engendered greater knowledge. As a consequence of this nobler philosophical association, touch seemed less frequently associated with taste than during previous periods. Only physiological studies continued to associate both these senses, seen as endowed with a similar organic function, the *mammelons du goût* (taste organs) being a specific form of those of the skin.[117] From then on, taste was more regularly linked to the sense of smell in the philosophic domain, where they constituted two "lower" senses, as well as in the medical realm, where their physiology was more and more envisaged together. The physiological difference between these two senses was simply that smell could detect food from farther away. According to Claude-Nicolas Le Cat, "smell seems to me less a particular sense, than a part of or an addition to that of taste, for which it is like the sentinel: in a word, smell is the taste of smells and is like the foretaste of flavors."[118] The collaboration between these senses is particularly optimal in animals and savages.[119] At a period when sight was being readily defined as a distant form of touch, smell appeared to be a distant form of taste.

In conclusion, the character of taste that emerged was a heterogeneous composition in which older and newer ideas got intertwined. One finds the traditional criteria of taste as animal sense, necessary sense, sense of contact, sense of childhood, sense of the ineffable immediacy. But its value changed: after the turn of the eighteenth century, taste was seen as a necessity and was thus valued for its role in the conservation of the bodies and for its essential role in gaining knowledge. Its association with bodily need did not translate into a condemnation of an animal sense anymore, but rather became a celebration of a providential Nature, an association between sensual delight and the sense that allows its preservation. These new ideas did not inevitably question older values, as taste remained disregarded compared with the other senses.

The Disturbing Materiality of the World

Sensualist theories were widely disseminated in eighteenth-century France. They influenced the most diverse thinkers, in particular the encyclopedists, but also the materialists, the latter composing a broad spectrum of thought and gathering dissimilar authors with diverse opinions, all provocative in their questioning of knowledge. In the seventeenth century, Descartes distinguished the soul from the body; human and animal bodies were by then reduced to the rank of automatons, working as machines. The superiority of humans to the rest of nature was preserved by the fact that the former was the only one to have an immortal soul. Taking up the conception of the body as a machine, materialists in the eighteenth century radicalized Cartesian thought by eliminating the specificity of the soul, from now on considered as a material entity as well. So, as stressed by Yves Charles Zarka in a collective study of French materialists, Julien Offray de La Mettrie "recovered the theory of the animal-machine and, contrary to Descartes, conceived of the man-machine."[120] As a result of this revolutionary philosophical theory, the secular duality of the human being was abolished, since humans and animals were perceived as similarly mechanistic.

According to these thinkers, the world consisted entirely of matter, devoid of any transcendence and consequently of God. How was gustation represented within this new context that emphasized the materiality of the body?

Condillac's contemporaries wondered about the influence of the body and the senses on the mind. The physical body was perceived as able to influence moral and intellectual behavior, which tended to strengthen the issue of feeding and, indirectly, of taste.[121] Materialists such as Claude-Adrien Helvétius were inspired by Condillac, who strongly denied being a materialist. As in sensualist theory, the senses occupied a central place in materialists' analysis. Once again, it was the argument of necessity that was most generally used in reference to taste. Being essential to the preservation of the bodily machine, feeding explains the intensity of pain engendered by hunger as well as the delights of repletion. La Mettrie underscored the power of the sense of the taste, associated with a physical need and henceforth, when satisfied, accompanied by the most vivacious sensations:

> The human body is a machine. . . . Without it [food] the soul languishes, enters in fury and dies worn out. . . . But feed the body, pour strong juices into its pipes, and strong liqueurs: then the soul . . . arms itself with a proud courage, and the soldier that water had scared off, becomes wild, runs cheerfully to death in the sound of drums. . . . What a power than that of a meal! Joy is reborn in a sad heart, it passes in the soul of the dinner guests who express it by pleasant songs, where the Frenchman excels. . . . It looks at times that *the soul lives in the stomach*.[122]

The concept of taste's necessity, formerly used to devalue it as a lower sense, was within materialist discourses the very crux of its value.

Helvétius considered that men were machines guided by self-interest. The main part of their existence consisted in the satisfaction of bodily needs and in the search for pleasure. Culinary refinement mattered little, for gustatory delights resulted essentially from personal habits. A delicate dish was thus exactly the same as an unrefined one. This was actually a very old idea; many authors of the Christian tradition, such as Jean-Baptiste de La Salle or Malebranche, already considered taste a useless sense. Whatever the quality of the dish, what caused pleasure was the satisfaction of hunger, which tended to decrease the importance of cookery, as Helvétius explains:

> Shall happiness be placed in the delicacy of the table? But the various cuisines of nations prove that good food is only the accustomed food. . . . Whoever is hungry and can satisfy this need is happy. . . . The poor man enjoys, as for physical pleasures, all those of the rich. . . . I know that there are expensive pleasures out of reach . . . but one can always replace them with others, and fill in an as pleasant way the interval which separates a satisfied need from a returning need, that is a meal from another meal.[123]

However, not all materialists would agree. Recognized for the delicacy of his table, the Baron of Holbach was a famous gourmet very attentive to the quality and refinement of food. Contrary to Helvétius, he valued the delicacy of high cuisine, which held an important place in his life. He was, however, very much aware of the fleetingness of the senses' delights. In his works, he thus insisted on the necessary moderation of pleasures—an everlasting topos—which becomes here a rational strategy to enjoy even more all the sensual enchantments of life:

> Although food is necessary to him, he [the man] finds some pleasure in food only at intervals; it is the same for all pleasures, the senses of the man are susceptible to these only with a certain quantity of movement proportional to their strength; so the too lively pleasures tire him and disturb the order in him; the continued or too often repeated pleasures become insipid, bother him, and consequently turn into pain. . . . It follows that the man must, in order to be happy, exercise some choice in his pleasures—save them, resist the too vivacious passions, and avoid all which can disturb the order in his machine either immediately either by later consequences.[124]

The commonplace tenet of gustatory moderation is revived here in a totally new context. It has nothing to do with moral or spiritual virtue anymore, nor with social and polite behavior, but with material and bodily mechanics; moderation is necessary for the good preservation of life.

It is interesting to see that despite the provocative nature of their theories, most materialists actually used very old ideas and stereotypes in their arguments, which were just articulated and endorsed in different ways. For taste, it was the traditional cultural value of necessity that was most often emphasized, with bodily needs leading to intense pleasures precisely because they were essential to the maintenance of the bodily machine. However, according to most materialists, these pleasures more often came from animal repletion than from delicate consumption. Humans, just like animals, need to fulfill these bodily needs, which is why they feel pleasure. The borders between human and animal were not justified anymore, nor was haute cuisine since the main part of food was to satisfy hunger. Let us, however, note the importance granted to feeding, since it can have an influence on thought. But the issue here was not to stimulate the gustatory pleasures, for the delight comes from animal repletion more than greedy refinement.

Conclusion: Taste at the Peripheries of Sensory Cultures

One of the five traditional senses, taste's history joins the long tradition of the hierarchy of the senses peculiar to a deeply dualistic Western culture. The distribution of roles leaned on a partition of the senses into two subgroups, bringing into opposition the lower and the higher forms of senses. The latter—sight and hearing—were connected with the intellectual and spiritual spheres. Sight and hearing were thought to be favorable to the development of knowledge, revealing the superiority of humans in the world as well as the unique dimension of human interiority. Since these senses act at distance from the sensory objects they apprehend, they were considered as more objective and reliable. At the other end of the scale were the lower senses—taste and touch—which, on the contrary, disclosed the similarity of the physicality of humans and animals. Necessary senses, they were deeply involved with the satisfaction of bodily needs, which justified not only their proximity with their sensory objects but also the intense pleasures they provided. These senses' direct contact was, however, perceived as a weakness for it also granted subjectivity; the subject and object of sensation were mingled to the point that they got confused.

The study of the senses was obviously unbalanced in early modern Europe, as evidenced by the general theories of perception and also by discreet little details in the ways in which each of the senses was investigated. In treatises of the senses, the order of the chapters generally followed that of the classic hierarchy. The passage dedicated to taste was, systematically, less rich than the others. Very often, the authors referred to bodily functions or to the chapters relative to touch or smell for additional development, as if taste alone were not enough, not worth discussing. In the end, it appears that scholars held taste in the lowest estimation, even if it traditionally occupied the next-to-last position on the traditional sensory scale. Touch, situated in the lowest rank, was indeed awarded a central and founding role. Because it was endowed with a founding value, it had a much higher status; it appeared as the most reliable sense, which granted touch much more significance for authors than the gustatory sense.

The depreciation of taste was so deeply rooted that this sense seemed nearly unaffected by the philosophical and sensory revolutions that took place at the turn of the eighteenth century. By then, new ideas spread that were rooted in empiricism and sensualism, both of which considered sensory experience as the foundation of all knowledge. The idea of a hierarchy of the senses was revised into a new perspective on collaboration between the sensory organs. But in spite of the extraordinary presence of sensation in the thought of the Age of the Enlightenment, taste somehow remained in the shadows in theoretical works discussing the importance of sensory knowledge. Locke used the example of flavors to demonstrate that the senses led to knowledge of the world, but sight still remained the noblest and highest sense of all. Condillac emphasized the power of an essential sense that, when in pain, was capable of annihilating all the others; yet he reserved only a minor place to taste in his survey, granting nearly all his attention to the sense of touch.

Despite the apparent silence toward taste that we find in a number of texts, a consistent characterization of taste comes to light in between the lines: taste

was almost unresponsive to philosophical changes, and its nature was dominated by the ideas of necessity, of immediacy, and of ineffability. Yet, although
taste remained a "lower" sense, the values attached to it were gradually evolving, notably because of the radical changes in the way the body and the senses
were conceived. In this new context, the necessary gustatory sense was not
depreciated anymore, but on the contrary was valorized for its essential role in
the preservation of the animal mechanics of humanity, providing, for that very
reason, the most intense form of pleasure.

4 From a Material to a Spiritual Taste

TASTE . . . Among the five senses of nature it is the one through which one distinguishes flavors . . . TASTE is figuratively used in Morality regarding the judgment, choice, and discernment of the mind . . . One constantly talks and hears talking about *taste*; good *taste*, bad *taste*. One often says that a person has no *taste*, without understanding what it actually is. Because it is much easier to say what *taste*, and good and bad *taste* are not, than to clearly indicate what they are.

—*Dictionnaire de Trévoux*, 864–865, s.v. "Goût"

For centuries the meaning of the word *taste* was simple and unequivocal: it referred to the bodily sense discriminating flavors. The concept of taste as used in a broad and figurative way, and familiar to us today, only became widespread during the early modern era. Since antiquity—in the case of Quintilian, for instance—there were a few examples of a figurative use of the word *taste* as well as other uses that more generally spoke of food, but these were exceptions. Although there were countless references relating to the inner eye of the mind, taste was limited for centuries solely to the bodily and culinary fields. It was only in the sixteenth century that a figurative meaning of the word appeared within discourses, and from the mid-seventeenth century onward, these gradually entered into common use. The first examples appeared in Italy and Spain, before reaching France, Britain, and Germany.[1] From the Renaissance through the Enlightenment and beyond, taste became a metaphor employed in a range of different contexts, thus carrying multiple meanings.[2]

Surprisingly, the first figurative uses of the word *taste* emerged in religious and especially mystical literature. Food-related metaphors actually existed for centuries within the Christian tradition to refer to spiritual realities.[3] "Food was . . . a central metaphor and symbol in Christian poetry, devotional literature, and theology because a meal (the Eucharist) was the central Christian ritual, the most direct way of encountering God."[4] Likewise, it would be in the spiritual and religious context that discourses would multiply and start expanding the meanings of the word *taste*. Metaphors of taste became particularly frequent in the sixteenth century, notably thanks to the influence of mystical authors such as Teresa of Avila and John of the Cross, who were abundantly read and rapidly translated into French in the early seventeenth century. The term then progressively left the specific context of mystical literature and spread within the frame of the *savoir-vivre* (politeness). Treatises of civility frequently referred to the *honnête homme's bon goût* (good taste), which designated a moral quality of the mind required for advancement in elite social spheres. Finally, in the eighteenth century, this moral quality evolved, and taste was more often used in the aesthetic judgment of fine arts.

There is already an extensive literature on the diverse uses of taste in a number of particular contexts. The aim of this chapter is thus not to redraw in detail this huge cultural movement with all its many local variations. Rather than thoroughly investigating all these metaphors individually, the objective is here to analyze them in an integrated approach and to explore the ways in which they reveal a shift in meanings regarding the sense of taste, which from the seventeenth century onward was endowed with a figurative logic.

The *Je ne sais quoi* of Mystical Writings

The idea of a spiritual form of taste, and of spiritual senses more generally, is deeply rooted within the Christian tradition; the Bible contains many traces of the spirituality of the senses. According to specialists, Origen was the first author to formulate a doctrine on the spiritual senses; this doctrine was later adapted by Gregory of Nyssa, mentioned by Augustine, developed by Bonaventure, and subsequently revisited over and over again.[5] According to this theory, humans are endowed with five bodily senses that allow them to know the world and, similarly, with five spiritual senses through which the soul seeks communication with God. This old theory was for a long time used only in specialized theological treatises. It enjoyed an unprecedented expansion in the sixteenth century when certain mystics—most of them from the Carmelite tradition—decided to use a more sensory and sensual language to relate their personal supernatural experience.[6]

Among the spiritual senses, "spiritual taste" is not easily defined, especially since its descriptions vary from one author to another.[7] It usually referred to an especially intimate and personal experience of religion.[8] The expression mostly covered two possible meanings. On the one hand, the term designated a spiritual sense similar to the spiritual sight or the spiritual touch. Taste was here considered as a "*spiritual sense* of the inner soul, thanks to which the latter would comprehend and experience supernatural realities with a way of knowing similar to the taste sensation provided by the physical sense of the same name."[9] Alternately, the expression "spiritual tastes"—in this case readily used in the plural—was employed "to express the agreeable, the delightful character of certain cognito-affective phenomena that appear within the *oraison* (orison, prayer) or in the course of spiritual life."[10] In their writings, early modern mystics often underscored the ambivalent nature of spiritual tastes. They explained that these supernatural delights were given by God as a consolation, a reward for the soul suffering on the arid path of contemplation. The author of the *Imitation of Jesus Christ* sees in them a foretaste of the eternal life, as he explains to his readers in a dialogue between the soul and Jesus Christ, in which the latter states: "This fully sweet affection that you sometimes feel is an effect of my grace's presence, and like a taste of the heavenly goods that I make you feel in advance; on which you should not lean on too much, because I give it and redraw it as it pleases me."[11] Likewise, according to Francis de Sales, these spiritual rewards are "little foretastes of the immortal sweetness which God gives to the souls who seek him. They are sugar-plums which he gives his little children when he entices them."[12] Several mystics, however, advised the faithful to remain cautious regarding supernatural delights, for these could easily lead to a consuming desire to renew them and consequently produce the vice of *gourmandise spirituelle* or spiritual *gula* (spiritual gluttony). Supplicants beginning their contemplative life were the most likely to give in to this weakness, which "finds its way within the taste they have for the inner life."[13] Moreover, as the extremely influential sixteenth-century Carmelite nun Teresa of Avila constantly stated, it is impossible to know where these pleasures come from: "We do not know if these tastes are from God, or if it is the Devil that gives them."[14] According to Teresa, an evil spirit is able to imitate these supernatural sensations, creating illusions of the senses and deceiving the Christian, who sees them as a gift of God while actually under the power of the demon. Teresa of Avila was especially anxious about this, and repeatedly recalled how important it was to remain detached from spiritual tastes whose origins may not be confirmed. Besides, she states, "perfection is not located in the tastes, but in the greatness of love."[15]

Nonetheless, the expression "spiritual taste" is not to be reduced to the spiritual *gula*; it was used in very different contexts within mystical literature. The same word could have multiple definitions, depending mostly upon the writer. In her work *The Interior Castle* (often translated as *The Mansions*), which was a guide for spiritual development, Teresa of Avila describes seven "mansions" or "dwelling places," each level being a step to get closer to God. According to her, the possession of the "tastes of God" is peculiar to a specific stage of the spiritual life that is related to what she calls the "fourth mansion," where souls have achieved some level of progress. Teresa states that "as they approach the prayer of quiet, and start savoring the tastes and consolations given by our Lord, they think it is a great thing to always be tasting. But they should believe me, and not dive too much ahead . . . life is long, and there are many labors within it."[16] These tastes only occur at an intermediate stage of the contemplation path, a stage in which "the soul is not strong yet, it is still like a little child that starts to get breastfed, from which one can only expect death if he goes away from his mother's breasts."[17] Only very few would have the chance to achieve the long and arduous journey leading to the ultimate mystical union with God. Furthermore, according to Saint Teresa, this spiritual labor could only be partially accomplished by the Christian who wishes to communicate with heaven. Beyond a certain limit, it is God himself who chooses to elect the entirely passive soul and to elevate it toward himself. Teresa distinguishes the "tastes"—which are supernatural pleasures—from the *contentements* (satisfactions)—coming from human nature:

> It seems to me that the satisfactions may be said about what we acquire ourselves through our meditation, and by the prayers we make to our Lord, which come and proceed from our nature, although it is always with the help of God (because it must be understood regarding everything I will say, that we cannot do anything without him) . . . and rightly so, we receive satisfaction for working with these matters: but if we consider it rightly, we may receive the same satisfaction from many other things on earth. . . . It seems to me that . . . these satisfactions are natural . . . and that they start within our nature and finish in God. Tastes, however, begin in God, and our nature feels them and enjoys them as much as the other ones [the satisfactions], and actually much more.[18]

In this extraordinary experience of the divine, which is simultaneously "natural and supernatural," God alone provides mystical ecstasy.[19] The impalpable, inexplicable spiritual taste is the gift of a "supernatural grace" that brings "great peace, harmony, and sweetness within the innermost part of ourselves, and I do not know how nor why, and . . . it fills up everything, and flows into all the mansions and powers . . . which is why I said it [supernatural grace] comes from God and ends in us: because certainly (as the one who will feel it will see) the whole external human enjoys this taste and sweetness."[20] This particular taste, Teresa explains, takes its origin "from a place even more intimate, like something very deep, and I think it must be the heart of the soul."[21] The subsequent stages leading to contemplation are only more delightfully ineffable. "I think it would be better," she adds, "not to say anything about the [mansions] that remain, since it will be impossible to say anything about them, and will even be difficult for the mind to understand them [the mansions]."[22] The wonderful experience of the divine is necessarily ineffable; it "produces goods that we could not explain, and the soul itself could not understand what it is that is given to it."[23] Since taste is a particularly indescribable sense, it can easily be used to relate to the ineffable spiritual delights delivered by God.

Similarly, John of the Cross explains that the path leading to contemplation goes through two dimensions, both active (called *the active night of the senses and of the mind*, described in *The Ascent of Mount Carmel*) and passive (named *the passive night of the senses and of the mind*, explained in *The Dark Night*). Just like Teresa—who had an immense influence on his own writings—Saint John also insists on the passivity of the soul, entirely submitted to God's will:

> The soul could not reach these notions through any of its comparisons or imaginations, because . . . they are above all that; thus God releases them within the soul without its help, and sometimes whenever it thinks about it and pretends it the least, God sends these divine features within the soul. . . . They are so effective that they sometimes make the soul and the body shiver . . . these notions suddenly enter the soul, as we said, and without any choice . . . but to be humble and resigned. God would operate there when and how it pleases him . . . they are a part of the union toward which one heads the soul.[24]

Taste was, however, even more significant to John than to Teresa; John considers spiritual taste to be felt at the exact moment of mystical union with God, a supreme experience beyond any other one, where "it is God himself that we feel and taste: however it [this perception] is not clearly and obviously like in his glory; nevertheless it is such a high and intense feature of notion and flavor that it penetrates the most intimate part of the soul and the devil cannot intervene nor imitate it, because there is nothing similar to that nor anything approaching these flavors and delights. These notions have a certain taste of the divine being and of the eternal life, and the devil could not counterfeit such high things."[25] Although quite close in their mystical writings, Teresa of Avila and John of the Cross did not share exactly the same conceptions of the "taste of God": Teresa's intermediate stage of the spiritual life could be imitated by Satan, while for John, the ultimate outcome of contemplation was that the taste of heaven could only come from God himself.

There were actually many different ways of defining this particularly fleeting concept. For Jean-Joseph Surin, a French Jesuit priest, mystic, and devotional writer of the seventeenth century, the "sweet taste of God" was also of an extreme value.[26] According to him, the height of mystical experience precisely consists in feeling "the taste of God's presence inside," which brings tremendous joy.[27] As he stresses in his work on the *Fondements de la vie spirituelle* (Foundations of Spiritual Life), tasting God once is savoring him forever: "The man enjoying God does not savor anything as sweet in the world as the will and the good pleasure of his Lord, in which he finds his Heaven, which he never leaves, because in everything and everywhere he sees and finds this divine will; he is deprived of any other taste, purpose and feeling."[28] God, he adds, "fulfills the soul with his sweetness which cannot be understood . . . the solely divine will tasted and savored is the food of the faithful and true lover of Our Lord."[29] The "taste of God" is hence a crucial concept in Surin's mystical writings.

To all these early modern mystics, the words related to the sense of taste seemed perfectly appropriate to refer to their supernatural experience, extraordinary as well as ineffable. They used a sensual and sensory language in order to express the spiritual delights rewarding the soul seeking God. It is difficult to find words when describing a transcendental experience necessarily exceeding language. The expression *Je ne sais quoi* (I don't know what), readily associated with the sense of taste, is used often in these texts, relating the unutterable aspects of the divine.[30]

The use of words inspired from the senses may seem surprising, given the fact that renouncing physical pleasures was the first step of a good religious life. Countless injunctions toward humility could be found within devotional and mystical literature, where the soul was encouraged to leave everything behind in order to reach God. The most important thing for beginners in their spiritual life is, according to John of the Cross, to renounce to oneself "from the outside and the inside, practicing suffering for J.C. and annihilating oneself in everything."[31] It is essential to forget oneself, to ignore the body and the world, leaving the soul "empty . . . and purified of all appetite" so that God can fill it with his ineffable delight.[32] Since the pleasures of eating were thought to detach men from spirituality, renunciation of food was actually considered the beginning of self-despoilment. As Benoit of Canfield, an English mystic, explains in his *Rule of Perfection*—a work on contemplative prayer—senses' gratifications "prevent [one] from thinking of God . . . when one wants to eat delicate dishes, pleasant fruits, and all that one finds pleasing to taste, even when the thing is neither rare nor dear, it is necessary to refrain from it by way of mortification."[33] The suffering that such abstinence provides feels delectable to the penitent, for it recalls the Christ's agonies and contributes to mastering the flesh. Annihilation was actually, Jacques Gélis explains, "one of the four rules of mystical discourses, with humility, indifference, and poverty. This will of annihilation, of self-despoilment, this requirement that led to stripping oneself of the 'inner cloth,' was not new: since Meister Eckhart, the agony of the self was a rule of life." Several mystical texts thus reveal a true aspiration to martyr.[34]

Early modern mystics explained how vital it was to make the void in oneself in order to feel God's completeness. Abandoning the flavors of the earth gives the soul the only hope of living a supernatural experience, which would bring spiritual pleasures so much more delightful than every other sensory gratification accessible in the world. As John of the Cross advises his followers: in order "to taste everything, do not take pleasure in anything." In failing to renounce "this sensual taste and appetite," the soul might lose "the taste of God," for two conflicting and contradictory ideas cannot coexist in the same place at the same time.[35] Between the taste of God and the taste of the world one must choose. Indeed,

> this food of the Angels is . . . not given to the palate seeking flavors in the one of the humans; and not only does the soul that takes delight in foreign tastes become incapable of the divine spirit, but it greatly irritates his Majesty by laying claim to spiritual food while not contenting oneself with God alone, but willing to interpose appetite and affection for other things. . . . O if the spirituals only knew which goods they lose . . . for not withdrawing their appetite in childless things, and that they would find in this simple spiritual food the taste of everything, if they did not want to enjoy them anymore: and because they persist in doing this they do not taste it.[36]

Bodily tastes, peculiar to the childhood of the soul, need to be left behind for the hope of "tasting God" one day.[37] Surin, who explains that it is crucial "to keep a great disgust of all creatures" in order to "taste God completely," defends the same idea. He distinguishes two kinds of taste: "One is vile, and satisfies nature with imperfection; the other is high and sublime. This low and vile taste opposes the true taste of God" and must thus "be completely removed, so that one becomes capable of the true experience of the sovereign good." It is all the more crucial to reach the "taste of God" because this kind of taste is "universal, it has the power to make all things in particular taste" delightful. One then "savors everything that appears. . . . The man who tastes God entirely, hence also tasting everything inside him, is always happy, because this general taste of God elevates his spirit, and removes the particular tastes of the things that could bother him."[38] According to Surin, the taste of God being truly "universal" brings in return "the general taste of everything"[39]—all the more reason to let go of the tastes of the world.

Despite the multiple definitions of spiritual tastes, the metaphor of the "taste of God," prolifically used within mystical writings—especially those influenced by the Carmelite trend, such as Teresa, John, and Surin, who was inspired by the two former—was most often employed to refer to the unutterable delights felt when encountering the divine. Mystical literature hence reveals the indefinable character of the sense of taste, which escapes language and rational analysis. Because the mystical taste of God brings such extraordinary delights, it may sometimes be hard for the soul to come back to reality afterward. Teresa and John describe the pain of the mystic, who after tasting "heavenly delights" comes back to a world in which he can only notice the vacuity.[40] As Teresa confesses, "having felt the tastes of God, she [the soul] sees that those of the world are only smoke and vanity, and she slowly leaves them and withdraws."[41] According to John of the Cross, on the way back everything arouses repulsion: "[A]fter having tasted spiritual matters once, the whole flesh is disgusting, which means that tastes and sensory ways are useless."[42] Heavenly appetites give John a *hunger*, Teresa a *thirst*, always unfulfilled.[43] Only the divine bread—God's Spirit—can permanently satisfy the soul. Those who stay attached to the creatures earthly pleasures] are "always starving like dogs," because only God can bring "repletion" and "satiety" to the faithful.[44] The soul must thus choose, says John, between "the affection of God and the affection of the creature. . . . Which proportion is there from the creature to the Creator, from the sensual to the spiritual, the visible to the invisible, the temporal to the eternal, from the heavenly, pure, spiritual food to the sensible food of the senses . . . as long as the soul is subjected to the sensory and animal spirit, the pure spiritual spirit cannot enter it."[45] The communion is an important symbolic moment in this respect. It emphasizes the idea of God's fullness compared to the world's emptiness, here expressed through the metaphor of hunger. Thomas à Kempis fervently describes the soul invited to the "feast" of God, which is "the bread of heaven, *the bread of the Angels . . . the bread which came down from heaven, and gave life to the world. . . .* O sweet feast, in which you give yourself in food!"[46]

These food-related metaphors were actually a traditional way of relating to higher spiritual realities in religious writings. As Priscilla Parkhurst Ferguson points out, Augustine had already relied "on the terrestrial to reach the divine. Far from renouncing the senses, time and again Augustine draws on them to raise himself above mere sensual pleasure." He uses several metaphors of food to relate to the divine's presence and words, like when he pens God's declaration: "I am the food of the fully grown; grow and you will feed on me. And you will not change me into you like the food your flesh eats, but you will be changed into me." Sensuality, Ferguson explains, "has traditionally figured mystical unions with the godhead, an allegorization or metaphorization that resolutely decorporealizes the sense experience. Yet, in his insistence on the imagery of nourishment along with the constant invocation of known earthly delights, Augustine, like so many others, incessantly appeals to the familiar foundation of taste. Paradoxically but empathically, humans accede to the divine through the terrestrial, the material, and the social."[47] In the book they edited on *Religion and the Senses*, Wietse de Boer and Christine Göttler have addressed the sensory and affective dimensions of religion and demonstrated in a large variety of ways how in early modern Europe religious experience was actually "overwhelmingly mediated by sensory discourses and practices."[48]

All of these suggestive metaphors also recall, once again, the ambiguous relationship the Christian tradition had toward food, the senses, and the body. Several specialists in the fields of history of religion and Christianity have stressed the profound ambiguity of Christian discourse on the body, which was, as Jacques Gélis explains, "a double movement of ennoblement and of low esteem of the body. The body is double and inconsistent, like the one that inhabits it." Christian discourse on the body was moreover very diverse, depending on the author and his sensibility and influences, as well as on context: "A pessimist interpretation of the earth, a negative approach to the body inherited from Saint Augustine and Gregory the Great and developed by certain mystical threads or by the Jansenist trend in the seventeenth and the eighteenth centuries, is opposed to the positive image and more measured appreciations of a body that is balanced, seen in Jean Gerson's late-fourteenth century and de Sales' seventeenth-century texts."[49] It is thus not uncommon to find inconsistencies within religious writings related to the senses and to the body.

As demonstrated in chapter 2, the association of God with repletion was also found within the demonological universe. The devil was renowned for only offering tasteless feasts during Sabbath. The food provided was not salted and in the end did not fulfill the witch, who starved when leaving the diabolical feast. Mystical and demonological writings were, of course, very different forms of literature, yet these shared a common image of God represented as wholeness as opposed to the void of the devil. Only God was thought to be capable of appeasing hunger, nourishing the body and the soul of the world. Taste was a delight offered by God's grace, which the devil, master of illusion, failed to imitate. Although the devil's enterprises were facilitated by the sin of gluttony, Satan himself could neither procure nor reproduce taste. It is quite intriguing that even if the pleasures of taste may lead to the devil, taste itself in the end only referred to God.

We can spot discussions of the spiritual taste within several devotional texts. These discussions are frequent within Teresa of Avila's and John of the Cross's works, particularly when they describe the exultations of the divine union; however, spiritual taste was not ubiquitous with other authors. Benoit of Canfield, for instance, sometimes mentions the idea that "the soul neither sees nor tastes anything but God, his sweet pleasure and will."[50] During contemplation, "this will, pleasure, and satisfaction of God is something so delicious and pleasant to the soul (when it tastes it perfectly) that it draws, illumines, expands, extends, raises, ravishes, and intoxicates her. Hence she no longer feels any will, affection, nor inclination of her own. Rather, wholly stripped of herself and of all self-will, interest, and benefit, she is plunged into the abyss of this will and swallowed up in its engulfing pleasure, and so is made one spirit with it."[51] But this English mystic only occasionally referenced taste; he was much fonder of visual metaphors, as evidenced, for instance, in the *Rule of Perfection*, in which God is described as a light or a sun illuminating the soul, burned by a heavenly fire. Benoit describes the proper will of the soul as "the darkness of a tenebrous night," failing to "sympathize with the clarity of the Sun . . . the light of the Divine will."[52] Sight actually occupies a far more important place than taste in this book. The same may be said of Pierre de Bérulle, one of the most important mystics of seventeenth-century France, who only sporadically used taste as a figure of speech in his work. For him, taste refers more to the resistance of self-esteem than to the presence of God, "which is fed by the proper content and pleasure and by a spiritual gluttony and despicable abuse of holy things that converts it in its own delights and pleasures and adapts them to its own taste and feeling. But very dangerous and occult from which proceed several indulgences, presumptions, illusions, and diabolic disappointments."[53] The founder of the French Oratory seems to prefer the metaphors referring more generally to the spiritual food, like when he refers to the soul attracted and entirely converted "to the breast of the divine piety through the sweetness of the milk deriving from it."[54] Yet light, vision, and sun are far more frequently used here as examples by the author in order to enlighten his ideas.[55] These differences between mystical authors who frequently used the example of taste and those who did not can partly be explained by the fact that these authors came from different spiritual and cultural traditions, opposing a sensual Spanish mystique inspired by Teresa of Avila and more rational spiritual trends of Northern Europe, represented, for instance, by Benoit of Canfield.

In sum, the mystical literature of the sixteenth and seventeenth centuries reveals utterly new uses of the word *taste*, from now on endowed with a figurative meaning. Since it appeared in a very specific religious context, it was not yet of common use in the sixteenth century. But already one century later, the expression "tasting God" could be found in dictionaries, which lets us assume an important diffusion of the term.[56] *Foretaste* is defined in the 1694 edition of *Dictionnaire de l'Académie françoise* as "the taste one has in advance of something pleasant. God fulfilled him with spiritual consolations and gave him a foretaste of bliss. It is only a foretaste of the peaceful fruit."[57] This definition, however, disappears in later editions, which tends to suggest that it fell out of use. The 1762 edition of the *Dictionnaire* only mentions the phrase "He has no taste for the things of Heaven."[58] But in 1762, this expression relates to something very different from the mystical "taste of God" mentioned above.

If food-related metaphors could be found already in ancient theological writings—in the Bible or in the works of Church fathers—the peculiarity of early modern mystical literature is on the one hand an insistence on taste (not just on food), and on the other hand a broad diffusion that these writings would deliver for taste metaphors, so popular that the idea of a figurative sense of taste would enter the common use of language. The new uses of the word *taste* diffused in the sixteenth and seventeenth centuries are also and foremost a sign of transformations of the representations of this sense. For a long time limited to the concrete domain of food, taste entered for the very first time a more spiritual universe—and it is, paradoxically, within the religious context, which one would have thought the most reluctant to celebrate this bodily sense, that it first emerged. One may wonder why it was a lower sense—an object of deadly sin—that was chosen to verbalize the highest spiritual transcendence accessible to humans on earth. But the spiritual taste referred to something very different than the bodily sense from which it proceeded: it was related to the spirit and had nothing to do with food. Further, it was not connected to any physiological need. The "hunger of the soul" was only a metaphor referring to higher supernatural realities. Needless to say, there was also no animality within the act of tasting God.

However, the bodily and the spiritual tastes share certain features and one may find traces of the material sense's heritage. For gustation as well as for the "taste of God," taste is characterized by an intense pleasure. The spiritual sense is, just like the bodily one, especially personal and somehow indefinable, so strongly delightful that words fail to fully describe it. As stressed by Surin, "the pleasures and the delights of these souls are unexplainable."[59] Teresa constantly insists on her own "simplicity" and on her incapability to describe mysteries so much greater than her, readily claiming: "[T]he same way I don't know what I have to say, I cannot say it with good order, and . . . it is extraordinary that I do such a thing."[60] She shows this "simplicity" through the form of her writing itself and demonstrates how the whole mystical language is in fact grounded in the unutterable, which is probably the reason why taste's lexicon, deeply ineffable, flourished favorably in that context.[61]

The "taste of heaven" was moreover a spiritual delight that was felt more than rationalized. It was a gift of God to the passive soul that abandoned itself to him. Taste thus became for the very first time a higher form of knowledge, since it helped to communicate with God. Material and spiritual tastes were, furthermore, both characterized by embodiment or unification. The same way food melts in the mouth before transforming itself into the body, the soul gets lost in God and confused with him, transforming the mystic, who incorporates it with rapture. Within this exceptional mystical union, the soul tastes God while being tasted by him.[62]

All these early modern mystics described contemplation as the foretaste of heaven, using the means of a very carnal language. It is as though only the words related to the pleasures of the senses were capable of describing the intimate and magnificent experience of the divine ecstasy, referred to as "tasting God."[63] This indescribable spiritual union was the ultimate reward reserved to a small minority of chosen souls able to communicate with God himself. The journey toward the divine was nevertheless full of difficulties; very few arrived at their destination. Although mystical literature theoretically offered the same method to everybody, the spiritual path, just like bodily taste, was deeply personal. Paradoxically, while pleading for the renunciation of oneself, the mystics hence revealed the unique nature of their personal experience, disclosing through the self-expression of their writing the deeply idiosyncratic character of the sense of taste, in its spiritual just like in its physical expression.

By displacing the traditional meanings of the spiritual taste, sixteenth- and seventeenth-century mystical texts also gave these metaphors an unprecedented diffusion. These metaphors quickly entered France in the seventeenth century, thanks to the translations and broad diffusion of Teresa of Avila's and John of the Cross's works, widely read at the time.[64] The latter influenced several writers, notably Francis de Sales, whose *Introduction to the Devout Life* became a bestseller in early modern France. The idea of a figurative sense of taste was widely diffused through this spiritual literature.

From the *Honnête Homme*'s *Bon Goût* to the Aesthetic Taste of Beauty

Originating from mystical literature, the expression *taste* used in a figurative way gradually spread outside the properly religious context to enter general use in the French language in the mid-seventeenth century. New metaphors were invented, using the same word to refer to very different realities. One of the most popular was the expression *bon goût* (good taste), which flourished within polite society in the classical period. This concept, shaped in early modern guidebooks on polite behavior, became fashionable with Gracian, whose works on the ideal courtier were translated and well known in France.[65] The *bon goût* designated a quality of the mind of the *honnête homme*—also called the *galant homme*, or the *gentleman* in English—which allowed him to adopt in every circumstance the most appropriate behavior and language, depending on people, moment, and place. Based on a set of undetermined common rules, the *bon goût* was thus at the same time a form of knowledge and an intuition, helping mannerly people adjust their conduct and, as a result, succeed socially. This was also a new strategy of distinction peculiar to high society—as theorized by Norbert Elias and Pierre Bourdieu—for the success and large diffusion of literature of civility spread the codes of politeness outside the limited circle of initiated members of the late seventeenth- and eighteenth-century elites. Jean-Baptiste de La Salle's *Règles de la bienséance* were used in schools to teach students how to read, while many conduct manuals were published in the *bibliothèque bleue* (blue library) in Troyes, spreading a myriad of texts that widely disclosed the rules of politeness into lower social strata.[66] As a result, theorists of honesty would start distinguishing civility—a universal concept—from politeness—a true distinction of the elite minority.[67] The *bon goût* had the advantage, for the upper classes, of relating to more implicit qualities difficult to define with words, which could only be acquired by constantly observing those who possessed it. According to David Bensoussan, the notion of *bon goût* inherited from Guicciardini's notion of *discrezione*, Castiglione's *grazia* and *sprezzatura*, Della Casa's *leggiadria*, and Gracian's *despejo* and *gusto relevante*, all words used to refer to the courtier's grace. Bensoussan explains that all these concepts present "the same implicit mixture of idealism and pragmatism, which hinges on this idea of 'je-ne-sais-quoi' that is their common feature and that allows, through its vague and mysterious character, to legitimize all the opportunistic strategies of active insertion within society as it is, at the same time validating the myth of a qualitative superiority relying on an election of a quasi-supernatural order."[68] Hence, precisely because of its vagueness, the development of the *bon goût* became an ideal of perfection intended to define an elite.

This particularly refined form of polite behavior was not only meant to preserve appearances by showcasing the paragon of impeccable conduct; indeed, since the sixteenth century, theories of honesty were deeply intertwined with moral ethics. The visible outside had to be a faithful reflection of the invisible inside. This reflection was very important to Erasmus, who endowed each gesture or bodily behavior with a moral value and disciplined the bodies of children in order to perfect their souls.[69] The Erasmian ideal was still present in Antoine de Courtin's mind, who suggests that his readers please not only "the eyes of the body" but also "the eyes of the soul." Indeed, he explains, "the principle of true politeness" is not only the "external charm . . . we must aspire to something stronger, which marks the good disposition of the inside, rather than the beautiful disposition of the outside."[70] Ethics and etiquette, ways of being and ways of displaying, were indissolubly joined.[71] The *bon goût* likewise referred to the outside as well as to the inside of the *honnête homme*, revealing an art of living in which spirit and conduct were in perfect harmony.

This harmonic ideal did not, however, prevent theories of honesty from becoming more complex during the baroque period. From the mid-seventeenth century onward, writers increasingly pointed out the tension between appearance and being, underscoring the possible dissimulation of true thoughts—people may be lying and disclosing their true selves. Critiques of this *fausse politesse* (false politeness) came especially from religious circles—Christians such as Bossuet, Fénélon, Jacques Esprit, and La Rochefoucauld.[72] The solution offered by conduct manuals was to emphasize a true politeness grounded on Christian values like charity, revealing in the end a true "Christian civility," which was the name of a book written by Pierre Nicole.[73] The insistence on this tension between inside and outside was even more accentuated after 1680 when the whole court moved to Versailles; the transformation of social life that occurred there might explain these evolutions within theoretical discourse.[74]

In its relation to good manners, the new expression *bon goût* testifies to a change in use, a transformation of taste's meanings. Most importantly, this moral form of taste became a fashionable topic in mid-seventeenth-century France. Countless debates were held to discuss this new expression and its content and uses, which had to be defined. After lurking for a long time at the peripheries of discourses, taste was thus for the first time decisively an object of great interest in high society. It was not reduced anymore to the limited scope of mystical writings; an array of books was published that discussed this notion of good taste along with broad considerations on honesty and polite behavior. Authors reflected on the meanings of this new expression, different theorists (among them cultivated *mondains*) furthered a variety of polemics on the notion.[75] These authors, for the most part used to frequenting the royal court and/or the salons, were very much aware of the existing rules of social behaviors peculiar to these visible spaces. Conversing about taste was a fashionable recreation at popular salons, such as in Madame de Scudéry's[76] or Madame de Sablé's, where, according to Claude Chantalat (who has thoroughly investigated popular salons of the era), the guests "took pleasure in analyzing with great subtlety several aspects of the life of the mind and of the heart." They offered "quintessential definitions" of many notions related to taste, such as "the *agrément*, the *bel air*, or the *justesse*," and differentiated between taste and analogous expressions like "the *bel esprit*, the *bon esprit*, the *esprit plaisant*, the *esprit fin*."[77] The phrase *bon goût* was likewise regularly addressed in these polite conversations.

As with mystical notions of taste, theorists offered many different definitions of the notion of *bon goût*. Progressively, the word *taste* acquired an aesthetic value. Art and literature were indeed an important part of high society's universe: aesthetic critiques were made at court and within the Parisian salons. Taste would thus gradually designate a new elite faculty that entailed judging the value of literary or artistic works, just like the tongue and the palate were able to appreciate the quality of dishes tasted. The faculty of the tongue was thus attributed to the mind. As Roger de Piles, French painter and art critic, explains, "the same way we say that the mind sees, we say again that it tastes. It is employed to judge books, like it is the task of the tongue to judge flavors."[78] In the eighteenth century, the aesthetic role of taste became more and more distinct from the one it played in social life.[79] Discussions moved away from the morality of taste to address beauty, while taste's initial meanings were gradually left behind. Taste was from then on defined as a new faculty of the mind distinguishing the good from the bad within works of art. The public concerned with these questions expanded to include philosophers, especially theorists of beauty. This change laid the foundations of aesthetics and philosophy of art, a new discipline facilitated by this new fascination with the topic of taste from the late seventeenth century onward.[80]

Debates initiated during the previous century on the question of the *bon goût*—which was progressively altered to *Goût*—went on throughout the eighteenth century. Placed within the frame of aesthetic discussions, the question of taste was central at the time; it mobilized the intellectual elite, among whom were the encyclopedists and the philosophers of the Enlightenment. Voltaire, Montesquieu, Jaucourt, and D'Alembert each wrote a part of the entry for "taste" in the *Encyclopédie*, which enlarged the debate around this concept.[81] Associated with beauty and with art, taste became truly fascinating for scholars like Denis Diderot, David Hume, and later, Immanuel Kant.[82] In this context, taste entered the universe of philosophy for the first time. Treatises on taste thrived in many European languages, as the whole of Europe was interested in the topic. The spread of translations and contact between contemporary scholars facilitated an ongoing exchange of views. National traditions developed in the Germanic, British, and French schools regarding theories of taste. Due to the spread of treatises and availability of translations, scholars tackled new themes and offered contrasting opinions on taste.

From sixteenth-century mystical writings to eighteenth-century aesthetic works, several metaphors endowed taste with a figurative sense, inventing new spiritual forms of taste. They were related to very different universes—devotion, etiquette, and art. What kinds of meanings did these varying uses produce? What was it that connected quotation to aesthetic judgment, the social *bon goût* to the mystical *je ne sais quoi*? Why was such a despicable material sense such as taste chosen as a means of engaging with such heterogeneous and noble topics?

Good and Bad Taste

By definition, the word *taste* is always implicitly referring to something good and enjoyable. As stated by Richelet in his dictionary, taste "is to like what is good. . . . One does not use *the taste* and *to taste* regarding sad and disagreeable matters."[83] Taste is therefore necessarily inscribed within a dialectic frame: the concept of *good taste* is inextricably bound up with that of *bad taste*, whatever the context considered. Bodily or physical taste naturally distinguishes the dishes considered "good" from all those that are judged "bad." The same opposition is also present in the figurative sense of the word, as evidenced by the expression *bon goût* itself, where the use of the adjective *bon* (good) underscores this dialectic nature, which seems peculiar to the sense of taste. Positive and negative valences certainly exist for each of the five senses—there are beautiful and ugly scenes to look at, agreeable and disagreeable sounds to listen to—yet it seems somehow different for taste because in this case, the antimony becomes an operative value. The dialectic of good/bad is implied in the very definition of taste; this is not the case for the senses of sight or hearing. Taste, always qualified as good or bad, is never neutral.[84] The taste of the body as well as the taste of the mind is perceived through an immediate sensation of pleasure or repulsion, as indicated, for instance, by the examples proposed in the entry "taste" of the aforementioned *Dictionnaire de la langue françoise*: "a meat of good taste, of bad taste, that is of an excellent taste, of a refined taste, of a delicate taste, of an exquisite taste, of a spicy taste. . . . This man has taste; he does not have any taste; he has a delicate, refined, exquisite taste."[85] The knowledge provided by the sense of taste is always associated with a value judgment.

However, in early modern France, distinguishing good taste from bad taste was not only a matter of personal preference: a larger debate was at stake on the nature of taste. First of all, seventeenth-century educated elites were convinced that a good and a bad taste existed in and of itself—that is, that good and bad taste dwelt in the realm of the absolutes, which elicited discussions on the topic.[86] La Bruyère writes of the commonly held belief that "there is a point of perfection in art, like there is one of goodness or maturity in nature. He who feels and enjoys it has a perfect taste; he who does not feel it, and enjoys less or more, has a defective taste. There is thus a good and a bad taste, and disputes about taste are well-founded."[87] Classical artistic and literary works originating from antiquity were especially seen to embody beauty and good taste. They were an absolute and an ideal, an example to be followed. The proof of their remarkable quality was that they survived throughout centuries without losing society's admiration. Yet in the late seventeenth century, controversies arose when contemporary works were compared to these antique models; intellectual conflicts lasted for decades and were ultimately dubbed *La Querelle des Anciens et des Modernes* (The Quarrel between the Ancients and the Moderns).[88] This *Querelle* had a huge influence on taste debates, for these discussions, while examining the value of art works, also questioned the nature and value of the faculty of taste.

The Ancients felt that taste embodied a perfect and impassable state, leading afterward to an inevitable process of corruption; the only possibility of achieving good taste for contemporaries was thus to faithfully imitate the antique models.[89] The Moderns, on the contrary, although they acknowledged and were inspired by the quality of works from antiquity, suggested that it was possible to perfect taste in their own time. Ancients and Moderns, however, recognized that good taste was not present in all times and places; some periods of artistic genius were especially favorable to the growth of taste. Value judgments were hence numerous and referred to the tastes of people, social groups, and entire nations. In seventeenth-century France, the *bon goût* was a classical taste characterized by order and nature, for art and literature as well as for cuisine. Bad taste was one of excesses, of exaggerated artifice; bad taste involved breaking aesthetic rules, like Spanish taste, which had a reputation among the French as being favorable to singularity and excess. Clearly, a preference for nature and sobriety would remain in eighteenth-century France. Voltaire, for instance, considered that the artistic taste, as well as the culinary one, needed to be sober and natural, avoiding a profusion of useless ornaments: "The same way the bad physical *taste* consists of being flattered only by spicy and studied seasonings, the bad *taste* in Arts is to only be pleased with studied ornaments, and not feel the beautiful nature of a work. Depraved *taste* in foods is choosing the ones [foods] that disgust others; it is a kind of illness. Depraved *taste* in the Arts is liking subjects that revolt the *esprits bien faits* (refined/proper minds); to favor the comic over the noble, the precious and affected over the simple and natural beauty: it is a mental illness."[90]

As already underscored above, French subjects living under the reign of Louis XIV were convinced of the superiority of their taste and felt that their cuisine and the quality of their literature and fine arts were a testament to this superiority. They explained this higher taste as resulting from the development of a refined form of civility in their country, reflective of a preeminent political and military structure.[91] They, however, conceded that France had previously not been spared from periods in which taste declined, as Jean-Baptiste Morvan de Bellegarde, author of influential books on ethics, polite behavior, and conversation, stresses: "Good taste has its trials as does the mind; not so long ago, taste was very depraved in France"[92] The idea of a corruption *du goût* (meaning that peoples tastes became vulgar) is, in fact, a literary commonplace, as we can see in Molière's 1663 play *La Critique de l'École des Femmes*, in which Climène complains that "the taste of people is strangely spoiled" and "*le siècle s'encanaille furieusement*" ([people of] the century become terribly vulgar).[93] But generally speaking, the early reign of *Louis le Grand* was seen as a period of glory for taste. The cultural propaganda the Sun King used to reinforce his political power was, of course, not independent from the shared belief in the triumph of French taste.

In the seventeenth century, the criteria for judging the value of a work of art were not very specific. A work was generally judged as good if it pleased the man of taste. The judgment of taste thus depended on the *subject* more than on the *object* considered. To please the *honnête homme*, the artistic or literary work needed to be in accordance with the norms of classical aesthetics, attached to the principles of order and unity, as we already saw in chapter 1.[94] With manners as well, taste consisted of recognizing what was expected of the *bienséances* (proprieties). Custom therefore played a considerable part, since "custom makes proprieties and proprieties make what is pleasing; and so our taste which finds good what is according to proprieties and bad what is against it, is ruled by the custom."[95] The importance of custom and habits was very often stated in discourses on taste, which could be found in the widest variety of registers. As illustrated in chapter 3, the empiricist and sensualist philosophers and the cooks before them all insisted on the power of habits and customs that ruled taste preferences, whether in the domain of food, morality, or aesthetics.

Also of crucial importance in these debates is the origin of the ability to judge. Was taste an innate or acquired faculty? The question gave rise to intellectual discussions with important social and aesthetic stakes. Some theorists argued for a taste given at birth, while others emphasized the education required for the development of the judgment of taste. Most authors compromised between the two previous hypotheses, combining a natural gift with a taste acquired through experience. Interestingly, within this debate, taste frequently appeared to be a frontier between nature (the "natural taste") and culture (the "acquired taste"), such as within the *Réflexions sur le goût* (Reflections on Taste) of Nicolas Gédoyn, a cultivated Jesuit and member of the French Academy.[96] He considered that taste, either physical or spiritual, was a natural gift susceptible to progress through experience: "In the physical, and in the moral," he writes, "there is a natural taste, and an acquired taste," the former being "a gift of nature," while the latter was "the fruit of experience and reflection." Gédoyn uses the example of champagne to clarify his thoughts: "If I drink Champagne wine for the first time, I will say if it pleases me or not. The feeling only is enough for that. But I will never be able to say if it is a good Champagne wine, because since I never drank any I don't know the taste and quality Champagne wine must have." For the moral taste, it is the same because "the natural taste . . . is not anything else than the right reason, and what we call common sense, because nature supposedly gave it to all men."[97] Only the experience of tasting could increase the level of discernment. However, Gédoyn summarizes that the "natural taste" is always more reliable because "it never fools us"; it

consists in a sensation, or a feeling. . . . The same way I will distinguish sweet and bitter if my palate is well disposed, if I have sense and reason I will taste a sensible speech as necessarily as I will see light when I open the eyes in broad daylight. It is not like that for the acquired taste. This taste is the fruit and the effect, not only of art and as a consequence of knowing the rules, but even more of the just idea of perfection to which one needs to bring back all the things we do or judge about. These conditions are rarely found together. . . . Which is why the good taste is so rare, and the bad one so common.[98]

The faith granted to taste as a sensation is not surprising in this cultural context influenced by sensualism, investigated in the previous chapter. The senses indeed played an important part in aesthetic judgment, as testified by the etymology of the term *aesthetics*, which comes from the Greek work *aisthesis*, meaning sensation, feeling, what the senses can perceive.

Nevertheless, many scholars considered bodily taste to be inferior to spiritual taste, which could be cultivated. Voltaire, for instance, thinks that only the "*taste* in Art" could really be developed, "because in the physical *taste*, although one sometimes ends up liking things for which one first felt repugnance, yet nature did not want men in general to learn to feel what was necessary to them; but the intellectual *taste* needs more time to train."[99] It is thus the old idea of the "necessary sense" that explains that the "sensual taste" could not be refined.

Whatever the value granted to the natural and acquired tastes, most theorists agreed that not all men were capable of distinguishing the value of works.[100] Taste was a very rare quality. It was believed to be the prerogative of a minority of distinguished and cultivated men considered to be genuine connoisseurs and the only ones able to perceive beauty. According to David Hume, widely read in France, these connoisseurs were the reference point of a standard of taste.[101] Members of high society were privileged in this matter, since they received a good education. By daily circulating within a sphere of highly educated people, they developed their own taste. These individuals were not exclusively aristocrats, but members of a community of cultivated persons who shared mutual tastes and customs. As emphasized by Charles de Saint-Evremond, essayist and literary critic, "the most essential point is to acquire a real discernment, and to give oneself a pure light. Nature prepares us to do so, while experience and the company of delicate people completes our training for this."[102] Members of the royal court in the seventeenth century and of the Parisian salons in the eighteenth century supposedly possessed the *bon goût* and, later on, taste. Taste was thus contemplated within an elitist sphere, excluding those who did not have it.

With time, the audience recognized as possessing *good taste* would increase and become more complex and diversified. Academies of Arts and Sciences were founded in the course of the seventeenth century—such as the Académie française, the Académie royale de peinture et de sculpture, or the Académie royale des sciences—and these would become what Pierre Bourdieu and other sociologists have called "instances of legitimization."[103] These academies would have much power in defining the authors, artists, and works labeled with "good taste." They would, however, gradually compete with the development of the press; an increasing number of journals dedicated to book reviews and art criticism flourished in the late seventeenth and eighteenth centuries that discussed the quality of works of art. According to Anne Goldgar, the readership of these new *journaux*—for instance, the Parisian *Journal des sçavants*—were mostly people "too poor to afford the books they discussed, too isolated—even in major cities—to see books from all corners of Europe, and those with too little time to read every book that came off the European presses."[104] An increasing number of readers and spectators were thus consuming and criticizing art and literature, composing what Jürgen Habermas has theorized as the "public sphere," notably linked to the rise of the bourgeoisie.[105] This public sphere united a variety of learned people from differing classes and social strata, gathered due to the way in which they made "public use of reasoning"—discussing the rules of taste and making judgments on the works submitted by artists and writers.[106] All the members of this new public literary sphere would meet to discuss in cafés and in salons. The debate over taste changed in these contexts; as Anne Goldgar has shown in her study of Parisian journalists as censors, the issue of taste was absolutely fundamental to the French literary world's judgment on which books deserved to be published and which censored.[107] Journalists, she writes, "directed the tastes, interests, and activities of readers."[108] They were censors in the Republic of Letters. The increasing number of people claiming to possess taste, however, did not go unchallenged. Several scholars among the Republic of Letters—like Voltaire, for instance—would react harshly toward these "judges" and against journalists in particular: they lacked legitimacy.[109]

A Sensory and Undetermined Discernment

The moral and aesthetic tastes actually shared many common features with bodily taste; features of bodily taste were also valid within the mystical context of taste, though very distant from the social universe. First of all, in whichever context considered, taste appeared to be a concept difficult to define. Several theorists attempted to put words to this impalpable sensation, but they always necessarily came back to this *je ne sais quoi*, impossible-to-describe characteristic, which taste had retained from its mystical origin. In the polite universe, after stating the numerous qualities a *honnête homme* was supposed to possess, the authors of conduct manuals or treatises of taste emphasized that knowing the rules was not enough. To socially succeed, according to Dominique Bouhours—a Jesuit priest who was also an essayist and critic, a regular guest at the Parisian salons—one needs a little something more, a unique "good taste" to make the difference, a sort of "grace," charisma, or mysterious aura.[110] The indeterminacy of taste remained salient in relation to aesthetic judgment, for the feeling of beauty was also beyond words. As a matter of fact, the indeterminacy of taste is part of what defines and constitutes this sense, no matter the domain considered. As Bouhours accurately states, "it is much easier to feel it than to know it. . . . It would not be a *je ne sçay quoy* [sic] if one knew what it was; its nature is to be incomprehensible and inexplicable."[111] The expression *je ne sais quoi* referred to the impossibility of fully defining taste, an elusive concept with multiple and often contradictory meanings. Many authors actually used the word without providing any definition.[112] This *je ne sais quoi* was a real topos associated with the sense of taste—and later on, with beauty—which one finds in the most various and least-expected contexts, such as Jacques Rohault's *Traité de physique*.[113] This ineffability was also a commonplace in polite conversation.

Nonetheless, some writers tried to go beyond the indeterminacy of taste and to identify the main features of this concept. They described it like a new faculty meant to distinguish the bad from the good, whether in cuisine, in social behavior, in conversation, or in artistic and literary works. Authors accentuated the singularity of this form of judgment, characterized by its rapidity as a sense that is felt before it is registered. The idea of an instantaneous polite, literary, and artistic taste originated from the tongue's gustatory capabilities: as soon as it enters in contact with food, the tongue experiences a feeling of pleasure or repulsion that precedes intellectual reflection. So too, in the same way the tongue immediately knows if a meal is pleasant or not, the mind spontaneously judges the value of a work or a person, discriminating, almost without thinking, good from bad taste. As Bouhours explains, "these *je ne sçay quoy* in beauty and in ugliness, so to speak, excite in us some *je ne sçay quoy* of inclination and aversion, where reason does not see anything and about which the will is not the master: they are the first movements preceding reflection. . . . *These feelings of sympathy and antipathy are born in one instant*, and when we think about it less; we love, and hate before, without the mind noticing it, and if I dare say, without even the heart knowing."[114] The instantaneousness of perception is hence another essential feature of taste that factors into its undetermined nature. The gustatory assessment is so fast that it is hardly defined. As mentioned in chapter 3, physicians and philosophers studying the five senses usually also stressed the spontaneity of taste, explaining that taste was a sense of contact: the gustatory sensation provokes an immediate response of pleasure or repulsion—or, following Bouhours, a natural sympathy or antipathy, in accordance with the old humoral theory. As illustrated in the previous chapters, for a very long time—and still, actually, in the seventeenth and eighteenth centuries in other contexts—the rapidity of taste was a criterion that led to the depreciation of this sense, the lack of distance between the sensory organ and its object being considered as an obstacle to the development of knowledge. But within the specific domain of taste theory and aesthetics, the spontaneity of taste was underscored as a positive quality of a particular form of discernment. As Voltaire emphasizes in the *Encyclopédie*, "this sense, this capacity for discriminating between different foods, has given rise, in all known languages, to the metaphor which expresses through the word taste the feeling of beauty and defects in all the arts; it is a quick discernment like that of the tongue and the palate, and which, like them, anticipates reflection; like the palate, it voluptuously relishes what is good and it rejects alike the bad with loathing; like the palate it is also uncertain and doubtful, ignoring even if what is presented to it must please it, and sometimes requires habit to become formed."[115]

Spiritual taste, although a discernment of the mind, was in reality a judgment grounded in the senses, for it was accompanied by a physical sensation, a reaction to an artistic or literary work. As a result, a problem arose regarding the immediacy of taste within the sphere of aesthetic judgment. Was reason or feeling the principle arbiter of taste? Several polemics opposed the rationalist versus the sensitive trends. The stakes were high because a taste founded on feeling suggested the possibility of a relativity of tastes, which was contradictory to the classical and Cartesian conviction of an ideal and absolute beauty. Yet in the seventeenth century, the classical authors who underscored aspects of feelings, of the heart's delicacy, did not deny reason's role in the judgment of taste.[116] As Morvan de Bellegarde points out, "taste is exquisite when it is ruled by reason, and those who only follow their inclination as a guide usually have a bad taste, because in a certain way they look like beasts, which only act by instinct and by temperament."[117] The spiritual taste considered here was thus a very different form of taste than the animal sense traditionally despised. "The good taste," Morvan continues, "is the effect of a right and enlightened reason, which always takes the good side in doubtful or ambiguous matters."[118] The classical *bon goût* as well as the aesthetic taste were consequently grounded in reason. The ability to judge beauty was possible thanks to the internalization of aesthetic rules, realized by constantly observing art works and the people able to judge them.

Seran de la Tour, an eighteenth-century French critic, explains that "every feeling inspired by Taste is an effect of Beauty. Yet there is no Beauty devoid of fixed, invariable, eternal rules."[119] Nevertheless, most taste theorists recognized that knowing the rules alone was not enough to determine the quality of art works.[120] For many authors, taste was a specific form of judgment localized in between sense perception and intellectual understanding. Jean le Rond D'Alembert believes that the "true philosopher . . . lets himself go to the lived and quick pleasure of the impression; but convinced that true beauties always win the examination, he soon retraces his steps, goes back up to the causes of his pleasure, gets to the bottom of it, distinguishes what was an illusion from what deeply hit him, and is able through this analysis to give a healthy judgment of the entire work."[121] That spiritual taste was also a sensory taste did not make taste an arbitrary form of judgment. The intervention of reason in the elaboration of aesthetic taste makes the latter superior to physical taste, in which individual sensibility is more significant. In these theories, taste became a true faculty of judging, a discernment, a form of knowledge in its own right. As Seran de la Tour underscores, there is a "knowledge through taste,"[122] which consists in discerning between the natural gift and the assimilation of rules through experience and habit, at the frontier between nature and culture.

Yet starting in the eighteenth century, some authors increasingly started to highlight the major importance of the senses, feelings, and pleasure in the elaboration of the judgment of taste. Jean-Baptiste Dubos—also referred to as l'Abbé

Du Bos—is a representative figure of this empiricist trend, opposed through lived polemics to other writers who favored a rationalist perspective.[123] What is new in the eighteenth century is the idea that taste could be entirely used to reference pleasure and sensation.[124] In this sense, the example of cookery was especially relevant, as Dubos highlights in a famous passage:

> Does one reason to know if a *ragoût* is good or if it is bad, and does it ever occur to anyone, after having determined the geometrical principles of flavor and defined the qualities of each ingredient which make up the composition of this dish, to discuss the proportions of their mixture, to decide if the *ragoût* is good? We never do such a thing. There is inside us a sense designed in order to know if the Cook operated following the rules of his art. One tastes the *ragoût* and even without knowing these rules, one knows if it is good. It is the same in a certain way for works of the mind and paintings made to please us by moving us.[125]

According to Dubos, taste is an "inner feeling" and a "natural discernment"[126]—in short, a "sixth sense" that "is inside us without us seeing its organs. It is the portion of us which judges on the impression it feels, and which . . . pronounces without consulting the rule and the compass. It is finally what we commonly call *le sentiment* (feeling)."[127] It was quite common in the eighteenth century to consider that the aesthetic taste worked like an additional sense. The objects of beauty were seen as affecting taste in the same way that the visual objects affected sight, or flavors affected the bodily taste. The taste of beauty was thus clearly distinguished from the gustatory one. Seran de la Tour explains that "the proportion that is found between the senses and their objects is the same as the one observed between the faculty of feeling Beauty, which is Taste, and the power of exciting love about it which resides sovereign in Beauty."[128]

Taste is, moreover, a deeply affective sense, characterized by the pleasure it gives, as much in the literal as in the figurative sense. The mystical "taste of God" referred to a supernatural delight as well. The aesthetic taste is accompanied by a different emotion, but it is also a higher form of pleasure. Generally speaking, taste is a sense that allows a savoring of delights, as Claude-Nicolas Le Cat significantly asserts: "Taste in general is the movement of an organ that delights in its object and feels all its goodness; which is why Taste is of all sensations; one has taste for Music and Painting, just as for ragoûts, when the organ of these sensations savors, so to speak, these objects."[129] Taste therefore came to symbolize pleasure in general, the ability to savor an object, and the delight taken in consuming it, whether food or the arts—or anything else, for that matter, as evidenced by the *Dictionnaire de Trévoux*, which defines taste as "feeling, pleasure."[130] Moreover, taste brings "the most sensitive" pleasures, which is why "one has transferred this word from its ordinary meaning to all sensual delights of the senses and even of the mind."[131]

The aesthetic taste was, furthermore, manifested through a physical pleasure, since it had to touch the person observing the work of art; yet despite this physical manifestation, it was a higher form of sensory emotion, since it concerned the noble senses of sight, hearing, and the mind—and not, or at least not yet, the tongue or the palate. Seran de la Tour writes:

> The musical beauty affects the sense of hearing; it knows how to estimate its strength and melody, because the ear is made to feel its perfection. The optical beauty enchants sight; because the audacity and the regularity of its whole present to this sense what the mind and the imagination can offer of most finished in this genre. The intellectual beauty, which is the object of Taste within the Arts, the Letters, and the Sciences, this Beauty whose appeal determines it so absolutely that it makes it enthusiastic, when the mind knows, or even thinks being able to untangle it from the difficulties that surround it, produces the same effect on it.[132]

The sensory pleasure of the judgment of taste had therefore nothing to do with the tongue. At no point was cookery considered as an art in these aesthetic works. When taste finally entered art and philosophy, it still concerned the higher senses, which reveals the survival of the secular devaluation of gustation. As Crousaz stressed in his *Traité du Beau* (Treatise on the Beautiful), "it is not surprising that men, in order to express what they thought to be pleasant regarding the objects of Sight and Hearing, used different terms than the ones used to indicate what they like regarding the objects of the other Senses," because when seeing colors or hearing sounds, "our Soul gets out of ourself [*sic*], so to speak; it seems that it goes to grasp the objects, that it is uniting itself to them, that it carries itself or expands where the colors are, and where the Sounds are formed; It [the soul] believes to be feeling them less from the inside than from the outside." This is not the case for the other senses, according to Crousaz, because men feel the sensations of cold or warm, of flavors, or odors, "in their organs: they conceive that something escapes the objects to come and make an impression, and the pleasure they feel by receiving these impressions, through the way the external objects send to them, disposes them to look at these objects as beneficial, and to give them the praise of *good*."[133]

As for Dubos, he considers that "there is inside us a sense destined to judge about the merit of these works, which consists of the imitation of natural objects. This sense is the sense itself that would have judged the object that the Painter, the Poet, or the Musician imitated. It is the eye when it concerns the colors of a painting. It is the ear when it is about judging if the accents of a story are touching or if they suit the words, and if the singing is melodious."[134] The aesthetic taste is obviously associated with visual and auditory judgment, and not with gustatory discernment.

The problem, however, of a sensory taste lacking a rational grounding is that it presupposes the possibility of a relativity of tastes, thus contradicting the idea of a true and absolute beauty. The diversity of tastes was striking. In his classic *L'Idée de Nature en France*, Jean Ehrard demonstrated that in the eighteenth century, the notion of the diversity of people—announced by Montaigne—replaced the traditional attachment to the idea of human universality. The discovery of the New World led to countless travels and exchanges that transformed the perceptions of the world: people were diverse in time—as evidenced by the Quarrel—and in space—the myth of the *bon sauvage* being one of the many references in these discussions.[135] "The eighteenth century," writes Ehrard, "discovers with wonder what the previous times had had premonitions about: the incredible diversity of mores and customs, of lifestyles and forms of thought. So the moral world was not less rich and varied than the physical world."[136]

Taste was believed to depend on individual humors and temperaments, but also on fashions, uses, and customs. Some went even further, like Morvan de Bellegarde, for instance, who suggested that there was an organic—if not materialistic—cause explaining the diversity of tastes. Food itself was considered by some thinkers to be one of the favorable items leading to the development of the mind. Indeed, Morvan explains, the *"personnes de qualité* (quality people, respectable persons) usually have more refinement, sharpness, brightness, delicacy, than the ones from an obscure condition." Education plays an important role in this supremacy, of course, but it's not the only factor: "It is obvious that good food, and that the juices of exquisite meat, which mingle with the blood and the other humors of the body, subtilize them, and make them more suitable to the functions of the mind."[137] Although this remark concerned the domain of food more than taste, it announced new perspectives that would become more important within the forthcoming years. We will see in chapter 5, then, that some authors felt that taste also depended on the anatomical or physical disposition of the brain. As Morvan de Bellegarde emphasizes, "such as the organs are differently disposed in most men; the objects too act differently on their senses," which explains the various tastes and dislikes in foods among different eaters and among differing food habits and customs. "That is why properly one can say with good reason that tastes must not be disputed, because the same objects excite different sensations, depending on the various dispositions of the fibers; and what flatters the taste of some people causes disgust and a sort of pain to others. . . . The difference that can be noticed between the minds comes from the disposition of the organs and the diversity of the temperament, the fibers of the brain, and the substance from which it is filled up with. . . . All these things, however purely material, contribute to the beauty, neatness, and sharpness of the mind, because the soul when it is engaged and like wrapped in the mass of the body, depends on the organs; these organs when they are well disposed help it fulfill its functions."[138]

In the end, he concludes, "the mind does not depend less on the disposition of the climate than on the disposition of the humors and the organs."[139] With food preferences reduced to material individual differences, communication on this topic becomes irrelevant.[140] The text of Morvan de Bellegarde testifies to the emergence in the eighteenth century of the first hypotheses in favor of the relativity of tastes, which appeared despite the common belief in a true beauty. The diversity of tastes, in either food or aesthetics, became commonplace, though variously assimilated during the Enlightenment. Tastes were then considered to be an example among many others of individual differences of judgment.[141] As Seran de la Tour submits: "since nature is the same within the productions of a species, all men are thus born with a particular portion of Taste. But the quality of the judgment from which is formed the one of Taste, is as different as the constitutions and the temperaments."[142]

Aside from one's organic configuration, the environment would also play a part in perceptions, in accordance with climate theory—developed notably by Montesquieu—which, in the eighteenth century, justified the many differences observed between peoples. The "climate" was considered from a very broad perspective and concerned geography as well as the quality of air or food. As Jean-Baptiste Dubos explains, in a certain country,

> the air might be . . . adverse to the physical education of children whose delicate organs would destine them to become men of a great spirit one day. . . . It is possible that in a certain country, the emanations of the earth are too rough. All these faults one conceives to be possibly infinite, must make that the air of a country, which temperature seems the same than the one of a neighbor land, is not as favorable to the physical education of the children as the air one breaths in the latter . . . since the air's difference in a neighbor land where men are tall makes the inhabitants small, why would it not make them more spiritual in a country than in another? The height of men must vary with more difficulty than the quality and the competence of the organs of the brain. The more an organ is untied, the more the blood that nourishes it easily changes it. Yet of all the organs of the human body, the most delicate are the ones that serve the spiritual soul to do its functions. What I am saying here is just the explanation of the general opinion, which has always attributed to the different qualities of the air the difference noticed between the peoples.[143]

Physical causes—that is, the quality of the air or of food—might also have moral consequences. Whichever explanation, whether relating to the physiology or to the climate, these propositions suggest the relativity of tastes, slowly emerging during the eighteenth century and evidenced, for instance, by Voltaire in the entry "beauty" of his *Philosophical Dictionary*. In this entry, he explains that should a toad be asked to define beauty, he would answer that beauty is "his toad wife with her two great round eyes issuing from her little head, a wide and flat mouth, a yellow belly, a brown back."[144] This example shows that taste and beauty would progressively be more and more related to personal feelings and experience. *Le sentiment* (feeling), notably under the influence of empiricism and sensualism, would become one of the most important concepts debated in eighteenth-century Europe.

A Spiritual Taste

In the late seventeenth and eighteenth centuries, taste was the object of an un-precedented enthusiasm. Debates and books on the topic increased, while taste entered the realms of art and philosophy that to date were considered inaccessible to this lower sense. If likes and dislikes were long banished from table talk, the spiritual taste became one of the most popular themes for polite conversation of the elite. However, these new representations did not necessarily question all the older and traditional values. The theoretical interest indeed concerned a very different, figurative form of taste. Whether mystical, *mondain*, or aesthetic, taste did not refer at all to an enlightened judgment regarding the quality of food. It was on the contrary very specifically related to the mind, composing a sort of "spiritual taste"[145] of the inside and liable to numerous different forms depending on the context considered. The mystical taste had certainly nothing to do with the low material pleasures of the senses—any more than did the *bon goût* of the *honnête homme*, whose value did not depend on physical skill but on a moral ability to read situations and interlocutors—while the aesthetic taste concerned the higher productions of human intelligence.

Additionally, these new forms of taste went far beyond the simple natural needs, and justified the superiority of humans versus animals, for man was the only acculturated being. Hence these creations all referred to the mind and not the physical body, as exemplified by Seran de la Tour: "Beauty in every genre is the food of the soul, like foodstuff is the one of the body."[146] If the gustatory taste was turned toward the body and the exteriority of the world, the spiritual taste, on the contrary, referred to the true interiority of the soul, which was much more valued in early modern cultures still deeply influenced by dualistic epistemologies, as highlighted in chapter 2. Indeed, as D'Alembert stresses, "the source of our pleasure and of our boredom is only and entirely in ourselves; we will thus find inside ourselves, by looking at it carefully, the general and invariable rules of *taste*, which will be like the touchstone in the trial of which all talented productions will be submitted."[147]

Now endowed with a spiritual dimension, taste was worthy enough to be discussed by philosophers. It even became a philosophical category, referring to the judgment of beauty. But it was only by getting outside of itself, so to speak, that taste entered the philosophical realm, leaving gustation as always in the peripheries of knowledge. The celebration of the bodily taste was found solely in culinary literature; elsewhere, it remained at the margins of the world of thought. The bodily taste, linked to the physical constitution, was the one taste that could not be discussed or taught—quite a surprising fact actually, considering the refinement of cookery in this period. Voltaire, although himself a gourmet, considered that "the sensual *taste*," which is the preference or the repugnance one has for certain food, is not to be disputed, "because a defect of organs cannot be corrected. It is not the same for the Arts; since they have real beauty, there is a good *taste* that discerns them, and a bad *taste* that does not; and one often corrects the fault of the mind that gives a wrong taste. There are also cold souls, false minds, which cannot be excited nor set upright: it is with them that one must not dispute over *tastes* because they do not have any."[148] Despite the wide range of intellectual discussions on taste, gustation thus remained in a lower esteem.

Nevertheless, the invention of multiple figurative senses of the word is an indication of a transformation of the representations of taste. These authors were using new expressions and innovative vocabulary and categories, which is why they thought it was important to define spiritual taste and to reflect on its origin and nature. By doing so, they inevitably came back to the physical taste, mentioning the sources of metaphors and establishing connections and comparisons between bodily and spiritual tastes. Thanks to these parallels, gustation emerged, albeit only discreetly in the discourses, subtle yet intensely present. Morvan de Bellegarde, for instance, working on artistic judgment, evokes "a Lady which finds relish in eating oak-leafs, Spanish wax, lime, and plaster" in order to give his readers an example of bad taste.[149] Further on in his text, when mentioning mockery, he insists on the importance of measure and dosage, just like in cookery, because "the salt of fine mockery makes all the agreement of civil society; but this salt needs to be spread with a lot of circumspection: the same way one spoils a ragoût by throwing too much salt in it; one makes oneself hated when the mockery is too bitter."[150] Returning to the bodily sense was a particularly effective strategy to elaborate theories on the spiritual form of taste.

The abbot Gédoyn, in a speech on taste designed for the members of the French Academy, builds his whole demonstration starting from the corporeal taste to explain in what consists the spiritual taste: "Let's always compare the moral taste to the material and physical taste. It is, I think, the way to reason on it certainly."[151] By confronting the two uses, he draws the conclusion that taste works "always by way of comparison, and by bringing one thing back to another of the same kind."[152] He proceeds likewise when presenting his whole theory, generally illustrating each hypothesis with two examples, one food-related and the other inspired by aesthetics. All authors, however, were not so systematic in referring to the literal taste. The President Du Gas, for instance, prevost of the merchants of Lyon, author of a dissertation entitled "On Taste"—published just after the abbot Gédoyn's dissertation in the same volume—does not make any allusion to the origins of the metaphor.

In the course of the eighteenth century, references to physical taste would become less frequent. The concept was assimilated, and from then on analysis was almost exclusively related to aesthetics. Although Voltaire, influenced by Gédoyn and additionally a true gourmet, readily made comparisons referring to the physical taste, his contemporaries would not often follow his lead. There is only one allusion to bodily taste in Montesquieu's entire *Essay on Taste*.[153] As for D'Alembert, he does not say anything about gustation in his "Reflections on the Use and Abuse of Philosophy in Matters of Taste."[154] His discussion focused rather on the nature of beauty, which became the true object of taste, and from which the material taste was rejected, as highlighted by Denis Diderot, for instance, who excluded from beauty all "the qualities related to taste and smell . . . one does not call *beautiful* the objects in which they reside, when one only considers them relatively to these qualities. One says *an excellent dish, a delicious odor*; but not *a beautiful dish, a beautiful odor*. When one says, *here is a beautiful turbot, here is a beautiful rose*, one considers other qualities within the rose and the turbot than the ones relative to the senses of taste and smell."[155] Just like Voltaire, Diderot was a renowned gourmet, but to him as to most theorists of taste and beauty, flavors had nothing to do with art or with beauty, and thus had nothing to do with aesthetics either.

Still, gustation sometimes appeared within small disparate remarks, discreetly recalling the origin of the term. Generally, these were found within the passages where questions of delicacy were discussed—for instance, in the writings of Montesquieu and Seran de La Tour. Both these authors wanted to demonstrate that all men did not share a universal appreciation for the qualities defining taste. Some people naturally had a higher refinement, meaning they perceived more subtleties than others. They were able to detect the slightest nuances among different flavors and to recognize an exceptional dish through little details invisible to ordinary palates. The same may be said of art experts when looking at exceptional works of art. Montesquieu uses the example of the delicacy of Apicius's and Philoxenus's tastes, famous gourmands of antiquity: "Delicate people are the ones that to every idea or every taste add a lot of ideas or a lot of accessory tastes. Rude people only have one sensation; their soul cannot compose nor decompose; they do not add nor remove anything to what nature gives. . . . Philoxenus and Apicius carried at the table many sensations unknown to us vulgar eaters; and the ones which judge with taste the works of the mind have and receive an infinity of sensations that other men do not have."[156]

Criticized for centuries because of their unrestrained gluttony—as demonstrated above—Philoxenus and Apicius were now being celebrated for the delicacy of their taste, therefore suggesting an ongoing transformation of the representations of taste. Interestingly, the refinement of the palate of a connoisseur reveals what truly constitutes the knowledge of taste: a form of discernment that allows those who possess it to assert an enlightened judgment on what is consumed—no matter the object—detecting the slightest details, invisible to the rest of the world. This discernment happens in just an instant, for it is, above all, a feeling. Voltaire explains that

> it is not enough for *taste* to see, to know the beauty of a work; one must feel it, be touched by it. It is not enough to feel, to be touched confusedly, one must untangle the different nuances; nothing can escape the rapidity of the discernment; and it is again a resemblance between this intellectual *taste*, this *taste* of the Arts, and the sensual *taste*; because if the gourmet quickly feels and recognizes the mixture of two liqueurs, the man of *taste*, the connoisseur, will see in a quick glance the mixture of two styles; he will see a fault next to an agreement.[157]

This immediate sensation of pleasure is a form of knowledge. If the common man contents himself with the satisfaction of the senses, the man of taste, in addition to the delightful sensation, enjoys determining in what taste consists. Seran de la Tour stresses that

> the imperfect Taste enjoys these masterpieces of art, without knowing its price. It is not made to analyze the pleasant effects it feels; it feels them and is content with this. The *jouissance* [enjoyment] of the pleasure it feels interests it much more than its cause. The delicate Taste, like the rude Taste, enjoys; but its enjoyment has much more perfection and much more extent. It distinguishes in the same dish what is insipid and what has a lot of Taste, what is bitter and what is sweet, what is tasteless and what has perfume; it would make the history of its decomposition should it be necessary, so much wisdom it has to uncover art's mysteries.[158]

Taste is a form of discernment, in art as in cookery, which grants this sense a much higher value than gustation alone could never acquire.

Nevertheless, if some authors occasionally referred to the delicacy of the bodily taste to prove the value of the taste of the mind, the passages relating to gustation only occupied a very small portion of their texts. The essential nature of the demonstration of taste was elsewhere. Consistently, within the works explicitly defining the sense of taste, material taste was only briefly mentioned without any thorough investigation. Gédoyn himself recognizes that "acquired taste is always grounded on the natural taste, which is like its base and foundation; but which besides does not ever lead us very far of its own accord. One easily understands that it is here only a question of the acquired taste. It is generally only a matter of that one."[159]

As the studies moved further away from the first treatises on taste, the topic of gustation receded to a point of near absence. The individual character of material taste was one of the most frequent reasons invoked to justify its rejection. Physical taste appeared to be an especially subjective and idiosyncratic sensation, more so than aesthetic taste. The latter seemed apparently more suitable to intellectual discussions and to intersubjective communication, whereas the former was reduced to the intimate silences of each individual. This idea was defended by Immanuel Kant, who, in his *Critique of Judgment* (1790), rejected the singularity of the judgment of gustation—a judgment he considered to be subjective—and then developed an entire analysis on the universal faculty of the aesthetic judgment of taste. Gustation, he explains, is linked to a material need. It is a "satisfaction in the pleasant . . . bound up with [self-] interest. That which pleases the senses in sensation is pleasant" and therefore depends on individual appreciation.[160] Physical taste follows desires and fulfills bodily needs; it seeks personal gratification, which is why "everyone says that hunger is the best sauce, and everything that is edible is relished by people with a healthy appetite; and thus a satisfaction of this sort does not indicate choice directed by taste. It is only when the want is appeased that we can distinguish which of many men has or has not taste."[161] The pleasant is therefore a purely subjective judgment, based on inclination alone. This is the case for taste in wine as well as for the appreciation of colors or sounds: it is a sensory judgment. There is no knowledge in agreement and enjoyment—Fontenelle had already made this argument in the seventeenth century.

In contrast, according to Kant, aesthetic judgment is drawn from satisfaction in the beautiful, which is a disinterested (i.e., not subjective) form of satisfaction, as it is not bound up with any individual desires or gratification of the senses. This is the reason why aesthetic taste is free and allows for the approval of all men and philosophical dispute on the subject. Kant considers that "the Pleasant, the Beautiful, and the Good designate three different relations of representations to the feeling of pleasure and pain, in reference to which we distinguish from each other objects or methods of representing them. . . . We may say that of all these three kinds of satisfaction, that of taste in the Beautiful is alone a disinterested and free satisfaction; for no interest, either of Sense or of Reason, here forces our assent."[162] According to Kant, the Beautiful is that which is represented as "the object of a universal satisfaction."[163] Since the Beautiful is not self-interested, "hence it must be regarded as grounded on what he [the man judging] can presuppose in every other man."[164] He continues:

> As regards the pleasant therefore the fundamental proposition is valid, everyone has his own taste (the taste of Sense). The case is quite different with the Beautiful. . . . [A man] judges not merely for himself, but for every one, and speaks of beauty as if it were a property of things. Hence he says, "the thing is beautiful"; and he does not count on the agreement of others with his judgment of satisfaction, because he has found this agreement several times before, but he demands

it of them. (He blames them if they judge otherwise and he denies them taste, which he nevertheless requires from them.) Here then we cannot say that each man has his own particular taste. For this would be as much as to say that there is no taste whatever; i.e. no aesthetical judgment, which can make a rightful claim upon every one's assent.[165]

In the end, Kant excludes bodily taste, subjective and interested, from philosophical investigations. Only the aesthetic taste can be the object of a public and universal judgment. Several theorists of beauty and taste had already disdained the material taste when discussing spiritual taste, but the German philosopher is the one with whom the dismissal of gustation would be the most radical and the most final. Prior to Kant's intervention, many authors of aesthetic treatises based their primary arguments on gustation before leaving it behind in order to explore more thoroughly the sense of beauty. Kant, on the contrary, escapes this subtle curious movement where gustation alternatively appears and disappears. The physical sense was not even considered as the foundation of aesthetic sense anymore. It was the object of a different appreciation that had nothing to do with the aesthetic judgment, the only appreciation considered as pure, disinterested, universal, and worthy of philosophical inquiry.

Conclusion: A New Sense Modality

During the early modern era, taste became the object of a thriving interest. This new attention rose when figurative meanings of the word *taste* were created and largely spread into common usage, thus leading to the spiritualization of taste. Once endowed with new meanings and values, taste was liberated from the sole realm of food and entered, for the very first time, a less material universe.

Taste, like most concepts, is understood inside an "extensive, mobile, and variable semantic field."[166] From the sixteenth to the eighteenth centuries, the taste metaphors spread toward very different contexts, morphing from the initial spiritual and mystical uses into broader references to states of civilization, respectable and cultured behavior, and ideals of beauty. In mystical literature, the Taste of God referred to the ineffability of the divine, suggesting the elusive delights of meeting God. Completely passive, the soul reaches spiritual nirvana that words alone cannot describe, a type of *je ne sais quoi* that can only be understood when personally experienced. To relate to the bliss of the mystical union, it is the sensory vocabulary of bodily pleasures that was elected to refer to the highest spiritual experience accessible on earth, a foretaste of the joys of heaven. The expression "tasting God" was first limited to theological writings, but thanks to the massive spread of mystical works in the seventeenth century, notably in France, the idea of a spiritual taste became more widespread while its meanings were transformed. Other figures of taste emerged that were not necessarily linked to theology, notably in polite society, where taste became a fashionable issue and one of the most popular topics of honest conversation. This lexical enthusiasm came along with new uses. Taste then referred to standardized though indefinable qualities of the *honnête homme*. The *bon goût* elaborated in this context involved a series of qualities leading one to adopt the most suitable behavior in all circumstances. The bodily taste had thus given birth to a spiritual and a moral taste, before evolving later on toward the aesthetic sense of beauty in the eighteenth century.

All these many different uses of the word *taste* led to thriving discussions in a variety of cultural and social settings among theologians, taste theorists, moralists, philosophers, and writers of all sorts. Taste thus became the object of an exceptional curiosity between the seventeenth and eighteenth centuries. For the first time, this lower sense was the object of a specific discourse and therefore was being investigated apart from all of the other senses. Numerous reflections on taste contributed to extend a concept that was obviously far from monolithic; it engaged various connotations, depending on contexts, uses, or applications.

This metaphorical shift or spiritualization of taste is a complex matter. It is perhaps quite difficult to distinguish clearly taste as a linguistic metaphor and taste as a literal thing. Put it is important to stress here that metaphors are not only linguistic changes affecting language; they are also, Mark Johnson underscores, "more fundamentally, a conceptual and experiential process that structures our world."[167] Carolyn Korsmeyer's previous work on the philosophy of the bodily sense of taste has already demonstrated how meaningful metaphors are and how changes in words relate to the ways in which people understand and experience the world surrounding them.[168] This is especially true when new social practices emerge that embody the metaphors, as with taste—developing and displaying good taste in Parisian salons is one example of these new embodied practices; likewise, "tasting God" not only relates to a rhetorical metaphor but to very specific practices of mystical contemplation. However, this is not to say that all forms of taste were alike or that one form of taste was determined or necessarily led to another, like a cause to a consequence. Rather, all these metaphors reveal new regimes of contiguity between fields that to date were remote from one another, hence disclosing deep though implicit evolutions that otherwise would remain invisible. Words and expressions circulate while referring to different things, but they share the same vocabulary and especially the idea of a spiritual taste, though the latter would be differently defined according to the context considered.

All these various uses of taste involved different settings, practices, and values. Yet, interestingly, whichever domain considered—whether the realm of the mystical, of aesthetics, or of honest society—all these different forms of spiritual tastes shared common features, all of which originating from the bodily taste, the source of all metaphors. The indeterminacy of taste was one of these features, as demonstrated by the frequent use of the expression *je ne sais quoi* associated with this particular sense. There is a part of taste that escapes words, analysis, and reason, and that is precisely a part of what defines it: "It would not be a *je ne sais quoi* if one knew what it was."[169] Taste is perhaps a more pliable sense, open to ambiguity, which would explain why the topic does elicit discussions, although many considered that taste existed in the realm of absolutes.

In the appreciation of dishes as well as in the observation of the others and the admiring of a work of art, there is a particular form of knowledge about the world that is displayed. Taste is felt before being thought, which makes it faster than reason. In theories of perception, in treatises on the soul or on the senses, philosophers and physicians had already stressed the immediacy of the gustatory taste. Taste, along with touch, had long been defined as a "contact sense," a material sense directly entering into contact with its object, giving it a lower state of value and objectivity than the noble distance senses of sight and hearing. But, within the polite and aesthetic universes, the spontaneity of taste, endowed with a spiritual value, was now perceived positively. The spontaneous taste was accompanied by reflection, for the judgment of taste had to be justified by objective criteria. It was only in the eighteenth century that the first pleas for the relativity of tastes would appear, where the palate's judgment was seen to rely entirely on feeling, as evidenced in the writings of Dubos and Diderot.

The notion of pleasure was also central to qualify taste, perceived as the supplier of a higher form of individual delight. The "taste of God" is an intensely singular and supernatural ecstasy, superior to any earthly pleasure available in the world; this rapture engaged the mystic's body and mind entirely. The *bon goût* of the *honnête homme* refers to a more moderate pleasure, but nevertheless applies alike to very positive qualities, an agreement and a politeness composing the harmony of an individuality where the inside and the outside of the person were combined to reveal an art of living and an ideal of perfection. Aesthetic judgment, likewise, also involved pleasure; this pleasure, although spiritual, was also a sensory delight, revealed, according to the context, through different organs, delighting the mind, the eye, and/or the ear. Depending on the context, time, and metaphor involved, it is perhaps not literally the same kind of taste, nor is the same organ perform-ing—the tongue or the mind, the ear or the eye, the inner feeling engaging the entire body—but it is somehow a similar kind of intense, personal, immediate, and sensible judgment that is performed. These judgments are all an aesthetic form of knowledge and experience, if one considers the original meanings of *aesthesis* as referring to sensation or sense perception.

Gifted with a figurative meaning, taste began to refer to very positive qualities, which may seem surprising when confronting these theories with the predominantly negative representations that were presented in previous chapters. But in this transposition of meanings, taste lost the features associated with gustation's derision. Divorced from any bodily need, taste was not solely material anymore. There was no longer any association with animality: spiritual taste was specifically human. Taste was now being defined as a discernment of the mind that spontaneously recognized, through a mechanism of comparison, the good from the bad. The many metaphors of taste hence reveal the emergence of new representations of the taste sense. For a long time taste was specifically limited to the realm of exteriority, referring to the animal nature of a despicable bodily sense. But now a spiritual and inner form of taste was born, provoking a significant transformation of the values associated to this sense. For the very first time, taste acquired a dimension of interiority, defining its properly human superiority.

Moreover, among humans themselves, taste became a distinctive quality of the members of an elite constituted of connoisseurs, as opposed to the rest of the world. No matter the context, taste systematically appears indeed to be used as a reference to define small communities of taste and distinction, whether a spiritual and religious elite, a social elite of the polite world, or an intellectual elite of those accredited to judge the works of art. Taste thus remains the object of a distinction, a social distinction as much as a distinction of the self. Taste is indeed perhaps the sense providing the most intense sensation of self. The expression *je ne sais quoi* itself demonstrates how the sense of taste is deeply connected to the sphere of intimacy, true indication of the subjectivity of individual sensation, which isolates each subject in his or her own truth. Taste is, more than any sense, the world of the individual subject.

Nonetheless, these new ideas did not necessarily annihilate all former conceptions that had originated from the physicality of taste. The shameful values of gustation remained despite the development of new meanings. It is revealing in this regard to see that the bodily taste, although briefly mentioned, was systematically relegated to the boundaries of discourses: taste theorists frequently recalled the origin of the metaphor, but without ever making this the heart of their inquiry. It is as though taste, in order to be thought of and discussed, had to get outside of itself—so to speak—to be defined as something else. Moreover, taste theorists insisted, aesthetic judgment was perceived through the eyes and the ears, and consisted in an internal discernment of the mind, while perceptions of the tongue were eliminated from the discussion. There was no place for cookery as an art within the treatises of aesthetics that celebrated the beauty of the fine arts, particularly the arts of painting and music. So despite the profusion of references and debates on taste, gustation still remained at the margins of knowledge. An abundance of metaphors appeared that relied on gustation to explore taste but only to reject gustation afterward. In texts from this era, there is obviously a lingering tension between the two dimensions constituting the sense of taste, its corporeal and intellectual forms.

Nevertheless, it remains very significant to find learned discourses on bodily taste, even if these discourses mostly discuss the spiritual forms of taste, because for long there was no discourse at all. Hence I argue that the debates and the invention of spiritual forms of taste were what allowed the emergence of discussions on the bodily taste itself. All these various works on taste indeed demonstrate the rise of a new interest in matters of taste, which would not be without impact on the ways in which the bodily sense itself would be conceived. Discussions on material taste and spiritual taste were porous, all the more as spiritual taste was built, invented, and developed in relation to the bodily sense of taste. Additionally, even when recalling the origin of the metaphor was not considered useful anymore, reminiscences remained, signs of the metaphor's material foundations. The early modern era saw the constitution of a new sense modality characterized by its ineffability, its immediacy, and its close connection to individual emotion. Each criterion defining taste was endowed with a higher value. The immediacy of taste, long perceived as rooted in the animality and materiality of a lower sense, became the place of a stronger and more positive emotion, originating from the individual and not needing to be reasoned. The same goes for the speechless character of taste. First eliminated from polite conversations because it embodied a bestial triviality, taste then became a *je ne sais quoi*, exchanging one silence for another one much more positive in order to become the place of the ineffable. This expression reveals that taste would now go beyond words, relating to a reality that is higher than words and not under them anymore, as was earlier the case. Although founded on reflection, taste went beyond reason, since it was grounded on emotion. Finally, it became the metaphor of an individual subject that could only be defined by the emotion moving him or her. The true revolution of taste that occurred in the early modern era consisted in the invention of taste as the seat of a system of representations defined as a new sense modality that was no longer perceived as being exclusively material.

5 Toward an Art and Science of Taste

The animals feed; the man eats; only the man of wit knows how to eat.
—"Aphorismes du Professeur pour servir de prolégomènes à son ouvrage et de base éternelle à la science," in Brillat-Savarin, *Physiologie du goût*, 19

After exploring the multiple metaphors of taste, we still need to understand why taste was the object of such intellectual enthusiasm in the seventeenth and even more in the eighteenth centuries. Which specific cultural, social, political, economic, and culinary contexts could explain this transformation regarding the meanings and values of taste? What made the emergence of this new sense modality of taste possible in early modern Europe? To answer this, we need to get back to eighteenth-century social history and especially to the history of food—from beauty go back to bouillon. The aim here is to examine how concerns about spiritual taste would interact with discussions on taste as a gastronomic sensation. We have seen indeed that debates on spiritual taste often included discussions on the bodily sense of taste. Likewise, did discourses on food, cuisine, and material taste include developments on spiritual taste? These debates provide a complementary picture of the complex and numerous relations between the taste of the body and the taste of the mind.

The *Nouvelle Cuisine*: New Discourses on Taste

First let us quickly recall a few important events regarding food history in the eighteenth century. After the period of culinary history dominated by La Varenne, Massialot, and L.S.R., a new generation of cooks and recipe books arose in the late 1730s, a period during which *nouvelle cuisine* emerged.[1] Those who claimed to embody culinary innovation in turn criticized the former representatives of mid-seventeenth-century modern cuisine. The recipe books and practices of *nouvelle cuisine* have already inspired a great deal of research from food and culinary historians like S. Mennell, B. Fink, and S. Pinkard. The aim here is to emphasize how this specific culinary context influenced the ways in which the concept of taste was discussed during the eighteenth century. *Nouvelle cuisine* actually inspired extensive literature on taste; beginning with recipe books, discourse on *nouvelle cuisine* would later spread to become the concern of the entire polite reading public in the Enlightenment. Thus, a new rhetoric of taste arose that would eventually lead to the invention of the art of gastronomy.

Nouvelle cuisine, according to its defenders, allegedly offered more refinement of food and taste through culinary innovation. Vincent de La Chapelle was the first one to suggest this idea in *The Modern Cook*, published in London in 1733 and translated into French in 1735 under the title *Le Cuisinier moderne*. Likewise, Menon, one of the most prolific culinary writers of his time, pleaded a few years later in favor of a new form of cookery, as evidenced in the title of his cookbook, *Nouveau Traité de la Cuisine* (New Treatise of Cuisine).[2] François Marin's *Dons de Comus*, published a little later the same year, held the same thesis.[3] These cooks wished to appear as innovators, promoters of a "modern cuisine,"[4] proposing recipes "in the newest taste."[5] They were convinced of the superiority of their technique in comparison to that of their immediate predecessors. As stated in the *Dons de Comus*, "there has been good food in France for more than two centuries, but one can [be] assure[d] without doubt, that it has never been so delicate, and that one has never worked [cooked] yet neither so properly, nor with such a fine taste."[6]

Cookery habits have certainly changed since the mid-seventeenth century. However, according to food historians, eighteenth-century practices did not represent an upheaval comparable to that of La Varenne's time. *Nouvelle cuisine* was especially characterized by the frequent use of bouillons, broth, sauces, and coulis, which were made through a process of reduction, in order to concentrate the flavors of meat, fish, and vegetables, used as cuisine *fonds* in most preparations.[7] Bouillon was "the soul of cuisine" in eighteenth-century France.[8] Regarding the taste of food, although the concern for respecting the authentic flavors of each ingredient rhetorically remained, in practice it seems that modern habits contributed, on the contrary, to a reduction in the range of possible flavors by giving most of the dishes a similar taste. As Susan Pinkard explains, "technique and organization focused on stocking the kitchen with basic preparations, sauces, and garnishes that could be combined with principal ingredients and with each other to produce an infinite array of dishes. . . . The search for novel combinations (often represented by fanciful names) could easily overwhelm the character and quality of principal ingredients, and the omnipresence of basic preparations could cause everything to taste the same."[9] According to the cooks, the keywords of *nouvelle cuisine* were simplicity and lightness, as highlighted, for instance, in the *Dons de Comus*: "Modern cuisine, established on the foundations of the ancient one with less artifice and less embarrassment, although with as much variety, is more simple, more appropriate, more delicate, and maybe even more learned. The former cuisine was very complicated and of an infinite detail."[10] This did not necessarily mean that the cook's work was any easier. On the contrary, all the coulis, bouillons, and restaurants were long, expensive, and difficult preparations, requiring technical command and a considerable number of ingredients. But on the plate, simplicity and lightness were displayed, leaving the eater unaware of the sophisticated preparation. The great variety of dishes was also crucial to the organization of meals in the new fashion; hors d'oeuvres, starters, and entremets multiplied; these aimed to offer the dinner guests a rich diversity of flavors, along with a spectacular visual effect produced by an array of dishes.[11] However, in spite of undeniable evolutions, the *nouvelle cuisine* did not represent the revolution its promoters asserted.[12] As a matter of fact, many of the cooks who wished to appear as innovators actually took back, even stole, numerous recipes from their predecessors in their own cookbooks. This stealing was the case, for instance, of Vincent de La Chapelle, who "borrowed" numerous recipes from Massialot, going as far as plagiarizing the latter in his preface before blaming him for the archaic character of the very cookery from which he was inspired. Instances such as these introduced for the first time the problem of intellectual property in the culinary domain.[13]

Most interestingly for this investigation on the history of taste, it was actually the discourse surrounding culinary practices rather than the culinary practices themselves, which dramatically changed in the eighteenth century. *Nouvelle cuisine* generated the publication of a new generation of cookery books, the construction of which was much more original than the actual recipes. The introductions, especially, changed. Recall that in the classical period, cooks decided to publish a preface to introduce their recipe books, and in these they left a few comments on their cuisine. Their successors would pursue this habit, while giving it an utterly new form and language. If La Varenne and his followers wrote a few lines or pages to quickly present their recipe book, eighteenth-century culinary writings went a lot further, as they offered much longer and more detailed introductions, some of them totaling more than fifty pages. These prefaces were more than just culinary introductions: they were philosophical, historical, and scientific essays on taste and cuisine, celebrating the fact that modern practices were superior to previous habits.

The evolution of introductory pages can firstly be explained by a change of author. In the 1730s, it was no longer the cooks (or their librarians) who wrote the prefaces, as in the previous century; rather, contemporary professional writers wrote them. This was the case, for instance, of the "Dissertation préliminaire sur la cuisine moderne" (Preliminary Essay on Modern Cuisine), attributed to Étienne-Laureault de Foncemagne, member of the Académie française, and published as the introduction of Menon's *La Science du Maître d'Hôtel Cuisinier*.[14] Likewise, the *Avertissement* (foreword) of the *Dons de Comus* (The Gifts of

Comus), an anonymous work recognized as François Marin's, was written by two Jesuits, Pierre Brumoy and Guillaume-Hyacinthe Bougeant, men of letters who were at that time momentarily exiled from Paris because of controversial publications.[15] Although the *Dons de Comus* was regularly modified and adapted in successive reissues of the work, the introduction was systematically entrusted to a professional writer.[16] As a consequence, culinary writings were conferred a much higher legitimacy. The intervention of literate characters endowed with a certain fame in the writing of cookbooks made the latter more erudite and hence more attractive for a variety of new readers, which reveals—or contributes to—the valuation of cuisine, the cook, and of culinary literature in the culture of the period. As Jean-Claude Bonnet states, this "accompanying discourse dissociated from practice proves that cuisine then becomes the object of a general knowledge and of a debate."[17] Initially addressed to professional cooks, recipe books became gradually the object of a more important and broad interest, and started to concern the polite public at large. As convincingly argued by Emma Spary, "Only by recruiting a polite readership could cookery writing as a genre become a matter of interest within the Republic of Letters."[18] This distinguished readership would later on contribute to making cookery the object of a worthwhile and specific literary genre—gastronomic literature.

From now on, members of the polite society would openly display their interest in the art of cooking, which had gradually ceased to be a morally suspect passion. Some of them even sometimes enjoyed cooking themselves—as the regent, a renowned gourmet,[19] or as the presumed author of the *Cuisinier gascon* (The Gascon Cook), whom specialists suspect of being a prince of royal blood.[20] The latter's preface, dedicated to the Prince de Dombes, actually presented the author as "one of the best cooks in France."[21] New cookbooks' culinary introductions often mentioned this new interest of aristocrats in cookery, like in the *Dons de Comus*: "We have in France several great Lords who, for their own diversion, do not disdain to sometimes talk about cuisine, and whose delicate taste contributes greatly to training excellent cooks."[22]

The interest in food, cuisine, and taste increasingly spread and generated important debates in the eighteenth century. Although published in cookbooks, the introductory discourses presented by *nouvelle cuisine*'s promoters were well known to contemporaries. The number of people likely to be interested in critical debates—notably on food—had dramatically increased since the previous century. Many historians and specialists of the Enlightenment have argued for the development of a public sphere in the eighteenth century, an argument inspired by the influential work of the German political philosopher Jürgen Habermas.[23] These scholars highlight the cultural, social, and political changes brought by the rise of print culture since the sixteenth century, which notably resulted in an increasing number of potential readers, especially among the urban bourgeoisie.

As a consequence, first, "good taste" was not defined exclusively by the king, his court, and the aristocracy anymore. Second, a much wider audience was now discussing taste as an object of debate. The model embodied by Louis XIV and the absolute monarchies of the Old Regime, Habermas argues, was dominated by the public spectacle of the king and courtiers, thought of as a representation of power. Succeeding this model, so the argument goes, was a "bourgeois" public sphere, composed of an increasing number of rational individuals who wished to participate in this new form of publicness that did not depend on nobility, rank, or status but on the ability to read, think, and debate in a critical manner; these abilities were the basis of this novel form of public life. These people—sometimes from very different socioeconomic backgrounds—would gather in cafés, Freemasonic lodges, salons, and provincial academies distinct from the traditional academies and institutions of knowledge.[24] These cultural and social changes most definitely impacted the ways in which the concept of taste was constructed and discussed during the Enlightenment. This new public was fond of debates on matters of food, cuisine, and taste, as long as they provided food for thought.

New writings on taste and cuisine therefore became much more learned than before, as was the case for *nouvelle cuisine*'s introductory discourses. Addressing a wider audience than former cookbooks, the authors of these texts shared the same culture as their readers; their writings were hence full of references, scholarly remarks, and antique authors' quotations, testifying to the intellectual and gustatory distinction of an eminent group of people.[25] The content of the forewords indicates very clearly that the anticipated audience was not one composed of cooks but of the polite reading public, of which contemporary readers were very much aware. Again, Spary has highlighted the established complicity between authors and their readers, all of whom were part of a community of educated members making public use of reasoning and critical scrutiny.

A Science of Taste

Let's consider the content of these learned discourses on taste more thoroughly. First of all, writers obviously celebrated the increasing sophistication of knowledge of taste and cuisine. According to the encyclopedic vision of knowledge peculiar to the Enlightenment, the ideal cook, presented as the specialist of food par excellence, had to develop a comprehensive science of every dimension of food; his expertise was to include both technical and intellectual skills.[26] This meant that he had to be able to identify precisely the properties of each ingredient used in a culinary preparation, as well as the ideal combination of the diverse elements of a given dish. The aim was to elaborate a sophisticated cuisine that would be best for taste and for health, therefore presented as a *science*—the word is everywhere. This pretentiousness was displayed in the titles of cookbooks and in the prefaces, and also more generally throughout the entire cookbook.[27]

Since the mid-seventeenth century, the content of the cookbooks had changed. In Menon's work, for instance, recipes alternate with general considerations on specific ingredients, regarding their cultivation, origin, history, taste, culinary, and therapeutic uses.[28] The form and presentation of the text, as well as the order and methods adopted in culinary preparations, were additional factors used to claim that cuisine should be elevated to the dignified status of a *science*. Indeed, new cookbooks had gradually adopted a more structured construction, proposing for the first time an alphabetical classification of recipes, which facilitated their use.[29] Technical culinary language also became more complex, as evidenced by the first food dictionaries.[30]

In order to make these "observations on the nature, virtues, and properties of foods of which cookery makes use," cooks—and especially the writers of the introductions—read numerous contemporary works in the fields of medicine and chemistry.[31] Louis Lemery's *Traité des alimens* (Treatise of Foodstuffs) represented an important reference, as Foncemagne underscored in his "Dissertation préliminaire."[32] This comprehensive knowledge of medicine was crucial to the cook, as the aim of *nouvelle cuisine* was to provide dishes good for taste and for health; this claim was then much stronger than when La Varenne underlined the dietary interest of the *Cuisinier françois*'s recipes. Reacting to the secular, unfavorable reputation of the "sauces' maker,"[33] who was accused of being responsible for diseases and premature deaths, the *Science du Maître d'Hôtel Cuisinier* wanted to offer "a solid answer to reproaches which [were] made for a long time to the art of cookery."[34] According to Foncemagne, the potentially bad consequences of cuisine should not be imputed to "the innocent art of cookery"[35] but to the intemperance and excesses of some "ignorant *Artistes*" who were unaware of *nouvelle cuisine*'s newest practices, which offered "a judicious and enlightened mixture of natural flavors" and dishes that were "as healthy as [they were] delightful."[36] The knowledge displayed by *nouvelle cuisine* was presented as the best remedy for diseases, as a complementary practice to medicine; the cook was responsible for the prevention of ailments, whereas the pharmacist was in charge of remedies. As already mentioned in chapter 1, cookery and medicine have traditionally had narrow though sometimes conflicting relationships. The introductory discourses of the *nouvelle cuisine*'s new recipe books reveal the increasing liberation of cuisine, a new autonomy from medicine asserting the cook as the real specialist of food and dietetics—though theoretically, these discourses indicated, cuisine was still subordinate to medicine.[37]

The modern culinary practitioner was not only a good cook but also a real scholar, guided, like the intellectual elites of the time, by the "lights" of reason:

One admits that the dexterity of hands, a healthy judgment, a discerning palate, [and] a sure and refined taste are qualities absolutely necessary to a good cook. I dare to say that this is still not enough. Such would possess all these talents, who in matters of cookery, would ever just be a laborer guided by the only *routine*, or what is in medicine an *empirique* [a practitioner]. An artist of this character, slavish slave of custom, will not dare to imagine some new *ragoût*, or to change anything from the practice he would have learned. . . . Give him the knowledge of the qualities and properties of the food he works with . . . you will spare him his time, work, and money. The *lights*[38] would guide him in his trials; he would know how to take advantage of his errors themselves.[39]

Knowledge was thus as important as technical skills to the modern cook. More precisely, the enlightened *nouvelle cuisine* was presented as a chemical concoction of flavors. Chemistry was indeed fashionable in eighteenth-century France. It had been a rising practice and discipline since the sixteenth and seventeenth centuries, notably thanks to the progressive questioning of former dietetics scholars. Paracelsus was one of the first to question Galen's theories and to favor chemistry. Likewise, the anatomist Andreas Vesalius famously promoted dissections as a way of getting a better knowledge of the body, and by doing so he contributed to the weakening of Galenic theories. The discovery of blood circulation by William Harvey in 1620 led to undervaluing the Galenic model even more, for he demonstrated that blood was produced by the heart and not by the liver, as Galen had thought. At the end of the seventeenth century, scholars perfected chemistry and used it to get a better understanding of the functions of the human body. One then spoke of "iatrochemistry," indicating a medical system explaining all vital acts by chemical operations.[40] Among others, Jan-Baptista Van Helmont explained digestion as a chemical process, one in which stomach acids decomposed food particles rather than a process initiated by heat, as the Galenists believed. Van Helmont was followed by Thomas Willis, who also studied fermentation and distillation in the stomach's functions. At the end of the seventeenth century, the iatrochemists opposed the iatrophysicists, who, like Philippe Hecquet, considered digestion as a process of trituration. The theories of digestion would give rise to long-lived debates between partisans of fermentation and defenders of trituration, which Der-Liang Chiou and Emma Spary, among others, have well explained in their works.[41]

What is important here with regard to the history of taste is that eighteenth-century scholars and the cultivated elite were passionate about the sciences and food-related questions. Medical books and chemical writings were widespread and read by anyone who wished to be or to appear as enlightened, including cooks.[42] The authors of the culinary writings of the 1730s—neither doctors nor chemists, and consequently not necessarily up to date regarding the most recent

scientific theories and events—proposed a personal interpretation of their read-
ings when they offered to adapt chemical concepts to culinary practices. They
identified the cook as an alchemist, as he was capable of transforming the raw
ingredients of nature, conferring these higher qualities and taste to them.
It was alleged that the most significant culinary evolution of the time was
the achievement of making food lighter, cleansing it from all harmful materials, which, cooks thought, would make food healthier, as it would become
easier to digest. The result of this process was called quintessence. As stated
in the *Dons de Comus*, "modern cuisine is a sort of chemistry. The science of
the cook today consists in decomposing, in making digest[ible] and in *quintes-
senciating* meats, pulling nourishing and light juices, and mixing and merging
them together so that nothing dominates and that everything is felt."[43] Just like
the seventeenth-century "true taste" of food, eighteenth-century discourses on
cuisine were not rhetorical only. All the bouillons and coulis, foundations of
the *nouvelle cuisine,* constituted the extracts or "quintessences" of meats and
were presented as a practical application of chemical theories.[44] The new culinary processes aimed at extracting the spirituous principles of foodstuffs in
order to concentrate these within elaborate dishes. This first purification of food
through culinary technique associated, once again, cookery with the digestive
process.[45] This association between cookery and digestion was not new; cuisine
had been considered for a very long time as a first cooking of food, in preparation for the second *coction* [cooking] of the stomach.[46] This rather ancient idea
was, however, adapted in the eighteenth century in relation to the evolution of
scientific knowledge—that is, to the conception of digestion itself as a chemical process.[47] After all, *nouvelle cuisine*, presented as a true form of chemistry,
allows "facilitat[ion]" of the digestion by the dressing and cooking of meats,"
which reinforced the therapeutic value of cookery.[48] Hence, considering the
theoretical and practical knowledge displayed by the cook, cookery demanded
the title of "science,"[49] as evidenced in *nouvelle cuisine*'s new cookbooks: "But
how much does the honesty of cookery not contribute to health? Nothing comes
out of the cooks' hands, which did not pass through a severe examination, and
which is not well purified. The most unrefined meats deposit there, by the fire's
action, their earthiness [*terrestréités*]."[50]
The stakes of this chemistry of flavors were actually much more important
than it seems. The idea of extraction and concentration of food essences sends
us back to the theories of the spirituous principles or the chemistry of the *esprits*
[spirits], particularly popular since the works of Descartes. In these theories,
communication between the body and the soul was thought to be possible
precisely by means of animal spirits, which were seen as extremely subtle, fluid
materials, "composing the most volatile mass of the blood volume which go to
the brain and, in particular, to the "pineal gland" where the soul has its center

of action. . . . Mutually, under the influence of its will, the soul has the power to cause various movements in the place where it is supposed to remain and to push so the animal spirits" toward the brain and then toward the muscles.[51] Nerves were seen as the vessels allowing the animal spirits to join every region of the body, acting as the vehicles of thought, of will, and of sensory impressions. Food played an important role because the animal spirits derived from foodstuffs through the digestion. Descartes considered that "the juice of meats, which passes from the stomach to the veins, getting mixed with blood, always communicates some of its qualities."[52] Certain foods, like fermented liqueurs, spices, and other highly flavored foods were thought to possess wide quantities of penetrating volatile principles or volatile salts, which were easily transformed into a spiritual principle in the blood during the digestion. The brain then took from the blood the subtlest parts of the spiritual substances to secrete them in the nerves as animal spirits. Animal spirits were thus the source of power that allowed the mutual action of the soul on the body, or of the body on the soul. In the seventeenth century, Cartesians, pleading for the government of the mind over the senses, only considered one part of this equation as possible: that of the power of the soul on the body. In the eighteenth century, an increasing number of scholars would return to the question and ask whether the reverse logic could not be true—whether the body, too, could have an influence on the soul—hence suggesting that cookery could interfere with the mind. With this theory, the culinary domain became of vital interest, which justified all the more the intervention of scholars in this sector, which had been formerly neglected when it concerned only the body. Modern cooks saw an opportunity here to underscore the positive outcomes of sophisticated cuisine, which, informed by bodily processes and medical theories, could be beneficial both to physical health and to the development of the mind:

> Cuisine subtilizes the unrefined parts of food, strips the mixed that it uses from the earthly juices which they contain: cuisine perfects them, purifies them, and spiritualizes them in some way. The dishes prepared must thus carry in the blood a greater abundance of purer and looser spirits. From there more agility and vigor in the bodies, more vivaciousness and fire in the imagination, more extent and strength in the genius, more delicacy and sharpness in our tastes. Would it thus be too much to advance, as to place the dressings of modern Cuisine among the physical causes which, from Barbary, have recalled among us the reign of politeness, the talents of the spirit, the Arts and the Sciences?[53]

Diet was thus presented as one of the physical causes influencing the development of the mind, along with climate, which had long explained the physical and moral variations between peoples, as highlighted, for instance, by Foncemagne: "Physics [teaches] us that the diversity of food, just as much as that of climates, puts variety and difference, not only in bodies, but also in genius, inclinations, and customs of nations."[54] Foncemagne then quotes a whole passage of Dubos,[55] a "man of wit,"[56] regarding the changes brought about by the development of commercial trade, which transformed culinary habits and hence modified the minds of the people:

> Which change does one not notice in the spirits of the Peoples of the North, since sugar, spices, wine, and other foodstuffs growing in warm Countries, are a part of their ordinary food. *Salts, and spirituous juices of these foodstuffs,* says a man of wit, *throw in the blood of northern Nations a soul, or to speak with the Physicists, an ethereal oil, which they could not pull from the food of their Country. These juices fill the blood of a man of the North with animal spirits formed in Spain and under the most blazing climates.*[57]

The important changes caused by the intensification of global trade since the sixteenth century were, of course, of essential concern to contemporaries. People not only worried about economic and political issues but also about social and cultural transformations likely to influence their health, even the development of their brain, notably through the import of new foodstuffs coming from abroad.

The mutual influence of diet and behavior is an old problem, traces of which one already finds in the Middle Ages and in the Renaissance, particularly in the "doctrine of similarity." This theory claimed that the characteristics of food were directly transferred into the consumer, who become what they ate: consuming rabbit makes one shy; eating fox makes one cunning; and absorbing deer brings longevity, for this animal lives on its own for a very long time. In the vast network of similarities, people's understanding of the world relied on analogy, in which every element of nature found its meaning within a network of sympathies and antipathies.[58] But the doctrine of similarity gradually weakened and was mocked by the end of the sixteenth century, though as Ken Albala stresses, many people still believed in it.[59] In the eighteenth century, although the idea of the influence of the physical on morality remained, the system explaining it had entirely changed, the theory of spirits or of the volatile principles being far different from the former theory of similarity. The debate reached an unprecedented scale during the Enlightenment.[60] Numerous philosophers got involved in this discussion, like Rousseau, who used the theory of the influence of diet on character in his plea in favor of vegetarianism: he asserted that the aggressiveness of the English people resulted from their frequent consumption of meat-based food,[61] an idea shared by the materialist La Mettrie.[62]

The *Médecine de L'Esprit* (Medicine of the Spirit), published in two volumes by Antoine Le Camus, is an interesting book regarding these discussions. The author sought to prove that "physical causes . . . modifying differently the bodies, also vary the capacities of the minds."[63] Indeed, "the age, the temperament, the way of living; the seasons arrange the inclinations of the soul by varying the dispositions of the bodies."[64] These words obviously had materialistic connotations, which is why the author was cautious enough to deny any potential accusation of materialism, by referring to God and to the immortal soul. This debate is crucial to an investigation on the history of taste, for it concerned not only food but also the gustatory sense. The ability to distinguish with delicacy the various nuances of flavors indeed appeared as the result of an ideal configuration of the organs as well. It testified to a bodily intelligence, closely connected to a spiritual intelligence. Gustatory and moral tastes were thus considered two aspects of one and same sense modality, the perfection of which rested on the physical organs and expressed itself through an intellectual sharpness, as evidenced both in cookbooks and theoretical works such as those of Le Camus: "As the bodily taste and the spiritual taste also depend on the conformation of fibers and on the organs intended to operate their diverse sensations, the delicacy of these two sorts of tastes undoubtedly proves the sharpness of the organs peculiar to them, and consequently one can . . . go back from the bodily taste to a very delicate principle which is common to it in some way with the purely spiritual taste."[65]

As a matter of fact, "more or less sensuality for the pleasures of the table, a more or less exquisite discernment of the dishes and the liqueurs often shows the quality of the judgment. . . . [T]hose who take the food without choice, without discernment, and who swallow them in a voracious way, are mostly cold men and of little genius."[66] The stakes of the science of flavors, defended in the prefaces of modern cuisine's books, were hence much more important, as they concerned not the body only but also, and more importantly, the mind. Taste was now part of both.

Cuisine among the Fine Arts?

According to *nouvelle cuisine*'s supporters, although new culinary practices required a high level of knowledge, these were not to be reduced to a simple technique, as they also needed the cook to display his own personal talent, his capacity to improvise and adeptly mix the various ingredients composing the most delicate dishes. In the forewords, cookery was presented as a true form of "art,"[67] and the cook as an "Artist in matters of Cuisine."[68] The words *art*, *artiste*, and also *science* did not have exactly the same meaning as they do today.[69] For centuries, the word "art" was closer to the idea of craftsmanship than to that one fine art, as evidenced by the Latin word *ars*—equivalent of the Greek word *techne*—which designated talent, skill, ability, know-how. It concerned abilities as much as professions. Science was considered to be pure knowledge, whereas art had the sense of technique. Then later on in the Middle Ages, mechanical arts would be distinguished from liberal arts, the former concerning practical activities and the latter theoretical knowledge.[70] Cuisine, in this process, was adjusted to an art craft—a rather low one because it was performed by slaves in antiquity and in later eras by servants—and was afterward further adjusted to be a mechanical art, often organized around corporations and companionship. Cuisine was moreover considered a lower activity because it related to the pleasures of senses and not to the mind. Eventually, the sense of the word *art* evolved in the Renaissance with the invention of the figure of the artist and the emergence of the idea of fine arts, which concerned noble arts such as painting and sculpture; an art of cooking was simply out of the question. Since antiquity, we can find examples of people defending the idea of a culinary art. But most of the time these instances were meant to be ironic, or at least they were received as such, up until the eighteenth century. By then, even though cuisine was still considered a "mechanical art" in the *Encyclopédie*,[71] a possible aesthetic of cuisine was discussed in the context of the *nouvelle cuisine*.

According to the writers of the famous prefaces, the objective of cookery was to achieve the perfect harmony of flavors, just like painting displays a harmony of colors.[72] This search for harmony was one of the main arguments used by the authors of these culinary narratives to raise cuisine to the rank of an art, alongside painting or music.[73] Such a scheme would have simply been unthinkable two centuries earlier. Before the eighteenth century, irony always accompanied attempts to inscribe haute cuisine among the fine arts, as when Michel de Montaigne laughed at the claims of Cardinal Caraffa's cook and his "*science de gueule*" (science of the mouth); he spoke about his practice as a subject of high theology. Montaigne's irony is evidenced in the title of the essay in which this passage appeared: "On the Vanity of Words."[74] For a long time, and still in sixteenth-century France, an art of cuisine was not really conceivable.[75]

One of the oldest formulations of the debate regarding a possible art of cookery went back up to Plato's *Gorgias*. In response to Polos's question, "What is cookery?" Socrates answered that it is "not an Art . . . it is a know-how . . . it is to know how to gratify and to please."[76] Unlike medicine, cuisine does not know "which food is better for the body" and "cannot offer any rational explanation on the nature of the regime which it administers to such or such patient; it is thus incapable to give the slightest justification. As for me," continues Socrates, "I do not call that an art, nothing but a practice, which acts without reason."[77] Although this extract was actually attacking rhetoric by way of the language of cookery, it nonetheless reveals important values attached to cuisine, which would have a lasting influence. The conception of cookery as deprived of any rational knowledge was both a symptom and a cause of the secular depreciation of the sense of taste. Cuisine was all the more underestimated as it pursued pleasure and not the Good as an end. As long as the cook ignored the properties of ingredients, he was incapable of determining the reasons for positive or negative effects of certain foodstuffs on the body. Only the doctor was granted this knowledge, for he had mastered dietetics, which allowed him to really take care of and heal the body. Consequently, cuisine appeared as a slavish practice, unworthy of a free man.[78] Plato exercised a considerable influence on food morality, provoking numerous debates on the value of cookery, which was often presented as deceit or "disguise" because of its use of seasonings. According to him, the objective of cuisine was to seduce the senses, to flatter the sensual taste, and not to contribute to the body's well-being, much less to that of the soul's. Writers in the Enlightenment are thus influenced by a very long tradition. Gradually detached from the discourse of medicine over the centuries, cuisine would in the end dedicate itself only to the pleasures of the palate but not without pretending to possess its own form of knowledge as well.

Considering all this historical and philosophical background, the idea of an art of cookery was quite audacious in the eighteenth century, and writers in the late 1730s were very much aware of the boldness of their aesthetic comparisons:

> One may have never dared to find a link between two apparently so distant objects such as the art of painting and of cuisine. But *except the boldness of the comparison and besides the irreverence,*[79] I did not find [an] image more appropriate to express my ideas. The union and break of colors [*couleurs*] that makes the beauty of color [*coloris*], represent well enough . . . this mixture of juices and ingredients with which the cook composes his ragoûts. These ingredients and juices have to be blended and melted, in the same way as the painter blends his colors, and the same harmony, which in a painting strikes the eyes of the connoisseurs, has to be felt by delicate palates in the taste of a sauce.[80]

Just like artists with colors, cooks aesthetically expressed a culinary harmony with flavors. Besides painting, cuisine was also readily likened to music, as in Foncemagne's "Dissertation préliminaire": "Shall one thus be blamed for suggesting that there is a harmony of flavors, like a harmony of sounds, and maybe that of colors and smells? . . . But who can find it wrong that I propose that there is a certain harmonious proportion between flavors, more or less similar to the one that the ear perceives in sounds, although of a different sort. If it is not, then one should tell me why such [a] mixture of flavors revolts the organ of taste, whereas such other one [flavor] flatters it pleasantly."[81]

Foncemagne insists not only on the talent of the cook but also on a good audience's ability to appreciate, educated palates being just like musical ears: "In the dressings of food, as in musical plays, there are dissonances that must be prepared and saved adeptly. For the most learned musician, provide an audience of Hurons, Hottentots, and other wild Peoples of America or Africa, and see if they will pleasantly be touched by the beauty and elegance of his learned chords. . . . A skillful cook as well only requires delicate and sensible palates to savor the harmony of juices with which he makes up his ragoûts."[82] Thus, it was believed that the art of cuisine also needed refined and experienced tasters to be truly appreciated; these tasters would identify the slightest nuances of flavors, so subtle that very few would be capable of evaluating the differences with the *delicate organs* of the connoisseurs, explored in the previous chapter.[83]

Several texts of the time offered similar theories and suggested the idea of correspondences between taste and music. *Le Festin joyeux, ou La Cuisine en Musique en vers libres* (The Joyful Feast, or Cookery in Music in Free Verse) is a particularly suggestive example, as this was a songbook made up of recipes.[84] Polycarpe Poncelet also supported in a rather unique way the idea of a sensory association between taste and music.[85] In his *Chymie du gout et de l'odorat* (Chemistry of Taste and Smell), he defined a *musique savoureuse* (tasty music),[86] based upon the correspondences between sound and flavor, a theory establishing links between the senses of taste and of hearing:

> The enjoyment of liqueurs depends on the mixture of flavors, in a harmonic proportion. Flavors consist in the more or less strong vibrations of salts, which act on the sense of taste, like sounds consist in the more or less strong vibrations of air, which act on the sense of hearing; there can thus be a music for the tongue and for the palate, as there is one for the ears; it is very likely that flavors, to excite a variety of sensations in the soul, have, as the sonic bodies, their tones that are generative, dominant, major, minor, low, high-pitched notes. . . . Seven full tones make the fundamental basis of the sound music; such [a] number of primitive flavors is the basis of the tasty music, and their harmonic combination is made in similar reason.[87]

Each note on the scale of C major was associated with a flavor (figure 5).[88] The demonstration continued with tasteful mixtures that corresponded to various possible musical chords.[89] Science and aesthetics were thus here also blended. The cook, a true artist, was compared to a musical composer and conductor: "In brief I naturally consider a Liqueur like a sort of musical air. A composer of *ragoûts*, jams, [and] ratafia liqueurs, is a symphonist in his kind, and he must master the nature and principles of harmony, if he wants to excel in his art, the object of which is to produce pleasant sensations in the soul."[90]

Music and cookery are alike, as they both yearn for harmony and composition.[91] Inspired by Rameau's harpsichord of colors, Poncelet suggested building a harmonic organ of flavors, on which one could "play any sorts of tasty tunes, if the new organist possesses with intelligence his keyboard."[92] The author never really specified how to build this instrument or how it actually worked,[93] but he disclosed here the idea of a possible control of flavors and tastes through technique, a fantasy of a potential mechanical reproduction of flavors. His ideas

Figure 5. Polycarpe Poncelet, *Nouvelle Chymie du gout et de l'odorat*, xxvij. University of Liège, Alpha Library, R02450B.

also testify to the tendency during the Enlightenment to associate the functioning of the body to that of machines.

A little earlier, Father Castel—a Jesuit defender of Rameau and Rousseau—had, based on the idea of an analogy between sounds and colors, proposed making an ocular harpsichord that would associate musical notes with colors.[94] The "music of colors" was by then the object of many contemporary debates addressed, for instance, by Diderot, Voltaire, and Rousseau. During the eighteenth century, the question of the senses was of primary interest, notably due to important transformations brought about by the empiricist and sensuality theory. The question of synesthesia and correspondences between the senses were especially chief matters of concern. Discussions on the harpsichords of colors and flavors were inscribed within these larger debates on the senses, and reveal the quest for a universal harmony, as indicated, for instance, by Father Castel: "The five senses are only one because they are necessary for the soul which is unique. . . . The harpsichord represents the total harmony, the harmony between all the arts and the sciences (literature, history, geometry, philosophy, morality, religion) thanks to our five senses; between the five senses and our body, itself in accordance with our soul, guarantee of our harmony with all beings."[95] By comparing cuisine to painting or to music, culinary authors obviously wanted to endow the gustatory sensation with an aesthetic dimension. These provocative claims pleaded for the reassessment of the sense of taste; by weakening the traditional idea of a "hierarchy of the senses," the bodily sense of taste was for the first time presented as an aesthetic sense. Indeed, previously, theories of taste had only considered the taste of the mind as endowed with an artistic discernment, connected with the eye and the ear, not with the tongue or the palate. Now, however, the tongue itself led to art, perceived through a bodily sense.

Using a variety of arguments, the writers of these essays offer quite elaborate demonstrations in order to emphasize the importance of taste. Numerous allusions are made, especially, to contemporary aesthetic theories.[96] For instance, the notions of diversity and unity, crucial to Jean-Pierre de Crousaz and Francis Hutcheson in order to define beauty, were here likened to culinary delicacy: "The *diversity* of flavors would be little . . . without unity. Here are two objects that nature offers in everything, and which, in the judgment of a famous Author,[97] are the unique foundation of all that is *beautiful*."[98] Foncemagne also mentioned extracts from the *Théorie des sentimens agreables* (Theory of Pleasant Feelings) by Louis-Jean Lévesque de Pouilly, friend of Shaftesbury, indicating that "the enjoyment of flavors and smells is not less matched to our needs than that of colors and sounds."[99]

Furthermore, not only did authors of culinary discourses make use of aesthetic and scientific knowledge of their time, but the very debates they were having in cookbooks were held elsewhere as well. Antoine Le Camus, member of the Faculty of Medicine, also defended the idea that taste "can be reduced to a science as positive as music or painting." He asserted that

> the ear gave us the science of sounds, the eyes made an art of colors, why would the mouth not form a science of tastes? There are maybe only seven primitive tastes in nature, as well as there are only seven colors and seven tones. Doubtless are there also semi-tones in flavors, as well as there are semi-tones both in sounds and colors. . . . It would be possible to have with flavors an even more true harmony, than the one that could form the harpsichord of colors. These sauces in which enter various seasonings, are they not a concert of flavors of which our palates are the judges?[100]

The idea of a science of taste was reinforced by the fact that if the practices of cookery and discourses on cuisine were formerly "relegated to vile handmaids, or to uneducated people . . . nowadays . . . this art [is] exercised by nobler hands, and embellished by more delicate tastes. *Comus* has students that he can admit, and enrich us of his gifts."[101] As a matter of fact, the intervention of men of letters and more generally of the polite world into the culinary domain enhanced its value. Cuisine was now considered a form of knowledge, of the body and of the mind, possessed by a small number of cooks and enjoyed by a minority of connoisseurs. The capacity to distinguish with delicacy the slightest nuances of flavors reflected a discernment of the educated man, who was capable of judging art and the world *avec esprit* (with wit). Spiritual and bodily tastes were hence two important and complementary dimensions of the same sense modality. Culinary literature restored the balance between taste and gustation, here for the first time endowed with an equal value. Consequently, taste could finally dare to align itself with painting and music, sight and hearing, two noble senses already long endowed with an essential dual dimension of body and mind.

However, one should keep in mind that most of these intriguing texts claiming cookery's access to the titles of science and art were often somehow meant to be ironic. The authors of the time were particularly fond of sarcastic texts and literary humor—especially when food was involved—as Spary has demonstrated in *Eating the Enlightenment*. Moreover, it should be noted that *nouvelle cuisine*'s writers did not sign the texts they published in cookbooks, which tends to show that these works were considered pleasant banter. Only from the nineteenth century onward, with the development of gastronomic literature, would cuisine really become the object of a specific literary genre, an inheritance of the ideas found in the culinary introductions of the late 1730s. But these documents nevertheless highlight new representations of taste and cookery, new ideas just starting to spread, even though they were not necessarily commonly shared. After all, although developed within the framework of cookbooks, taste was no longer reduced to the culinary register, in which it had been confined until then. Men of letters published discourses in recipe books involving the most diverse knowledge: dietetics, chemistry, and aesthetics, interwoven with culinary matters. Although these essays were published inside a cookbook, their impact reached far beyond this universe, as one also finds traces of this debate in other contemporary medical, philosophical, and aesthetic texts that had very little overt culinary content.

Members of the polite reading public were concerned with their health and endeavored to adapt the best, balanced diet. Therefore, they read works drafted by doctors, cooks, and anyone else likely to offer expertise; trying to determine the best regimen and reviving old ideas of self-medication, they celebrated, for instance, the figure of Cornaro, author of a very successful guide to health, diet, and long life (*On the Sober Life*), whom we have already met.[102]

Conflicting Models of Taste

Entrusted to professional writers, the cookbooks' prefaces of the *nouvelle cuisine* moved away from the narrow domain of cookery to raise other issues, in particular philosophical matters. One of the most frequent issues debated concerned the dialectic between nature and culture, often implicitly connected with discourses on taste. In the eighteenth century especially, discussions concerned the evolution of cookery throughout history. To *nouvelle cuisine*'s defenders, this evolution was perceived as a progress. For the Jesuits Brumoy and Bougeant, cuisine was an art arisen from a need, which "perfected with the genius of people, and became more delicate as they polished themselves. . . . The progress of cookery . . . followed among civilized nations the progress of all the other arts."[103] With the gradual rise of civility and politeness in the early modern era, talented chefs were able to transform a material need into a refined pleasure, a real sublimation of nature's raw ingredients through the art of cookery.[104] In turn, the artist was guided by nature in his work.[105]

But culinary sophistication was not to everyone's taste in the eighteenth century. The publication of *Dons de Comus* in 1739 provoked negative reactions, giving rise to a real "gastronomical polemic," in the words of Stephen Mennell, who edited the main texts of this debate.[106] A little after François Marin's publication, a writer named "Desalleurs"[107] anonymously published the *Lettre d'un pâtissier anglois au nouveau cuisinier françois* (Letter from an English Pastry Cook to the New French Cook), which was a direct attack against the *Dons de Comus*. The author mocked the scholarly claims of a simple cook, who reasons "in a manner, which is a little over the reach of people of this Profession . . . well versed in history, in metaphysics, and in the science of the world."[108] Contemporaries were perfectly aware that the cooks of the *nouvelle cuisine* had "used the pen of some man of letters."[109] Desalleurs criticized the scientific claims of this allegedly innovative cuisine, where "learned cooks would not miss the opportunity to use their methodical spirit to perfect cookery, by treating it, as the other sciences, with the rules of geometry. What a ragoût for the delicately voluptuous people, that a geometrically chemical dish, in which only enter reasoned quintessences, and cleared, with precision, of any *earthiness*."[110] The irony of Desalleurs against these "geometrically chemical dishes" is pretty clear and aims at the chemical pretentions of the cook who claims himself capable of purifying food and of extracting healthy and delicious principles from it.

The allusion to "geometrical knowledge" was directed against the Cartesians and those who used geometrical reasoning in all domains of knowledge, as well as against theorists of the physiology of taste. Contemporary physicians, such as Jacques Rohault and Claude-Nicolas Le Cat, indeed considered that flavors depended on the one hand on the configuration of the eater's organs, and on the other hand on the structure of the sapid particles composing the food ingested. This was called the iatrophysical doctrine, which suggested, following the works of the Florentine doctor Lorenzo Bellini in 1665, a "solidest interpretation of the taste buds' function. The particles of the salts, separated from food thanks to mastication, and dissolved by the saliva, would act differently according to their forms and their respective movements, on the papillae."[111] In his *Traité de physique* (Treatise on Physics), Jacques Rohault so explained that flavors depended on the structure of the tasted substance, a structure that "consists in the thickness, figure, and movement of its parts; and that it is from the diversity that one can imagine in these three things that are born the diverse flavors."[112] One finds similar ideas in Claude-Nicolas Le Cat's works in the eighteenth century.[113]

For Desalleurs, *nouvelle cuisine*'s dishes were in any case disappointing from a gustatory point of view: "The choice of food became very useless by the skill of our cooks. They know so well how to *quintessenciate* everything, that nothing dominates, and that one cannot distinguish, neither by taste nor by the eye, if what one eats is meat or fish. The great art of the nouvelle cuisine is to give fish the taste of meat, and meat the taste of fish, and to leave vegetables with absolutely no taste."[114] Besides the "geometrical" nature of this cuisine, Desalleurs found absurd the idea of a moral influence of food on customs. If this is so, then, he says, instead of encouraging children to study, one should just prepare each of them for their profession through a particular diet:

> The ideas of our mind depend on the organic constitution of the body. Yet the organic constitution of the body depends absolutely on the quality of the food that serves to fix it. Thus the ideas of our mind usually depend on the quality of our food. Of these very obvious principles . . . one might . . . take big advantages for the education of children . . . [young people] lose precious time in their childhood, to learn dead languages, with which they have nothing to do; one overloads their memory with fables, stories, and readings which disgust them . . . for all education . . . one should . . . only give young people foodstuff and foods relative to the state for which they are intended. This food would be measured and seasoned by a skillful and experienced cook, who would master the thoughts that produces in a soul the digestion of a soup à la Nivernaise, a sauce à la Chirac, and similar food.[115]

Meusnier de Querlon reacted a little later to this letter in an *Apologie des Modernes* (Apology of the Modern), which appeared after 1740. Although the text did not deal directly with food and cookery, it was nevertheless clearly a reaction to the debate, as revealed by the complete title of the document.[116] The author introduced himself as a "Philosopher Cook" and recapped all the remarkable inventions of the Moderns, celebrating the progress of the arts and sciences made possible by the rise of the philosophical spirit.[117] He argued in favor of the chemistry of flavors, "the utilities of philosophy and geometry in the nouvelle cuisine." Addressing the English pastry cook, he writes: "You apparently believe that a triangular ramekin, a parabolic pie, and similar ragoûts would be more unhealthy than others; but make no mistake, please, not only would they be more pleasant to the people of good taste, but they would certainly be healthier."[118] Nouvelle cuisine's dishes were thus presented as good for taste and for health. In fact, the controversy was not only a culinary one. The real stakes here actually concerned the wider debate between the Ancients and the Moderns—the defenders of tradition against the promoters of progress. This famous Querelle had started in the seventeenth century and continued through the Enlightenment. Born in the literary domain, this conflict, which we encountered in chapter 4, would gradually extend and affect all sectors of knowledge, including the culinary art, opposing "modern cuisine" to "ancient cuisine."[119] Defenders of ancient cuisine viewed the chemical foundations of modern cuisine with contempt. They associated culinary refinement with the corruption of society's health, reopening a secular debate and adapting it to contemporary conditions. In contrast, the promoters of nouvelle cuisine emphasized the culinary improvement observed over the centuries, made possible by the progress of technique and scientific knowledge. There was thus a new rhetoric and new discourses that arose in the eighteenth century that positively celebrated the sense of taste, presented as the object of a distinction, as a symbol of culture and modernity and endowed with a performative nature.

The "gastronomical polemic" actually exemplifies broader intellectual debates that were held on cookery in the Enlightenment. Culinary sophistication had its critics, as evidenced in the article "cuisine" by the Chevalier de Jaucourt published in the Encyclopédie. The encyclopedist delivered here a rather pejorative conception of what he nevertheless qualified as an "art to flatter taste, this luxury ... this lust of good food to which one attaches such a great importance."[120] The author stigmatized his contemporaries, who were fond of delicate and diversified dishes and hence corrupted by culinary refinement, since sophisticated preparations engaged the eater in conspicuous consumption, which then led to diseases and debauchery. He criticized this "deceiving art," a sign of the civilization's decline and of moral perversion, opposing the presumed moderation of the first humans, whose food was considered natural and adjusted to the strict limitations of need.[121] The nostalgia for a golden age collides here with the current food habits of Moderns perceived as depraved and consisting, according to Jaucourt, in a "secret reduced to a learned method, to cook beyond necessity."[122] The beginning of the encylopedist's analysis, at least, was not that different from that of the Dons de Comus's, which, in the presentation of the history of cookery, also recalled the old myth of innocence of the origins—a commonplace of gustatory discourses.[123] The temperance of the "first people" "was not long-term; the habit to always eat the same things, and more or less dress in the same way, gave birth to disgust, disgust created curiosity, curiosity encouraged experience, experience brought sensuality; the man tasted, tried, diversified, chose, and succeeded in *making an art of the simplest and the most natural action.*"[124] The main difference between Jaucourt and the *Dons de Comus* was the perception of the consequences of progress, considered as disastrous by the former and positive for the latter. If modern practices were seen by cooks as better for taste and health, the Chevalier de Jaucourt—a Protestant trained in theology and medicine in Geneva—delivered a rather pessimist discourse, in which cookery appeared as an art of disguise, creating "so many flattering poisons prepared to destroy the temperament, and shorten the course of life."[125] The author, however, recognized that the art of cookery also sometimes provided new methods for better preservation and digestion of food.[126] Interestingly, despite the clearly deprecatory nature of the text, cuisine still appeared here as a form of *art*—even if "deceptive"—and of *science*—although "des plus pénibles" (very difficult)—which indicates that the idea of a culinary knowledge had nevertheless began to spread.[127] Though the words "art" and "science" did not have exactly the same meaning they have today, a form of knowledge was nevertheless implied, intertwining intellectual and practical skills formerly denied to the sense of taste.

Moreover, questions of taste and cuisine were part of the wider debate held on luxury in the eighteenth century. The evolution of global trade and the important transformations of consumption practices led to discussions on the nature and consequences of the larger availability of luxury goods. Promoters of consumption and luxury goods as social, economic, and political incentives were at conflict with those who favored another model of society allegedly closer to nature. Cuisine was one among many examples of the issues caught in the crosshairs of these disputes. Moral discourse in favor of or against culinary refinement often more broadly implied economic and political opposition. Opponents of culinary sophistication readily criticized excesses of luxury, which was also often a way to condemn absolutism, confirming that debates about cuisine were definitely not only about food.[128]

Jean-Jacques Rousseau is a well-known illustration of these polemics, as he famously pointed to culinary refinement as an indication of society's corruption of nature. Disapproving of sophisticated cuisine, considered as pernicious, Rousseau pleaded for a return to simple foods. He excluded meat, considered as unnatural, from the ideal regime. The vegetarian diet seemed closer to the primitive state, as indicated by the instinctive taste of children for fruits, dairy products, and pastries.[129] According to Rousseau, knowing how to eat did not imply any aesthetic approach to cookery but meant a favoring of simplicity and sobriety, for complex seasonings and spicy flavors corrupted the sense of taste. He did not completely condemn *gourmandise*, but considered it to be solely "the passion of childhood," which should not last later on.[130]

For others, such as Voltaire, luxury had to be encouraged, as it favored the enrichment of great countries such as France.[131] Debates on luxury were more broadly inscribed within the major discussions related to nature. The different ways in which nature was being thought of and discussed indeed influenced the different values granted to luxury, according to the author considered—these disputes were of course not only visible in cookbooks.[132] In these disputes, each author employed rhetorical strategies to defend his point of view. The same themes and stories were used by a variety of authors, who could easily use the same story with a different conclusion, depending on the thesis they wished to demonstrate. For instance, against the idea of a corruption of contemporary cuisine as opposed to sobriety of the past, cooks highlighted the corruption of antique cookery as opposed the sobriety of the Moderns. People such as the Romans, Persians, and Greeks—and also individual personalities like Heliogabalus, Philoxenus, Apicius, and Cleopatra—constituted so many exempla of greedy immoderation. In counterpoint, contemporary gentlemen were models of sobriety. As mentioned above, the identity of modern cuisine was set directly against the allegedly profusions of medieval cuisine, as modern cooks claimed to offer a lighter, more natural cuisine that revealed the "true taste" of food. Seen through the eye of the cook, food reached in modern cuisine a stage of ultimate perfection. Culinary history was read here in a more positive way because it was presented as a process of improvement and progress. Such a claim would only grow as we move forward to the eighteenth century and would reach its height with the *nouvelle cuisine* of the late 1730s, when the debate again brought into conflict the Ancients (partisans of food sobriety in accordance with nature) and the Moderns (defenders of sophisticated cuisine and promoters of the idea that cultural progress requires an increase in luxury). To these debates were moreover added, as already mentioned, economical and political concerns.

In sum, the emergence of eighteenth-century *nouvelle cuisine* coincided with the invention of an innovative discourse on taste, which represented the first form of writings solely dedicated to bodily taste and the pleasure of eating, and heralded the emergence of gastronomical literature a little later. Whether despised or celebrated, one cannot deny that taste was for the first time the object of intense ideological and philosophical debates in mid-eighteenth-century France, affecting the whole learned society. How might we explain this enthusiasm around a theme formerly so neglected?

An Ideal Context for Discourses on Taste

During the classical period, taste, perceived as too trivial a subject, was banished from honest conversations and works of scholars. The real novelty in the eighteenth century was that by then members of polite society dared to openly display their interest in matters such as food or cuisine. Previously, even if one appreciated refined cuisine, the enjoyments of the table had to be kept silent, excluded from conversation and writings. In between the classical period and the eighteenth century, something had changed regarding the representations of taste that authorized—and encouraged. even—men of the polite world and of letters to speak freely about culinary delicacies.

Numerous factors can explain these important cultural and social changes. First of all, the economic context of eighteenth-century Europe was much more favorable than that of the previous century. There were fewer wars than before, while diseases and mortality decreased thanks to the progress of science and techniques, notably improvement of supply processes, which considerably decreased the risks of famines. The fact that hunger was becoming less of a dreadful threat most likely played a part in the rise of discussions on matters such as taste, all the more as consumption and luxury were now becoming an important concern to the polite world. Second of all, the political context of eighteenth-century France was especially favorable in raising the importance of taste. The death of Louis XIV in 1715 was perceived as the beginning of a new era.[133] People felt released "from an atmosphere of sad and heavy devotion."[134] The regent, Philippe, Duke of Orleans, who succeeded the Sun King, was a true gourmet, passionate about cuisine, just like Louis XIV afterward. Philippe was particularly fond of small intimate suppers, gathering just a few carefully chosen dinner guests. He preferred these sorts of intimate meals to those fancy meals displaying power that were so common during the reign of Louis XIV. The regency would remain famous in the history of cuisine, perceived as a golden age of refinement and portrayed with nostalgia by later gourmands, such as Grimod de La Reynière:

> [T]he long peace following the Treaty of Utrecht, the great fortunes of finance . . . the quiet and sensual life of a Monarch less concerned with his glory than with his private delights; the character of his courtiers, more friends with sensory pleasures than with those of the mind; the sensual and voluptuous tastes of Philippe, whose orgies had been used as models to the small suppers, everything contributed to give, under this Prince, a great importance to the food Arts. One knew all the enjoyments that procure a delicate and inventive food; one refined on all the parts of cookery and the office, and the suppers of the King, the Princes and some courtiers were mentioned as the ultimate word of what Comus' art could offer of most delicious and most learned.[135]

The eighteenth century was thus a particularly timely moment for "the food Arts," hence also for celebrations of the sense of taste.

What is more, with time the Church had gradually lost its influence in everyday life, although the idea of a "de-Christianization" in the Enlightenment must, of course, be carefully nuanced.[136] The sin of gluttony lost much of its gravity in the process, while the word *gourmandise* itself was now endowed with a double meaning, as it was defined as a "refined and disordered love of good food."[137] The idea of a food disorder is old and calls to mind the animal gluttony, discussed in chapter 2. But from now on, although the negative conception remained—which can notably be understood by the fact that this last quote was written by the Chevalier de Jaucourt—the word *gourmandise* now also supposed a "refined love" of food, susceptible to estimate the various nuances, which was something new.[138]

To these many changes, one must finally add the two important cultural phenomena discussed above: sensualism and the invention of metaphors of taste. Regarding sensualism, we saw that in comparison to other senses, especially sight and touch, scholars granted small interest to taste. Yet it cannot be denied that empiricism and sensualism represented an intellectual revolution that inevitably altered contemporaries' representations of the world. The central place the senses held in the development of knowledge contributed to a reevaluation of the importance of sensibility. As a result, the pleasures of the senses were no longer seen as dangers the Christian should worry about but as benefactions granted by God to allow the optimal preservation of the body. If the consequences of empiricism and sensualism were not immediately visible in the actual works of these philosophical movements, these new ideas most certainly contributed to a new consideration of the senses, hence also of taste—at least indirectly.

Locke and Condillac were abundantly read; their ideas influenced the philosophers of the Enlightenment, the encyclopedists, and the writers of aesthetic theories such as Dubos. There were obvious references to these works made in culinary discourses as well, like when Meusnier de Querlon announced the forthcoming publication of an "essay nouveau sur l'Entendement humain" (new essay on human understanding) demonstrating "in a new and metaphysico-géometrical way, that the diversity of our opinions comes only from the difference in our foods, and that in brief our food is the source and the unique origin of our ideas and thoughts, by where one can judge of which importance the art of cuisine is in a State, because the health and the way of thinking of societies depend on it."[139] Revisiting Locke's theories, Meusnier de Querlon then suggests considering food, instead of the senses, as the basis of all ideas: "In the meantime, I beg the philosophers, who will doubtless consider this a paradox, to be only three weeks without taking anything, and they will let me know; it is an experiment to be made, because one noticed well that people who eat too little, and who pretend to fast, often have very hollow ideas; but we still ignore which ideas would have a man who would not eat at all."[140] This text is ironic, of course, but these ideas are particularly suggestive and testify to contemporaries' appropriation of empiricist and sensualist theories.

The introductions of *nouvelle cuisine* also appeared after several decades of intellectual discussions about the multiple metaphors of taste, which contributed to a revaluation of this sense that was then transformed into a true sense modality. I argue that the aesthetic treatises of taste facilitated the emergence of a discourse on gustatory taste as well, because thanks to the theories of taste this sense was no longer unworthy of interest, even in its bodily form, as comparisons between the taste of body and of the mind were necessary to thoroughly define the taste of the mind. In the eighteenth century, writers on bodily taste would likewise rely on comparisons with spiritual taste to claim the aesthetic nature and value of taste and cuisine; we saw indeed that the authors of the prefaces of cookbooks drew support from the previous aesthetic theories to claim cookery's access among the fine arts, indicating that these authors were familiar with this theoretical literature on taste.

Finally, one should not forget that the culinary context itself was convenient to the development of interests in taste. As we have seen, French cuisine went through a decisive evolution from the sixteenth and seventeenth centuries onward, which continued into the Enlightenment. At the end of the early modern era, gustatory sensibilities were profoundly remodeled. Jean-Louis Flandrin has demonstrated that the transformations of culinary practices actually reveal a sharper attention to food delicacies among seventeenth- and eighteenth-century eaters. He argues that it is because French people in the classical period enjoyed the pleasures of the table that they started using the word *taste* in other domains, employing a concrete term with an abstract value, which led to an increasing number of taste treatises in the end of the early modern era.[141] According to Flandrin, discussing taste in a figurative sense was actually a way for contemporaries to speak about food delights in a time when the subject was still officially banned from polite conversations. This may well have been the case, of course, although it appears quite difficult to prove. But if the sharper attention to food delicacies might well have had an influence on the transformation of the representations of taste, the explanations of these transformations are likely much more complex. Debates on taste were indeed going on in other European countries as well, like in Britain and Germany, whose culinary history was not exactly the same as in France. What is especially interesting in this context is the cultural reinvention of the concept of taste that took place. Whatever the real causes of this reinvention, it is clear that issues like consumption and food preparation were understood differently and that the sense of taste was reinvented in the context of this new understanding.

A New Aesthetic of Life

What is more, food models and habits of dining—in and out—had changed. First of all, small intimate suppers represented "the archetypal eighteenth-century meal," favoring a more delicate cuisine among the elites.[142] As Florent Quellier underscores, "contrary to the food display of the Renaissance and the *grand siècle* (seventeenth century), the pleasure here [was] above all gustatory, and very secondarily visual and ostentatious," which was another significant evolution since the visual display of banquets in the time of La Varenne.[143] These intimate suppers could take various forms according to the dinner guests. The model private meal as practiced by the regent was also widespread among the libertines, who constantly sought to stimulate the pleasures of each of the five senses, creating an atmosphere of synesthesia where tasty delights, true instruments of seduction, were the prelude to intimacy and lovemaking.[144] The famous figure of Casanova, amateur of aphrodisiac dishes, embodied this trend, while Restif de la Bretonne gladly emphasized the natural connections between the practices of seduction and the delights of the senses—especially taste.[145]

Philosophical dinners represented one among many other forms of private suppers, where the finest cuisine accompanied good wines, freed tongues, and favored intellectual exchanges. According to the participants, the most delicate meal would be worth nothing if not enhanced with the spirit of the dinner guests, the essential salt to the success of a feast. The spiritual and the sensual tastes are no longer divorced from one another (like when the love of food was understood to obscure the brain) but instead now complement and strengthen each other (as eating delicate meals was now thought to reinforce the organs of the eater and liberate the mind). Taste of the body and taste of the mind intensify each other both in action—knowledge on taste led to a higher attention and enjoyment of flavors—and in words—speaking with *esprit*, since from now on one's ideas on taste could and had to be expressed through language.

The attitude of the scholar toward the pleasures of the senses profoundly changed, as exemplified by Voltaire. The renowned philosopher traveled a lot and met people of power and the great minds of his time, which allowed him to savor the delights of the best tables in Europe.[146] Voltaire was the opposite of the ascetic scholar who stereotypically shielded himself from the agitations of the world. On the contrary, he relished the finest food and purchased luxury goods for his cuisine; the philosopher was a prestigious host whose cuisine was recognized for its delicacy, and who liked to call himself "l'Aubergiste de l'Europe" (Europe's innkeeper).[147] Voltaire liked to indulge himself and enjoyed the sensual pleasures of taste as much as those of conversation, which he considered, along with theater, as one of the most refined forms of social life. He celebrated with the same enthusiasm the pleasures of the mind and of the body, "la *bouche parlante* et la *bouche mangeante*" (the talking mouth and the eating mouth).[148]

Shortly before the publication of the Menon's and Marin's controversial culinary texts, Voltaire published *Le Mondain, ou l'Apologie du luxe*[149] (The *Mondain* or the Apology of Luxury), a philosophically inspired poem in verse in which he did not conceal his enthusiasm for the pleasures of *gourmandise*: "Let us have supper;

that these brilliant services, / That these ragoûts are delights to me! / That a Cook is a mortal divine!"[150] Tasty pleasures appeared in this text as expedient for the pleasure of life, as demonstrated by the philosopher's conclusion: "[T]he heavenly paradise is where I am."[151] This provocative statement would lead to his short-term exile but nevertheless reveals the emergence of new values in eighteenth-century France, turned less toward ascetic devotion in preparation for the afterlife than toward the material enjoyments of the present day.

Generally speaking, it was the significance of life that dramatically changed in the eighteenth century. A new aesthetics of life emerged around the prospect of earthly happiness, which could take various forms according to the author.[152] Yet whether happiness would be found in pleasures, peace, reason, virtue, or sensual delight, happiness was a rising value during the Enlightenment, as highlighted in the entry "Bonheur" (happiness) of the Encyclopédie: "All men meet in the desire to be happy. Nature made us to all a law of our own happiness. All which is not happiness is foreign to us; only it has a power marked on our heart; we are all entailed there by a fast slope, by a powerful charm, by a victorious attraction; it is an indelible impression of nature that engraved it in our hearts, it is its charm and perfection."[153] Far from opposing the idea of God, the prospect of earthly happiness appeared as a gift of heaven, a prelude to the enjoyment of the afterlife. Sensualists had previously emphasized the decisive nature of pleasure, which was seen as the mainspring of human knowledge and behavior. Pleasure was easily connected with happiness, which is why many thought that "of all the arts there is not any one more important than that to be happy."[154] Culinary refinement was obviously part of this new cultural movement engaging in the pleasure of living, which became essential in the eighteenth century and still influences so much of contemporary Western ways of thinking and living.[155]

The possibility of earthly felicity encouraged those who had the means to seek, in a kind of hedonistic way, all material pleasures. The Enlightenment revealed an "obvious taste for lavishness and luxury."[156] In the eighteenth century, in the food domain, there were especially rare and exotic ingredients that embodied luxury, such as coffee, tea, and chocolate, but also products like refined wines, which saw great popularity. These luxury goods grew in tandem with debates on the economical and philosophical utility of consumer goods, which were pleasing precisely because they were not necessary.[157] The history of taste therefore intertwines with that of the history of consumption and participated in the development of a consumer society and of individualism, where the search for personal happiness became a social value.

It is clear that the intimacy of taste became increasingly important as one gets closer to the nineteenth century, as evidenced on one hand by the widespread use of the fork and the individual place setting, and on the other hand by the emergence of the restaurant. Rebecca Spang has demonstrated well the new place taste gradually received on the social stage with the *Invention of the Restaurant*.[158] The restaurant allowed the construction of an intimate space for taste where individual choice dominated, dictating the menu and the moment of consumption. Taste hence received a new place on the social scene, where it became the object of distinction and a new lifestyle, where the pleasures of the senses and the enjoyments of the mind combined to make possible the idea of a heaven on Earth.

Taste for Its Own Sake: Toward the Invention of Gastronomy

The new representations of taste, born in the course of the eighteenth century, found their achievement during the next century with the invention of gastronomy, simultaneously a discipline and a literary genre.[159] At that time, the authors of culinary writings did not consider it necessary to express their ideas in the introduction of a cookbook or a pamphlet, or to use an ironic or a playful tone to discuss a matter such as taste. As Frédéric Charbonneau stressed, cuisine—after having been reduced for centuries to the "un-noble" and secondary literature—was for the first time the object of a specific literary genre, celebrating the pleasures of the table, really conferring to taste the status of an object of thought and of discourse.[160] Cookery became a form of poetry, where the words got involved with the flavors to stimulate the sensual imagination of the reader. Gastronomic literature was born. Grimod de La Reynière, author of the *Almanach des gourmands*, published almost every year from 1803 to 1812, is considered as the inventor of *la Littérature gourmande*[161] (gastronomic literature) and of gastronomic critique. The ideas of art and science of taste, ironic when not controversial in the eighteenth century, triumphed after the French Revolution. Grimod de La Reynière spoke of the *grand Art alimentaire*[162] (the great food art) or the *Art de la cuisine*[163] (cookery art), asserting that "gastronomic science has become fashionable."[164] Grimod's perspective went beyond the rhetorical wish of the culinary prefaces from the late 1730s.

To some, such as Antonin Carême, the comparison of cuisine and the fine arts took a more concrete form, like when, in his *Pâtissier pittoresque* (Picturesque Pastry Cook), he compared pastry to architecture, a form of art recognized as the most lasting of all. As highlighted by Michel Delon, "the fragility of food was worth from now on the eternity of the stone. The perishable and edible object gave itself as monument."[165]

Finally, the many decades of discussions about taste and cuisine ultimately led to one of the most famous books ever written on gastronomy: Brillat-Savarin's *Physiologie du goût* [Physiology of Taste]. This work was not, strictly speaking, a cookbook, although the author delivered a few recipes, but actually belonged to a literary genre called the *physiologies*, popular during the first half of the nineteenth century. These were cheap, small-format, illustrated texts written by columnists, writers of vaudeville, and popular novelists nowadays forgotten, apart from Balzac.[166] The *physiologies* addressed the most diverse kinds of topics, from customs to sciences. In his book, Brillat-Savarin investigated the "new science" of gastronomy, the general principles of which he endeavored to specify.[167] He celebrated in particular those few individuals gifted with a refined taste, capable of perceiving the slightest nuances among flavors—an ability, he says, that most people lacked. These experts could be identified with "gastronomic test tubes" (particularly delicious dishes) that, based on whether they gave the eater pleasure, revealed those connoisseurs endowed with a superior sensibility; for indeed "there is also the blind and the deaf in the empire of flavors."[168] However, it is noteworthy to stress that for a long time the blind and deaf in the realm of taste had no lexical existence. It is significant that the word *ageusia*, which refers to the loss of the sense of taste, only appeared in the nineteenth century. Cuisine and taste had acquired by then a higher cultural and social meaning that made it necessary to have an appropriate word to refer to the gustatory handicap, nonexistent until then, whereas the words *deaf* and *blind* had existed for centuries.[169]

The knowledge associated with taste from the eighteenth century onward had deepened. Far from being a simple sensual pleasure, gastronomy was defined as "the reasoned knowledge of all which has report to the man, as he feeds."[170] This knowledge was intellectual as much as physical, just like the sense of taste itself, now considered a dual entity. A proper human dimension of taste was now commonly recognized. Consequently, "of all creatures . . . the man is the one whose taste is the most perfect. . . . The animals are limited in their tastes; some only live of vegetables, others only eat meat; others feed exclusively on seeds; none of them knows composite flavors. . . . Gourmandise is the exclusive privilege of the man."[171] The animality of taste gave way to gastronomy, the realization of which was made possible by the development of culture, revealing human taste's superiority to animals' palates as well as to the palates of less educated people. This was the reason why taste, far from being a trivial subject, was seen as a subject of study that should be reserved for the greatest minds:

> As long as the cooks only reserved this matter to themselves and one only wrote "dispensaires" [collections of pharmaceutical formulas], the results of these works were solely the products of an art. But finally, too late maybe, the scholars approached. They examined, analyzed, and classified foodstuffs, reduced them to their simplest elements. They sounded the mysteries of assimilation, and following the inert matter in its metamorphoses, they saw how it could take life. . . . They

appreciated its influence [of diet] so far as on the faculty to think, either that the soul is impressed by the senses, or that it feels without the help of these organs; and of all these works they deducted a high theory, which embraces all man and all part of the creation which can animalize itself.[172]

The access of cuisine to the rank of art meant that it could be represented by "Gastérea ... the tenth muse," who "presides over the enjoyments of taste."[173] After all, "taste, such as nature granted to us, is still the one of our senses which, all things considered, provides us the highest delights."[174]

Conclusion: Taste of the Body and Taste of the Mind

One can henceforth conclude that a real transformation of the representations of taste occurred in the eighteenth century, as evidenced by the number of innovative discourses on the sense of taste that constituted real philosophical and scientific essays on cookery and taste. Culinary practices had certainly evolved from the mid-seventeenth century onward, but in the late 1730s these discourses especially constituted a revolution. Considerations of taste did not just concern the culinary universe any longer but also interested the polite reading public at large—from cooks, artisans, and traders to writers, philosophers, and doctors—in short, anyone who wanted to appear as enlightened.

For a long time, gustation was left at the peripheries of knowledge. The first theories of taste in the late seventeenth century just briefly mentioned bodily taste, while focusing on aesthetic and spiritual forms of taste, connected mainly to the eyes, the ears, and the mind. A few decades later, on the contrary, it was physical taste itself that became for the first time the center of intellectual debates. Discourses on gustation were by then inspired by various facets of contemporary knowledge, originating mainly from the scientific and medical fields on the one hand, and from aesthetic theories on the other hand. The ideal cuisine was thought of as the locus of a chemistry of taste, the object of an art (that of the harmony of flavors) and of a science (the knowledge of the properties of food and of the functioning of the taste sensation). The result, according to cooks, was to provide dishes better for digestion and thus for health, as well as dishes that were more delightful to savor. The knowledge provided through the sense of taste was both a sensory and intellectual knowledge, practical and theoretical, a knowledge in which elite cooks and a minority of connoisseurs were experts. The comments on *nouvelle cuisine* were often ironic, sometimes political, but they nevertheless reveal the emergence of a new culture of taste. The stakes were significant because taste was not only peculiar to the animal nature of men; it wasn't just an object of a bodily need anymore. Rather, the sense of taste had acquired a much higher cultural and social value, especially as this sense was now at the center of debates regarding the relationship between body and soul, one of the oldest debates in Western philosophical thought. Food played a considerable role in this context, since it could act on thought through the means of the spirits.

The late seventeenth and eighteenth centuries represented a key moment in the history of the gustatory sense because it was at that time that the sense modality of taste was built for the first time as a dual entity, with a spiritual taste and a bodily taste seen as two complementary parts of one same sense modality; the sharp discernment of the former answered the sensual delicacy of the latter. Sight and hearing, traditionally considered as higher senses, consisted for centuries with this double identity—sensory and intellectual—which endowed them with a certain nobility, a value that taste lacked for a long time. The invention of a taste of the mind—the spiritual counterpart of gustation—may have been the very reason that made possible a celebratory discourse on the bodily sense of taste, depreciated for so long. Eating well became as important as thinking well. It was a form of judgment that displayed a higher discernment and that was a part from now on of the art of living in the Enlightenment. With the culinary "lights," taste left the material lowness to become a tangible sign of civilization's progress.[175]

A new rhetoric was invented that pleaded at the same time for a learned sophistication of cookery—which was illustrated in particular by chemical references—and for simplicity. It would seem moreover that the authors of the culinary writings of this time would have a long-lasting influence on the rhetoric of cookery in the whole history of gastronomy, up until today. The formula of *nouvelle cuisine*, just like the rhetoric that was connected with it, is indeed a recurring formula in food history. Those who would wish to appear as innovators would successively be inspired by these discourses in the future. Escoffier, at the beginning of the twentieth century, would repeat numerous slogans of the promoters of eighteenth-century *nouvelle cuisine*, as did the gourmets of the 1970s and of today. Whatever the context in which the expression *nouvelle cuisine* appears, it would seem that the same double reference to something more learned and simpler emerges. *Nouvelle cuisine* systematically presents itself as more favorable to the truth of food, reachable by science, which is of use to the growth and to the maintenance of the body. It aims to be an intellectual, abstract, cultural place, where nature and science agree, where the real truth of food and the most refined sophistication are reconciled.

However, the *modernity* of cuisine was not unanimously celebrated. Certain authors, such as Rousseau and the Chevalier de Jaucourt, on the contrary considered culinary refinement as the indication of a cultural decline, a sign of corruption of the goods of nature. Others, like Desalleurs, laughed at cooks' boldness; for him, these were simple craftsmen who dared to appear as scholars or artists. These debates reveal the insertion of taste within the framework of the Quarrel between the Ancient and the Modern. The opposition was lively and highlights the deep hesitation in the Enlightenment between the partisans of tradition—condemnatory of this new sophistication and supportive of more natural, instinctive food—and the promoters of progress, who saw the art of cooking as a justifiable enjoyment. In this culture dominated by naturalism, the question of taste was instrumental as symbolic of the dialectic between nature—(whether considered generous or corrupted) and culture (whether culture refers to progress through luxury or social decline), revealing the always lively presence of the dualisms, in spite of the appearance of philosophies that, like sensualism or materialism, had denounced its intellectual foundations. Or perhaps food is naturally a matter for polemics?

In any case, whether condemned or celebrated, taste was the object of an extensive production of texts in the eighteenth century, after having been left at the peripheries of knowledge for centuries. The turn of the late seventeenth century corresponds to the passage of the "silences" of taste—with all the nuances this supposes—to new discourses on taste.[176] From this moment, taste freed itself from the limited frame of culinary literature as the only appropriate place of expression. The observations of the *nouvelle cuisine* were certainly published within cookbooks, but they mobilized very rich knowledge borrowed from very different areas of expertise: chemistry, aesthetics, dietetics, physiology, empiricism, and sensualism. Besides, these texts were read by the whole cultivated elite, as indicated by numerous allusions in the most diverse sources.

The improvement of French culinary art had changed representations and attitudes toward food. The emergence of a figurative sense of taste generated plentiful discussions and contributed to transform the former figure of a material and animal sense into a full sense modality, a form of dialogue between the senses and the mind, body and thought, a reconciliation between the physicality and the interiority of taste. This sense modality was characterized by immediacy, ineffability, individuality, and emotional sensibility. The gustatory metaphors gave taste its respectability, authorizing speeches on the very art of cooking. The philosophers of the Enlightenment, such as Voltaire and Diderot, focused in their writings on the figurative sense of taste and its place in the judgment of beauty. But in their everyday life, they embraced the attitude of true gourmets and were frequent dinner guests at the finest meals. The pleasures of the body and the mind, the eating and the talking mouth combined, gave rise to a lifestyle that was also an aesthetics of life in the eighteenth century. *Gourmandise* ceased to be a sin to be hidden; it became a mark of intellectual distinction that one displayed for others. The evolution continued in the nineteenth century, when changes in representations were translated by the invention of new practices and new vocabulary. A new discipline, gastronomy, was created to refer to the knowledge of culinary delicacy. In this way, taste entered literature in the shape of the gastronomic discourse, appealing to the imagination and to the qualities of writing. At the same time, a word was created to refer to the deprivation of the sense of taste, ageusia, whereas for centuries the absence of an appropriate term did not seem to have mattered. In the eighteenth century, the sense of taste, a complex sense modality, had left the peripheries of the sensible to become the object of discourse that positively celebrated taste as the object of a human distinction.

Conclusion

Taste must indeed be discussed and disputed, as it is a profoundly
dialogical form of experience.
—Weiss, *Feast and Folly*, 87

Taste is a deeply idiosyncratic sense. Yet although taste is one of the most intimate sensations one can have, it does not mean that taste is not worth being
discussed. Today there is no doubt that Western contemporary societies have
a thriving interest—a passion even—for topics related to food, taste, and gastronomy. Nowadays, people are as fond of eating refined cuisine as they are of
debating their personal preferences and sharing their opinion—their enthusiasm, as much as their anxiety—about the present and future of food-related
matters. However, discussing taste has not always been such a natural social
and cultural practice as it is today; intellectuals and experts of all sorts have
not always so openly displayed their interest in food and taste. For centuries,
there was very little to be debated about taste, which was considered a "lower
sense" and therefore kept at the peripheries of knowledge. In the beginning of
this research, I was challenged by the surprisingly frequent absence of early
modern discourses on the bodily sense of taste, a phenomenon that I have
referred to by using the expression "the silences of taste." Silences of taste were
especially striking outside the culinary universe in more general writings on
sensibilities. Words and discourse on the sense of taste were scarce, and this
scarcity was suggestive, for it was one among many other indications that taste
was for a long time not considered a matter of interest worthy of scholars and
readers of the polite world.

Taste was traditionally conceived as a lower sense, probably, as I have argued,
the lowest sense of all. The absence of words and gestures referring to the vile
pleasures of gustation can be deliberate—as, for instance, when they concern
social rules dictated by etiquette or by books of manners—or indirect—such as
when cooks implicitly reveal their uneasiness in celebrating a sense too easily
associated with the sin of gluttony. But the silences of taste are most often not

immediately perceptible and are disclosed only by discreet signs: the concision, if not the lack of an entire chapter, on taste in the treatises of the senses; the exclusion of taste when theorists listed examples using the four other senses to emphasize general knowledge about sensory experience; the nonexistence, for centuries, of a specific word to refer to the lack of taste. The lower esteem of taste is also revealed through the tendency of authors investigating the senses to systematically consider taste within the framework of a sensory association with touch or smell. The easy association of taste with other senses makes of taste the *most relational sense*,[1] but this is also one of the reasons for the silences of taste: referring to taste by way of another sense was a way of avoiding a more thorough chapter on taste itself—as if taste alone was not worth investigating.

I have used the expression "the silences of taste" to refer to this cultural system, characterized by a tenuous presence of gustation in the general discourses relating to the senses. This expression must, of course, not be taken literally. A low interest in matters of taste certainly does not mean that people of the time did not enjoy eating or that there was absolutely no discussion at all on this subject. Food historians have highlighted the deep transformations of cuisine and taste sensibilities that occurred in the sixteenth and seventeenth centuries, during which medieval food practices evolved toward a modern art of cookery, which was presented as powerfully new in its culinary practices as well as in its books. Cooks were by then spreading new discourses celebrating taste and cuisine, which constituted the first examples of positive gustatory writings before the emergence of gastronomic literature in the nineteenth century. Culinary pleasures and discussions on taste seemed to flourish in this context—and indeed, they did. But outside of the proper culinary universe, taste was left at the margins of knowledge; the gustatory sense, culturally and historically, was seen as a lower sense, which made it a vulgar subject unworthy of interest for a long time. The inscription of the question of taste within a more general perspective hence reveals the deep tension existing in the early modern era between a nascent trend toward culinary celebration and a wider movement of depreciation of gustation, marked by the scarcity of words on taste.

In the past, gustation had been disturbing and despised when not simply silenced. Closely connected to the satisfaction of a bodily need, taste was primarily bothersome because of its material nature. Physical necessities naturally come along with pleasure, which easily leads to conspicuous consumption and generates dramatic consequences, one of these being the sin of gluttony—easily confused with the sense through which this sin occurs. The most diverse sources denounce the disorders and dangers of the mouth, as evidenced by the bestiary of greedy animals and the recurring figures of crazy gluttons of history. Cranes, ducks, turkeys, bears, pigs, wolves, and cats, along with Philoxenus, Apicius, Heliogabalus, and all the other voracious gluttons of history, illustrate well the extent to which gluttony took all the space, leaving the sense of taste and its potential expertise largely unexplored. The leading representation of taste was that of a disorder, revealing the permeability of the borders between humanity and animality. If not kept under control, gustatory pleasures were dangers to virtue, health, intelligence, and even to sensory pleasures themselves, threatening the order of God, of the world, and of the men and women affected by the bestial and demonic universes. Consequently, doctors, philosophers, men of God, and men of the polite world, as well as moralists and cooks, all constantly insisted on a necessary *mediocritas* (moderation) with regard to food. This recommendation is present everywhere, in all periods, all contexts, and by the most diverse authors from antiquity up until today. The stereotype of moderation is obviously adapted according to the context considered, but it is always implicitly present where bodily taste is concerned, as a kind of necessary barrier against the drift of gustation.

As demonstrated above, the association of taste with the sin of gluttony is not the only reason for taste's low esteem; there are deeper reasons explaining this distrust. Taste was mainly despised because it referred to the body, to matter, and to bestiality—all ambiguous objects in the early modern era, which inherited of a long philosophical and religious tradition characterized by dualism. Western culture is deeply influenced by this opposition between the conoible and the intelligible, an opposition that inevitably affected gustatory representations; the history of dualisms hence enlightens the history of taste. In the Renaissance, the understanding of the world was articulated by way of analogy. By then, taste had found its place within a rich universe of signs: the four temperaments, the four humors, the chain of being, the ages of life, the four elements, and the four seasons meant that flavors were distributed within a complex system in which the taste sensation was considered an indication of something else. For the human as for the animal, the gustatory sense was a necessary sense, intended to naturally distinguish edible elements from poisons. Flavors were thus thought to reveal the qualities the food would bring to the body, and the palate was a trustworthy organ for individual diet as well as for medical diagnosis. Consequently, culinary likes and dislikes were not supposed to be impeded, as evidenced by the liberty provided by the *service à la française*, leaving the eaters free to choose dishes according to their own temperament.

In the seventeenth century, the analogical system was gradually abandoned in favor of naturalism, notably due to the influence of Descartes. This was the moment of the *grand partage*, which installed a greater distance between humans and their environment and transformed all former representations of the world. Man was the only being allegedly endowed with interiority, a soul, thoughts, and reason. He was parted from then on from his environment, enabling the emergence of the idea of Nature. Humans shared the same physicality with non–human beings, existing within a body-machine. Taste belonged to this universal dimension of physicality, revealing the closeness of humanity with the animal realm, while losing in this context the value of a sign that characterized this lower sense until then; taste did not provide clear and distinct ideas and was perceived as useless to the development of knowledge and the sciences. From then on, diet was no longer determined by sensations or by temperaments but by reason—not by the eater but by his doctor. As a consequence, diversity of food would not be justified anymore by medical reasons but by gustatory pleasure. Taste was not the sign of anything else anymore, which is the reason why it was rejected to the peripheries of knowledge, along with the body, animals, and the materiality of the world. The Church's influence, especially powerful in the seventeenth century in the context of Catholic reform, only accentuated the depreciation of the senses that was concurrently established outside the religious domain.

Cartesian ideas would be increasingly questioned in the late seventeenth and early eighteenth centuries. The most radical opposition came from empiricism and sensualism, which brought the senses back to the center of philosophical investigations and weakened the dualistic system of thought, though without ever destroying it completely. Taste was a good specimen for Locke to prove that it was necessary to feel in order to think, and thus to taste in order to know—although taste did not produce the most useful knowledge, which explains the poverty of language concerning flavors. Although taste did not really receive much attention in the works of Locke and Condillac, even as touch was truly revalued in the Enlightenment, the intense intellectual interest regarding sensory experience in the eighteenth century necessarily influenced the ways in which taste itself was conceived. The former idea of a hierarchy of the senses was being questioned in favor of the idea of collaboration between the senses, while the traditional representation of "necessary" senses was now endowed with a more positive value. Taste became the sense of sensual delight, the gift of a providential nature providing through pleasure the satisfaction of bodily needs.

At the same time, in the late seventeenth and early eighteenth centuries, a new discourse appeared on taste that was instrumental in transforming this sense into a dual entity. Having been limited for centuries to a physical dimension, taste was finally endowed with a figurative meaning that inspired a variety of metaphors at the origin of an extensive literature; the mystical "taste of God," the *bon goût* of the *honnête homme*, and the aesthetic "taste" represented three important moments of this history. Despite their obvious differences, these metaphors indicate the birth of a form of spiritual taste closely bound to bodily taste. Both were intimately linked, creating a tension between two dimensions, which in their differences revealed a particular form of knowledge of the world characterized by the ineffability, the immediacy, the emotional, and the individual. The previous features of taste responsible for a depreciation of this lower sense were completely transfigured, endowing the new sense modality with a higher value. The absence of distance between the object and subject of perception that formerly led to the depreciation of this sense of contact was from now on conceived as the source of an immediate knowledge that was felt even before being thought. The silences of taste connected to a low materiality gave way to the ineffability of a sense modality that went beyond language. Taste was no longer only a matter of a shared physicality between humans and animals, according to the principles defended by naturalism. Its status had changed because it now also required the participation of the mind, henceforth also belonging to human interiority, being a specific kind of knowledge of the world inaccessible to animals.

Taste was more precisely defined as discernment based on a system of comparisons. First, taste was naturally a culinary discernment. Modern cuisine intended to reveal the "true taste" of food by highlighting each and every ingredient, in contrast to the allegedly disgusting culinary profusions and excesses of older practices. The lexicon of discernment, order, nature, and simplicity—peculiar to the aesthetics of classicism—was opposed to that of confusion, assimilated to the past, occasion of a variety of quarrels between the Ancients and the Moderns. Second, taste was also a moral discernment, that of the *honnête homme* touched by a form of grace, a man of *bon goût*, a quality allowing him to instinctively know the appropriate behavior and conversation to adopt in all circumstances. Third, taste became an aesthetic discernment, a judgment of beauty based upon the body and the mind, allowing one to identify valuable works of art.

Each of these theoretical works was certainly related to quite a different form of taste, but they nevertheless created a new space in which to discuss the bodily sense as well. In treatises of taste, the gustatory sense appeared at first only in the background, the main object of investigation being the taste of the mind. Yet in order to clarify the nature of spiritual taste, theorists systematically returned back to physical taste, the origin of multiple metaphors of taste. *From Gluttony to Enlightenment* argues that it was precisely these debates on spiritual taste that facilitated and yielded new discussions on bodily taste itself. Bodily taste became the main object of debates later on, like in the innovative discourses published in the late 1730s recipe books of *nouvelle cuisine*, which leaned on arguments previously stressed by (spiritual) taste theorists. In these discourses, as well as in other contemporary writings, bodily and spiritual tastes were reconciled and presented as two complementary parts of the same sense modality. An ideal configuration of the organs inside the body led as much to a refined taste in the perception of flavors as to a delicate taste in the appreciation of beauty. Taste was hence considerably rehabilitated during the eighteenth century and became an important focus of interest to scholars and polite readers, who were concerned about food and the ideal diet as well as about displaying an exquisite taste of the mind, notably in public conversations. People were now "tasting the world," which meant knowing the world with the body and with the mind; the one did not go without the other. Knowledge and science were as important as the pleasure of the senses. Sensualists had previously emphasized how intertwined these actually were. At table, words as much as flavors heightened the imagination and displayed *l'esprit* (wit) of the dinner guests. A poetics of food appeared, in which to know and to discuss cuisine was a way of savoring even more. As Allen Weiss stresses, "for any art, in particular that of the table, knowledge increases pleasure."[2]

The connection between the talking mouth and the tasting mouth had long been underscored in a variety of sources. But this connection did not always come along with a positive value. In a period during which gustation was despised, the union between the talking and tasting mouth was presented in a rather negative way. In sixteenth-century emblems, for instance, the sin of gluttony often led to the *péché de langue* (sin of the tongue), embodied by a greedy and screaming duck. The association remained but was then turned upside-down in the eighteenth century, when the harmony between tasting and talking testified on the contrary to a higher form of human distinction, embodied by an elite group of true connoisseurs.

All these discourses celebrating taste that spread in the eighteenth century only became possible because taste, for long confined to the strict dimension of physicality, the foundation of its bestiality, became equipped with a form of interiority, thought of as a human prerogative. The relegation of the animal part of taste was accompanied by the progressive disappearance of references to the bestiary from manner books and dictionaries, revealing the internalization of a radical difference that did not need to be said anymore: the difference between humans and animals. But in this process of rejection of the animal universe, bodily taste also lost a more positive dimension that had formerly qualified this sense, which allowed it to identify through pleasure the most favorable food for the body. From now on, physicians argued that only medical experts were able to determine the therapeutic quality of food, which was inaccessible knowledge to the misleading judgment of the palate—although cooks would keep on pleading for their own expertise. At the same time, the lower senses, which were ancient medicine's instruments of diagnosis, were little by little replaced by techniques perceived as safer—that is, more readily employing the sense of sight.

From the moment the human dimension of taste became more clearly emphasized and disjointed from its animal dimension, taste could receive more attention, as indicated by the emergence of a new public. If in the mid-seventeenth century it was most often the cooks who wrote the prefaces of their cookbooks, in the eighteenth century, the authors who published dissertations on taste and cuisine were professional writers who had nothing to do with the culinary universe, which demonstrates—or contributed to—the enhancement of cookery on the social stage. At first, culinary literature, a privileged place for gustatory discourses, was the only type of source revealing this process. But new conceptions of taste soon extended beyond the culinary register to concern all domains of knowledge. Taste became a subject of interest not only to cooks but also to scholars, philosophers, writers, and other thinkers—including churchmen—as well as polite readers. The extension of the public concerned with matters of taste is a significant indication of the cultural transformation of the representations of this sense. Taste had left the peripheries of knowledge to stand out as a new sense modality, a true grace possessed by elite connoisseurs only.

In the end, the seventeenth and eighteenth centuries represented a crucial period of transformations of the ways in which the sense of taste was conceived. Food historians had long underscored the revolution of sensibilities that occurred during the sixteenth and seventeenth centuries, ratifying the transition between a medieval and a modern art of cookery. *From Gluttony to Enlightenment*'s suggestion is that there was another, perhaps even more significant, upheaval that happened just a little later: the invention and construction of taste as a sense modality, constituted for the first time as a dual entity, uniting body and soul. Both the higher senses of sight and hearing were endowed for a long time with a physical and spiritual dimension; this was the case also for the sense of smell. Taste, on the other hand, was for centuries reduced to mere materiality. Associated with the human mind and with sensibility, taste gradually became a specific form of knowledge of the world. Actually, much further into the past, in Latin the word *sapor*—flavor—referred during antiquity to *sapere*—which meant to know and to savor in the sense of enjoying, tasting—as well as to *sapientia*—to encounter wisdom. Taste thus had already constituted at this point a particular form of knowledge associated with intelligence, just like smell. Constance Classen argues that "taste and smell furnish two basic terms of intelligence: sapience and sagacious. In Latin, taste did not merely stand for a sense of aesthetic discrimination, as in English, but for the faculty of intelligence. The verb to taste, *sapere*, also meant to know, giving us our sapience—wisdom—and sage—wise person. Thus *homo sapiens* is not only 'knowing man,' but also 'tasting man' . . . even the supposedly lower senses of taste and smell can stand for intellectual processes."[3] This is a quite surprising association, for in Western cultures it was most generally sight that was connected with knowledge. In the early modern era, the etymology of flavor was, however, forgotten: no allusion to the relations between flavor, knowledge, and wisdom can be found in the dictionary of Rochefort or the *Dictionnaire de l'Académie françoise*. Although Nicot, Furetière, and Richelet quickly mention in their entries dedicated to the term *saveur* (flavor) that this word comes from the Latin one, *sapor*, they do not deliver any translation or any further comment on what this origin might imply. One can only find a few discreet indications here and there that testify once in a while to this antique origin.[4] The new sense modality of taste established in the eighteenth century thus seems somehow to rehabilitate an ancestral value—since taste also appears as a form of knowledge in the Enlightenment—while exceeding the limits formerly attributed to the gustatory sense, as there was, at that time, also a proper taste of the mind.

The celebration of taste was, however, never unanimous. For other writers, such as Fontenelle, Descartes, and Kant, there was no possibility of knowledge through taste, which was seen as a deceitful sense only useful for enjoying, and not knowing, the world. Besides, many—for instance, Rousseau and the Chevalier de Jaucourt—criticized the sophisticated knowledge and practices displayed by believers in *nouvelle cuisine* while promoting a sober life closer to nature. The depreciation of gustation thus never totally disappeared, even in the eighteenth and nineteenth centuries, and indeed may still be found today—we may wonder, for instance, when considering the unbalanced interest toward each of the five senses today, if the "hierarchy of the senses" has really completely disappeared from our contemporary cultures. The history of taste, like any cultural history, is necessarily full of multiple and conflicting representations.

Furthermore, it would seem that there is a more structural dimension in the devaluation of taste: even when it is celebrated, taste never completely graduates from the peripheries of knowledge. One indication, among others, of this devaluation, besides the constant emphasis on moderation against the disorders of the mouth, is taste's (especially *gourmandise*'s) association with childhood.[5] Treatises of civility make it clear: manners are to be particularly strict in order to control the drives of the stomach, a control that needs to be acquired from the youngest age. The person who, once an adult, did not learn to master his or her appetite revealed a weakness and inability to govern the body by reason. Moreover, the figure of the child was frequently used in empiricist passages relating specifically to taste. John Locke, for example, readily referred to the example of the flavors felt by the child at the youngest age as an argument against innate ideas. Rousseau, among others, would also consider *gourmandise* the passion of childhood. This common view is so prevalent that one sometimes finds it as well in the figurative version of taste: Teresa of Avila considered the spiritual tastes as peculiar to the childhood of the soul on the path toward contemplation. Moreover, taste also frequently referred to the feminine universe, a phenomenon already emphasized by Korsmeyer, Classen, and Quellier.[6] The history of taste thus discloses a history of silences and of the margins. Even when intellectualized, gustatory knowledge is utterly instinctive, immediate, and irrational, supplied by a necessary, ineffable sense of contact. Figures of the woman (holy or witch), of the "savage," of the animal or the crazy glutton, the child, and the boorish all reveal taste to be a sense of the peripheries. Yet it is the same sense that would later be retranslated to embody the summit of human distinction: the aesthetic taste, denied for a long time to these categories of beings described as "inferiors," who were previously readily associated with the animal and bodily sense of taste. In contrast, a domesticated, intellectualized taste took shape, which became an object of discourse peculiar to a minority of connoisseurs. The figures of the *friand*, the gourmet, and the man of taste appeared, concealing the older idea of taste as a lower sense (which, however, never totally disappears).

For a long time, the absence of distance peculiar to a sense of contact made of taste an unreliable and unworthy sense. But it would be the same proximity between self and the world that would later make taste valuable in a society gradually promoting the cult of individualism. The history of taste also obviously participated in the construction of the modern subject. In the first chapters of this book, the texts we encountered were produced within a culture in which community represented an essential social and cultural value and in which signs of individuality were not socially approved. Such an idiosyncratic sense as that of taste could hardly be openly expressed in this context. This is one of the many reasons why personal preferences were not supposed to be communicated at the table, as conduct books clearly indicated. Also, the phenomenon of holy anorexia, as well as mystical writings, was disturbing at the time, for these revealed a unique experience peculiar to an exceptional soul, isolated in its privilege to "taste God." Yet a conflicting movement gradually emerged, revealing a trend toward displaying the singularity of the subject; in this movement, to exhibit one's tastes in cookery, art, and knowledge started to be increasingly valued. In the eighteenth century, even those who criticized the exaggerated delicacy of cuisine and who pleaded a return to nature demonstrated just as well their individuality, and displayed the same kind of self-fashioning actions as those who celebrated modern cuisine. Taste is by definition a "sense of differentiation,"[7] as it distinguishes the good from the bad—a dimension of taste thoroughly investigated by Pierre Bourdieu in his book *La Distinction*. As Gaëtan Brulotte explains, "while defining identity, taste consequently contributes to the construction of the otherness."[8]

Discourses on taste are not only words but also active forces endowed with a power of performativity, modeling both sensibilities and attitudes or ideas. The polite man who in the seventeenth century did not speak about taste because he had internalized the principles of politeness shows just as much his membership in a cultural elite as the eighteenth-century philosopher who would not hesitate to publicly display his culinary refinement in a time when this kind of behavior was expected. In the end, taste would therefore be celebrated for the very reasons that had formerly led to its dismissal.

In sum, the cultural history of taste obviously extends far beyond the history of food, cookery, and gastronomy. More than the history of a sense, *From Gluttony to Enlightenment* discloses the history of the relationship between early modern actors and the world. Using a multitude of sources borrowed from diverse registers, this study reveals the multiple connections that gustation actually maintained within universes apparently very remote from food, such as philosophy, medicine, mystics, demonology, and aesthetics. Despite their many differences, polite readers, mystics, philosophers, doctors, and cooks shared the same culture, and together disclose the transformation of the cultural representations of the sense of taste, from a lower animalistic and bodily sense into a sense modality, embodying the refinement of the human mind, employing knowledge of the body and of the soul. During the early modern era, a new experience of the sense of taste spread and was organized at the same time in religious, literary, and philosophical fields. As a result, the cultural definition of taste diversified, which authorized a new legitimacy of taste and cuisine. The invention of gastronomy was thus not only due to the mere evolution of cookery practices but also results from a much vaster cultural phenomenon.

Interestingly, taste became part of wider debates of crucial importance in the history of Western thinking, such as debates regarding the relationship between nature and culture, humans and nonhumans, progress and decline, the individual and society, and the singular and the universal—all important debates through which taste challenged the idea of a hierarchy of the senses. In this respect, taste is a quite peculiar sense that escapes the traditional divisions into well-defined categories. Taste obviously resists and questions the cultural construction of the hierarchy of the senses, within which this sense functions differently from the other ones: where to place taste when this sense ceases to be strictly material? Indeterminate, taste is a *je ne sais quoi* that ends up blurring all categories, cracking the carefully organized system dividing nature and culture, man and animal, sky and earth, material and spiritual, sensible and intelligible.

In the end, between silences and celebrations, *From Gluttony to Enlightenment* discloses a fragmented history of a sense that, despite its lower esteem, nevertheless highlights the beauty of the ephemeral, reminding us that we are perishable beings, inviting us to taste the world, just here and just now.

Notes

Introduction: De Gustibus Non Est Disputandum?

1. Havelange, *De l'œil et du monde*, 8.

2. Furetière, *Dictionnaire universel*, vol. 2, fol. T2 v, s.v. "Goust." There are marginal occurrences of a figurative sense of taste to be found since antiquity, but metaphorical references to taste did not really enter common usage before the seventeenth century.

3. "It also means the ways in which a thing is done, the particular character of a work. This work is of good taste, this furniture is of good taste, of bad taste." *Dictionnaire de l'Académie françoise*, vol. 1, 1694, 529, s.v. "Goust." All source translations are mine unless otherwise indicated.

4. Taste thus designates the "discernment, the refinement of judgment." *Dictionnaire de l'Académie françoise*, vol. 1, 1694, 529, s.v. "Goust."

5. Furetière, *Dictionnaire universel*, vol. 2, T3 v, s.v. "Gouster."

6. However, philosophers have recently started to investigate the bodily sense as well, following the lead of Carolyn Korsmeyer's *Making Sense of Taste*. For example, Champion, *Hors-d'oeuvre*.

7. On the historiography of food history, see Claflin and Scholliers, *Writing Food History*, notably the introduction and conclusion, as well as Claflin, "Food among the Historians." Also see Becker, *Studia Alimentorum*; Scholliers, "Twenty-five Years of Studying."

8. Scholliers, "The Many Rooms in the House," 61.

9. Parasecoli and Scholliers, *A Cultural History of Food*; Meyzie, *L'alimentation en Europe*; Quellier, *La Table des Français*; Albala, *Food in Early Modern Europe*; Flandrin and Montanari, *Food: A Culinary History*; Wheaton, *Savoring the Past*; Bonnet, "Les manuels de cuisine." There are specific bibliographic repertoires related to the rich production of food studies. See especially *The Food Bibliography* (http://www .foodbibliography.eu) launched in 2007 by the European Institute for the History and Cultures of Food (IEHCA), the Villa I Tatti of Florence (The Harvard University Center

for Italian Renaissance Studies), the Mellon Foundation, and the Bibliothèque Nationale de France (BNF).

10. Karila-Cohen and Quellier, *Le corps du gourmand*; Quellier, *Gourmandise*; Pinkard, *A Revolution in Taste*; Meyzie, *La gourmandise*; Freedman, *Food: The History of Taste*; Ferguson, *Accounting for Taste*; Flandrin, "La distinction par le goût," "Pour une histoire du goût," "La diversité des goûts"; Redon, Sallmann, and Steinberg, *Le désir et le Goût*.

11. There are a few exceptions, such as Spary, *Eating the Enlightenment*; Ferguson, "The Senses of Taste"; Korsmeyer, *Making Sense of Taste*; Chiou, *Homo gastronomicus*. I would like to thank Emma Spary for giving me a foretaste of her book before its official publication, Der-Liang Chiou for sending me an electronic copy of his thesis, and Georges Vigarello for recommending me this latter work.

12. Freedman, *Food: The History of Taste*, 7.

13. For example Classen, *A Cultural History of the Senses*; Krampl, Beck, and Retaillaud-Bajac, *Les Cinq sens de la ville*; "The Senses in History," *American Historical Review*; Gelard, *Usages et langages des sens*; Gelard and Sirost, *Langages des sens*; Quiviger, *The Sensory World*; Smith, *Sensing the Past*; Howes, *Empire of the Senses*; *I cinque sensi*; Summers, *The Judgment of Sense*.

14. Howes, *Sensual Relations*, 29; Howes, *Empire of the Senses*, 1.

15. Havelange, *De l'œil et du monde*; Classen, *Color of Angels*.

16. Corbin, *Le Miasme et la Jonquille*; Le Guérer, *Les Pouvoirs de l'Odeur*; Jaquet, *Philosophie de l'Odorat*; Dugan, *The Ephemeral History of Perfume*. Also see the collective research held by Classen, Howes, and Synnott on *Aroma: The Cultural History of Smell*. The three authors are members of the *Centre for Sensory Studies*, Concordia University, Montréal, http://www.centreforsensorystudies.org.

17. Rosenfeld, *Revolution in Language*; Rosenfeld, "Deaf Men on Trial"; Fritz, *Paysages sonores*; Corbin, *Les Cloches de la Terre*; Murray Schaffer, *The Tuning of the World*. Also see Carter, "The Sound of Silence"; Kisby, "Introduction"; Gutton, *Bruits et sons dans notre histoire*.

18. Additionally, several multisensory works related to all five senses often dedicate a place to taste, but taste systematically occupies a minor position compared to the other senses. Howes, *Empire of the Senses*; Jütte, *A History of the Senses*; Ackerman, *A Natural History of the Senses*; Bynum and Porter, *Medicine and the Five Senses*; Classen, *Worlds of Sense*; Nordenfalk, "The Five Senses"; Vinge, *The Five Senses*; Kermode, "The Banquet of Senses." This is, however, not the case in Serres, *Les cinq sens* and Smith, *Sensing the Past*. Recently, the study of touch is also starting to become an important research topic. See especially Moshenska, *Feeling Pleasures*; Classen, *The Deepest Sense*; Classen, *The Book of Touch*; Harvey, *Sensible Flesh*; O'Rourke Boyle, *Senses of Touch*.

19. Several scholars also underscore the gendered dimension linked to the qualification of the senses, where the lower senses tended to be closely connected to women's sensuality, while the higher senses were recognized as part of masculine rationality. Classen, "The Witch's Senses"; Korsmeyer, *Making Sense of Taste*, 30–36.

20. Du Laurens, *Discours de la conservation de la veüe*, 36.

21. "[T]aste and touch act by contact, while the other senses act from a distance." Aristotle, *De Anima*, 40 [423a].

22. Korsmeyer, *Making Sense of Taste*, 11.

23. The context can change along with the justifications. In the eighteenth century, for instance, sensualists would question the reliability of sight precisely because it never reaches its object; the eyes therefore need the warranty of touch to confirm their perception of the world. But in the beginning of the early modern era, taste, a contact sense, was held in lower esteem, as chapter 3 explains.

24. Havelange, *De l'œil et du monde*.

25. Febvre, "La sensibilité et l'histoire"; Mandrou, *Introduction à la France moderne*, chapter 3, "L'homme psychique: sens, sensations, émotions, passions," 75–89.

26. Smith, *Sensing the Past*, 2.

27. These are distinctions, one should keep in mind, that do not make much sense in most non-Western civilizations.

28. Descola, *Par-delà nature et culture*.

29. For instance, see Mennell, *All Manners of Food*; Flandrin, "La distinction par le goût"; or Spang, *The Invention of the Restaurant*.

30. Korsemeyer, *Making Sense of Taste*.

31. Varela, Thomson, and Rosch, *The Embodied Mind*.

32. Audouin-Rouzeau and Sabban, *Un aliment sain dans un corps sain*; Laurioux, "Cuisine et médecine au Moyen Âge"; Flandrin and Montanari, *Food*; Bynum and Porter, *Medicine and the Five Senses*; Chiou, *Homo gastronomicus*.

33. Grieco, "Food and Social Classes"; Flandrin, "Seasoning, Cooking, and Dietetics."

34. With all the precautions required while using contemporary terms and meanings to relate to early modern realities.

35. Spary, *Eating the Enlightenment*; Albala, *Food in Early Modern Europe*, chap. 6, "Diet and Nutrition," 213–230; Grmek, *Histoire de la pensée médicale en Occident*.

36. *Dictionnaire de l'Académie françoise*, vol. 2, 1762, 366, s.v. "Physique."

37. Aristotle's *De Anima*, related to the five senses, was already classified among his treatises of physics.

38. Viala, *La France galante*; Bury, *Littérature et politesse*, 6; Elias, *Civilisation des moeurs*. On the enduring reputation of French haute cuisine, see Ferguson, *Accounting for Taste*; Peterson, *Acquired Taste*.

39. [Courtin], *Nouveau traité de la civilité*, 20.

40. [Bonnefons], *Delices de la Campagne*, 216.

41. The French capital was considered as "the place where one can meet people of any nations, and provinces, who with a common voice agree that the best bread of the world is eaten in Paris." [Bonnefons], *Delices de la Campagne*, 1–2.

42. La Varenne, *Le Cuisinier françois* (1651), fol. a vij r. François-Pierre said La Varenne worked for Louis Châlons-de-Blé, Marquis d'Uxelles and governor of Chalon-sur-Saône. Both were native of the same region.

43. France, *Politeness and Its Discontents*, 54 (chap. 4, "Polish, Police, *Polis*").

44. Viala, *La France galante*, 356–391; Bury, *Littérature et politesse*, 45 *et seq.*

45. Regarding British debates on taste, see notably Woodruff Smith's study of consumption and respectability in Britain. Smith, *Consumption and the Making of Respectability*.

46. Classen, Howes, and Synnott, *Aroma*, 9.

Chapter 1. The "Silences of Taste"

1. For a synthesis on early modern food practices, see Flandrin and Montanari, *Food: A Culinary History*, which, in spite of the limited number of footnotes, remains a good starting point. Also see Kümin, *A Cultural History of Food*; Albala, *A Cultural History of Food*; Albala, *Food in Early Modern Europe*; Parasecoli and Scholliers, *A Cultural History of Food*; Wheaton, *Savoring the Past*; Flandrin and Hyman, *Le Cuisinier françois*. For more specific studies, the reader should consult the specialized bibliographical collections, in particular the *Food History Bibliography* (http://www.foodbibliography. eu), published by the IEHCA with the collaboration of the Villa I Tatti of Florence (The Harvard University Center for Italian Renaissance Studies), the Mellon Foundation, and the Bibliothèque nationale de France.

2. Pinkard, *A Revolution in Taste*.

3. Because they grow close to the ground, vegetables were indeed considered an ig-noble food. As Allen Grieco remarkably demonstrated, the hierarchy of food was sym-bolically and in practice organized according to the chain of being, in which meat and especially birds, close to the sky, were considered the most important dishes. Grieco, "Food and Social Classes."

4. Barbara Ketcham Wheaton considers it a "modular" culinary system. Wheaton, *Savoring the Past*, 116.

5. De Lune, *Le cuisinier* [1656], in Laurendon, *L'art de la cuisine française*, 242. Pierre de Lune is the cook of the duke of Rohan, grandson of Sully. In his cookbook, he delivered the first known recipe of the *bouquet garni*—which he calls *paquet d'assaisonnement*— and of roux, named *farine cuite*. Laurendon, *L'art de la cuisine française*, 242.

6. [Bonnefons], *Delices de la Campagne*, [209]. Nicolas de Bonnefons was the first valet of the young Louis XIV, in a time during which this office, originally reserved to the members of the royal family, had become a venal office.

7. "Differences in social standing were coming to be expressed not just through dif-ferences in quantity or variety of food served at the tables of different strata, but more subtly through styles of cooking and serving. There was food to be emulated and food to be disdained. Food had become, in sociological jargon, a vehicle for anticipatory socialization on the one hand, and for the expression of social distance on the other." In other words, people were "consciously or unconsciously adopting the ways, tastes and manners of a social group to membership of which" they aspired. Mennell, *All Manners of Food*, 75.

8. "In 1691 Countess d'Aulnoy visited Spain and immediately complained about the grand supper served her for St. Sebastian's Day, which was 'so full of garlic and saffron and spices' that she couldn't eat any of it. She also disliked the 'very nasty stews, full of garlic and pepper,' and a 'pastry [which] is so peppery that it burns your mouth.' At a dinner with the queen mother in Toledo, she found herself 'like Tantalus, dying of hunger but unable to eat a thing. For there I had no middle ground between meats reeking of perfume,' and therefore disgusting, and those 'full of saffron, garlic, onion, pepper, and spices', and therefore impossible to eat." Flandrin, "Dietary Choices," 410.

9. On the other hand, texts written in Latin were rather connected with dietetics and other forms of scholarly discourses. Girard, "Du manuscrit à l'imprimé," 108. Let us also

recall that unlike most servants, cooks could read, write, and calculate, as demonstrated by Takats in *The Expert Cook*.

10. *Le cuisinier Taillevent*, n.p.

11. Girard, "Le triomphe de 'La Cuisinière bourgeoise'"; *Livres en bouche.*

12. Girard, "Du manuscrit à l'imprimé," 108.

13. Platine (B. Sacchi), *Le Platine en François* [1505]. This is the French translation of a collection of Italian recipes from the mid-fifteenth century, appearing in Latin in 1473–1475 under the title *De honesta voluptate et valetudine*. The *Viandier* was the first printed French cookbook. It is a compilation of older recipes, the first version of which would date from the end of the thirteenth century, which is before the birth of its supposed author, the cook Guillaume Tirel, who worked for the kings of France in the fourteenth century. *Le Cuisinier françois*, ed. Flandrin, Hyman, and Hyman, 12, 31.

14. The *Ouverture de cuisine* of Lancelot de Casteau, published in Liège in 1604 by Léonard Streel, is one of the only indications of the culinary evolution in motion. Realized by the cook of the prince-bishops of the principality, the work was the first one written in French, testifying to a transformation of sensibilities, a transformation situated between medieval habits and culinary modernity. See Adam, "Précisions sur l'*Ouverture de cuisine*"; Leclercq, *La joyeuse entrée*. Jean-Louis Flandrin also mentions *Le Thresor de santé* as witnessing the new practices, but even though this book does contain some recipes, it is not strictly speaking a specialized cookbook such as those that would appear during the second half of the seventeenth century. *Le Thresor de santé, ou, Mesnage de la vie humaine. Divisé en dix Livres. Lesquels traictent amplement de toutes sortes de Viandes et Breuvages, ensemble de leur qualité et preparation* (The Treasure of Health, or Nurturing Human Life. Divided in ten books. These amply address all kinds of victuals and beverages, along with their quality and preparation) published in Lyon by J. Ant. Huguetan in 1607. Finally, the *Livre fort excellent de cuysine*, which appeared in Lyon in 1542 and was reprinted in 1576 under the name *Le grand cuisinier tres-utile et profitable*, is also an indication of the culinary changes. See Albala, "Introduction," in *A Cultural History of Food*, 17–18.

15. La Varenne, *Le Cuisinier françois*.

16. Only ten editions out of thirty-two published while the author was alive were printed by the Privilege's successive holders (Pierre David, his widow, and his son-in-law Jean Ribou). The book was already translated into English in 1653, only two years after its French publication, by an anonymous author identified by the initials I.D.G. This was the first time a French cookbook was translated into English. Hyman and Hyman, *The French Cook*. Besides the simple copy of the text, there were also other adaptations, which sometimes only borrowed the title and added completely different content (recipes of *l'Ecole des ragoûts* [the school of stews], used by the Italian publishers who did not see the confusion in *Il cuoco francese [. . .] Per il signor De La Varenne Cuoco Maggiore des Sig. Marchese d'Uexelles*). The English translation was really based on La Varenne's book under the title *The French Cook* (London: Adam, Ch., 1653). The popularity of this text was confirmed and reinforced when it was published in the *bibliothèque bleue* (blue library). La Varenne, *Le Cuisinier françois: D'après l'édition de 1651*, n.p.

17. Flandrin and Hyman, *Le Cuisinier françois*, 79–90.

18. This argument was sometimes only rhetoric, when used by cooks working in the service of the most illustrious families. It does not necessarily mean that all the bourgeois were by then always necessarily more concerned about savings than the aristocrats.

19. La Varenne, *Le Cuisinier françois*, fol. a vi v.

20. The dedication appears from the title "Aux Dames" (To the Ladies) in the *Iardinier françois*; "Aux Dames Ménageres" (To the Ladies Housewives) in *Les Delices de la Campagne*. In Liège, Lancelot de Casteau also dedicated his *Ouverture de cuisine* to women.

21. "I only wanted to write for those who have no knowledge at all, or only a little; particularly to educate so many poor people who would make their day, if they could take some care of the garden." [Bonnefons], *Le Iardinier françois*, fol. ē v.

22. [Bonnefons], *Le Iardinier françois*, fol. ã vii r.

23. La Varenne, *Le Cuisinier françois*; [Massialot], *Le Cuisinier roïal et bourgeois*; [Menon], *La Cuisinière Bourgeoise*.

24. Food historians do not know much about the cook who hides behind these initials. "Some people believed to find a Sir Robert in him, to whom there are discreet allusions made in the text. Others speak about a Sir Rolland. . . . What is certain is that he was one of the most famous cooks of his time, and that he served in the castle of Fontainebleau, in Saint-Cloud, in Rueil and in Vaux-le-Vicomte, maybe during the glorious times of Fouquet." Laurendon, *L'art de la cuisine française*, xii.

25. There are countless examples: "If you do not want to put any *garniture*, the *potage* will not be lesser, but there are two main things you cannot avoid, namely the *mitonnade* and the cullis; one is the foundation of the *bâtiment*, and the other is the cover and the crowning. To make things a little properly, it is necessary to go through this; otherwise, do not get involved, because serving a naked soup without any *garniture* and ornamental, good God, for a small saving what a vile act! Far from here these bourgeois seasonings! Egg yolks diluted with verjuice to embellish a soup of consequence and other ingredients of the same flour: is there nothing more mechanic and of more *rampant* [groveling] than this method?" L.S.R., *L'Art de bien traiter*, 63.

26. "This Book can bear good witness of this. It is a Cook who dares to qualify himself as Royal, and it is not without reason; because the Meals he describes for the different times of the year have all been recently served at Court, or at the tables of Princes, and persons of the first rank; And showing them how to practice what composed all these Meals, he gives the real manners of the King's officers, who have worked on it; so one can say that it is the most fashionable, and the most exquisite." [Massialot], *Le Cuisinier roïal et Bourgeois*, fol. ă iij v.

27. [Bonnefons], *Delices de la Campagne*, fol. ã 6 r–v.

28. La Varenne, *Le Cuisinier françois*, fol. a vi r.

29. Louis XIV was fond of spicy dishes and ate with his fingers.

30. The differences were sometimes tenuous between those who claimed to revolutionize cookery and their predecessors. So Massialot, who claims to reveal "everything that is most fashionable, and most exquisite" ([Massialot], *Le Cuisinier roïal et Bourgeois*, fol. ă iij v), copied several recipes from Pierre de Lune, whose cuisine is perceived as more archaic by specialists. Let us finally note that the term *modern* itself would only appear in the eighteenth century in the title of a cookbook: La Chapelle, *Le Cuisinier moderne*

(1735). The work was first published in London in English, in 1733, under the title *The Modern Cook*. Its author was at that moment a maître d'hôtel to Lord Chesterfield. He then passed into the service of Guillaume d'Orange.

31. [Massialot], *Le Cuisinier roïal et Bourgeois*, fol. ǎ iiij r.

32. Jean-Louis Flandrin, Mary Hyman, and Philip Hyman consider *L'Art de bien traiter* as the most refined and modern of all cookery books from the seventeenth century. *Le Cuisinier françois*, ed. Flandrin, Hyman, and Hyman, 13.

33. L.S.R. wanted to demonstrate that his technique was among the newest trends of the time, "with a method which was not yet seen nor taught, and which destroys all those that preceded, as abusive, obscure and of very difficult execution." L.S.R., *L'Art de bien traiter*, 19. The editorial success of the *Cuisinier françois* seems unjustified according to this author, because the recipes proposed were vulgar and untasty: "I believe that we shall not see here the absurdities and disgusting lessons which M. de Varenne dares to give and support, with which he has for so long deceived and bemused the foolish and ignorant populace. . . . [I]f we examine it a little more closely, we shall see so many lownesses and so many ridiculous manners . . . that we shall see few chapters where we should not find any disgusts, confusion and unbearable faults. . . . And to give some idea to your minds, glance through and read with me several and different articles in which one sees the establishment of this pleasant doctrine, but before any things take precautions of some good antidote and think of taking a singular preservative against the poisons and infamies which you will find there, fearing that in the discovery of so many impurities your heart escapes and meets death, where the center of life should be in the most perfect and the most eminent degree." L.S.R., *L'Art de bien traiter*, 22–23.

34. L.S.R., *L'Art de bien traiter*, 21.

35. [Bonnefons], *Delices de la Campagne*, fol. ã 6 r.

36. L.S.R., *L'Art de bien traiter*, 21.

37. L.S.R., *L'Art de bien traiter*, 21.

38. The *assiette volante* is "a selection of several articles on one plate, or a course consisting of a large number of assorted items; sometimes also used to refer to a dish passed from hand to hand without being placed on the table." Mennell, *All Manners of Food*, 336, n. 5.

39. L.S.R., *L'Art de bien traiter*, 21.

40. [Bonnefons], *Delices de la Campagne*, [209–210]. Emphasis added.

41. [Bonnefons], *Delices de la Campagne*, 213–214.

42. "Fats tend to magnify the flavour of the foods they accompany." Pinkard, *A Revolution in Taste*, xii.

43. [Bonnefons], *Delices de la Campagne*, 221.

44. "[T]he dishes became rather undifferentiated and broadly 'tasted the same.'" Mennell, *All Manners of Food*, 54.

45. "Cooks strove to produce dishes that fused many layers of flavor into a single, unitary whole, rendering individual ingredients unidentifiable to even sensitive palates. . . . The aim was to turn raw materials of all sorts into confections unlike anything in nature. . . . Cuisine *was* artifice: perfection was achieved when flavors fused so completely

that it was hard to guess what the individual components were." Pinkard, *A Revolution in Taste*, xii, 4.

46. Lune, *Le Cuisinier*, 284.

47. "[O]ne can serve bisque of young pigeons and potages of stuffed chickens any time . . . health soups of capon, of knuckle of veal, all furnished according to its species and its nature. But it is not always the time to eat green peas from the spring season, turnips, *choux pommés* [cabbages with a firm heart] of Milan and other particular things which nature can only give and produce with Gehenna and extraordinary constraints." L.S.R., *L'Art de bien traiter*, 44.

48. So, the small "corn-fed chickens, will be bled in the throat, scalded [*échaudés*], plucked, and completely emptied, then cooked again in water [*refait à l'eau*] for more cleanliness, but it takes with it much of their good taste: that is why if one wants to have the patience to pluck them dry, and to redo them on coals, or on grill, they will be much better than cooked in water [*eschaudez, et refaits à l'eau*]." [Bonnefons], *Delices de la Campagne*, 218.

49. [Bonnefons], *Delices de la Campagne*, 292.

50. L.S.R., *L'Art de bien traiter*, 47.

51. [Bonnefons], *Delices de la Campagne*, 238.

52. "Some stuff them [the small goslings] before putting them on a spit, and sew back on the opening of the stomach, but they are never that good; it is better to cook the stuffing apart, and to stick it afterwards in the body when serving." [Bonnefons], *Delices de la Campagne*, 237.

53. [Bonnefons], *Delices de la Campagne*, 265.

54. [Bonnefons], *Le Iardinier françois*, 241. So, for the lemonade, some people "add crushed almonds; but since it is a drink, the simplest that it can be is the best." [Bonnefons], *Le Iardinier françois*, 313–314.

55. "Monseigneur, although my condition does not fit me to aspire to the heroic spirit, it nevertheless gives me enough pride not to forget my duty. In your house I have, during ten years of employment there, discovered the secret of the most delicate preparation of dishes. I dare say that I followed this profession to great approbation from Princes, Marshals of France, and many persons of rank, who have greatly admired your table in Paris. . . . It seems to me that the public must benefit from this experience, so that it will owe you all the utility that it will receive from it. I thus put down in writing what I put into practice for so long time in the honor of your service, and made a small Book which has the title of *Escuyer* of your cuisine; but since as all that it contains is only a lesson that the desire to please you made me learn, I imagined myself that it should be honored with your Name. . . . Consider that it is a treasure of sauces whose taste contented you sometimes, and that after all it is a *chef d'oeuvre* [masterpiece] which comes from the hand of the one who will be all his life, your Grace, your very-humble, very-obedient, and very-grateful servant, François Pierre said La Varenne." La Varenne, *Le Cuisinier françois*, fol. a ij r–a iij v. Emphasis added.

56. La Varenne, *Le Cuisinier françois*, fol. a iij v.

57. *Le Cuisinier françois*, ed. Flandrin, Hyman, and Hyman, 67–68. The choice of the name "La Varenne" could be a reference to another famous cook, Guillaume Fouquet,

who worked for the Duchess of Bar, sister of Henri IV. The title of "Escuyer de Cuisine" refers to another illustrious predecessor, namely Taillevent, royal cook. Pinkard, *A Revolution in Taste*, 60. "Royal cook" is hence a more distinguished term than that of the simple "cook."

58. Cooks would not be the only ones stressing their own taste expertise at the time—and even more so in the eighteenth century—but the rise of their status is nonetheless obvious.

59. Takats, *The Expert Cook*. On the evolution of the cook's status, also see Cohen and Csergo, *L'artification du culinaire*; Champion, *Hors d'oeuvre*.

60. La Varenne, *Le Cuisinier françois*, 308.

61. [Bonnefons], *Le Iardinier françois*, fol. a viii r°.

62. Lune, *Le Cuisinier*, 241.

63. [Bonnefons], *Delices de la Campagne*, [209].

64. [Bonnefons], *Delices de la Campagne*, [216].

65. L.S.R., *L'Art de bien traiter*, 58–59.

66. [Bonnefons], *Le Iardinier françois*, 367.

67. L.S.R., *L'Art de bien traiter*, 61. The same can be said of wines, which must be tasted "every fortnight." L.S.R., *L'Art de bien traiter*, 33. "[T]aste if you like the seasoning, otherwise add what will be missing." L.S.R., *L'Art de bien traiter*, 33.

68. [Bonnefons], *Le Iardinier françois*, [214–215].

69. Carême's quotation, possibly apocryphal, remained famous: "There are five Fine Arts, namely painting, sculpture, poetry, music, and architecture, the main branch of the latter being pastry." Carême, *Le Cuisinier pittoresque*, 1815, rev. ed., Le Mercure de France, 2003. Quoted in Champion, *Hors d'oeuvre*, 72.

70. L.S.R., *L'Art de bien traiter*, 25.

71. L.S.R., *L'Art de bien traiter*, 19.

72. L.S.R., *L'Art de bien traiter*, 19.

73. L.S.R., *L'Art de bien traiter*, 45.

74. [Massialot], *Le Cuisinier roïal et Bourgeois*, fol. ã iij r.

75. L.S.R., *L'Art de bien traiter*, 25.

76. [Massialot], *Le Cuisinier roïal et Bourgeois*, fol. ã iijj r.

77. Among the different varieties, the "Choux à large Coste" (cabbages with thick ribs) have a "great delicacy. . . . To my taste, there is no sort of Cabbages that equals that one; because they cook quickly and are so delicate, that . . . [they] melt in the mouth." [Bonnefons], *Le Iardinier françois*, 153. Cooks elaborate the same distinctions about carrots and salsify ([Bonnefons], *Le Iardinier françois*, 169–171), as well as about most vegetables. Broadly speaking the wild version was often less appreciated: "Of the purslane, I find four sorts, the Green; the White; the Golden recently brought from the islands of saint Christophe, that is the most delicate; and the fourth is the Porcelaine [pourcelaine], or small wild Purslane, least to hold in esteem; the Earth producing it naturally without any work." [Bonnefons], *Le Iardinier françois*, 198.

78. [Bonnefons], *Delices de la Campagne*, 228. Certain preparations were also considered superior. So, of duck, "one makes all kinds of soups, but particularly with turnips which is their real taste" [Bonnefons], *Delices de la Campagne*, 239 (emphasis added). As for fishes, the "Esplans, said Esperlans" constituted "the most delicate, the most

excellent, and the only one of all fishes that has a good smell" [Bonnefons], *Delices de la Campagne*, 360.

79. [Bonnefons], *Le Iardinier françois*, 117, 136, 140; L.S.R., *L'Art de bien traiter*, 22, 34–35.

80. [Bonnefons], *Delices de la Campagne*, 11.

81. [Bonnefons], *Delices de la Campagne*, 6, 11, 12, 23.

82. [Bonnefons], *Delices de la Campagne*, 288.

83. [Massialot], *Le Cuisinier roïal et Bourgeois*, fol. ã iijj r; L.S.R., *L'Art de bien traiter*, 19; Lune, *Le Cuisinier*, 241.

84. [Bonnefons], *Delices de la Campagne*, 218; [Massialot], *Le Cuisinier roïal et Bourgeois*, fol. ã ij r–v.

85. [Bonnefons], *Delices de la Campagne*, [97–98].

86. The diet chosen by the monks is justified by reasons of austerity or necessity, not of taste. "My devout brothers . . . as you apply yourselves with much curiosity to the culture of gardens . . . also by your care you cultivate all kinds of good herbs and vegetables, of which most of the time you live happy, either that you do it by austerity, either that you lack more solid charities, yet by a wise policy you prefer taking such dishes (however badly prepared) than to be in the public's responsibility." [Bonnefons], *Delices de la Campagne*.

87. [Bonnefons], *Delices de la Campagne*, fol. ã 6 r.

88. On this topic, see Flandrin, "Médecine et habitudes alimentaires anciennes," 85–95.

89. Manuscript domestic cookbooks, also called "books of secrets," reveal heterogeneous sets of advice regarding all aspects of everyday life—from culinary recipes to medical remedies and magic formulae, as well as recipes for cosmetics, perfumes, coloring agents, and other technical items. I have chosen not to investigate this kind of source in this research, for they are less likely to reveal theoretical discourses on taste than are printed cookbooks.

90. "Red cabbages will also have some little place in your garden, for the necessity in certain diseases." [Bonnefons], *Le Iardinier françois*, 155. "Jerusalem artichokes are round roots that come all by knots, and that one eats in Fast in the shape of Artichokes; they do not need great culture, as long as they are placed in good earth . . . The Doctors found that they were not healthy; this is why they will be banished from the good Tables." [Bonnefons], *Le Iardinier françois*, 180–181.

91. "The Verjuice . . . is also crystallized without sugar, or with very little; but it is a very unpleasant jam, that rather disgusts the poor Sick to whom one gives them, than wake their appetite." [Bonnefons], *Le Iardinier françois*, 306–308.

92. [Bonnefons], *Le Iardinier françois*, 361–362.

93. [Massialot], *Le Cuisinier roïal et Bourgeois*, fol. ã ij v–ã iij r.

94. The modern cuisine "tends only to preserve and to maintain health in good condition and in good disposition, teaching to corrupt the vicious qualities of meats, by opposite and diversified seasonings, which aims only, as I say, to give man a solid, well prepared food, convenient to his appetites." "Le Libraire au Lecteur" (The Bookseller to the Reader), in La Varenne, *Le Cuisinier françois*, fol. a vi r–v.

95. "And as well as it is much more pleasant to preserve oneself in a praiseworthy health by a moderate use of a very healthy air, good food, and other dietary parts, which grow

here with us, and which depend on our arbiter; than to use a heap of foreign remedies which harm us, which vehemently purge us, and which cost a lot: besides that often they hardly displease, and disgust us, which nevertheless we are forced to use in the cure of our diseases." [Patin], *Traité de la conservation de santé*, "Preface au Lecteur," fol. a v r.

96. [Patin], *Traité de la conservation de santé*, "Preface au Lecteur," fol. a v r.

97. "Le Libraire au Lecteur," in La Varenne, *Le Cuisinier françois*, fol. a vij v.

98. The restaurant was by then a therapeutic food preparation (often meat concentrate), destined for the sick and people with a weak complexion. It was defined as a nourishing food that restores, allowing one to get one's strength back. *Le Dictionnaire de l'Académie françoise*, vol. 2, 1762, 620, s.v. "restaurant." The "Restauratif ou Restaurant" is defined in the *Encyclopédie* as a "medical term . . . a remedy liable to give strength and vigor." Diderot and D'Alembert, *Encyclopédie*, vol. 14 (1765), s.v. "restauratif ou restaurant." The restaurant was additionally the place in which these remedies were served. See Spang, *The Invention of the Restaurant*.

99. So, about the *"tortugat, ou restaurant de tortues"* (tortugat, or tortoises' restaurative), in which he specifies: "I do not put any seasoning, especially as it is the choice of doctors or of the sick." Lune, *Le Cuisinier*, 250. Also for the *"Eau de poulet"* (chicken water), where the chickens are cooked before going through a linen: "Some put in some 'buglosse' (Anchusa officinalis) and borage, others some violets, chicory, etc. . . . I leave it to the doctor." Lune, *Le Cuisinier*, 250. There is no real medical claim anymore on behalf of the cook. But the latter nevertheless gives remedies meant to heal, like the *"Gelée de ganules pour les maladies"* (jelly for the sick): "Put the ganules in slightly warm water, cook them for an hour and make them go through a linen. When well pressed, make them clarify with fried egg whites; season with salt, sugar, and a little of lemon." Lune, *Le Cuisinier*, 251.

100. [Bonnefons], *Le Iardinier françois*, fol. ã iij v–ã iiij r.

101. [Bonnefons], *Le Iardinier françois*, fol. ã iiij v.

102. [Bonnefons], *Le Iardinier françois*, fol. ã v r.

103. [Bonnefons], *Le Iardinier françois*, fol. ã v r–v.

104. [Bonnefons], *Le Iardinier françois*, fol. ã v v–ã vi r.

105. Delumeau, *Une histoire du paradis*, vol. 1, 15.

106. [Bonnefons], *Delices de la Campagne*, [98].

107. Boudier, *La Cuisine du peintre*; Quellier, *Gourmandise*, 105; Bendiner, *Food in Painting*; Nordenfalk, "The Five Senses," 2. On fruit and gardens in the early modern era, see Quellier, *Des fruits et des hommes*.

108. Ebert-Schifferer, *Natures mortes*, 63.

109. [Bonnefons], *Delices de la Campagne*, fol. ã 3 v–ã 4 r.

110. See chapter 3.

111. L.S.R., *L'Art de bien traiter*, 24.

112. L.S.R., *L'Art de bien traiter*, 22.

113. L.S.R., *L'Art de bien traiter*, 32.

114. Viala, *La France galante*, 91–92.

115. See notably *Le Mercure galant*, written by Jean Donneau de Visé until May 1710 and then afterward by Charles Rivière Du Fresnay, Paris, au Palais, 1678–1714. For a thorough analysis of this source, see Chiou, *Homo gastronomicus*, 223, 248–256; Wheaton, *Savoring the Past*.

116. The rules of hierarchical precedence also dictated the distribution of the dishes. The rank of the dinner guests actually influenced the food they received at table, depending on whether they were seated at the "high end" or at the "low end" of the table.

117. L.S.R., *L'Art de bien traiter*, 51.

118. L.S.R., *L'Art de bien traiter*, 63.

119. Corbin, "Histoire et Anthropologie sensorielle," 19.

120. Quellier, *Gourmandise*, 141, 145.

121. Chiou, *Homo gastronomicus*, 261.

122. The meal was initially the main object of the literature of civility, originated from the medieval *contenances de table*.

123. Elias, *Über den Prozess der Zivilisation*. Norbert Elias has notably argued that the control of individual affectivity and emotions was linked to social order. On the history of the body, see, for instance, Vigarello, *Histoire du corps*; Courtine and Haroche, *Histoire du visage*. Literature on notions of civility and politeness in the early modern period include Karila-Cohen and Quellier, *Le corps du gourmand*; Quellier, *Gourmandise*; Losfeld, *Politesse*; Viala, *La France galante*; Romagnoli, "Mind Your Manners"; Bierlaire, "Colloques scolaires et civilités puériles"; Bury, *Littérature et politesse*; Montandon, *Bibliographie des traités de savoir-vivre*; Montandon, *Pour une Histoire des traités de savoir-vivre*; France, *Politeness and its Discontents*; Marenco, *Manières de table, modèles de mœurs*; Chartier, "Distinction et divulgation"; Revel, "Les usages de la civilité"; Flandrin, "La distinction par le goût"; Bonnet, "La table dans les civilités."

124. "A sphere of silence and secret is organized around the body." Revel, "Les usages de la civilité," 190.

125. Chiou, *Homo gastronomicus*, 238. Courtine and Haroche, *Histoire du visage*, 211 *et seq.*

126. "It is unrefined to demand something that is on the table, particularly if it is some delicacy; and in the same way it is a person subject to his mouth who requires the best piece when asked for the choice of something; one usually answers: Whatever will please you." [Courtin], *Nouveau traité de la civilité*, 169. Antoine de Courtin is inspired here by Erasmus. Érasme de Rotterdam, *La civilité puerile*, 59.

127. [Courtin], *Nouveau traité de la civilité*, 162–166; Érasme, *La civilité puérile*, 61; La Salle, *Rules of Christian Decorum*, 66–69 ("How to carve and to serve meat").

128. Érasme, *La civilité puérile*, 61.

129. "It is a very improper weakness to say out loud: I do not eat this, I do not eat that, I never eat roast, I never eat rabbit, I could not eat anything in which there is pepper, nutmeg, onion, etc. As these are only imaginary aversions, that could easily be corrected, if one had had in one's youth some good friend; and which one can still overcome every day, if one wants to suffer hunger a little, or not to love so much ones person and appetites: so such disgusts should never be known; it is necessary to civilly take all that is presented to you." [Courtin], *Nouveau traité de la civilité*, 170.

130. La Salle, *Rules of Christian Decorum*, 64–65.

131. Flandrin, "From Dietetics to Gastronomy," 419.

132. L.S.R., *L'Art de bien traiter*, 21.

133. [Massialot], *Le Cuisinier roïal et Bourgeois*, 2. It was considered important to "avoid the proximity of two dishes of a similar kind, without one of another sort in

between; for otherwise the thing would be done with bad grace, and could force the taste of some of those at table, since everyone does not like the same thing." [Massialot], *Le Cuisinier roïal et Bourgeois*. "The notion of choice is all the more central . . . as food insecurity remains the daily lot of the largest number." Quellier, *Gourmandise*, 119.

134. Flandrin, "From Dietetics to Gastronomy," 418–432.

135. L.S.R., *L'Art de bien traiter*, 41.

136. [Bonnefons], *Delices de la Campagne*, [212].

137. Epistle to the Philippians, 3:19: "Whose end is destruction, whose God is their belly, and whose glory is in their shame, who mind earthly things."

138. La Salle, *Rules of Christian Decorum*, 57.

139. "Criticizing the dishes is a sign of bad education and an unpleasant thing for the host. If you are receiving, politeness demands you to apologize for the little of magnificence of the feast. To praise your dinner or to recall what it cost you is an unpleasant sauce offered to your guests." Érasme de Rotterdam, *La civilité puérile*, 65.

140. La Bruyère, *Les Caractères*, 289–290.

141. Quellier, *Gourmandise*, 102–137 (chap. 4, "Le règne des friands et des gourmets").

142. We shall return more in more detail to the concept of *bon goût* in chapter 4.

143. Bury, *Littérature et politesse*, 152.

144. "The method that teaches [one] to follow the real order, and to calculate exactly all the circumstances of what we see, contains all which gives some certainty to the rules of arithmetic. But what satisfied me most with this method, was that, by it, I was insured to use in all my reason, if not perfectly, at least the best that was in my power; and so that I felt, by practicing it, that my spirit became little by little used to conceive more clearly and more distinctly its objects." Descartes, *Discours de la méthode*, 53.

Chapter 2. Pleasures, Disorders, and Dangers of an Animal Sense

1. The history of *gourmandise* is today well-known, thanks to recent important contributions such as Karila-Cohen and Quellier, *Le corps du gourmand*; Quellier, *Gourmandise*; Meyzie, *Gourmandise*; Casagrande and Vecchio, *Histoire des péchés capitaux*; N'Diaye, *La Gourmandise*; Yeomans and Derville, "Gourmandise et gourmandise spirituelle."

2. Furetière, *Dictionnaire universel*, vol. 2, fol. T2 v, s.v. "Gourmandise."

3. Richelet, *Dictionnaire*, vol. 1, 771, s.v. "Gourmand."

4. *Dictionnaire de l'Académie françoise*, vol. 1, 1694, 528, s.v. "Gourmand."

5. Furetière, *Dictionnaire universel*, vol. 2, fol. M3 v, s.v. "Friand." Same register for the *friandise* (delicacy), defined as a "passion that one has for delicate or tasty foods . . . is also said of all things one eats for pleasure only, and not for feeding." Furetière, *Dictionnaire universel*, vol. 2, fol. M3 v, s.v. "Friandise."

6. Furetière, *Dictionnaire universel*, vol. 1, fol. Dddd2 r, s.v. "Delicat."

7. Furetière, *Dictionnaire universel*, vol. 2, fol. T2 v, s.v. "Gourmet, ette." The word *gourmet* was still limited to wine expertise in the fourth edition of the *Dictionnaire de l'Académie françoise*, vol. 1, 1762, 829.

8. For more details on the theoretical elaboration of the sin of gluttony, along with the vocabulary of food intemperance in the Middle Ages, see Montanari and Prosperi, "Entre le ventre et la gueule," 37–55.

9. Casagrande and Vecchio, *Histoire des péchés capitaux*, 210.

10. Gregory of Nyssa, *De virginitate*, chap. 21, PG46, col. C. Quoted in Bynum, *Holy Feast*, 38.

11. Crespet, *Deux livres de la hayne de Satan*, fol. 359 r.

12. [Kempis], *Imitation de Jesus-Christ*, 92.

13. It is the case, for instance, of Cesare Ripa, who chose this fruit as the symbol of the sense of taste in his *Iconologie*. Ripa, *Iconologie ou les principales choses*, 48.

14. Quellier, *Gourmandise*, 29. Dante describes the torments of the gluttons in canto VI of *Inferno* (Hell). He relates how cold and dark the third circle is, always flooded with heavy rain, hail, and snow, in which "Cerberus, hideous monster and cruel dog, barks terribly with his three gullets at the sinners submerged in this circle. His eyes are red and enflamed; his beard dirty and disgusting; his belly large, and his paws armed with sharp claws: he dashes toward these shadows, tears them up and smashes them to pieces." Dante Alighieri, *Divine Comédie*, [134] (Canto VI, Lines 7–18).

15. Pascal, *Pensées*, 74. Pascal was an "antihumanist," largely influenced by Augustinian pessimism. Bury, *Littérature et politesse*, 14.

16. Casagrande and Vecchio, *Histoire des péchés capitaux*, 209. Vegetables and fish were less and less associated with fast and punishment, as evidenced not only by the attention they received among the promoters of modern cuisine but also by the popularity of pleasure gardens and kitchen gardens from the seventeenth century onward.

17. Renaudot, *Recueil général*, vol. 2, 314, 69th conference (no. 20), "Du Ieusne" (On Fasting), 313–320.

18. Lessius, *Conseils pour vivre longtemps*, 172. Emphasis added. This quotation comes from a work of Lessius published in 1647, shortly before the books of La Varenne and Nicolas de Bonnefons, who also insisted on "the true taste" of food.

19. In ancient representations of the body, the *esprits* (spirits) were connected with the humors, of which they constituted the most airy, the most volatile part. They transmitted the decisions of the soul. "Spirit, in terms of Medicine, describes the light and volatile atoms, which are the most subtle parts of bodies, give them movement, and are in the middle between the body and the faculties of the soul, which serve to make all its operations. It is the vital and animal spirits that swell the muscles to support the bodies, and make them move. The spirit is a very subtle body [entity], always mobile, engendered of blood and vapors, carrier of the faculties and commander of the soul by means of the nerves and muscles." Furetière, *Dictionnaire universel*, vol. 1, fol. Ddddd2 v, s.v. "Esprit." "Spirits, in the plural, are small light, hot, and invisible bodies, which carry life and feeling in the parts of the animal. Vital spirits, animal spirits, the spirits get lost with blood, the vital spirits go to the extremities by the arteries. The nerves are the vehicle of the animal spirits." *Dictionnaire de l'Académie françoise*, vol. 1, 1694, 400, s.v. "Esprit."

20. Aristotle, *Nicomachean Ethics* [Book VII].

21. Renaudot, *Recueil général*, vol. 2, 315.

22. Quoted in Bierlaire, "Érasme, la table et les manières de table," 150.

23. Quellier, *Gourmandise*, 19–20.

24. The authors of conduct books emphatically insisted on discretion in this respect.

One should not, "when serving oneself, make noise and scrape dishes, or rake one's plate by drying it out to the last drop. These are rattles of weapons, which disclose as a signal our gluttony to those who might have not been attentive otherwise." [Courtin], *Nouveau traité de la civilité*, 171–172.

25. La Salle, *Rules of Christian Decorum*, 58.

26. The author refers here to the passage of the Epistle of Paul to the Philippians already mentioned above.

27. La Salle, *Rules of Christian Decorum*, 57.

28. Casagrande and Vecchio, *Histoire des péchés capitaux*, 193–228.

29. Boaistuau, *Le Théâtre du Monde*, 77.

30. Sales, *Introduction to the Devout Life*, 340–341.

31. La Bruyère continues: "Not only does he occupy at table the first place, he alone occupies that of two others; he forgets that the meal is for him and for all the company; he gains control of the dish, and makes his own of every service: he does not become attached to any of the dishes until he finished trying them all; he would want to be able to savor them all at the same time. He uses only his hands at table; he handles meats, alters them, dismembers them, tears them up, and uses them in a way that guests, if they want to eat, have to eat his leftovers." La Bruyère, *Les Caractères*, 289. There were also actual conduct books entirely built on this principle of an antithesis of civility, exposing the exact opposite of the ideal behavior, such as the *Grobianus*: "When you shall be served at table some delicious little dishes, see that your hand is the first one on the tray: do not think twice! Seize the piece that seems tasty to you, otherwise another might outstrip you and eat it; if you are wise, do not forget to always observe this custom, it is beneficial and suited to your stomach. And if somebody addresses you a sidelong look, you can just tell him: 'Each is to himself his own fellow man.' Maybe the chosen portion you lust after is on the distant part of the tray and there is nobody by your side to present it to you: stretch out your arm right in front and catch it! What importance indeed, since it was not arranged in front of you, as it should have been?" Dedekind, *Grobianus*, 66.

32. Furetière, *Dictionnaire universel*, vol. 2, fol. T2 v, s.v. "Gourmand."

33. Pierre Boaistuau gives several examples of gluttonous churchmen: "I wanted to describe and to put to the rank of the others, the prodigious banquet of this Prelate, not to imitate him, but to hate him: because maybe while he had his loins on fire, and while he was so fully enjoying these delights, the poor Lazare was at his door, who was chilled by cold, hunger, and thirst: but good Lord? What could have said or thought . . . the Apostles who were forced by hunger, to eat ears of corn all raw, if they had seen their successor (but not imitator) in a cuisine so hot, and so populated with foods?" Boaistuau, *Histoires prodigieuses*, fol. 112 r–v. On the cultural tradition of the gluttonous monk, see Rosé, "Le moine glouton," 191–219.

34. As testified by the secular association between gluttony and tyranny, on which there already is an extensive literature. See Karila-Cohen and Quellier, *Le corps du gourmand*, 18.

35. Churchmen are particularly severe against these behaviors: "What is more shameful than being the slave of one's mouth and stomach? What is more insane than giving up all the goods of the spirit and of the body, which sobriety brings us, for such a small

pleasure as that of drinking and eating, and getting exposed to all the discomforts and all the troubles which intemperance overwhelms us with? Miserable fate of mortals, to be subject to something so vain and so frivolous, to the darkness of such a blindness, and to such errors, and to let their spirit become the toy of goods that are only imaginary, like those whom one enjoys only in dreams!" Lessius, *Conseils pour vivre longtemps*, 192–193.

36. "Gastrimargia, id est gula, est excessus in cibo et potu. Item gula sive gastrimargia est vorax edacitas, nauseanti stomacho applaudens, naturae finibus non contenta. Item gula est solius causa corporis, illecebrosus et avidus appetitus cibi et potus. Ventris ingluvies est immoderata ciborum concupiscentia satisfactio." (Gastrimargia, that is gluttony, is the excess in eating and drinking. The same way, the gula or gastimargia is the voracious piggishness, applauding to the disgusting stomach, unsatisfied with the limits of nature. The same way, gluttony is the cause provoked by the only body, it is also the captivating and greedy appetite of food and drink. The stomach's gluttony is a satisfaction of food produced by an excessive concupiscence.) Vincent de Beauvais, *Speculum Doctrinale*, ed. Douai 1624, repr. Graz, 1965, vol. 4, clv, 389. Quoted in Laurioux, *Gastronomie*, 259, n. 14.

37. Ferrières, *Sacred Cow, Mad Cow*.

38. Institoris and Sprenger, *Marteau des Sorcières*, 187. The first edition mentioned neither the date nor the editor.

39. Institoris and Sprenger, *Marteau des Sorcières*, 187.

40. Institoris and Sprenger, *Marteau des Sorcières*, 302.

41. Boguet, *An Examen of Witches*, 3 (chap. 1). Henry Boguet was a judge from the end of the sixteenth and the beginning of the seventeenth century, active in Franche-Comté. His *Examen of Witches* was largely inspired by his own experience in witchcraft trials. There are a dozen known editions of this influential book, which was widely used in the beginning of the seventeenth century.

42. Boguet, *An Examen of Witches*, 11 (chap. 5).

43. The saints were particularly supported. Jean Bodin thus gave the example of a holy man guided in each act of everyday life by a good angel, who went as far as managing his taste: "when he wanted to drink, or to eat something that was bad, he felt the signal" of the angel, who touched his right ear if he ate something bad, his left ear in case of a good deed. Bodin, *De la Démonomanie des sorciers*, 24.

44. Bodin, *De la Démonomanie des sorciers*, 12.

45. "Let us learn, then, when we are about to eat and drink, to think of Him who is the author of all, and to bless our food with the sacred sign of the Cross as we have been taught by the Holy Fathers, who held the Cross in such reverence that they said it delivered us from devils and made them flee from before us." Bodin, *Démonomanie des sorciers*.

46. Boguet, *An Examen of Witches*, 103 (chap. 35).

47. Boguet, *An Examen of Witches*, 103.

48. Institoris and Sprenger mention the testimony of a "young converted witch," a victim of the evil spells of her aunt, who ends up burned at the stake. The witness explains that "the greatest harms come from midwifes, who are obliged to kill or to of-

fer the demon the biggest number of small children. She also maintained that she was severely beaten by her aunt for, while discovering a hidden cooking pot, finding the heads of several children . . . some sorcerers had cooked their own children and had eaten them." Institoris and Sprenger, *Marteau des Sorcières*, 254–255.

49. Classen, "The Witch's Senses," 70–84.

50. Institoris and Sprenger, *Marteau des Sorcières*, 253.

51. Classen, "The Witch's Senses," 71–73.

52. Boguet, *An Examen of Witches*, 57 (chap. 21).

53. A man was victim of a "terrible demon, who forced him to eat his own excrements." Institoris and Sprenger, *Marteau des Sorcières*, 302.

54. On disgust, see Delville, Norris, and von Hoffmann, *Le Dégoût*; Korsmeyer, *Savoring Disgust*; Kelly, *Yuck!*; Menninghaus, *Disgust*; Miller, *Anatomy of Disgust*; Kolnai, *On Disgust*.

55. Lancre, *On the Inconstancy of Witches*, 210–211. See especially book 3, Discourse III, "The Sabbath Feast and the Wonderful Meats Eaten There."

56. Boguet, *An Examen of Witches*, 58 (chap. 21). Bodin also stated that "the devels are horrified by salt." Bodin, *De la Démonomanie des sorciers*, 136.

57. Lancre, *On the Inconstancy of Witches*, 214.

58. On earlier religious meanings and symbolic uses of salt, see Tarot, "De l'Antiquité au monde Moderne: Le sel du baptême," 281–302.

59. Boguet, *An Examen of Witches*, 58 (chap. 21).

60. Boguet, *An Examen of Witches*, 58 (chap. 21).

61. Boguet, *An Examen of Witches*. "But all witches are agreed that there is no taste at all in the dishes of which they eat at the Sabbath, and that the meat is nothing but horseflesh. And nearly all declare that when they leave the table they are as hungry as when they went to it. Antide Colas said that the food was cold; Clauda Vuillat, of the village of Mirebeau, that they ate nothing but wind at the Sabbath; Christofle of Aranthon that it seemed to her as if she had eaten nothing." Boguet, *An Examen of Witches*, 58–59 (chap. 21).

62. Boguet, *An Examen of Witches*, 59 (chap. 21).

63. Havelange, *De l'œil et du monde*, 109–145 ("L'œil du diable").

64. "[W]itches cause hurt and injury by a touch of the hand." Boguet, *An Examen of Witches*, 84 (chap. 28).

65. "[B]esides the ordinary effect of fasting, the raising up of the spirit, the keeping down of the flesh, the practice of virtue, and the gaining of a great reward in Heaven, it is a very good thing to keep possession of the power of mastering gluttony itself, and for holding the sensual appetite and the body subject to the law of the spirit; and though we do not fast much, yet the enemy fears us more when he recognises that we know how to fast." Sales, *Introduction to the Devout Life*, 269.

66. Because of this "resemblance between shameful pleasures and those of eating, for both concern the flesh," Francis de Sales decided, in his chapter dedicated to "the Modesty of the Marriage Bed" (chapter 34), to explain everything "which I cannot say of the one, by that which I say of the other." Sales, *Introduction to the Devout Life*, 337.

67. Albala, "Historical Background," 14.

68. Bynum, "Fast, Feast and Flesh," 130.

69. Albala, "Ideology of Fasting," 51.

70. Du Chesne, *Le pourtraict de la santé*, 196. Joseph Du Chesne was adviser and ordinary doctor of the king.

71. "In the borders of India . . . on the oriental side, near the source of the Ganges" lives "the tribe of the Astomes, which are deprived of mouth, hairy on all the body and get dressed with a down of leaves; they live on air and on perfumes they inhale by the nostrils. They do not take either food nor drink, contenting themselves with diverse perfumes of roots, flowers, and wood apples [*pommes des bois*], which they take with them if the journey has to last, so that they would not lack smells to breath; a slightly too strong scent kills them without difficulty." Pline l'Ancien, *Histoire naturelle*, livre VII, 45–46 (Book VII, II, [18]).

72. Examples of holy anorexia were especially numerous in the thirteenth and fourteenth centuries, with a peak around 1500, followed by a decline in the sixteenth century. Bell, *Holy Anorexia*; Bynum, *Holy Feast and Holy Fast*; Gélis, "Le corps, l'Église," 45–51; Meuret, *L'anorexie créatrice*.

73. Saint Catherine of Siena was reputed to feed solely on the host.

74. Holy anorexia was a way for women to assert their own personality, in reaction to a world that tried to dominate them. Bell, *Holy Anorexia*.

75. Vigliano, *Humanisme*.

76. Théophraste Renaudot was a French doctor and surgeon trained in Montpellier who was best known as the founder of the *Gazette*, one of the first French newspapers. The Bureau d'Adresse was a learned academy of doctors, lawyers, and cultivated people originating primarily from the bourgeoisie. Debates organized as conferences on the most diverse topics were held every week for ten years beginning in 1632. The year after, in 1633, Théophraste Renaudot started publishing the reports of the conferences every week; these reports were later compiled into four volumes about hundreds of conferences, titled *Centuries des questions traitées és conférences du Bureau d'Adresse*. The fifth volume, gathering fifty-one conferences, was published by Eusèbe Renaudot, Théophraste's elder son. These conferences were very successful, as evidenced by the numerous (including English) editions and translations of the reports. The speakers of these debates are very difficult to identify because their anonymity was voluntarily protected so as to encourage the liberty of reasoning and speaking; the aim of these gatherings, after all, was to constitute "an honest recreation" ("Avis au Lecteur," in Renaudot, *Recueil général*, vol. 1, fol. A ij). The content of the conferences suggests that a majority of doctors were among the speakers and the participants; however, they were not the most exceptional members of the Republic of Letters, the latter—people like Descartes or Gassendi—gathered elsewhere in selected Parisian salons. Thus, these conferences of the Bureau d'Adresse are all the more revealing of common conceptions about knowledge in the first half of the seventeenth century. On the Bureau d'Adresse, see the comprehensive studies of Suzanne Mazauric (*Savoirs et Philosophie*; *Théophraste Renaudot*).

77. On medieval bestiaries, notably see the work of Michel Pastoureau.

78. Vinge, *The Five Senses*.

79. The ape is, for instance, represented in the foreground of the series The Lady and the Unicorn, a tapestry of the end of the fifteenth century illustrating the sense of taste (Musée national du Moyen Âge, Paris). On this work, see Delahaye, "Les tapisseries," 57–64.

80. Renaudot, *Recueil général*, vol. 1, 424, 24th conference, "1. Quel est le plus noble des cinq Sens?" (Which Is the Noblest of the Five Senses?), 416–426. Let us note that for Ripa the hawk appears to be the "true Symbol of Taste," because it "has such a good one [taste], that according to S. Grégoire, however hungry it is, it prefers to endure it than to feed on rotting carcass or rotten flesh." Ripa, *Iconologie ou les principales choses*, 47.

81. We shall return in the following chapter to the traditional associations of the senses of taste and touch.

82. Janson, *Apes*, 239–260 (chap. VIII). Quoted in Kulbrandstad Walker, "Appetites," 116.

83. "Adage IV V 42/LB II 1075D," in Erasmus, *Collected Works: Adages*, 170.

84. The pike was also considered as a gluttonous animal. It was mentioned as an example in the definitions of the words *gourmand* and *vorace*: "The pike is a very greedy fish" [*Dictionnaire de l'Académie françoise*, vol. 1, 1762, 829, s.v. "Gourmand"]. Nicolas de Bonnefons justified this reputation by the fact that pikes "eat all the fish of the place they're in, and a little number of big pikes is enough to ruin a big pond." [Bonnefons], *Delices de la Campagne*, 330.

85. Many emblems represented gluttony by the figure of the bear, which, when seeking honey, is punished because of its weakness by the violent attack of bees: The bear's *gourmandise* "is proverbial and makes it commit carelessnesses." Pastoureau, *L'ours*, 90.

86. The fox is "of a gluttounous nature, / And [wants] everything for itself." Richelet, *Dictionnaire*, vol. 1, 771, s.v. "Goulu."

87. The article related to voraciousness also referred to the "lions and other fierce and carnivorous beasts." Furetière, *Dictionnaire universel*, vol. 3, fol. Ooo03 r, s.v. "Vorace."

88. On the symbolic figures used in bestiairies, see notably Cohen, *Animals as Disguised Symbols*; Connor, "Menagerie of the Senses;" Tervarent, *Attributs et symboles*; Bierlaire, "Zoologie," 179–188; Nordenfalk, "*The Five Senses*," 1–22.

89. A voracious person "eats without chewing, greedily, with avidity. The lions and other wild and carnivorous beasts are voracious animals. Sharks in the sea, pikes in the rivers, are voracious fishes. One also says it of big birds of prey, and even people who are big eaters." Furetière, *Dictionnaire universel*, vol. 3, fol. Ooo03 r, s.v. "Vorace." "[I]t is the proper of voracious animals to eat gluttonly." Furetière, *Dictionnaire universel*, vol. 2, fol. T2 r, s.v. "Goulument."

90. Furetière, *Dictionnaire universel*, vol. 2, fol. Ddd r, s.v. "Loup." The proverbial expressions originated from the wolf's behavior make for the greater part reference to food and hunger: "One says that hunger drives the wolf out of the wood; to say, that necessity forces people to work, or to beg. One says that one puts people in the wolf's mouth, to say, that one exposes them to obvious dangers. One says, whom is made ewe, the wolf eats him, to say, that when one is too easy or patient, one is subject to

be pillaged, or insulted. . . . One also says, that war is very strong, when the wolves eat each other: what is said about authors or people from the same profession, when they tear each other apart, or plead against one another." Furetière, *Dictionnaire universel*, vol. 2, fol. Ddd v. The wolf is a scary animal that has "a dreadful mouth with a double row of teeth and fangs that cut like steel." Furetière, *Dictionnaire universel*, vol. 2, fol. Ddd r. The step between the dreadful wolf to the werewolf man-eater is easily crossed: "Some people believe that there are real werewolves, who are wolves, who eat only human flesh." Furetière, *Dictionnaire universel*, vol. 2, fol. Ddd r.

91. The duck is a "very gluttonous bird" (*Dictionnaire de l'Académie françoise*, vol. 1, 1762, 829, s.v. "Goulu"; *Encyclopédie méthodique. Médecine*, 345).

92. The *coq d'Inde* (turkey) is also a greedy bird. Bodin, *Théâtre de la nature*, 179.

93. Ripa, *Iconologie ou les principales choses*, 47. The association of gluttony with birds may be linked to the success of fowls in banquets, where they were considered as the most delicate foods.

94. Bobis, *Histoire du chat*, 245.

95. Richelet, *Dictionnaire*, vol. 1, 771, s.v. "Goulu." The definition of this animal still appeared in the dictionary of Trévoux in 1743, which also mentioned a bird bearing this name: "Gulo. Aldrovand speaks of a bird that has some report with the cormorant, in the fact that he devours fish with a lot of greediness, and it is the only reason why one gave it the name of Goulu [glutton]." *Dictionnaire de Trévoux*, vol. 3, col. 859–860, s.v. "Goulu." Let us note that there is actually an animal named *glouton* (the wolverine in English), the scientific name of which is *gulo gulo*, which more or less corresponds to the physical description that Richelet made of the *goulu*. Living at present in Scandinavia and in the north of Eurasia and American continent, it is probably the origin of the *goulu* mentioned here.

96. For example in Alciat, *Emblematum libellus*, fol. 36 r–v. When representing Avarice, Ripa makes the following comment: "This woman who has the stomach so big, who holds a purse, and who is accompanied by a skinny wolf, does not poorly represent the nature of the misers, who similar to the hydropiques, cannot extinguish the thirst they have for wealth, but like the . . . wolves have for the things of the world an insatiable or even enraged hunger." Ripa, *Iconologie ou les principales choses*, 147.

97. Pastoureau, *Le cochon*.

98. Ripa, *Iconologie ou les principales choses*, 46. The pig was represented in the allegory of "gluttony," next to a character with a long neck and a big belly. Ripa, *Iconologie ou les principales choses*, 156.

99. Buffon, *Histoire naturelle*, in *Œuvres*, 627–628.

100. Ripa, *Iconologie ou les principales choses*, 157.

101. Ripa, *Iconologie ou les principales choses*, 156.

102. The Florentine whom Dante meets in the third circle of Hell (canto VI), where the gourmands are punished, is called Ciacco, which in Tuscan means "pig." Let us note besides that the pig was also considered as "the closest animal to the man, the most similar to him" in the Middle Ages. Alexandre-Bidon, "Trop gourmand," 135.

103. Bodin, *De la Démonomanie des sorciers*, 18.

104. Bodin, *De la Démonomanie des sorciers*, 18.

105. Saint Augustine, *Confessions*, trans. H. Chadwick (Oxford: Oxford University Press, 1991), 171. Quoted in Shapin, "The Philosopher and the Chicken," 29.

106. Shapin, "The Philosopher and the Chicken," 29.

107. Shapin, "The Philosopher and the Chicken," 29.

108. Renaudot, *Recueil général*, vol. 2, 84, 55th conference, "1. Du Goust" (On Taste), 81–86.

109. The crocodile, according to Pline, is "the only animal on earth which has no use of the tongue." Pline l'Ancien, *Histoire naturelle*, ed. E. Ernout, Paris, 1952, p. 54 [Book VIII, XXXVII, § 89]. "[T]he starving wolf eats earth": Pline l'Ancien, *Histoire naturelle*, 52 [Book VIII, XXXIV, § 84].

110. Porta, *La magie naturelle*, 20. The ostrich is another commonplace: "One proverbially says of a glutton, that he has the stomach of an ostrich, that he would digest iron." From that came the expression "to have a cast-iron stomach." Furetière, *Dictionnaire universel*, vol. 1, 1690, fol. Kkkk4 r, s.v. "Digerer."

111. Ripa, *Iconologie ou les principales choses*, 130–131.

112. "[A]ppetites as disordered as those of pregnant women, who prefer coal, chalk, and ashes to the good food." Renaudot, *Recueil général*, vol. 2, 465, 78th conference, "1. Pourquoy l'Appetit sensitif domine sur la raison" (Why the Sensitive Appetite Dominates on Reason), 449–458.

113. On this issue, see Thomas, *Man and the Natural World*; Fontenay, *Le silence des bêtes*.

114. Homélies, *Sixième Homélie sur la Deuxième Epître aux Corinthiens* chap 9. Quoted in Burton, *The Anatomy of Melancholy*, 43 ("Democritus to the Reader").

115. Érasme de Rotterdam, *La civilité puérile*, 59–63.

116. [Courtin], *Nouveau traité de la civilité*, 176.

117. [Courtin], *Nouveau traité de la civilité*, 171.

118. Furetière, *Dictionnaire universel*, fol. T2 v, s.v. "Gourmandise."

119. Jaucourt, "*Gourmandise*," in Diderot and D'Alembert, *Encyclopédie*, vol. 7, 754. Let us note, however, that the article "Glouton" does not refer to the gourmand but to the animal previously mentioned (200n95). "I." [Daubenton], Diderot and D'Alembert, *Encyclopédie*, vol. 7, 722, s.v. "Glouton."

120. La Salle, *Rules of Christian Decorum*, 319. "It is so natural for people to seek pleasure in eating and drinking that . . . it is difficult to eat without offending God. Most people eat like animals to satisfy their appetite." La Salle, *Rules of Christian Decorum*, 57.

121. Pascal, *Pensées*, 136.

122. See, for instance, the work of Emmanuelle Raga, "Bon mangeur, mauvais mangeur."

123. Laurioux, *Gastronomie, humanisme*, 219, n. 98.

124. Bayle so tells that Apicius "had held, so to speak, a School of the mouth and of greed in Rome; that he had spent two and a half millions to eat well; that seeing himself hardly put into debt, he had finally thought of examining the state of his good; and that having found that he would only have 250 thousand livres (pounds), he poisoned himself, as if he had been afraid of starving with such a sum." Bayle, *Dictionnaire historique et critique*, vol. 1, 303, s.v. "Apicius."

125. Renaudot, *Recueil général*, vol. 2, 81. Emphasis added.

126. Renaudot, *Recueil général*, vol. 1, 418.

127. "For the enjoyment of the cena the Roman possessed a special organ whose sole function was to experience culinary pleasure: the gula, located between the throat and the beginning of the esophagus. Because pleasure was not experienced in the mouth, one could not spit out a piece of meat after tasting it. The delicious rottenness had to be ingested in order to be savored." Dupont, "Grammar of Roman Dining," 125.

128. "In fact, all the pleasures of taste do not excite animals—it is not the ones that they perceive at the end of the tongue but in the throat, and the sensation felt looks more like touch than taste. This is why the gourmands do not ask the gods to have a big tongue but to have the gullet of a crane, as reported Philoxenus, son of Eryxis." Aristotle, *Ethique à Eudème*, 1231a13 *et seq.*, quoted in Wilgaux, "Gourmands et gloutons," 27.

129. "Temperance and Profligacy are therefore concerned with those pleasures which man shares with the lower animals, and which consequently appear slavish and bestial. These are the pleasures of touch and taste. But even taste appears to play but a small part, if any, in Temperance. For taste is concerned with discriminating flavours, as is done by wine-tasters, and cooks preparing savoury dishes; but it is not exactly the flavours that give pleasure, or at all events not to the profligate: it is actually enjoying the object that is pleasant, and this is done solely through the sense of touch, alike in eating and drinking and in what are called the pleasures of sex. This is why a certain gourmand [Philoxenus] wished that his throat might be longer than a crane's, showing that his pleasure lay in the sensation of contact." Aristotle, *Nicomachean Ethics*, 176–179 [III, 1118a].

130. Emblem books did not represent the five senses as such, but there were numerous moral allegorical representations connected with gluttony, and other moral implications intertwined with sensible pleasures. On emblems, see the commented database and the sources digitized by the University of Glasgow, The Stirling Maxwell Centre for the Study of Text/Image Cultures, online at http://www.gla.ac.uk/schools/mlc/research/stirlingmaxwellcentre/.

131. Alciat, *Emblemes d'Alciat*, 112, 117.

132. "Philoxenus, this famous gourmand of the antiquity, contemporary of Denys the Tyrant, who only served extremely warm dishes on the table, and who wished to have a long gullet like a crane to be able to taste wines; Philoxenus, as I say, doubtless had in the internal tunic of the esophagus the mammelons [organs] of taste finer than elsewhere." [Jaucourt], Diderot and D'Alembert, *Encyclopédie*, vol. 7, Paris, 1757, 759, s.v. "Goût (Physiolog.)."

133. "Aristotle widens taste up to the esophagus or to the throat; but it must only be understood as the bottom of the mouth, or the borders of the throat; because the canal of the throat seems to be incapable of enjoying pleasure, sweetness, or bitterness. . . . And in vain Philoxenus would have had a crane's gullet, as he wished, to enjoy much longer the pleasure of drinking and eating." Bernier, *Abrégé de la philosophie de Gassendi*, vol. 6, 94. The author was a doctor of the Faculty of Montpellier.

134. There are other versions of Philoxenus's story with similar conclusions. The character is for instance described demanding boiling hot dishes, which he became used to consuming. Richelet, *Dictionnaire de la langue françoise*, vol. 1, 771, s.v. "Gourmand."

Rabelais also mentioned Philoxenus and Gnathon who, in order to receive the best piece, "boldly spat in the dishes" so as to disgust the other hosts. Rabelais, *Quart Livre*, 1548, quoted by Dedekind, *Grobianus*, 216, n. 18.

135. The woodcut published in the edition of 1549 was, however, not the one that had been planned at first for the emblem. It is presumed that Bonhomme had not yet received the right engraving, which would appear in the Latin edition in 1550, although the erroneous image continued to be used in the French editions. I would like to thank Alison Adams for pointing this out to me, and for her help in translating some of the verse epigrams and their comments into English.

136. Alciat, *Emblemes d'Alciat*, 117.

137. Casagrande and Vecchio, *Les péchés de la langue*.

138. Alciat, *Emblemes d'Alciat*, 114. The *escornifleurs* are the people who try "to eat at the expense of others." *Dictionnaire de l'Académie françoise*, vol. 1, 1694, 387, s.v. "Escornifler."

139. Alciat, *Emblemes d'Alciat*, 116. Here is the beginning of the epigram: "The Rat reigning in the storeroom, eating everything away, / Saw oysters opened by an end: / Put his beard in it: and false bone he catches, / which touched brought the trapdoor down, / And the thief in prison held, / Who came by himself in his pit." Alciat, *Emblemes d'Alciat*, 116.

140. "Magnificent and sumptuous, the baroque cult favored scenic and sumptuous games. By means of intensely expressive stages, of a spectacular liturgy and of preachings using abundantly scenic solutions, it [the baroque] plays with the senses and strikes the hearts." Delfosse, "Exciter les sens pour bouleverser les cœurs," 26; Delfosse, *La "Protectrice du Païs-Bas."*

141. The work circulated before as a manuscript, and the exact date of publication is not known. Platine, *Le Platine en François*, vol. 1. On this founding text, the reader should consult the remarkable study of Bruno Laurioux, *Gastronomie, humanisme et société à Rome*.

142. Girard, "Du manuscrit à l'imprimé," 108.

143. Desdier Christol de Montpellier adapted Platina's text, which he translated into French while adding his personal comments.

144. Quellier, *Gourmandise*, 105–107.

145. Cornaro, *De la sobriété*, 89.

146. Gélis, "Le corps, l'Église," 17–18.

147. Foucault, *Histoire de la sexualité*, vol. 2.

148. Plato, *Le Banquet*.

149. Plato, *The Republic*, 305–306 (Book IX, [585d–586c]).

150. O'Rourke Boyle, *Senses of Touch*; Fontenay, *Silence des bêtes*.

151. Mayr, *Authority, Liberty, and Automatic Machinery*; Maurice and Mayr, *The Clockwork Universe*.

152. Dear, "A Mechanical Microcosm," 58–60.

153. Dear, "A Mechanical Microcosm," 69, 59.

154. Claude Perrault as well considered the physical organs as machines led by the soul and studied by mechanics: "The soul uses the organs of the body, which are real

machines," and is "the main cause of the action of each part of the machine." Just like an organ, "which however able to provide different sounds, by the arrangement of the pieces of which it consists, never makes it but under the conduct of the organist." Perrault, *Essais de physique*, vol. 3, 1. Doctor in medicine from the Faculty of Paris, Claude Perrault (1613–1688) was a member of the Académie Royale des Sciences.

155. On Descartes, see Cottingham, "'A Brute to the Brutes?'"; Guéroult, *Descartes selon l'ordre des raisons*; Kambouchner, *L'homme des passions* and *Descartes et la philosophie morale*. I would like to thank Noëlie Vialles for these references and for her many valuable insights on Descartes's works.

156. Descartes, *Méditations métaphysiques*, 59 (1st Meditation). Emphasis added.

157. Descartes, *Méditations métaphysiques*, 93 (3rd Meditation).

158. Descartes, *Méditations métaphysiques*, 59 (1st Meditation).

159. The physicality/exteriority does not concern the body only but also all the physiological and physical processes: the temperaments, customs, habitats, ways of feeding, and so forth.

160. Carl Havelange has stressed the implications of this theory for the history of sight. Havelange, *De l'œil et du monde*. Philippe Descola developed a wide analysis of the analogist ontology of premodern cultures. Descola, *Par-delà nature et culture*, 280–320. On the same subject, see also Foucault, *Les mots et les choses*, 32 *et seq.*

161. Renaudot, *Recueil général*, vol. 2, 687, 92nd conference, "1. Quel est le plus sain de l'humide ou du sec" (Which Is the Healthiest of Wet or Dry), 681–689. This was a common idea in the Middle Ages. Aldebrandin of Siena had already written in the thirteenth century that "the body of the man is healthy; all the things which have a better flavor in the mouth feed him better." Quoted in Flandrin, "De la diététique à la gastronomie," 692.

162. Descola, *Par-delà nature et culture*, 98.

163. Descartes, *Discours de la méthode, Sixième partie*, quoted in Descola, *Par-delà nature et culture*, 103. Emphasis added, in order to stress all the nuances that were originally present in Descartes's hypotheses.

164. Descola, *Par-delà nature et culture*, 97.

165. In the seventeenth century, "everybody needed a doctor to indicate him the best suitable diet, while in the Middle Ages we were directly informed by our own body, in other words by our appetite." Flandrin, "De la diététique à la gastronomie," 691–692.

166. Aziza-Shuster, *Le médecin de soi-même*.

167. Cornaro, *De la sobriété*, 55.

168. Cornaro, *De la sobriété*, 45–46.

169. "No, never in the course of my irregular youth, excited with pleasures, never did I taste the joy of living as today! And however I did not spare either care or expenses, but all the pleasures seemed vain to me, filled with disappointments and with inconveniences. O life truly happy, besides the many favors you grant your beloved old man, you give his stomach such a perfection that he finds dry bread more delicious today than he formerly found the most delicate dishes, and where does this come from? It is because Reason, which lies in you, persuades him that bread is the most suitable dish for the man, when the appetite wishes it." Cornaro, *De la sobriété*, 86.

170. Cornaro, *De la sobriété*, 68–69.

171. Malebranche, *Traité de morale*, 184 [part 1, chap. 11, § XI].

172. St. Luke, X, 8, "Manducate quae apponuntur vobis." Sales, *Introduction to the Devout Life*, 271–272. "It is . . . a greater virtue to eat without choice what is set before you, and to take it also in the same order as it is set before you, whether it be according to your taste or not, than to choose always the worst. For though this latter way of living seems more austere, yet the other has in it more resignation, for by it we not only give up our taste but our choice. Thus it is no small austerity to turn our taste every way, and to hold it subject to occasion. Added to this, mortification of this kind makes no show, inconveniences no one, and is specially fitting for civil life. To put back one dish to take another, to pick and scrape at everything, to find nothing well prepared or well cleaned, to make a mystery of every mouthful, this betokens a heart soft and attentive to dishes and basins. I think more of St Bernard's drinking oil instead of water or wine, than if he had drunk the water of wormwood on purpose, for it was a sign that he did not think about what he was drinking." Sales, *Introduction to the Devout Life*, 271–272.

173. Malebranche, *Traité de morale*, 183–184 [part 1, chap. 11, § X]. Emphasis added.

174. Renaudot, *Recueil général*, vol. 2, 44–45, 52nd conference, "2. Si quelques autres animaux que l'homme usent de raison?" (If Other Animals Than Man Use Reason), 41–48.

175. The temperance of animals was a common idea: "Besides that it [nature] charged the man with such an insatiable appetite, that he does not stop looking constantly for new meats, and having found one good to his taste, he can only with great difficulty refrain from taking more than needed, from which afterwards result colds, catarrhs, and other infinite sorts of diseases. But as for animals they content themselves with those that nature prepared them, without disguising them, or forcing their nature to please their appetite. Moreover, nature gave them such a well-ordered constitution that they never take more than required to feed, neither in drink nor in food. But as for the man, all the fruits of the earth, of the trees, any sorts of herbs, vegetables, and roots, fishes of the sea, birds of the sky, are not enough for him to devastate nature, he has to disguise, mask, and sophisticate them, to change the substance into accident and nature into art; so that by such temptations nature is irritated and almost forced to take more than needed: then when the ship is overloaded, and when the stomach is very full, all the senses are disturbed so that none of them can exercise its office." Boaistuau, *Le Théâtre du Monde*, 76.

176. Boaistuau, *Le Théâtre du Monde*, 80.

Chapter 3. The Lowest Sense of All

1. Renaudot, *Recueil général*, vol. 2, 49–55, 53rd conference, "1. S'il y a plus de cinq sens externes" (If There Are More Than Five External Senses).

2. Lamy, *Explication mechanique et physique*, 7.

3. Lamy, *Explication mechanique et physique*, 28–29. François Bernier also questions the number of senses. Bernier, *Abrégé*, vol. 6, 14–18.

4. Perrault, *Essais de physique*, 22 (note in the margin). One finds the same idea in Lamy, *Explication mechanique et physique*, 6.

5. Renaudot, *Recueil général*, vol. 2, 53.

6. Du Laurens, *Discours de la conservation de la veuë*, 33; Renaudot, *Recueil général*, vol. 2, 50.

7. Du Laurens, *Discours de la conservation de la veuë*, 36.

8. Korsmeyer, *Making Sense of Taste*, 3.

9. Romeyer Dherbey, "La construction de la théorie aristotélicienne du sentir," 144.

10. Sanger and Kulbrandstad Walker, "Making Sense of the Senses," 3.

11. Sanger and Kulbrandstad Walker, *Sense and the Senses*; Ferino-Pagden, *I cinque sensi nell'arte*.

12. [Tomkis], *Lingua*. This is an allegorical play on the five senses, personified and distinguished by their clothes. We find the symbols commonly associated with the sense organs. Gustus is represented at the head of an army of monkeys—the analysis of the bestiary in the previous chapter has already shown the frequency of this animal to represent taste in iconographic and literary sources. In relation to the other senses, Gustus claims supremacy because he is essential to the subsistence of all: "Since the whole Microcosme I maintaine, Let mee as Prince, above the Senses raigne." [Tomkis], *Lingua*, fol. I2 (act 4, scene 5). The tongue—considered in this case as the organ of speech and not of gustation—demands in this play to become a sense in its own right. This is actually an old idea of antique origin. To consider speech as a sense did not shock anybody since the senses were not only considered as passive but also as active. Lady Lingua faces the other senses in a war to determine the superiority of one of them. In this battle, Appetitus—companion of Gustus, thus recalling the profound connection of taste and appetite—claims the extension of the seven liberal arts to eight, to be able to include the art of cookery. But in the term of the confrontation, the appetite and the tongue are defeated. Lady Lingua is condemned to remain locked in Gustus's house, kept prisoner behind the teeth. She fails to become a true sense, for the number of senses has to correspond to that of the elements, to which is added the sky. Let us note that Lady Lingua is in the end recognized as the sense of speech for women only. The access of cookery to the aesthetic discipline is, on the other hand, denied. It is sight, the expected winner, which triumphs after all over his opponents.

13. Romeyer Dherbey, "La construction de la théorie aristotélicienne du sentir," 138.

14. Renaudot, *Recueil général*, vol. 2, 101–102, 56th conference, "1. De l'Odorat" (On Smell), 97–104.

15. Aristotle, *De Anima*, 40 [423b].

16. The division of the senses within two subgroups, according to the presence or to the absence of a medium, is explained in book III of Aristotle's *De Anima*, whereas book II offers a unified vision of sensory perception, proposing a medium in the functioning of all the senses. The contradictions in the philosopher's thought can be explained by the fact that he worked on this topic for numerous years, refining his reflections throughout his life. See the works of the specialists of the subject, such as Romeyer Dherbey, *Corps et âme*.

17. Contemporaries of Aristotle and followers of both Aristotle and of Plato would have been the transmitters of this theory of opposition. See Romeyer Dherbey, "La construction de la théorie aristotélicienne du sentir," 135.

18. Bernier, *Abrégé*, vol. 6, 92. Claude Perrault explains as for him that "since the objects are generally either close and joined to the body, either remote from it, the joint objects make their movement, figure, size, gravity, hardness, coldness, heat, and other qualities of this nature known by touch, and their flavor by taste. The separate objects make their smell known by the sense of smell, the rustle which the shock makes them suffer by hearing; their color, movement, size, and figure by sight." Perrault, *Essais de physique*, vol. 3, 23–24.

19. The status of the sense of smell is not fixed and varies from one author to the other.

20. "Indeed there is no need for images nor for *espèces* (species) when the object and the faculty can join immediately, because the species and the images are only there to compensate for the distance of the objects. That is why they are only necessary to the senses of sight and hearing, because their objects are distant. But they are useless to the others, especially as their objects unite immediately with them. The warmth, cold, and other tactile qualities join touch by themselves, the flavors taste, the smells the sense of smell. . . . It is certain that sight cannot be without them [the species], and that bodies must send their images to the eyes to be perceived by them. . . . So much must be said of hearing, because it is necessary that the sound's image multiplies in the air to be heard." Cureau de la Chambre, *Le système de l'âme*, 43, 57.

21. "Taste, a necessary sense, which perceives all savours by the tongue and palate, and that by means of a thinne spittle, or watry iuyce." Burton, *Anatomy of Melancholy*, 23 (part 1, section 1, member 2, subsection 6).

22. Rochefort, *Dictionnaire general*, s.v. "Goust," 221. "The heat of the man which lasts as much as his life preserves him by feeding him . . . which is made by means of food. . . . Yet as the air repairs our spirituous parts; so, food (namely meat and drinks) restores our solid and liquid parts, a continual decrease of which happens. And because their repair was absolutely necessary for the animal's preservation, nature gave him an appetite and a desire of these: which if it is of meats [food] is called hunger, if of drinking, is called thirst, the one and the other accompanied with pain and with pleasure: of pain, to warn when it is time to take his meals; of pleasure to make him exercise all the more gladly these natural actions." Renaudot, *Recueil général des questions traittées*, vol. 2, 177–178, 61st conference, "1. Lequel est le plus mal aisé à endurer la faim ou la soif" (Which Is the Most Difficult to Endure of Hunger or Thirst), 177–184.

23. "And this sense of touch which nature gave to animals for the preservation of their species, the most unrefined, the most earthy of all, and consequently the most delicious, does it not often make us become beasts?" Du Laurens, *Discours de la conservation de la veuë*, 42.

24. "Because what says the Philosopher [Aristotle] that the sensible object applied to the organ is not felt, must only be understood of the three senses which are for the convenience of the animal; namely of sight, hearing, and smell; and not of the other two, which are for his absolute necessity, in consideration of what nature wanted to judge closer, exercising these two senses by a way internal and inseparable of the organ." Renaudot, *Recueil général des questions traittées*, vol. 2, 72, 54th conference, "1. Du Tract" (On Touch), 65–72.

25. Du Laurens, *Discours de la conservation de la veuë*, 36–37.

26. Aristotle, *De Anima*, 33 [420b].

27. Du Laurens, *Discours de la conservation de la veuë*, 36–37.

28. Du Laurens, *Discours de la conservation de la veuë*, 43.

29. "I want, so that each would know the perfection of this sense, to champion it, and make it almost similar to the intellect. . . . The intellect includes the whole universe without occupying any space, contains the sky and the earth . . . sight receives the sky without it occupying any space, the greatest mountains of the world enter all at the same time and entirely whole through the pupil." Du Laurens, *Discours de la conservation de la veuë*, 52–53.

30. Korsmeyer, *Making Sense of Taste*, 16.

31. Havelange, *De l'oeil et du monde*.

32. Du Laurens, *Discours de la conservation de la veuë*, 43.

33. Du Laurens, *Discours de la conservation de la veuë*, 44.

34. Lamy, *Explication mechanique et physique*, 91.

35. Du Laurens, *Discours de la conservation de la veuë*, 52.

36. "The intellect judges at the same time of two opposites, of right and wrong, accommodates them both in itself, understands one by the other, organizes them under one same science. The eye at the same moment receives the black and the white, and discerns them perfectly without one preventing the knowledge of the other, which does not happen with the other senses." Du Laurens, *Discours de la conservation de la veuë*, 53–54.

37. Bernier, *Abrégé*, vol. 6, 128.

38. Du Laurens, *Discours de la conservation de la veuë*, 54.

39. Perrault, *Essais de physique*, vol. 3, 62.

40. Gassendi published studies on optics and astronomy, but also on Epicurus's philosophy, which he endeavored to rehabilitate, refusing the image of depraved *pourceau* often attributed to the philosopher of "the Garden."

41. We find thirteen pages on touch, eight pages on taste, and the same on smell, with twenty-one pages on hearing. Bernier, *Abrégé*, vol. 6.

42. Perrault, *Essais de physique*, vol. 3, 26–41. Let us note that Claude Perrault is also the author of a treatise entitled *Du bruit et de la musique des Anciens* (On the Noise and Music of the Ancients, 1721). Rohault, *Traité de Physique*. Jacques Rohault is a popularizer of Descartes's works, which he helped disseminate. He is a secondary character in the classical period's scientific movement, but is particularly significant because his *Traité de physique* (Treatise on Physics) would be read in schools. He also organized public weekly sessions at his home, where he practiced experiments intended to explain physical phenomena.

43. Le Cat, *Traité des Sens*; Le Cat, *Traité des sensations*.

44. Le Cat, *La théorie de l'ouie*.

45. "Nescio an improbae sorti, vel potius occula cuidam majestati sit referendum, Linguam que Artis, et Naturae panduntur arcana in ignota et obscura sui compositione latitare" (I do not know if it is necessary to refer to an adverse fate, or rather to some hidden greatness; the tongue hides by its composition the secrets of art and nature spread in ignorance and darkness). Malpighi, *Opera omnia*, 13. See the chapter dedicated to the study of the tongue in this work: "Marcello Malpighii Exercitatio Epistolica De Lingua,"

13–20. Also see on this Korsmeyer, *Making Sense of Taste*, 68–102 (chap. 3, "The Science of Taste"); Grmek, *Histoire de la pensée médicale*, vol. 2, 28–31; Jütte, *History of the Senses*, 232–233.

46. Condillac, *Traité des sensations*, 77. Condillac was an eighteenth-century sensualist philosopher. His important work is more thoroughly addressed later in this chapter.

47. Renaudot, *Recueil général*, vol. 2, 65–66.

48. Bernier, *Abrégé*, vol. 6, 79.

49. Renaudot, *Recueil général des questions traittées*, vol. 2, 69.

50. "Since sensory life is spread all over the body, touch, which is inseparable from the former, does not have like the other senses a particular and limited organ, but one that is diffuse in all parts of the body. Because among the objects of all the senses only the tangible qualities give the being and constitute the animal by their proportion and temperature; so they only destroy it by their excess and overindulgence. Just like there is only a small part of our body that sees, another that hears, smells, and tastes; if there had been as well just a single part of the body which had been able to discern by touch the quality of its object, it would have happened that whereas the only part intended for the feeling of touch would have been delighting in one of these objects, the excess of some other could have destroyed all the rest of the animal without it feeling anything; and so would have died without knowing it nor consequently without being able to avoid it; which is the main purpose of its senses: which represent themselves on this matter death as so terrible, so that its horror would oblige them to take a greater care of their preservation." Renaudot, *Recueil général des questions traittées*, vol. 2, 66–67. The author is here inspired by Aristotle's *De Anima* [435b].

51. Renaudot, *Recueil général*, vol. 2, 67–68.

52. "[T]he refined touch denoting the flesh's softness and tenderness, on which consequently the tangible qualities easily make their impression: and this tenderness denotes the good temperance of the body, which is followed by the actions of the mind; which, unable to do anything without the ministry of the body when it is united to it, is forced to follow its arrangements. And it is also for that reason that great minds usually have delicate and weak bodies, which stupid and oafish have more strong and tough. Thus as touch distinguishes men from beasts, so it does between the people, what sight does not, nor the other senses; for on the contrary it often happens that great minds are shortsighted and have less refined senses." Renaudot, *Recueil général*, vol. 2, 67–68. Again, the author is actually referring to Aristotelian ideas: "[T]ouch . . . is in man the most precise sense. In the case of the other senses indeed man is far behind most animals, but by touch he has a precision much higher than the others; which is why he is the wisest of all animals. This is evidenced by the fact that, even in the human race, it is because of this sense's organ . . . that there are gifted and non-gifted beings. Indeed, the individuals with hard flesh are hardly gifted for reflection, whereas those who have a soft flesh are very talented." Aristotle, *De Anima* [421a].

53. Renaudot, *Recueil général*, vol. 2, 69–70.

54. Buffon, *Œuvres completes*, 172.

55. Reacting to the publication of John Locke's *Essay on Human Understanding*, Molyneux wonders whether a blind person from birth who would have suddenly recovered

sight would be capable of distinguishing, at distance and only by looking at them, a cube from a sphere, which he formerly perceived by touch. Both philosophers answered negatively, but the question generated an important debate in the eighteenth century.

56. Renaudot, *Recueil général des questions traittées*, vol. 2, 50–51.

57. Renaudot, *Recueil général des questions traittées*, vol. 2, 51.

58. "If, then, the rest of the flesh perceived flavour, taste and touch would seem to be one and the same sense. But as things are they are two, because they are not interchangeable." Aristotle, *De Anima*, 40 [422b].

59. Renaudot, *Recueil général*, vol. 2, 67–68.

60. Bernier, *Abrégé*, vol. 6, 91.

61. Cureau de la Chambre, *Système de l'âme*, 61.

62. [Jaucourt], "Goût (Physiolog.)," 760.

63. Burton, *Anatomy of Melancholy*, 23 [First partition, section 1, member 2, subsection 6].

64. "Nasal organs are only wide membranes spread on thin bones. . . . In dogs and in most beasts which have a much more delicate sense of smell than man, these membranes . . . are in largest number." Perrault, *Essais de physique*, vol. 3, 50–51.

65. Renaudot, *Recueil général*, vol. 2, 97–104.

66. "Just as flavours are sweet or bitter, so are smells . . . But . . . because smells are not very distinct, as flavours are, they have taken their names from the latter in virtue of a resemblance in the things; for sweet [smell] belongs to saffron and honey and bitter to thyme and such like, and similarly in the other cases." Aristotle, *De Anima*, 35 [421a]).

67. Lamy, *Explication mechanique et physique*, 47–48.

68. Rosenfeld, *Common Sense*, 18.

69. Howes, *The Sixth Sense Reader*.

70. On the history of this concept see the comprehensive study of Heller-Roazen, *The Inner Touch*.

71. There is already an extensive literature on this topic, that include Corbin, *Le Miasme et la Jonquille*; Le Guérer, *Pouvoirs de l'Odeur*; Classen, Howes, and Synnott, *Aroma*.

72. Cassirer, *Philosophie des Lumières*, 117.

73. Locke, *Essai philosophique*.

74. Locke, *Essay Concerning Human Understanding*, vol. 1, 77 (book 2, chap. 1, § 2).

75. Locke, *Essay Concerning Human Understanding*, vol. 1, 261 (book 2, chap. 23, § 32).

76. "I think it will be granted easily that, if a child were kept in a place where he never saw any other but black and white till he were a man, he would have no more ideas of scarlet or green than he that from his childhood never tasted an oyster or a pineapple has of those particular relishes." Locke, *Essay Concerning Human Understanding*, vol. 1, 79 (book 2, chap. 1, § 6).

77. Locke, *Essay Concerning Human Understanding*, vol. 1, 91 (book 2, chap. 2, § 2).

78. Locke, *Essai sur l'entendement humain*, 167, n. 1; Silver, "Locke's Pineapple," 43–65.

79. *Le Spectacle de la Nature* was published in 1732 and widely translated in Europe.

80. [Pluche], *Le Spectacle de la Nature*, vol. 5, 96–99.

81. Locke, *Essay Concerning Human Understanding*, vol. 1, 124 (book 2, chap. 11, § 3).

82. "I think it will be needless to enumerate all the particular simple ideas belonging to each sense. Nor indeed is it possible if we would, there being a great many more of

them belonging to most of the senses than we have names for. The variety of smells, which are as many almost, if not more, than species of bodies in the world, do most of them want names. Sweet and stinking commonly serve our turn for these ideas, which in effect is little more than to call them pleasing or displeasing; though the smell of a rose and violet, both sweet, are certainly very distinct ideas." Locke, *Essay Concerning Human Understanding*, vol. 1, 92–93 (book 2, chap. 3, § 2).

83. Locke, *Essay Concerning Human Understanding*, vol. 1, 186 (book 2, chap. 18, § 7).

84. Locke, *Essay Concerning Human Understanding*, vol. 1, 185–186 (book 2, chap. 18, § 5–7).

85. "[T]he ideas of hunger and warmth . . . probably are some of the first that children have and which they scarce ever part with again." Locke, *Essay Concerning Human Understanding*, vol. 1, 113 (book 2, chap. 9, § 5). Taste was also an opportunity for the author, in his "Epistle to the Reader," to defend his work and say he was aware that his book would probably not be well-received by all readers because it is impossible to please everybody. To this end, he used the metaphor of cookery and the variability of tastes: "Everything does not sit alike upon every man's imagination. We have our understandings no less different than our palates; and he that thinks the same truth shall be equally relished by everyone in the same dress, may as well hope to feast everyone with the same sort of cookery: the meat may be the same, and the nourishment good, yet everyone will not be able to receive it with that seasoning; and it must be dressed another way, if you will have it go down with some, even of strong constitutions." Locke, *Essay Concerning Human Understanding*, vol. 1, xxxiii–xxxiv (The Epistle to the Reader).

86. Locke, *Essay Concerning Human Understanding*, vol. 1, 16 (book 1, chap. 2, § 15).

87. Locke, *Essay Concerning Human Understanding*, vol. 1, 23 (book 1, chap. 2, § 27). Indeed, "[t]heir notions are few and narrow, borrowed only from those objects they have had most to do with, and which have made upon their senses the frequentest and strongest impressions. A child knows his nurse and his cradle, and by degrees the playthings of a little more advanced age; and a young savage has, perhaps, his head filled with love and hunting, according to the fashion of his tribe." Locke, *Essay Concerning Human Understanding*, vol. 1, 24.

88. Locke, *Essay Concerning Human Understanding*, vol. 1, 24.

89. Locke, *Essay Concerning Human Understanding*, vol. 1, 23 (book 1, chap. 2, § 25).

90. Locke, *Essay Concerning Human Understanding*, vol. 1, 50–51 (book 1, chap. 4, § 13).

91. Locke, *Essay Concerning Human Understanding*, vol. 1, 115 (book 2, chap. 9, § 9).

92. "For the understanding, like the eye" judges "of objects only by its own sight." Locke, *Essay Concerning Human Understanding*, vol. 1, xxxi (The Epistle to the Reader).

93. Locke, *Essay Concerning Human Understanding*, vol. 1, 120, 129 (book 2, chap. 10–11).

94. Locke, *Essay Concerning Human Understanding*, vol. 1, 306 (book 2, chap. 29, § 2).

95. Locke, *Essay Concerning Human Understanding*, vol. 1, 100 (book 2, chap. 7, § 4).

96. "The ideas we get by more than one sense are of space or extension, figure, rest, and motion. For these make perceivable impressions, both on the eyes and touch; and we can receive and convey into our minds the ideas of the extension, figure, motion, and rest of bodies, both by seeing and feeling." Locke, *Essay Concerning Human Understanding*, vol. 1, 97 (book 2, chap. 5).

97. Locke, *Essay Concerning Human Understanding*, vol. 1, 143 (book 2, chap. 13, § 25).

98. Condillac, *Traité des sensations*, 11.

99. Condillac, *Traité des sensations*, 11.

100. Condillac, *Traité des sensations*, 87.

101. Condillac, *Traité des sensations*, 69.

102. Condillac, *Traité des sensations*, 69–70.

103. Condillac, *Traité des sensations*, 70. Condillac still adds, as a note: "There is nobody unable to notice that he sometimes tends to attribute to a dish that he is eating the smells which strike his sense of smell. But what proves moreover this analogy [between taste and smell], is that we have more taste as we have a finer smell." Condillac, *Traité des sensations*, 70, n. 1.

104. For example, when he says that the power of sight is such that once endowed with it, "it is almost not possible anymore for the statue to think of smelly, sonic, or palpable objects. . . . Hearing, smell, and touch are consequently less exercised." Condillac, *Traité des sensations*, 188. Also, chapter 9 of the third part is dedicated to "the chain of knowledge, abstractions and desires, when sight is added to touch, hearing, and smell." Condillac, *Traité des sensations*, 211.

105. Locke, *Essay Concerning Human Understanding*, vol. 1, 99 (book 2, chap. 7, § 2).

106. Condillac, *Traité des sensations*, 18.

107. Condillac, *Traité des sensations*, 11.

108. Condillac, *Traité des sensations*, 11. If Condillac only makes a reference to smell and hearing here, it is because he has not yet evoked sight and touch, which are the last two senses to affect the statue.

109. Condillac, *Traité des sensations*, 70.

110. Condillac, *Traité des sensations*, 215.

111. Buffon, *Œuvres complètes*, 173–179. Emphasis added.

112. Condillac, *Traité des sensations*, 199.

113. Fontenelle, *Nouveaux dialogues des morts*, 320–321. The dialogue between Apicius and Galileo is in the second part of this work, related to the dialogues between "ancient and modern deads," no. 3, 318–325.

114. Fontenelle, *Nouveaux dialogues des morts*, 321.

115. Fontenelle, *Nouveaux dialogues des morts*, 322. Emphasis added.

116. [D'Alembert], "Discours préliminaire," ij–iij.

117. "The *mammelons nerveux* are here again the organ of Sensation. All that is new is that their structure is a little bit different from that of the *mammelons* of skin, and this proportionally to the disparity of their objects. The *mammelons* of skin, organs of Touch, are small, their substance is compact, thin; they are covered with a quite polished membrane, and with a tight tissue; the *mammelons* of the organ of taste are much bigger, more porous, more open; they are watered with many of limphe, and covered with a skin, or set in very uneven gaines, and so very porous." Le Cat, *Traité des Sens*, 23.

118. "The membrane which covers the nose and which is the organ of this sensation is a continuation of the one that covers the throat, the mouth, the esophagus, the stomach, and the difference of sensations of these parts is more or less as their distances to the Brain; I mean that the sense of smell does not differ more from taste, than taste from hunger and thirst; the mouth has a finer sensation than the esophagus, and the Stom-

ach; the Nose has it even finer than the Mouth, because it is closer to the source of the feeling." Le Cat, *Traité des sensations*, 230.

119. On sensibilities developed by the so-called savages—in particular, children having grown up away from any society—see Strivay, *Enfants sauvages*; Classen, *Worlds of Sense*, 37–49 (chap. 2 "Natural Wits. The Sensory Skills of 'Wild Children'").

120. Zarka, preface, vii.

121. See chapter 5 for the development of this question, in particular within the context of iatromechanism and Montesquieu's climate theory.

122. La Mettrie, *L'Homme-Machine*, 152–153. Emphasis added.

123. Helvétius, "De l'Homme," 74–75, 212, 223.

124. Holbach, *Éléments de morale universelle*, 20–22.

Chapter 4. From a Material to a Spiritual Taste

1. Interestingly, the figurative sense of taste exists in most foreign languages, including in non-Western discourses, like in India. Chantalat, *À la recherche du goût*, 22–26; Montandon, *Du Goût*; Korsmeyer, *Making Sense of Taste*, 44–45.

2. Like Carolyn Korsmeyer, I use the word *metaphor* in the sense of "its general connotation," and not in the stricter sense of the figure of speech theorized by linguistics. Korsmeyer, *Making Sense of Taste*, 38–39.

3. Many references were made, for instance, to the Christ's *dulcedo* (sweetness), as in Psalm 119:103: "How sweet are your words to my taste, sweeter than honey to my mouth!"

4. Bynum, "Fast, Feast, and Flesh," 122.

5. Canivet et al., *Les sens spirituels*.

6. On mystics, see Certeau, *Fable mystique*; Henneau, "À corps perdu;" Houdard, *Invasions mystiques*; Lebrun, *La jouissance et le trouble*; Bord, *Jean de la Croix*; Bajomée, Dor, and Henneau, *Femmes et livres*.

7. For more information on the theological developments of spiritual sense, see Adnès, "Goût spirituel."

8. Yeomans and Derville, "Gourmandise et gourmandise spirituelle."

9. Yeomans and Derville, "Gourmandise et gourmandise spirituelle," col. 627.

10. Yeomans and Derville, "Gourmandise et gourmandise spirituelle," col. 627–628.

11. [Kempis], *Imitation de Jesus-Christ*, 236–237.

12. Sales, *Introduction to the Devout Life*, 388.

13. Yeomans and Derville, "Gourmandise et gourmandise spirituelle," col. 622–626.

14. D'Avila, *Chemin de Perfection*, fol. 84 v.

15. D'Avila, *Traicté du chasteau*, fol. 43 v.

16. D'Avila, *Traicté du chasteau*, fol. 67 r; fol. 163 r.

17. D'Avila, *Traicté du chasteau*, fol. 68 v–69 r.

18. D'Avila, *Traicté du chasteau*, fol. 48 r–49 r.

19. D'Avila, *Traicté du chasteau*, fol. 71 v.

20. D'Avila, *Traicté du chasteau*, fol. 57 r–v.

21. D'Avila, *Traicté du chasteau*, fol. 57 v.

22. D'Avila, *Traicté du chasteau*, fol. 72 r.

23. D'Avila, *Traicté du chasteau*, fol. 58 r–v.

24. La Croix, "Degré du Mont Carmel," 318–319.
25. La Croix, "Degré du Mont Carmel," 317.
26. [Surin], *Fondemens*, 149.
27. [Surin], *Fondemens*, 3.
28. [Surin], *Fondemens*, 31–32.
29. [Surin], *Fondemens*, 44.
30. On the *je ne sais quoi*, see the comprehensive study of Scholar, *The Je-Ne-Sais-Quoi*.
31. La Croix, "Degré du Mont Carmel," 171.
32. La Croix, "Degré du Mont Carmel," 84.
33. Canfield, *Regle de perfection*, 123; Canfield, *Renaissance Dialectic*, 143.
34. Gélis, "Le corps, l'Église," 62; Le Brun, "Mutations de la notion de martyr."
35. La Croix, "Degré du Mont Carmel," 130, 118.
36. La Croix, "Degré du Mont Carmel," 82–83.
37. La Croix, "Degré du Mont Carmel," 149.
38. [Surin], *Fondemens*, 166–168.
39. [Surin], *Fondemens*, 171.
40. [Surin], *Fondemens*, 18.
41. D'Avila, *Traicté du chasteau*, fol. 68 r–v.
42. La Croix, "Degré du Mont Carmel," 207. In Benoit of Canfield's *Rule of Perfection*, God says: "If by the drawing of my spirit I do not make you abandon false pleasure; if by the experience of true pleasure I do not make you abandon false pleasure; if by the taste of heavenly delights I do not give you distaste for earthly delights . . . and if by supernatural satisfaction I do not make you cast off the repose you seek in nature, you will remain in yourself, the feet of your affections soiled with earthly mire, and consequently you will have no part with me in that beautiful city, wherein 'nothing defiled will enter' (Apocalypse, 21:27)." Canfield, *Renaissance Dialectic*, 164.
43. Teresa compares the difficulties of the *orison* and the desire of contemplation with "those who are very thirsty, and see water from far away, and when they want to reach it, they find somebody who defends their passing." D'Avila, *Chemin de Perfection*, fol. 95 r.
44. La Croix, "Degré du Mont Carmel," 89–90.
45. La Croix, "Degré du Mont Carmel," 88.
46. [Kempis], *Imitation de Jesus-Christ*, 506–507.
47. Augustine of Hippo, *Confessions*, trans. H. Chadwick (Oxford, 1998), book 6, 3, 3 (p. 92); book 7, 10, 16 (p. 124). Quoted in Ferguson, "The Senses of Taste," 375–376.
48. Boer and Göttler, *Religion and the Senses*, 2.
49. Gélis, "Le corps, l'Église," 18.
50. Canfield, *Renaissance Dialectic*, 126.
51. Canfield, *Renaissance Dialectic*, 156.
52. Canfield, *Renaissance Dialectic*, 23.
53. Bérulle, *Bref discours*, 30.
54. Bérulle, *Bref discours*, 45. "After the soul got rid of the affection of the external and indifferent things, she abundantly receives consolations and inner feelings that God ensues from it, like a sweet milk to nourish her in her childhood, and a tender dew to fertilize the sterile earth of her heart." Bérulle, *Bref discours*, 29.

55. "Jesus is the true sun, source of all light. The sun . . . is only an image of Jesus, who is a sun in the world of grace and glory, and is the Sun of so many suns that there will be saints in Heaven, which all receive from him their splendor and their illustration like from a vivid source and an inexhaustible fountain of light. . . . Jesus is the Sun not only of men, but also of the angels." Bérulle, *Discours de l'état*, 290–292.

56. Richelet, *Dictionnaire*, s.v. "Goûter," 772.

57. *Dictionnaire de l'Académie françoise*, vol. 1, 1694, 529, s.v. "Goust" [avantgoust]. There are no mentions of this particular meaning of the word *taste* in Nicot's 1606 dictionary. Nicot, *Thresor de la Langue françoyse*, 317, s.v. "le Goust."

58. *Dictionnaire de l'Académie françoise*, vol. 1, 1762, 830, s.v. "Goût."

59. [Surin], *Fondemens*, 101.

60. D'Avila, *Chemin de Perfection*, fol. 177 r, fol. à IIII v.

61. On the question of language and the ineffable within mystical literature, see Houdard, *Invasions mystiques*, 124 *et seq.*

62. In other contexts, the desire of spiritual incorporation would sometimes take other forms, closer to the idea of a self-inflicted disgust through mortification, such as the "pious manducation," which consists of ingesting "holy vinegar" (a beverage originating from maceration of holy relics in wine), consumed to get closer to the saint, with the hope of incorporating his spiritual essence. Gélis, "Le corps, l'Église," 48.

63. La Croix, "Degré du Mont Carmel," 149; [Kempis], *Imitation de Jesus-Christ*, 62, 139. Ignatius of Loyola also used a sensory language to relate to prayer and contempla-tion. See Marty, *Sentir et goûter*.

64. The works of Teresa of Avila were translated from 1601 by Jean de la Quintana-doine de Brétigny, later on by Arnauld d'Andilly. As for John of the Cross, René Gaultier translated his texts in 1621–1622.

65. Montandon, "Goût," 441. There are numerous works on the figurative sense of taste, such as, for instance, Chantalat, *À la recherche du goût*; Blanco, "Le goût des Espagnols"; Dens, *L'honnête homme*.

66. These *livres bleus* (blue books), printed in low quality and small format with a blue paper cover, are a type of popular literature published in early modern France. Chartier, "Distinction et divulgation," 61–70; Chartier, "Bibliothèque bleue."

67. Chartier, "Distinction et divulgation," 70; Losfeld, *Politesse*, 391.

68. Bensoussan, "Le goût selon Saint-Evremond," 24.

69. Chartier, "Distinction et divulgation," 53.

70. [Courtin], *Nouveau traité de la civilité*, 16.

71. Romagnoli, "La courtoisie dans la ville," 34.

72. Losfeld, *Politesse*, 57 *et seq.*; Bury, *Littérature et politesse*, 129 *et seq.*

73. Bury, *Littérature et politesse*, 129–130, 137. Pierre Nicole was a Jansenist who criti-cized the notion of honesty in his works. He writes that "charity thus has everything necessary to be sincerely civil; and one can say that it contains an inner civility toward all men, which would be infinitely agreeable to them if they could see it." Nicole, "Civilité chrétienne," 114. Antoine de Courtin, greatly influenced by Pierre Nicole, also pleads for the "Civility of a Christian." [Courtin], *Nouveau traité de la civilité*, 21.

74. Bury, *Littérature et politesse*, 169. The critique of politeness would become even stronger in the eighteenth century, notably with Jean-Jacques Rousseau. Losfeld, *Politesse*, 283–313.

75. Bury, *Littérature et politesse*, 176.

76. On Mme de Scudéry and her *académie sabbathine* (called this because meetings were held each Saturday), see Viala, *La France galante*. Her salon was considered a perfect "model of mondain literary societies." Losfeld, *Politesse*, 283.

77. Chantalat, *À la recherche du goût*, 30–31.

78. Piles, *Conversations*, 35.

79. Several works have been published on aesthetic taste, including Gigante, *Taste*; Ferry, *Homo Aestheticus*; Knabe, "Esthétique et art culinaire."

80. The first mention of the term appears in the work *Aesthetica*, published by Alexander Gottlieb Baumgarten in 1750.

81. Montesquieu, *Essai sur le goût*, 55. This essay was a posthumous and unfinished text, edited for the first time in 1757 in the article "taste" in the *Encyclopédie*. It was by then entitled "Essay on Taste Regarding the Things of Nature and Art." Voltaire, "Goût"; Voltaire, "Le Temple du Goût"; Diderot and D'Alembert, *Encyclopédie*, vol. 7, 1757, 761, s.v. "Goût (Gramm. Littérat. and Philos.)." The fourth part, signed "O," is attributed to D'Alembert, who published it later in the *Mélanges de littérature, d'histoire et de philosophie*. Le Ru, "La méthode des éléments de D'Alembert," 92.

82. [D'Alembert], "Réflexions sur l'usage," 767–770; Diderot, *Traité du Beau*; Hume, "Standard of Taste"; Kant, *Critique de la Faculté de Juger*.

83. Richelet, *Dictionnaire*, s.v. "Goût," 772.

84. At least in France and more generally in Western cultures, not necessarily in non-Western cultures, like in Asia. In his *Eloge de la Fadeur*, Julien has demonstrated that an absence of taste and flavor—an insipidy or blandness—is, for instance, crucial to Chinese pictorial and culinary aesthetics.

85. Richelet, *Dictionnaire*, s.v. "Goût," 772.

86. "One calls a depraved taste, the one that is contrary to the ordinary taste of other men. . . . The good taste consists in forming the most perfect idea possible of things, and in following it." Furetière, *Dictionnaire universel*, vol. 2, fol. T2 v, s.v. "Goust."

87. La Bruyère, *Caractères*, 83.

88. Viala, *La France galante*, 234 *et seq.*; Lecoq, *Querelle des Anciens et des Modernes*; Bury, *Littérature et politesse*, 156–168. These conflicts were not only ideological; they also encompassed oppositions between writers competing for widely envied positions, as well as people with different political and religious convictions (moderate Catholics vs. Jansenists, for instance). Viala, *La France galante*, 246 *et seq.*

89. "[T]he most certain way to form one's taste is to study these excellent originals, and to always offer them to oneself as a model; and the shortest and the most infallible way to corrupt it, is to despise them and lose them from sight." Mme Dacier, *Causes de la corruption du gout*, 437. She also wrote *Homere défendu contre l'Apologie du R.P. Hardouin, ou Suite des causes de la Corruption du Goust* in 1716. In her work, Madame Dacier tried to demonstrate the quality of Homer's texts against those who dared to criticize their quality, such as M. de la Motte and the Père Hardouin.

90. Voltaire, "Goût (Gramm. Littérat. et Philos.)," 761.

91. "One can say, without flattering ourselves too much, that . . . the Arts and Sciences are more cultivated there [in France] than in all the other Nations of Europe." Morvan de Bellegarde, *Lettres curieuses*, 32.

92. Morvan de Bellegarde, *Lettres curieuses*, 32–33.

93. Molière, *La Critique de l'École des Femmes*, scene 6.

94. On the importance of order and the disgust for excess in classical French culture, see France, *Politeness and Its Discontent*, 11 et seq.

95. L. Bordelon, *Remarques ou réflexions critiques, morales et historiques*, 1690. Quoted in Montandon, "Goût," 442.

96. Gédoyn, "Reflexions sur le Goût," 222. For a thorough analysis of this source, see Chantalat, "Deux monographies," 41–54.

97. Gédoyn, "Reflexions sur le Goût," 222–223.

98. Gédoyn, "Reflexions sur le Goût," 226–227.

99. Voltaire, "Goût (Gramm. Littérat. et Philos.)," 761.

100. "The good taste is of a great extent, and supposes rare qualities; it enters everything, and seasons all things; but it is not as common as one thinks; thousands of people flatter themselves to have it very refined, although they only follow their whim and their prejudices." Morvan de Bellegarde, *Lettres curieuses*, 11–12.

101. "Thus, though the principles of taste be universal, and nearly, if not entirely the same in all men; yet few are qualified to give judgment on any work of art, or establish their own sentiment as the standard of beauty." Hume, "Standard of Taste," 228.

102. Saint-Évremond, "Quelques observations," 130.

103. Bourdieu and Passeron, *Reproduction*; Champion, *Hors d'œuvre*, 34.

104. Goldgar, "Absolutism of Taste," 88.

105. Habermas, *Espace public*.

106. Habermas, *Espace public*, 38.

107. It could be argued that the very corpus of primary printed materials addressed here was in fact a product of the exercise of the rules of taste that are analyzed here. It would certainly be interesting to enlarge this investigation by addressing book reviews, in order to trace the boundary between good and bad taste in literature, art, and elsewhere. Such an investigation, however, is beyond the scope of the present book, which does not intend to determine which books were judged as good or bad in their time but to highlight the general conceptions of taste that were being discussed within all these theoretical works.

108. Goldgar, "Absolutism of Taste," 97.

109. What authors criticized about censorship and government control "was not so much its limitation of freedom, but rather its violation of literary hierarchy. Literary journals offended scholars because of their unelected exercise of power over the Republic of Letters. . . . To be judged was not a problem; who the judges were, however, was." Goldgar, "Absolutism of Taste," 103–104. Voltaire considers that "the Temple of Taste" is "a place . . . of which everybody talks about, where few people go, and which most of those who travelled to it almost never really well examined it." Voltaire, "Le Temple du Goût," 207.

110. [Bouhours], *Entretiens*, 255.

111. [Bouhours], *Entretiens*, 239. "[T]he *je ne sçay quoy* is maybe the only matter about which one did not write any books, and that scholars did not take the trouble to enlighten: there have been discourses, dissertations, and treatises on the strangest subjects; but no author that I know of has worked on this one . . . this matter being of the nature of those that have an impenetrable core, and that one can only explain through admiration, and through silence. I am delighted . . . that you're finally taking the right side, and that you are contenting yourself with what you first wanted to understand. . . . we will say nothing more of a thing, which only subsists because one cannot say what it is." [Bouhours], *Entretiens*, 256–257.

112. "However, to say the truth, this word Taste, which is so familiar to us, does not at first present a very clear idea, and those who use it the most, would maybe be embarrassed to tell us what it means, because it is not as easy as one thinks to define Taste well." Gédoyn, "Reflexions sur le Goût," 220.

113. "Flavor . . . by this word one means a 'je ne sçay quoy' that is on the side of food itself, in which consists the power they have to excite the feeling of flavors inside us." Rohault, *Traité de Physique*, 203.

114. [Bouhours], *Entretiens*, 250. Emphasis added.

115. Voltaire, "Goût (Gramm. Littérat. et Philos.)," 761.

116. "Taste, however uncommon, is not arbitrary: this truth is also acknowledged by those who reduce taste to feeling, and by those who want to pressure themselves into reasoning." [D'Alembert], "Réflexions sur l'usage," 768.

117. Morvan de Bellegarde, *Lettres curieuses*, 13–14

118. Morvan de Bellegarde, *Lettres curieuses*, 14.

119. [Seran de La Tour], *Art de sentir*, vol. 1, xxj.

120. "But spirit alone is not enough to make me judge a work of art, the same way as the well-disposed palate is not enough to let me know if a dish that I have never ate, and a wine that I have never drank, have the taste and the quality that is their own." Gédoyn, "Reflexions sur le Goût," 228.

121. [D'Alembert], "Réflexions sur l'usage," 770. "[T]he 'bon goût' is the first movement, or so to speak, a sort of instinct of the right reason that leads it with speed and that drives it more certainly than all the reasonings it could make. It is a first glimpse that reveals the nature of things in one moment. In a word, taste and judgment are indeed only one same thing, a same disposition, a same habit of the soul, to which one gives different names, depending on the different ways it takes to act. One calls it taste when it acts by feeling, and at the first impression of the objects; one calls it judgment, when it acts by reasoning, and after examining the works with the rules of the art and the lights of truth. So that what can say that taste is the judgment of nature, and that judgment is the taste of reason." *Dictionnaire universel françois et latin*, vol. 3, col. 865–866, s.v. "Goût."

122. [Seran de La Tour], *Art de sentir*, vol. 1, x.

123. The supporters of the rationalist perspective include La Bruyère, Boileau, Perrault, Fontenelle, La Rochefoucauld, the Chevalier de Méré, Madame de Sévigné, Pascal, Nicole, Malebranche, and Crousaz. These rationalists were opposed to the empiricist trends that insisted on the importance of feeling and subjective pleasure regarding

the judgment of taste—the aesthetics of feelings—represented, for instance, by Dubos, Montesquieu, or Bouhours. They also conflicted with relativists who refused the idea of an absolute taste, like Saint-Evremond or Fenelon. Fenelon writes, for instance, "by expressing you my thoughts with such freedom I do not pretend to contradict nor to correct anyone: I historically say what my taste is, like a man, during a meal, naively says he likes one ragoût better than the other one. I don't blame the taste of any man and I consent to have mine blamed. If the politeness and the discretion necessary to society's peace demand that men mutually tolerate each other regarding the variety of opinions related to the most important things of human life, all the more reason must they tolerate each other regarding the variety of opinions related to what matters very little to the security of humanity. I see well that by disclosing my taste I take the risk of displeasing passionate admirers of the Ancients and the Moderns, but, without intending to anger the ones and the others, I give myself to the critics of both sides." Fenelon, *Letter to La Motte*, May 4, 1714, *Correspondance de La Motte et Fénelon*, in La Motte, *Réflexions sur la critique*, vol. 1, 121–123. Quoted in Chantalat, *A la recherche du goût*, 58.

124. The public judges "through the way of feeling, and depending on the impression that the poem or the painting makes on him. Since the first aim of poetry and painting is to touch us, poems and paintings are only good works in proportion as they move us. . . . Yet the feeling teaches much better if the work touches and if it makes on us the impression that a work must make, than all the dissertations composed by the Critics to explain its merit and to calculate its perfections and faults. The way of discussion and analysis used by these Gentlemen, is good truthfully, when it is about finding the causes that make that a work pleases or does not please, but this way is not as good as the one of the feeling when it is about deciding this question. . . . Reason does not want us to reason on such a question, unless one reasons to justify the judgment that the feeling made." [Dubos], *Reflexions critiques*, vol. 2, 323–324.

125. [Dubos], *Reflexions critiques*, vol. 2, 325.

126. [Dubos], *Reflexions critiques*, vol. 2, 331, 360.

127. [Dubos], *Reflexions critiques*, vol. 2, 326.

128. [Seran de La Tour], *Art de sentir*, vol. 1, 3–4.

129. Le Cat, *Traité des Sens*, 20.

130. *Dictionnaire universel françois et latin*, vol. 3, 1743, col. 866, s.v. "Goût."

131. Letter CLVII from Costar to the marquise de Lavardin, in *Lettres*, vol. 1, 416. Quoted in Chantalat, *A la recherche du goût*, 20, n. 9.

132. [Seran de La Tour], *Art de sentir*, vol. 1, 4–5.

133. Crousaz, *Traité du Beau*, 127–128.

134. [Dubos], *Reflexions critiques*, vol. 2, 325–326.

135. Ehrard, *L'Idée de Nature*, 231–232.

136. Ehrard, *L'Idée de Nature*, 251.

137. Morvan de Bellegarde, *Lettres curieuses*, 29.

138. Morvan de Bellegarde, *Lettres curieuses*, 23–28.

139. Morvan de Bellegarde, *Lettres curieuses*, 30.

140. "It is not only the flavors that make different impressions on the organ of taste: it is likely that the other objects do almost the same effect." The author then suggests the

hypothesis of a differential perception of colors. Morvan de Bellegarde, *Lettres curieuses*, 25–26.

141. "The great variety of Tastes, as well as of opinions, which prevail in the world, is too obvious not to have fallen under every one's observation." Hume, "Standard of Taste," [203]. "One says proverbially that one must not dispute about tastes, to say, that they change depending on the diverse inclinations." Furetière, *Dictionnaire universel*, vol. 2, fol. T3 r, s.v. "Goust."

142. [Seran de La Tour], *Art de sentir*, vol. 1, 117.

143. [Dubos], *Reflexions critiques*, vol. 2, 292–294.

144. Voltaire, "Beau," 48.

145. *Dictionnaire universel françois et latin*, vol. 3, col. 865, s.v. "Goût."

146. [Seran de La Tour], *Art de sentir*, vol. 1, 228–229.

147. [D'Alembert], "Réflexions sur l'usage," 768.

148. Voltaire, "Goût," in [D'Alembert], "Réflexions sur l'usage," 761.

149. Morvan de Bellegarde, *Lettres curieuses*, 10.

150. Morvan de Bellegarde, *Lettres curieuses*, 47. There are several examples to be found in this work. "When one disputes about tastes, and one cannot reach an agreement, instead of defending one's own with obstinacy, one must use the method employed to enlighten doubts that can arise with language: it is necessary to resort to a surarbitre [arbitrator], and to refer to the good Authors; the same way one refers to the refined connoisseurs to judge the quality of wine." Morvan de Bellegarde, *Lettres curieuses*, 65–66.

151. Gédoyn, "Reflexions sur le Goût," 239. "I remember that Quintilien, willing to explain what one meant by salsum, which means the salt of discourse, considers first the word literally, from which he draws a sort of consequence for the figurative. By following the same method we will maybe find what Taste is. Literally it is the one of our five senses through which we distinguish flavors. Figuratively it will thus be what makes us distinguish the good and the bad in the works of the mind and of art. Indeed, like the flavors are the object of the material and physical taste, the same way the works of the mind and of art are the object of the moral taste." Gédoyn, "Reflexions sur le Goût," 221–222.

152. Gédoyn, "Reflexions sur le Goût," 224. He is, of course, not the only one to say that "the true cause of taste . . . is the accuracy in comparing." [Seran de La Tour], *Art de sentir*, vol. 1, 57.

153. The allusion to the bodily taste figures in the part entitled "On Delicacy." Montesquieu, *Essai sur le goût*, 55.

154. [D'Alembert], "Réflexions sur l'usage," 767–770.

155. Diderot, *Traité du Beau*, 68–69.

156. Montesquieu, *Essai sur le goût*, 55. Seran de La Tour agrees: "There is, regarding the material Taste, some dishes so delicate that one needs a faculty gifted with the same delicacy to feel them." [Seran de La Tour], *Art de sentir*, vol. 2, 164–165.

157. Voltaire, "Goût (Gramm. Littérat. et Philos.)," 761.

158. [Seran de La Tour], *Art de sentir*, vol. 2, 165–166. "One should not be surprised if those who find their occupation and their delight in the most refined research regarding

the material Taste are so sensitively affected, when they encounter dishes of a perfect delicacy: their taste used for easy and common things became insensitive to these. But when one presents them dishes of which they measure the price from their difficulty and their rarity, their senses seem to be reborn with all their brightness. They are in a sort of rapture, and they do not leave any doubt that if they seem so little sensitive it is because their sensations are extremely difficult to excite. That is how the material taste made a delicate pleasure from the simple satisfaction of a natural need. One sees that two things are required for this delicacy. The Art of the one that prepares it, the sensation in the one that judges: in both of them this delicacy must be so refined and so certain, that the most imperceptible defect and imperfection does not escape them." [Seran de La Tour], *Art de sentir*, vol. 2, 166–167.

159. Gédoyn, "Reflexions sur le Goût," 223.

160. Kant, *Critique of Judgement*, chap. 1, § 3: "The satisfaction in the pleasant is bound up with interest." http://oll.libertyfund.org/title/1217/97443 (accessed April 8, 2013).

161. Kant, *Critique of Judgement*, chap. 1, § 5: "Comparison of the three specifically different kinds of satisfaction." http://oll.libertyfund.org/title/1217/97447 (accessed April 8, 2013).

162. Kant, *Critique of Judgement*, chap. 1, § 5.

163. Kant, *Critique of Judgement*, chap. 1, § 6: "The beautiful is that which apart from concepts is represented as the object of a universal satisfaction." http://oll.libertyfund.org/title/1217/97452.

164. Kant, *Critique of Judgement*, chap 1, § 6.

165. Kant, *Critique of Judgement*, chap. 1, § 7: "Comparison of the Beautiful with the Pleasant and the Good by means of the above characteristic." http://oll.libertyfund.org/title/1217/97454.

166. Chartier, "Distinction et divulgation," 45.

167. Mark Johnson, "Introduction: Why Metaphor Matters to Philosophy," in *Metaphor and Symbolic Activity* 10, no. 3 (1995): 157. Quoted in Korsmeyer, *Making Sense of Taste*, 39.

168. Korsmeyer, *Making Sense of Taste*, 38–29.

169. [Bouhours], *Entretiens*, 239.

Chapter 5. Toward an Art and Science of Taste

1. The first mention of the term *nouvelle cuisine* appeared in the title of the third volume of Menon's *Nouveau Traité de la Cuisine*, published in 1742. We know very little about Menon's life—not even his first name.

2. [Menon], *Nouveau Traité de la Cuisine*.

3. François Marin worked as a *chef de cuisine* to the Duchesse de Gèsvres, before becoming the maître d'hôtel to the Marshal de Soubise.

4. Foncemagne, "Dissertation préliminaire," i, xix.

5. [Marin], *Dons de Comus*. The expression appeared on the title page of the work. Menon also claimed to offer a cuisine "dans le goût de la Cuisine nouvelle" (in the taste of new cuisine). [Menon], *Science du Maître d'Hôtel*, xxxj.

6. [Marin], *Dons de Comus*, 29.

7. "This very subtle and very complex conquest consists in separating and reintegrating, deacidifying and sieving." Bonnet, "Les manuels de cuisine," 60.

8. [Marin], *Dons de Comus*, vol. 1, 1758, [1]. This is the reason why the recipe of broth was the first and most complete recipe presented in the entire volume of the first edition of the *Dons de Comus* [1739], which was conceived as an *aide-mémoire* for professional cooks.

9. Pinkard, *A Revolution in Taste*, 156.

10. [Marin], *Dons de Comus*, vol. 1, 1758, xxij. The same idea was expressed in [Menon], *La Nouvelle Cuisine*, n.p.

11. There are numerous works on culinary practices of the era. See, for instance, Pinkard, *A Revolution in Taste*, 153–235 (third part, "Cooking, Eating, and Drinking in the Enlightenment, 1735–1798"); Meyzie, *Table du Sud-Ouest*; Flandrin and Montanari, *Food*, 347–432 (Part 6, "The Europe of Nation-States (15th–18th centuries)"; Wheaton, *Savoring the Past*, 194–219 (chap. 1, "Mid-Eighteenth-Century Trends and Controversies").

12. "These innovations which only represent a slow progress of detail on prior practice can only constitute little convincing evidences in favor of a culinary revolution." Mennell, *Lettre d'un pâtissier anglois*, xv.

13. "La Chapelle was one of the boldest liars in history. . . . [H]e took 480 recipes out of the 1476 that the first edition of his book contains (that is a proportion of one third of the whole) directly from Massialot." Hyman, "La Chapelle and Massialot."

14. Foncemagne, "Dissertation préliminaire," i–xxx.

15. For more information on the writers of culinary introductions, see Spary, *Eating the Enlightenment*, 195–242 (chap. 5, "The Philosophical Palate"); Pinkard, *A Revolution in Taste*, 158–159; Fink, *Les liaisons savoureuses*, 24; Mennell, *Lettre d'un pâtissier anglois*, xx.

16. Anne-Gabriel Meusnier de Querlon wrote the introduction of the *Suite des Dons de Comus* (1742), as well as the preface of the new edition of the same work in 1750.

17. Bonnet, "Les manuels de cuisine," 57. See also Mennell, *All Manners of Food*, 62–83 (chap. 4, "From Renaissance to Revolution: Court and Country Food").

18. Spary, *Eating the Enlightenment*, 197.

19. "The Regent was the most illustrious of these aristocrats who wished to be cooks." Mennell, *Lettre d'un pâtissier anglois*, xxv.

20. Fink, *Les liaisons savoureuses*, 89.

21. *Le Cuisinier gascon*, Amsterdam, 1740, in Fink, *Les liaisons savoureuses*, 92. "I have seen you a hundred times busy in the kitchen, a hundred times I have had the honour of working under your orders." Fink, *Les liaisons savoureuses*, 92.

22. [Marin], *Dons de Comus*, 1739, 30.

23. Habermas's *Strukturwandel der Öffentlichkeit*, published in 1962, was translated into English in 1989 as *The Structural Transformation of the Public Sphere*.

24. On this model, see notably Spang, *The Invention of the Restaurant*, and Mennell, *All Manners of Food*. On the importance of cafés as new places favorable to the creation of innovative forms of knowledge, see Spary, *Eating the Enlightenment*.

25. The title of the work itself could be symbolic, as in the *Dons de Comus*, which was an allusion to the Roman god of cookery and comedy.

26. Takats, *The Expert Cook.*

27. As exemplified in the title of Menon's work: *Science du Maître d'Hôtel Cuisinier, avec des Observations sur la connoissance & propriétés des Alimens* (Science of the Cook Maître D'hôtel, with Observations on Knowledge and Properties of Food). The author quickly published another volume as the sequel to the first one; it was related to confectionary and to the art of the office, and was entitled *La Science du Maître d'Hôtel Confiseur.*

28. An explanation on the properties of spices hence follows the recipe of the "*Potage de Bisque en gras & en maigre.*" Menon, *Science du Maître d'Hôtel Cuisinier*, 8–11.

29. The first example of a culinary work presented under the shape of a dictionary was Massialot's *Cuisinier royal et bourgeois*, which, in the second part, proposed an "Instruction according the alphabetic order. Teaching the way to dress all sorts of meats fat and meager, and how to serve them as first courses, entremets, and for roast, or of any other ways." This was the first time that recipes were classed by alphabetic order and not according to the order of services.

30. [M.C.D.], *Dictionnaire des alimens*; [Aubert de La Chesnaye des Bois], *Dictionnaire portatif de cuisine.* "For example, at the word Beef, one will find the definition of this animal, the use made of it in cookery; and, at the [entries referring to the] different parts of this animal, [will be mentioned] their diverse possible preparations." "Avis indispensable, Pour servir de Préface," in [Aubert de La Chesnaye des Bois], *Dictionnaire portatif de cuisine*, vj. The dictionary itself was preceded by an "Explanation, by alphabetic order, of the terms of Cuisine and of the Office, the use of which is not familiar to those who are not from the Art." [Aubert de La Chesnaye des Bois], *Dictionnaire portatif de cuisine*, ix–xvj.

31. Foncemagne, "Dissertation préliminaire," xxv.

32. Foncemagne, "Dissertation préliminaire," xxv. The many references made to Lemery's works reveal the survival of Hippocratic theories in the eighteenth century. Although Galenism was being questioned since a century or two by scholars, the habit of classifying foodstuffs according to temperaments remained, even if the theory explaining it was quite different from ancient dietetics. For an example of neo-Hippocratic survival, see Havelange, "Manger au XVIIIᵉ siècle," 155–161.

33. [Marin], *Dons de Comus*, vol. 1, 1758, xviij.

34. Foncemagne, "Dissertation préliminaire," x.

35. [Marin], *Dons de Comus*, 1739, 30.

36. Foncemagne, "Dissertation préliminaire," xj.

37. Foncemagne, "Dissertation préliminaire," xxviij–xxx.

38. Emphasis added.

39. Foncemagne, "Dissertation préliminaire," xxv–xxvj.

40. "It is the art to cure diseases with chemical remedies." "Iatrochimie & Iatrochimistes," in *Encyclopédie méthodique ou par ordre de matières, par une société de gens de lettres, de savans et d'artistes*, vol. 7, *Médecine*, 1798, 460.

41. Spary, *Eating the Enlightenment*, 17–50 (chap. 1, "Intestinal Struggles"); Chiou, *Homo gastronomicus*, 32–59 (chap. 1, "Le corps mangeant"). See also Albala, *Food in Early Modern Europe*, 213–230 (chap. 6, "Diet and Nutrition"); Debus, "La médecine chimique," 37–59.

42. Spary, *Eating the Enlightenment*; Takats, *The Expert Cook.*

43. [Marin], *Dons de Comus*, 1739, 29.

44. "[T]he basis of cuisine and the soul of sauces . . . is the bouillon, or quintessence, like one names it in modern cuisine." [Marin], *Dons de Comus*, 1739, 31.

45. The cook intends "to help the functions of the stomach by exciting its faculties, and often to change the solid food in a sort of artificial chyle, as one sees with extracts and restaurants." [Marin], *Dons de Comus*, 1739, 30.

46. See all the symbolic, literary, and material productions the metaphor caused in Alexandre-Bidon, *Archéologie du goût*.

47. About gastric digestion, Borelli suggested to replace the traditional notion of "coction" by that of chemical solvent: from the stomach wall would pass by a juice causing the dissolution of food, like etching causes that of metals. Grmek and Bernabeo, "La machine du corps," 26.

48. [Marin], *Dons de Comus*, 1739, 30. Some chemists, such as Polycarpe Poncelet, tried to chemically reconstitute the digestive process in a laboratory. The author proceeded to experiment with the aim of determining the effect of liqueurs on food, putting several preparations in jars in order to observe the process of putrefaction. [Poncelet], "Dissertation préliminaire," x–xviij.

49. [Marin], *Dons de Comus*, 1739, 29.

50. [Marin], *Dons de Comus*, 1739, 30.

51. Steinmetz, "Conceptions du corps à travers l'acte alimentaire," 8.

52. Descartes, "Traité de l'homme," in *Œuvres et lettres*, Paris, 1953, 843. Quoted in Steinmetz, "Conceptions du corps," 9.

53. Foncemagne, "Dissertation préliminaire," xxvij–xxviij.

54. Foncemagne, "Dissertation préliminaire," xx.

55. [Dubos], *Reflexions critiques*, vol. 2, 290–292.

56. Foncemagne, "Dissertation préliminaire," xx–xxj.

57. This passage was drawn from [Dubos], *Reflexions critiques*, vol. 2, 291–292.

58. Havelange, *De l'œil et du monde*; Descola, *Par-delà nature et culture*, 280–320; Foucault, *Les mots et les choses*.

59. Albala, *Food in Early Modern Europe*, 222.

60. The idea is persistent over the centuries, up until Brillat-Savarin, who considered that the people who eat fish were less brave than those who fed on meat. Brillat-Savarin, *Physiologie du goût*, 97. The famous aphorism "Tell Me what you eat, I shall tell you what you are" is another evidence of this lasting way of thinking. "Aphorismes du Professeur," 19. Contemporary research in behavioral psychology tends to show a survival of this "magic thinking" in our own contemporary representations. Fischler, "Editorial: Magie, charmes et aliments," in Fischler, *Manger Magique*, 10–19.

61. "It is certain that great eaters of meat are generally crueler and wilder than the other men; this observation is of all places and times: the English barbarity is known." Rousseau, "Émile ou De l'éducation," 411. About Rousseau and food, see Bonnet, "Le système de la cuisine et du repas chez Rousseau"; Bonnet, "Le réseau culinaire dans l'*Encyclopédie*," 909. Jean-Claude Bonnet indicates on this matter that engraved plates of the *Encyclopédie*, dedicated on the one hand to confectionary and pastry, on the other hand to butchers and their "killing," were particularly revealing of the values attributed to these practices. Bonnet, "Le réseau culinaire dans l'*Encyclopédie*," 910. The debate thus also took ideological forms, diet being used to disqualify other civilizations.

62. "Raw meat makes animals ferocious, as men would become by the same food; this is so true that the English nation, which does not eat meat as cooked as us, but red and bloody, appears to participate in this more or less great ferocity, which partially comes from such food and other causes, that education only can make powerless. This ferocity produces in the soul the pride, the hatred, the contempt of the other nations, the unruliness and other feelings which deprave the character, just like unrefined food makes a heavy, thick spirit, of which laziness and the indolence are the favourite attributes." La Mettrie, *L'Homme-Machine*, 152. It was also the point of view of Cheyne, promoter of the vegetarian diet.

63. Le Camus, *Médecine de L'Esprit*, 1, vij–viij.

64. Le Camus, *Médecine de L'Esprit*, 1, xv.

65. [Marin], *Dons de Comus*, 1739, 30.

66. Le Camus, *Médecine de L'Esprit*, 2, 81–82.

67. [Marin], *Dons de Comus*, 1739, 30; Foncemagne, "Dissertation préliminaire," i, vij, x.

68. Foncemagne, "Dissertation préliminaire," ix. On the relations between art and cuisine, see Cohen and Csergo, *L'artification du culinaire*. Caroline Champion also addressed the aesthetic dimension of cookery in her book *Hors d'œuvre*. I have tackled this question with more details in Von Hoffmann, "Le Sensible et le Culinaire".

69. Csergo, "L'art culinaire ou l'insaisissable beauté"; Champion, *Hors d'oeuvre*.

70. Champion, *Hors d'oeuvre*, 26 *et seq.*

71. Jaucourt, "Cuisine," ʒʒʒ

72. "The science of the cook consists" in giving flavors "this union that painters give to colors, and to make them so homogeneous, that from their various flavors only results a *goût fin et piquant* (refined and spicy taste), and if I dare to say, a harmony of all the tastes combined together." [Marin], *Dons de Comus*, 1739, 29.

73. On the relationship between harmony and cuisine, see Spary, *Eating the Enlightenment*, 224.

74. "He gave me a discourse on this science of the mouth, with a grave and magisterial countenance, as if he were speaking of some grand point of Theology. He unraveled differences in appetite for me; the appetite one has at the outset, and that which one has after the second and third courses . . . the rules regarding sauces, first in general and then particularizing the qualities of ingredients and their effects; the different salads according to their season, the one that must be warmed up, the one that must be served cold, and the ways of decorating and embellishing them to make them even more pleasing to [the] sight. After that, he embarked on the order of courses, full of important and fine considerations . . . And all this bloated with grand and magnificent words, such as one might use in describing the government of an empire." Montaigne, *Essais*, vol. 1, 609–610 [chap. 51]. According to Florent Quellier, "Montaigne's surprise in front of this learned cook reveals a cultural gap between Italian and French elites regarding the pleasures of the table." Quellier, *Gourmandise*, 106.

75. Cookery was often disdained for its useless character. When it was not set against medicine, it was perceived as inferior to agriculture. Unlike the "real arts" that are "necessary to life, as agriculture and sheep barn, which supply us with earth and animals to live and dress," the art of cookery, like that of perfumes, is "only for sensual delight."

Renaudot, *Recueil général*, vol. 2, 364–365, 72nd conference, "2. Quel est le plus necessaire de tous les Arts" (Which Is the Most Necessary of All Arts), 361–368 [pages 361–362 are wrongly numbered 347–348].

76. Plato, *Gorgias*, 160 [464c–464d].

77. Plato, *Gorgias*, 164.

78. "With regard to the activity dedicated to the body, it is a slave's job, in the service of others, which no free man practises." Plato, *Gorgias*, 295 [517d–518b].

79. Emphasis added.

80. [Marin], *Dons de Comus*, vol. 1, 1758, xxij–xxiij. Emphasis added. The addition was in the 1742 edition in the *Suite des Dons de Comus*, foreword of which is attributed to Meusnier de Querlon. Mennell, *Lettre d'un pâtissier anglais*, 50.

81. Foncemagne, "Dissertation préliminaire," vj–vij.

82. Foncemagne, "Dissertation préliminaire," vij–viij.

83. Foncemagne, "Dissertation préliminaire," iv–v. "The most skillful Artists are sometimes those who manage least to satisfy the common taste: they need discerning palates, like a profound Musician needs fine and learned ears." Foncemagne, "Dissertation préliminaire," vij.

84. Lebas, *Le Festin joyeux*.

85. Oratorien priest, author of works in agronomy on wheat and flour. Spary, *Eating the Enlightenment*, 224 *et seq.*; Csergo, "L'art culinaire ou l'insaisissable beauté," 24 *et seq.*

86. [Poncelet], "Dissertation préliminaire," xix.

87. [Poncelet], "Dissertation préliminaire," xviij–xx.

88. In the scale of flavors, *do* corresponds to "acid," *re* to "bland," *mi* to "sweet," *fa* to "bitter," *so* to "bittersweet," *la* to "astringent," and *ti* to "hot." [Poncelet], "Dissertation préliminaire," xx.

89. "In the sound music the tierces, the fifths, and the octaves, form the most beautiful consonances: the same effects are exactly in the tasty music: mix the acid with the bittersweet . . . lemon for example with sugar, you will have a simple, but charming consonance, in major fifth. . . . The dissonances are not less similar in one and the other music; in the acoustics strike the fourth, you will produce an unpleasant cacophony: in the tasty music mix the acid with the bitter; some vinegar for example with some absinthe, the compound will be terrible." [Poncelet], "Dissertation préliminaire," xx–xxij.

90. [Poncelet], "Dissertation préliminaire," xxij.

91. "I call composition the matching blend of ingredients which constitute liqueurs; it is mainly in this part that it is necessary to know the report of the flavors between them and the principles of harmony in order to avoid discordant combinations; the tastes are so strange! You should not thus consult them indifferently. Good taste only must govern the composition. . . . Happy the one who will have received from nature an exquisite taste: he can censor, reform, order, and pronounce without appeal on the just proportion of mixtures." [Poncelet], "Dissertation préliminaire," 43. The conception of cuisine as a harmony of flavors was, however, not generalized. There was no allusion to this in the article "harmony" published in the *Encyclopédie*, for instance—which is not that surprising considering this entry was written by Rousseau, a music lover but particularly severe toward haute cuisine. Diderot and D'Alembert, *Encyclopédie*, vol. 8,

1765, 50–54, s.v. "Harmonie." Signed "S," the part dedicated to grammar and music is attributed to Rousseau, whereas the passage concerning painting, signed "G," is the work of Mallet (1713–1755), a priest and a man of letters who wrote several articles on trade, history, literature, and religion. Kafker, *The Encyclopedists as Individuals*, xx, xxvii.

92. [Poncelet], "Dissertation préliminaire," xxiv–xxv.

93. "We shall say nothing of the harpsichord of flavors, the harpsichord of smells, and finally the harpsichord for all the senses, theoretically proposed by the same father Castel. Like the abbot Poncelet, who built an organ of flavors; nobody, as far as we know, ever had the madness to realize such an extravagant idea." G. E. A., *Encyclopédie des gens du monde*, 159, s.v. "Clavecin oculaire."

94. Castel, "Clavecin pour les yeux," 2552–2577. See Mortier and Hasquin, *Autour du Père Castel*; Franssen, "The Ocular Harpsichord."

95. Quoted in Mortier and Hasquin, *Autour du Père Castel*, 20.

96. Foncemagne was familiar with the philosophical discussions of his time: "He quotes Bayle, Crousaz, Dubos, Lévesque de Pouilly, Hutcheson, and many others. In his line of argument and his terminology he closely follows the movement of the Moderns." For example, he refers to *An Inquiry into the Original of Our Ideas of Beauty and Virtue* (1725), written by Francis Hutcheson, which had just been translated into French in 1749 (*Recherches sur l'origine des idées*). Knabe, "Esthétique et art culinaire," 130–131.

97. A footnote reference explicitly refers here to Crousaz's *Traité du Beau*. Foncemagne, "Dissertation préliminaire," vi, note a.

98. Foncemagne, "Dissertation préliminaire," v, vij. "[A]n object deserves the name of Beautiful, when it contains diversities which are reduced to some unity, and which hence occupy the mind without tiring it." Crousaz, *Traité du Beau*, 102.

99. [Lévesque de Pouilly], *Theorie des sentimens agréables*, 25. This sentence was reproduced in Foncemagne, "Dissertation préliminaire," iij–iv. Levesque de Pouilly besides considered that "analogy which rules in the entire Nature, lets us speculate that the law which regulates the pleasure of sounds, influences other objects of our senses. There are colors the assortment of which pleases the eyes; for apparently their impression on the fibers of the eye forms, so to speak, a consonance there. Maybe even this law extends to smells and flavors. It is true that those which are salutary, are pleasant; but their salubrity does not always seem to be an accurate measure of their enjoyment." [Lévesque de Pouilly], *Theorie des sentimens agréables*, 39.

100. Le Camus, *Médecine de L'Esprit*, vol. 2, 82–83.

101. Le Camus, *Médecine de L'Esprit*, vol. 2, 83. The author obviously read François Marin.

102. Spary, *Eating the Enlightenment*, 243–289 (chap. 6, "Rules of Regimen").

103. [Marin], *Dons de Comus*, 1739, 26. Foncemagne would agree. Foncemagne, "Dissertation préliminaire," [i]–ij.

104. [Marin], *Dons de Comus*, 1739, 26.

105. [Marin], *Dons de Comus*, xj.

106. Menon's work also appeared in 1739, the same year as that of Marin—just a little earlier actually, as revealed by the privileges of the two books. But if both works suggested similar ideas, the pages of the *Dons de Comus* were especially disputed. See

Mennell, *Lettre d'un pâtissier anglais* for more details on the authors and different editions of these texts.

107. Roland Puchot, Comte des Alleurs (1693–1754), future ambassador of France in Constantinople.

108. [Desalleurs], "Lettre d'un pâtissier anglois," in Mennell, *Lettre d'un pâtissier anglois*, 12. The mention of the "*nouveau cuisinier François*" (new French cook) does not appear in the printed title page of the *Dons de Comus*. This remark may have been added later onto a pirated edition.

109. [Desalleurs], "Lettre d'un pâtissier anglois," 12.

110. [Desalleurs], "Lettre d'un pâtissier anglois," 13.

111. Grmek and Bernabeo, "La machine du corps," 28. It is well known that Marcello Malpighi, while working with Bellini and using the microscope, discovered the existence of *gustatorys papillae*. Grmek and Bernabeo, "La machine du corps," 31.

112. Rohault, *Traité de Physique*, 205.

113. Le Cat, *Traité des Sens*; Le Cat, *Traité des sensations*.

114. [Desalleurs], "Lettre d'un pâtissier anglois," 16.

115. [Desalleurs], "Lettre d'un pâtissier anglois," 13–14.

116. [Meusnier de Querlon], "Apologie des Modernes ou Reponse du Cuisinier françois auteur des Dons de Comus, à un patissier anglois" (Apology of the Moderns or Response from the French Cook Author of the Gifts of Comus to an English Pastry Cook).

117. [Meusnier de Querlon], "Apologie des Modernes," 27.

118. [Meusnier de Querlon], "Apologie des Modernes," 34. The author continues: "I have for guarantees the great Newton, Descartes, Hartroker, Malpishy [*sic*], Mussembrock, and the most learned Physicists of the world who mathematically demonstrated that . . . generally all the bodies, solid as well as fluids, differ between them only by the configuration of their parts; from which results that if one Ragoût hurts more than another one, it comes only from the shape and configuration of its parts: yet inevitably . . . a little Pâté parallelipipede necessarily has different properties and qualities than a little Pâté of another form, unless one wants to argue that the essence and the properties of bodies do not depend only on the configuration of their parts; which would revolt all Physicists." [Meusnier de Querlon], "Apologie des Modernes," 35.

119. "One distinguishes today among professionals and people who like to pretend they have a good table, the ancient cuisine and the modern cuisine. The ancient cuisine is the one that the French put in fashion throughout Europe, and that one generally followed less than twenty years ago. The modern cuisine, established on the foundations of the ancient . . . is simpler . . . and maybe even more learned." [Marin], *Dons de Comus*, 1739, 29.

120. Jaucourt, "Cuisine," 537.

121. Jaucourt, "Cuisine," 538.

122. Jaucourt, "Cuisine," 537. See Bonnet, "Le réseau culinaire dans l'Encyclopédie," 891–914.

123. The same idea was defended in the *Dictionnaire des alimens*: "One must admit that in the first times, one did not know yet table delicacy. Temperance and frugality were there in all their prestige. . . . Using without much seasoning, and even with moderation, the benefactions of Nature, they were stronger and more robust; and exposed to

less diseases, they lived longer." The author then quoted several extracts of the *Dons de Comus* before embracing the critical point of view of the Chevalier de Jaucourt. [M.C.D., pseudonym Briand], *Dictionnaire des alimens*, vol. 1, v.

124. Jaucourt, "Cuisine," 537. Emphasis added, for this was commonplace at the time, and was defended, for instance, in [Marin], *Dons de Comus*, vol. 1, 1758, x.

125. "So, the simple cuisine in the first ages of the world, which became more complexe and more refined from century to century . . . is at present a study, a science among the most difficult, on which we ceaselessly see appearing some new treatises under the names of Cuisinier François, Cuisinier royal, Cuisinier moderne, Dons de Comus, Ecole des officiers de bouche, and many others which changing perpetually of method, prove enough that it is impossible to reduce to a fixed order, that which the whim of men and the disorder of their taste, search, invent, imagine, in order to mask food." Jaucourt, "Cuisine," 538.

126. Jaucourt, "Cuisine," 538.

127. Jaucourt, "Cuisine," 538.

128. "New models of 'the natural' as frugal and austere can be identified in the writings of moral and medical reformers from the start of the eighteenth century onward, long before they became general among a polite reading public in the middle of the eighteenth century. . . . These reform programs were explicit responses to a political program of civility and politesse closely associated with the court of Louis XIV and manifested in culinary writings." Spary, *Eating the Enlightenment*, 12.

129. Bonnet, "Le systéme de la cuisine et du repas chez Rousseau," 244–267; Bonnet, "Le réseau culinaire dans l'Encyclopédie," 909.

130. Figeac, "À la recherche du goût," 25.

131. On the history of luxury, see Berg and Eger, *Luxury in the Eighteenth Century*; Berry, *The Idea of Luxury*; Smith, *Consumption and the Making*; Ehrard, *L'Idée de Nature*.

132. Foncemagne repeatedly celebrates "the wisdom and fertility of nature," encouraging "the contemplation of nature's wonders." Foncemagne, "Dissertation préliminaire," iv–v. On the question of nature in the eighteenth century, see the work done by Jean Ehrard, Emma Spary, and Philippe Descola.

133. Roche, *La France des Lumières*, i–iii.

134. Delon, *Le savoir-vivre libertin*, 166.

135. La Reynière, *Manuel des Amphytryons*, 1808, 9–10.

136. Delumeau and Cottret, *Le catholicisme entre Luther et Voltaire*, 398–443 (chap. 5, "Déchristianisation?").

137. Jaucourt, "Gourmandise," 754.

138. On the evolution of the meanings of *gourmandise* in the eighteenth century, see the special issue on the subject in the journal *Lumières*, no. 11 (*La gourmandise entre péché et plaisir*), already quoted.

139. [Meusnier de Querlon], "Apologie des Modernes," 36.

140. [Meusnier de Querlon], "Apologie des Modernes," 36.

141. Flandrin, "La distinction par le goût," 261–302. "[T]he loan of that word [taste] suggests that the honest people cared about the taste of what they ate and that they did not hesitate to discuss it." Flandrin, "De la diététique à la gastronomie," 699.

142. Wheaton, *Savoring the Past*, 156. *Tables volantes* (flying tables) were very popular in the eighteenth century. This technical device was used to move the table up or down between the dining room and the kitchen, thus freeing the dinner guests from the presence of any servants and creating an atmosphere of intimacy and freedom of thought.

143. Quellier, *La Table des Français*, 96.

144. "After the pleasures of lust, there are no pleasures more divine than those of the table. . . . They help each other out so well that it is impossible to the followers of the former not to adore the latter." Sade, *Œuvres*, vol. 2, 862. Delon, *Le savoir-vivre libertin*, 174–179.

145. Restif de la Bretonne, *Sara*, 104. See Von Hoffmann, "Le goût et le toucher de la ville," 131–138; Delon, *Le savoir-vivre libertin*, 169, 173–174; Figeac, "À la recherche du goût," 17–18, 25. The sensual pleasures of the table and the bed, which succeed one another for the libertines, are completely mixed in the pornographic novel, where the meal becomes the place for all the excesses, as evidenced, for example, in the work of the Marquis de Sade. Figeac, "À la recherche du goût," 26–27.

146. The same thing was true for Diderot, who was "familiar with dinners offered by the baron of Holbach at the Grand'val." Bonnet, "Le réseau culinaire dans l'Encyclopédie," 907.

147. Wheaton, *Savoring the Past*, 215. There are numerous works dedicated to Voltaire's relationship with gustatory pleasures that analyze the place of food and culinary metaphors in his work and correspondence. See particularly Mervaud, *Voltaire à table*.

148. This expression is from Christiane Mervaud. Mervaud, *Voltaire à table*, 109–123.

149. "I like luxury, and even languor, / All the pleasures, the arts of any sort, / The cleanliness, the taste, the ornaments, / every honnest man has such feelings. / [. . .] Everything is of use to luxury, to the pleasures of this world; / Ah the good time in this iron century! / The non-essentials, very-necessary things / gathered both hemispheres." Voltaire, "Le Mondain," 295–296.

150. Voltaire, "Le Mondain," 301–302.

151. Voltaire, "Le Mondain," 303.

152. (C.), "Bonheur," in Diderot and D'Alembert, *Encyclopédie*, vol. 2, 1751, 322. According to Frank Kafker, the letter "C" refers to Pestre (1723–1821), a private tutor, member of the Catholic clergy, and author of nine philosophical articles and other contributions to the *Encyclopédie*. Kafker, *The Encyclopedists as Individuals*, xxvii, xxi, 304–306.

153. [C.], "Bonheur," 322.

154. [Lévesque de Pouilly], *Theorie des sentimens agréables*, 7.

155. On the history of happiness, see Mauzi, *L'idée du Bonheur*; Camporesi, *Le Goût du chocolat*; North, *Material Delight and the Joy of Living*; Ehrard, *L'Idée de Nature*, 541–606.

156. Hyman, "Printing the Kitchen," 399.

157. Berg and Eger, *Luxury in the Eighteenth Century*.

158. Spang, *Invention of the Restaurant*.

159. The first occurrence of the word, derived from Greek, famously appeared in 1800 in a poem of Joseph Berchoux entitled "La Gastronomie, ou l'homme des champs à table."

160. Charbonneau, *L'école de la gourmandise*.

161. La Reynière, *Manuel des Amphytryons*, 18.

162. La Reynière, *Almanach des Gourmands*, 1812, x.

163. La Reynière, *Almanach des Gourmands*, xi.

164. La Reynière, *Manuel des Amphytryons*, 19.

165. Delon, *Le savoir-vivre libertin*, 173.

166. Stiénon, *La Littérature des Physiologies*; Stiénon, "Lectures littéraires du document physiologique."

167. Brillat-Savarin, *Physiologie du goût*, 59.

168. Brillat-Savarin, *Physiologie du goût*, 164, 49.

169. The word *ageusia* was first mentioned in English in 1812 (*Oxford English Dictionary*). In French, the first example is the use of the word *agueustie* in 1836, followed by *agueusie* in 1897 (Rey, *Dictionnaire culturel*). Let us note that there is no entry to the word in the eighth edition of the *Dictionnaire de l'Académie françoise* in 1932. Alain Rey himself does not mention the word in his *Dictionnaire historique* (1992).

170. Brillat-Savarin, *Physiologie du goût*, 62.

171. Brillat-Savarin, *Physiologie du goût*, 56–57.

172. Brillat-Savarin, *Physiologie du goût*, 61.

173. Brillat-Savarin, *Physiologie du goût*, 297.

174. Brillat-Savarin, *Physiologie du goût*, 55.

175. Brillat-Savarin, *Physiologie du goût,* 55.

176. Der-Liang Chiou uses the suggestive term of *goût parlant* (talking taste). Chiou, *Homo gastronomicus*, 199.

Conclusion

1. I owe this idea to David Howes, whom I would like to thank for suggesting this.

2. Weiss, *Comment cuisiner un phénix*, 8.

3. Classen, *Worlds of Sense*, 59.

4. For instance, in Renaudot, *Recueil général*, vol. 2, 81: "Since the word of sapience or wisdom takes its name from flavors by the Latins, wise men professing it [wisdom] seem to be also experts in this matter [flavors]."

5. Florent Quellier has stressed that in the Old Regime, the child was represented as an imperfect and unfinished being, therefore associated with the animal, which is the reason why he had a disordered appetite. Quellier, *Gourmandise*, 193, 188–211.

6. Classen "The Witch's Senses"; Korsmeyer, *Making Sense of Taste*, 30–36; Quellier, *Gourmandise*, 162–187.

7. Le Breton, "Du goût en bouche," 15.

8. Brulotte, "Pour un imaginaire du goût," 25.

Bibliography

Primary Sources

Agrippa, H. C. *La magie naturelle*, ed. J. Servier. Paris: Berg International, 1982 [1533].

Alciat, A. *Emblemata*. Paris: J. Richer, 1584.

Alciat, A. *Emblematum libellus*. Venice: Aldus, 1546.

Alciat, A. *Emblemes d'Alciat, de nouveau translatez en françois, vers pour vers, jouxte les latins, ordonnez en lieux communs avec briefves expositions et figures nouvelles appropriées aux derniers emblemes, par Barthelemy Aneau*. Lyon: M. Bonhomme, 1549.

Aristotle. *De Anima, Books II and III (with certain passages from book I)*, ed. D. W. Hamlyn. Oxford: Clarendon Press, 1968.

Aristotle. *De l'âme*, ed. P. Thillet. Paris: Gallimard, 2005.

Aristotle. *Nicomachean Ethics*, ed. H. Rackham. Cambridge, MA: Harvard University Press, 2014.

Aristotle. *The Complete Works of Aristotle: The Revised Oxford Translation*, ed. J. Barnes. Princeton, NJ: Princeton University Press, 1984.

[Aubert de La Chesnaye des Bois, F.-A.]. *Dictionnaire portatif de cuisine, d'office, et de distillation, contenant la maniere de préparer toutes sortes de viandes, de volailles, de gibier, de poissons, de légumes, de fruits, etc. La façon de faire toutes sortes de gelées, de pâtes, de pastilles, de gâteaux, de tourtes, de pâtés, vermichel, macaronis, etc. Et de composer toutes sortes de liqueurs, de ratafias, de syrops, de glaces, d'essences, etc. Ouvrage également utile aux Chefs d'Office et de Cuisine les plus habiles, et aux Cuisinieres qui ne sont employées que pour des Tables bourgeoises. On y a joint des Observations médicinales qui font connoître la propriété de chaque Aliment, relativement à la Santé, et qui indiquent les mets les plus convenables à chaque Tempérament*. Paris: Vincent, 1767.

Aubert de La Chesnaye Des Bois, F.-A. *Dictionnaire universel d'Agriculture et de Jardinage, de Fauconnerie, Chasse, Pêche, Cuisine et Manège*. 2 vols. Paris: David le Jeune, 1751.

[Audiger]. *La maison réglée et l'art de diriger la maison d'un grand seigneur tant à la ville qu'à la campagne*. Paris, 1692.

Bayle, P. *Dictionnaire historique et critique*, 2 vols. Rotterdam: R. Leers, 1697.

Berchoux, J. *La gastronomie, ou l'homme des champs à table.* Paris: Giguet and Michaud, 1803 [1800].

Bernier, F. *Abrégé de la philosophie de Gassendi*, 7 vols. Lyon: Anisson and Posuel, 1678 [1674].

Bérulle, P. de. *Bref discours de l'abnégation intérieure*, in *Œuvres complètes*, tome 2, vol. 6, ed. M. Dupuy. Paris: Ed. du Cerf, 1997 [1597], 9–66.

Bérulle, P. de. *Discours de l'état et des grandeurs de Jésus*, in *Œuvres complètes*, t. 3, vol. 1, ed. R. Lescot and M. Join-Lambert. Paris: Ed. du Cerf, 1996 [1623].

Bérulle, P. de. *Œuvres complètes*, ed. M. Join-Lambert, R. Lescot, and M. Dupuy. Paris: Ed. du Cerf, since 1995.

Boaistuau, P. *Histoires prodigieuses extraictes de plusieurs fameux autheurs, Grecs et Latins, sacrez et prophanes, diuisees en six Tomes, le premier par P. Boasituau: Le 2. par C. de Tesserant: Le 3. par F. de Belleforest: Le 4 par Rode. Hoyer: Le 5. traduit du latin de M. Arnauld Sorbin Euesque de Neuers, par F. de Belleforest: Et le sixiesme recueilly par I. D. M. de diuers autheurs anciens et modernes. Augmentées de plusieurs portraicts et figures oultre les precedentes impressions*, vol. 1. Paris: Veuve G. Cavellat, 1598.

Boaistuau, P. *Le second tome des Histoires prodigievses, recueillies par Claude de Tesserant Parisien. Auec les pourtraicts et figures, et la table d'icelles mise à la fin.* Paris: Veuve G. Cavellat, 1597.

Boaistuau, P. *Le Théâtre du Monde*, ed. M. Simonin. Genève: Droz, 1981 [1558].

Bodin, J. *De la Démonomanie des sorciers. Reueüe diligemment, et repurgee de plusieurs fautes qui s'estoyent glissees és precedents impressions. Plus y est adioustee de nouueau une ample table des choses plus memorables contenues en ce liure*, 4th ed. Lyon: A. de Harsy, 1598 [1580].

Bodin, J. *Le Théâtre de la nature universelle.* Lyon: J. Pillehotte, 1597.

Boguet, H. *An Examen of Witches, drawn from various trials of many of this sect in the district of saint Oyan de Joux commonly known as saint Claude in the county of Burgundy including the procedure necessary to a judge in trials for witchcraft . . . by Henry Boguet chief Judge in the said county*, trans. E. Allen Ashwin, ed. M. Summers, and J. Rodker. [London]: 1929 [1602].

Boguet, H. *Discours exécrable des sorciers*, preface by M. Preaud. Marseille: Laffitte Reprints, 1979 [Réimpression de l'édition de Rouen, 1606] [1601].

[Bonnefons, N. de]. *Le Iardinier françois. Qui enseigne a cultiver les Arbres, et Herbes Potageres; Auec la maniere de conseruer les Fruicts, et faire toutes sortes de Confitures, Conserues, et Massepans. Dedie' Aux Dames.* Paris: P. Des-Hayes, 1651.

[Bonnefons, N. de]. *Les Delices de la Campagne. Suitte du Jardinier françois, ou [sic] est enseigné a preparer pour l'usage de la vie, tout ce qui croît sur Terre et dans les Eaux*, 2nd ed. Amsteldan [sic]: R. Smith, 1655 [1654].

[Bouhours, D.]. *Les Entretiens d'Ariste et d'Eugene.* Paris: S. Mabre-Cramois, 1671.

Brillat-Savarin, J.-A. "Aphorismes du Professeur pour server de prolégomènes à son ouvrage et de base éternelle à la science," in *Physiologie du goût*, 19–20.

Brillat-Savarin, J.-A. *Physiologie du goût*, introduced by J.-F. Revel, rev. ed. Paris: Champs/Flammarion, 2001 [1826].

Buc'hoz, J. P. *L'art de préparer les aliments.* Paris: Chez l'auteur, 1787.

Buffon, G.-L. Leclerc. *Œuvres*, preface by M. Delon, texts selected and commented by S. Schmitt with the collaboration of C. Crémière. Paris: Gallimard ("La Pléiade"), 2007.

Buffon, G.-L. Leclerc. *Œuvres complètes de Buffon*, vol. 3, *Histoire des Animaux*. Paris: F. D. Pillot, 1831.

Burke, E. *Recherche philosophique sur l'origine de nos idées du sublime et du beau*, ed. B. Saint Girons. Paris: Vrin, 2009 [1757].

Burton, R. *Anatomie de la mélancolie*, 3 vols., trans. B. Hoepffner, and C. Goffaux, preface by J. Starobinski, and afterword by J. Pigeaud. Paris: J. Corti, 2000 [1621].

Burton, R. *The Anatomy of Melancholy: What it is, with all the kinds, causes, symptonnes, prognostickes and seueral cures of it. In three partitions, with their severall sections, members and subsections. Philosophically, medicinally, historically, opened and cut vp.* Oxford: Printed for Henry Cripps, 1632.

Canfield, B. de. *Regle de perfection, contenante [sic] un abrege, de toute la vie Spirituelle reduite à ce seul point de la volonté de Dieu*, 5th ed. Paris: I. de Bats, 1696 [1608].

Canfield, B. de. *Renaissance Dialectic and Renaissance Piety: Benet of Canfield's Rule of Perfection: A Translation and Study*, ed. Kent Emery Jr. Binghamton, NY: Medieval and Renaissance Texts and Studies, 1987

Castel, L.-B. "Clavecin pour les yeux avec l'art de peindre les sons et toutes sortes de pièces de musique." *Mercure de France* (November 1725): 2552–2577.

Castiglione, B. *Le Courtisan de messire Bartazar de Castillon nouvellement reveu et corrigé*. Lyon: F. Juste, 1538 [1528].

Castiglione, B. *Le parfait courtisan du comte Baltasar Castillonnois [sic], Es deux langues, respondans par deux colomnes, l'une à l'autre, pour ceux qui veulent avoir l'intelligence de l'une d'icelles. De la traduction de Gabriel Chapuis Tourangeau*. Lyon: J. Huguetan, 1585.

Centre for Emblem Studies (Glasgow University). *Glasgow Emblem Studies*, [online], http://www.emblems.arts.gla.ac.uk.

Condillac, E., Abbé de. *Essai sur l'origine des connaissances humaines*, ed. Ch. Porcet, preceded by J. Derrida. *L'archéologie du frivole*. Auvers-sur-Oise: Galilée, 1973 [1746].

Condillac, E., Abbé de. *Traité des sensations, traité des animaux*, ed. M. Serres. Paris: Fayard (coll. "*Corpus des oeuvres de philosophie en langue française*"), 1984 [1754].

Cornaro, L. *De la sobriété. Conseils pour vivre longtemps*, ed. G. Vigarello. Grenoble: J. Milon, 1991 [1558].

[Courtin, A. de]. *Nouveau traité de la civilité Qui se pratique en France parmi les honnêtes-gens. Nouvelle édition revuë, corrigée, et de beaucoup augmentée par l'Auteur*. Paris: L. Josse and Ch. Robustel, 1728 [1671].

Crespet, P. *Deux livres de la hayne de Satan et malins esprits contre l'homme, et de l'homme contre eux*. Paris: G. de la Noüe, 1590.

Crousaz, J.-P. de. *Traité du Beau*, ed. F. Markovits. Paris: Fayard, 1985 [1715].

Cureau de la Chambre, M. *Le système de l'âme*, ed. M. Le Guern. Paris: Fayard, 2004 [1664].

Cureau de la Chambre, M. *Traité de la connaissance des animaux*, ed. O. Le Guern. Paris: Fayard, 1989 [1648].

[D'Alembert, J.]. "Discours préliminaire des Éditeurs," in *Encyclopédie ou Dictionnaire raisonné des sciences, des arts et des métiers, par une société de gens de lettres*, vol. 1, ed. D. Diderot and J. D'Alembert, i–xlv. Paris: 1751.

[D'Alembert, J.]. "Réflexions sur l'usage et sur l'abus de la Philosophie dans les matieres de goût," in *Encyclopédie*, vol. 7, ed. D. Diderot and J. D'Alembert, 767–770. Paris, 1757.

D'Avila, T. (Saint). *Le Chemin de Perfection, composé par la Ste. Mre. Terese de Iesus Fondatrice des Religieuses et Religieux Carmes deschaussés et de la premiere regle. Nouvellement traduicte D'espagnol en Françoy's par I.D.B.P. et L.P.C.D.B.* Paris: D. Langlois, 1623.

D'Avila, T. (Saint). *Les œuvres de Sainte Therese divisees en deux parties. De la Traduction de Monsieur Arnauld d'Andilly, premiere partie.* Paris: P. Le Petit, 1670.

D'Avila, T. (Saint). *Traicté du chasteau ou Demeures de l'ame, composé par la Mere Terese de Iesus Fondatrice des Religieuses et Religieux Carmes deschaussés et de la premiere regle. Nouvellement traduicte D'espagnol en Françoy's par I.D.B.P. et L.P.C.D.B.*, trans. J. de Brétigny. Paris: G. de La Noue, 1601.

Dante Alighieri. *La Divine Comédie de Dante Alighieri, L'Enfer; traduction françoise. Accompagnée du Texte, de Notes historiques, critiques, et de la Vie du poëte, par M. Moutonnet de Clairfons.* Paris: Le Clerc, Le Boucher, 1776.

Dedekind, F. *Grobianus. Petit cours de muflerie appliquée pour goujats débutants ou confirmés*, ed. T. Vigliano. Paris: Les Belles Lettres, 2006 [1549].

Descartes, R. *Discours de la méthode*, ed. L. Renault. Paris: Flammarion, 2000 [1637].

Descartes, R. *Méditations métaphysiques*, rev. ed., ed. J.-M. Beyssade and M. Beyssade. Paris: Flammarion, 2002 [1641].

Descartes, R. *Traité des passions*, in *Œuvres et lettres*, ed. A. Bridoux. Paris: Gallimard, 1987 [1649].

Dictionnaire général de cuisine française ancienne et moderne, de l'office et de la Pharmacie domestique, ouvrage où l'on trouve les prescriptions nécessaires à la confection de tout ce qui concerne la cuisine et l'office, à l'usage des plus grandes et des plus petites fortunes, 2nd ed. Paris: Plon Frères, 1853.

Dictionnaire universel françois et latin . . . vulgairement appelé dictionnaire de Trévoux, 6 vols. Paris: Veuve Delaulne, 1743.

Diderot, D. *Lettre sur les aveugles à l'usage de ceux qui voient (1749). Suivi de: Addition à la lettre sur les aveugles (1782)*, ed. R. Niklaus, 3rd ed. Geneva: Droz, 1970 [1749].

Diderot, D. *Œuvres*, ed. A. Billy. Paris: Gallimard, 1951.

Diderot, D. *Traité du Beau (Recherches philosophiques sur l'origine et la nature du Beau).* Amsterdam, 1772 [1st ed. 1751 in the *Encyclopédie*, s.v. "Beau"].

Diderot, D., and J. D'Alembert (eds.). *Encyclopédie ou Dictionnaire raisonné des sciences, des arts et des métiers, par une société de gens de lettres.* Paris: Briasson, 1751–1780.

Du Chesne, J. *Le pourtraict de la santé.* Paris: C. Morel, 1627.

Du Laurens, A. *Discours de la conservation de la veuë: Des maladies melancholiques: des catarrhes: & de la vieillesse, Reveus de nouveau et augmentez de plusieurs chapitres.* T. Samson, 1598 [1594].

[Dubos, J.-B.]. *Reflexions critiques sur la poésie et sur la peinture*, 3 vols. Paris: P.-J. Mariette, 1733 [1719].

Dumas, A., and D.-J. Vuillemot. *Petit dictionnaire de cuisine.* Paris: A. Lemerre, 1888.

Encyclopédie des gens du monde, répertoire universel des sciences, des lettres et des arts, avec des notices sur les principales familles historiques et sur les personnages célèbres, morts et vivants; par une société de savans, de littérateurs et d'artistes, français et étrangers, vol. 6. Paris: Treuttel et Würt, 1836.

Encyclopédie méthodique ou par ordre de matières, par une société de gens de lettres, de savants et d'artistes, précédée d'un Vocabulaire universel, servant de table pour tout l'ouvrage. Paris: Panckoucke, 1782–1832.

Encyclopédie méthodique. Médecine. Par une société de médecins, vol. 4. Paris: Panckoucke, 1792.

Érasme de Rotterdam. *Collected Works,* Toronto: University of Toronto Press, 1969–.

Érasme de Rotterdam. *La civilité puérile. Petit manuel de savoir-vivre à l'usage des enfants,* new and rev. trans. F. Bierlaire. Brussels: La Lettre volée à la Maison d'Érasme, 1999 [1530].

Érasme de Rotterdam. *Les colloques d'Érasme,* ed. L.-E. Halkin. Brussels: Presses Académiques Européennes, 1971 [1522].

Erasmus. *Collected Works: Adages IV iii 1 to V ii 51,* vol. 36, trans. J. N. Grant and B. I. Knott, ed. J. N. Grant. Toronto: University of Toronto Press, 2006.

Faret, N. *L'Honneste-Homme ou l'art de plaire à la cour.* Paris: T. Du Bray, 1630.

Foncemagne, Étienne-Laureault de. "Dissertation préliminaire sur la Cuisine moderne," in [Menon], *La Science du Maître d'Hôtel Cuisinier,* i–xxx.

Fontenelle, B. Le Bouyier de. *Nouveaux dialogues des morts,* ed. J. Dagen. Paris: Librairie Marcel Didier, 1971 [1683].

Furetière, A. *Dictionnaire universel, contenant generalement tous les mots françois tant vieux que modernes, & les termes de toutes les sciences et des arts,* 3 vols. La Haye–Rotterdam: A. and R. Leers, 1690.

Galien, Cl. *Œuvres.* Paris: Les Belles Lettres, 2000–.

Galien, Cl. *Œuvres médicales choisies I. De l'utilité des parties du corps humain,* trans. Ch. Daremberg, comments by A. Pichot. Paris: Gallimard, 1994.

Galien, Cl. *On the Properties of Foodstuffs (De alimentorum facultatibus),* ed. O. Powell. Cambridge: Cambridge University Press, 2003.

Gassendi, P. *Vie et mœurs d'Épicure,* 2 vols., ed. S. Taussig. Paris: Les Belles Lettres, 2006 [1647].

Gédoyn, N. "Reflexions sur le Goût," in *Recueil d'opuscules littéraires, avec un Discours de Louis XIV à Monseigneur le Dauphin, tirés d'un Cabinet d'Orleans,* 225–286. Amsterdam: E. van Harrevelt, 1767 [1745].

Gerard, A. *Essai sur le goût,* ed. P. Morère. Grenoble: ELLUG (Université Stendhal), 2008 [1759].

Gesner, C. *Tresor de Evonime Philiatre des Remedes secretz. Livre Physic, Medical, et Dispensatif de toutes substantiales liqueurs, et appareil de vins de diverses saveurs, necessaires à toutes gens. Principallement à Medecins, Chirurgiens, et Apothicaires.* Lyon: B. Arnoullet, 1555.

Gilliers, J. *Le cannaméliste français, ou nouvelle instruction pour ceux qui desirent d'apprendre l'office, dirigé en forme de dictionnaire.* Nancy: J.-B.-H. Leclerc, 1768 [1751].

Gracian, B. *Le Héros,* trans. J. de Courbeville. Paris: Champs libre, 1973 [1637].

Gracian, B. *L'homme universel.* Paris: Ed. Ivrea, 1994 [1646].

Gracian, B. *Traités politiques, esthétiques, éthiques,* trans. and comments by B. Pelegrin. Paris: Seuil, 2005.

Helvétius, Cl.-A. *De l'esprit.* Paris: Fayard, 1988 [1758].

Helvétius, Cl.-A. "De l'Homme, de ses facultés intellectuelles, et de son éducation," in Cl.-A. Helvétius, *Œuvres complètes*, vol. 10. Paris: P. Didot l'Aîné, 1795 [1773].

Holbach, P. H. D., Baron de. *Éléments de la morale universelle, ou Catéchisme de la nature*. Paris: O. de Bure, 1790.

Houdry, V. *La bibliothèque des prédicateurs qui contient les principaux sujets de la morale chrétienne mis en ordre alphabétique par le R. P. Vincent Houdry de la Compagnie de Jésus, seconde ed., reveuë et corrigée*, 4 vols. Lyon: A. Boudet, 1716–1717.

Hume, D. *Four Dissertations*. London: A. Millar, 1757.

Hume, D. "Of the Standard of Taste," in Hume, *Four Dissertations*, 203–240. London: A Millar, 1757.

Institoris, H., and J. Sprenger. *Le Marteau des Sorcières Malleus Maleficarum*, ed. A. Danet. Grenoble: J. Millon, 2005 [1486–1487].

Jaucourt, L. de. "Cuisine," in *Encyclopédie*, vol. 4, ed. D. Diderot and J. D'Alembert, 537–539. Paris: Briasson, 1754.

[Jaucourt, L. de]. "Goût (Physiolog.)," in *Encyclopédie ou Dictionnaire raisonné des sciences, des arts et des métiers, par une société de gens de lettres*, ed. D. Diderot and J. D'Alembert, vol. 7, 758–761. Paris: Briasson, 1757.

Journal encyclopédique, par une société de gens de lettres. Liège: Bouillon, 1756–1793.

Kant, E. *Critique de la Faculté de Juger (Kritik der Urteilskraft)*, ed. A. Philonenko. Paris: Vrin, 2000 [1790].

Kant, E. *Critique of Judgement*, 2nd ed., rev., trans. with introduction and notes by J. H. Bernard. London: Macmillan, 1914. http://oll.libertyfund.org/title/1217/97443 (accessed April 8, 2013).

[Kempis, Th. à]. *De l'imitation de Jesus-Christ. Traduction nouvelle, Par le Sieur De Beüil, Prieur de saint Val*. Paris: G. Desprez, 1679.

L.S.R. *L'Art de bien traiter* (Paris: J. Du Puis, 1674) in *L'art de la cuisine française*, ed. G. L. Laurendon. Paris: Payot (Les grands classiques de la gastronomie), 1995.

La Bruyère, J. de. *Les Caractères de Théophraste traduits du grec avec Les Caractères ou les mœurs de ce siècle*, rev. ed., ed. R. Pignarre. Paris: Flammarion, 2005 [1688].

La Chapelle, V. de. *Le Cuisinier Moderne, Qui apprend à donner toutes sortes de repas, En Gras et en Maigre, d'une manière plus délicate que ce qui en a été écrit jusqu'à présent; Divisé en cinq volumes, avec de nouveaux Modèles de Vaisselle, et des Desseins de Table dans le grand goût d'aujourd'hui, gravez en Taille-douce. Dedié à Son Altesse Serenissime Monseigneur le Prince d'Orange et de Nassau, etc., Par le Sieur Vincent La Chapelle, son Chef de Cuisine*, 2nd ed., vol. 5. The Hague: A. de Groot, 1742 [1735].

La Chapelle, V. de. *The Modern Cook*. London, 1733.

La Croix, J. de. "Le Degré du mont Carmel," in *Les œuvres spirituelles pour acheminer les ames à la parfaicte union avec Dieu. Du bienheureux P. Iean de la Croix premier Religieux deschaussé de la reforme de Notre Dame des Carmes; Et coadiuteur de la Ste Mere Therese de Iesus Fondatrice de la mesme reforme. (Traduictes d'Espagnol en françois, par M.R. Gaultier)*, 52–434. Paris: M. Sonnius, 1621.

La Croix, J. de (Saint). *Les œuvres spirituelles pour acheminer les ames à la parfaicte union avec Dieu. Du bienheureux P. Iean de la Croix premier Religieux deschaussé de la reforme de Notre Dame des Carmes; Et coadiuteur de la Ste Mere Therese de Iesus Fondatrice de la mesme reforme. (Traduictes d'Espagnol en françois, par M.R. Gaultier)*. Paris: M. Sonnius, 1621.

La Croix, J. de (Saint). *Les œuvres spirituelles pour acheminer les ames à la parfaicte union avec Dieu. Du bienheureux P. Iean de la Croix premier Religieux deschaussé de la reforme de Notre Dame des Carmes; Et coadiuteur de la Ste Mere Therese de Iesus Fondatrice de la mesme reforme. (Traduictes d'Espagnol en françois, par M.R. Gaultier).* Paris: M. Sonnius, 1628.

La Croix, J. de (Saint). *Œuvres complètes*, trans. Cyprien de la Nativité de la Vierge, ed. Lucien-Marie de Saint-Joseph. Paris: Desclée de Brouwer, 1959 [1st French trans. 1641].

La Mettrie, J. Offray de. "La Volupté, par Mr. Le Chevalier de M***, Capitaine au régiment Dauphin," in *Œuvres philosophiques de La Mettrie*, new ed., vol. 3, 15–93. Berlin: Ch. Tutot, 1796.

La Mettrie, J. Offray de. *L'art de jouir*, ed. G. Collet. Paris: Ed. du Boucher, 2002 [1751].

La Mettrie, J. Offray de. *L'Homme-Machine*, rev. ed., ed. P.-L. Assoun. Paris: Denoël/Gonthier, 1999 [1748].

La Reynière, G. de. *Almanach des gourmands, servant de guide dans les moyens de faire excellente chère. Par un vieil amateur. Contenant un grand nombre d'Articles de morale Gourmande et de Considérations Gourmandes inédites et curieuses; la Description de plusieurs espèces de ragoûts, tant exotiques qu'indigènes; la Petite Revue Gourmande, ou troisiéme Promenade d'un Gourmand dans Paris, les Découvertes Gourmandes et Friandes de l'année 1805; la Nécrologie Gourmande de 1805, etc.*, fourth annual edition. Paris: Maradan, 1806.

La Reynière, G. de. *Almanach des Gourmands, servant de guide dans les moyens de faire excellente choix. Par un vieil amateur. Contenant, parmi un grand nombre d'Articles intéressans sur l'Art alimentaire, une petite Dissertation sur les Truffes; une sur les Grillades, sur les Réductions, sur le Beurre, le Vin de Madère, les Repas de Noces, les Cuisinières, les Œufs, les progrès de la Cuisine dans le 18ᵉ siècle, le Kirschwasser, etc.; l'éloge des Cure-dents; les Découvertes nouvelles de 1810 et de 1811; des Poésies et des Anecdotes gourmandes; la Correspondance gourmande; la Petite Revue de l'année 1811, formant la Septième Promenade d'un Gourmand dans la bonne ville de Paris, quelques Articles de Gastronomie étrangère, etc. etc. etc.*, eighth annual edition. Paris: J. Chaumerot, 1812.

La Reynière, G. de. *Écrits gastronomiques*, ed. J.-Cl. Bonnet. Paris: Union générale d'éd., 1997.

La Reynière, G. de. *Manuel des Amphytryons, contenant un Traité de la Dissection des viandes à table, la Nomenclature des Menus les plus nouveaux pour chaque saison, et des Elemens de Politesse gourmande. Ouvrage indispensable à tous ceux qui sont jaloux de faire bonne chère, et de la faire faire aux autres.* Paris: Capelle et Renand, 1808.

La Salle, J.-B. de. *Règles de la bienséance et de la civilité chrétienne*, ed. F. Albert-Valentin. Paris: Ligel, 1956 [1703].

La Salle, J.-B. de. *The Rules of Christian Decorum and Civility, Divided into Two Parts, for Use in the Christian Schools*, trans. Richard Arnandez, ed. Gregory Wright, repr. Romeoville, IL: Christian Brothers Conference, 2007 [1703].

La Varenne, F.-P. de. *Le Confiturier françois*. Paris: J. Gaillard, 1660.

La Varenne, F.-P. de. *Le Cuisinier françois. D'après l'édition de 1651*, preface by M. and Ph. Hyman. Houilles: Manucius, 2001 [1651].

La Varenne, F.-P. de. *Le Cuisinier françois, enseignant la manière de bien apprester et assaisonner toutes sortes de Viandes grasses et maigres, Legumes, Patisseries, et autres mets qui se seruent tant sur les Tables des Grands que des particuliers. Par le Sieur de LA VARENNE Escuyer de Cuisine de Monsieur le Marquis d'Uxelles.* Paris: P. David, 1651.

La Varenne, F.-P. de. *Le Pâtissier françois.* Paris: J. Gaillard, 1653.

Lamy, G. *Explication mechanique et physique des fonctions de l'ame sensitive ou des sens, des passions, et du Mouvement Volontaire. Où l'on a ajoûté une Description des organes des Sens,* 2nd ed. Paris: L. Roulland, 1681 [1677].

Lancelot de Casteau. *Ouverture de cuisine.* Liège: Streel, 1604.

Lancelot de Casteau. *Ouverture de Cuisine,* introduction by H. Liebaers, trans. L. Moulin and J. Comm. Kother. Brussels: De Schutter, 1983 [1604].

Lancre, P. de. *On the Inconstancy of Witches. Pierre de Lancre's Tableau de l'inconstance des mauvais anges et demons (1612),* trans. H. Stone and G. ScholzWilliams, ed. G. Scholz Williams. Tempe, AZ: Brepols/ACMRS, 2006.

Lancre, P. de. *Tableau de l'inconstance des mauvais anges & demons, ou [sic] il est amplement traicté des Sorciers & de la Sorcelerie [sic]. Livre tres-utile et necessaire, non seulement aux Iuges, mais à tous ceux qui viuent soubs les loix Chrestiennes.* Paris: J. Berjon, 1612.

Le Camus, A. *Médecine de L'Esprit, Où l'on traite des Dispositions & des Causes Physiques qui, en consequence de l'union de l'ame avec le corps, influent sur les opérations de l'esprit; et des moyens de maintenir ces opérations dans un bon état, ou de les corriger lorsqu'elles sont viciées,* 2 vols.. Paris: Ganeau, 1753.

Le Cat, Cl.-N. *La théorie de l'ouie: supplément a [sic] cet article du traité des sens.* Paris: Vallat-la-Chapelle, 1768.

Le Cat, Cl.-N. *Traité des Sens. Édition corrigée, augmentée, & enrichie de Figures en Taille douce,* Amsterdam: F. Wetstein, 1744 [1739].

Le Cat, Cl.-N. *Traité des sensations et des passions en général, et des sens en particulier.* Paris: Vallat-la-Chapelle, 1767 [1739].

Le Cuisinier françois, ed. J.-L. Flandrin, Ph. Hyman, and M. Hyman. Paris: Montalba, 1983.

Le Cuisinier gascon. Amsterdam: L'Arche du Livre, 1740.

Le cuisinier Taillevent. Toulouse: J. de Guerlins, c. 1518–1520.

Le Dictionnaire de l'Académie françoise, 2 vols., 4th ed. Paris: Veuve Bernard Bruner, 1762.

Le Dictionnaire de l'Académie françoise, 2 vols. Paris: Veuve Jean-Baptiste Coignard, 1694.

Le Mercure galant. Paris: Au Palais, 1678–1714.

Le Thresor de santé, ou, Mesnage de la vie humaine. Divisé en dix Livres. Lesquels traictent amplement de toutes sortes de Viandes & Breuvages, ensemble de leur qualité & preparation. Œuvre autant curieuse & recerchee [sic], qu'utile & necessaire. Faict par un des plus celebres & fameux Medecins de ce siecle. Lyon: J. Ant. Huguetan, 1607.

Lebas, J. *Le Festin joyeux, ou, La Cuisine en Musique en vers libres.* Paris: Lesclapart, 1738.

Legrand d'Aussy, P. *Histoire de la vie privée des Français.* Paris: Pierres, 1782.

Lemery, L. *Traité des alimens, où l'on trouve la différence, & le choix, qu'on en doit faire; les bons, & les mauvais effets, qu'ils peuvent produire; leurs principes; les circonstances où ils conviennent. Revue, corrigée, & augmentée sur la seconde de l'auteur, par M. Jacques Jean Bruhier,* 2 vols. Paris: Durand, 1755 [1702].

Lemery, L. *Traité des alimens, où l'on trouve par ordre, et separement, La difference & le choix qu'on doit faire de chacun d'eux en particulier; les bons & les mauvais effets qu'ils peuvent produire; les principes en quoi ils abondent; le temps, l'âge & le temperament où ils conviennent.* Paris: P. Witte, 1705 [1702].

Lessius, L. *Conseils pour vivre longtemps,* in L. Cornaro, *De la sobriété. Conseils pour vivre longtemps,* ed. G. Vigarello. Grenoble: Jérôme Milon, 1991 [1647].

[Lévesque de Pouilly, L.-J.]. *Theorie des sentimens agréables. Où après avoir indiqué les régles que la Nature suit dans la distribution du plaisir, on établit les principes de la Theologie naturelle et ceux de la Philosophie morale.* Geneva: Brillot & Fils, 1747 [1736].

Locke, J. *An Essay Concerning Human Understanding,* 2 vols., ed. J. W. Yolton. London: Everyman's Library, 1961 [1690].

Locke, J. *Essai philosophique concernant l'entendement humain, ou l'on montre quelle est l'étendue de nos connoissances certaines, et la maniere dont nous y parvenons. Traduit de l'Anglois de Mr. Locke, par Pierre Coste, sur la Quatriéme Edition, revûë, corrigée, & augmentée par l'Auteur.* Amsterdam: H. Schelte, 1700.

Locke, J. *Essai sur l'entendement humain (Livres I et II),* ed. J. M. Vienne. Paris: Vrin, 2001 [1690; 1st French ed. 1700].

Lune, P. de. *Le cuisinier.* Paris: P. David, 1656.

Malebranche, N. *De la recherche de la vérité,* 2 vols., ed. J. C. Bardout. Paris: Vrin, 2006 [1674–1675].

Malebranche, N. *Traité de morale,* rev. ed., ed. J. P. Osier. Paris: Flammarion, 2006 [1684].

Malpighi, M. "Marcello Malpighii Exercitatio Epistolica De Lingua," in *Opera omnia, Figuris elegantissimus in aes incisis illustrate,* vol. 2, 13–20. London: R. Scott, 1686.

Malpighi, M. *Opera omnia, Figuris elegantissimus in aes incisis illustrate,* vol. 2. London: R. Scott, 1686.

[Marin, F.]. *Les Dons de Comus ou Les délices de la table. Ouvrage non seulement utile aux officiers de bouche pour ce qui concerne leur art, mais principalement à l'usage des personnes qui sont curieuses de savoir donner à manger, et d'être servies délicatement, tant en gras qu'en maigre, suivant les saisons, et dans le goût le plus nouveau* (Paris: Prault Fils, 1739), in B. Fink, *Les liaisons savoureuses. Réflexions et pratiques culinaires au dix-huitième siècle,* Saint-Étienne: Publications de l'Université de Saint-Étienne, 1995, 21–32.

[Marin, F.]. *Les Dons de Comus, ou l'art de la cuisine, réduit en pratique.* Paris: Pissot, 1758.

[Marin, F.]. *Suite des Dons de Comus ou l'art de la cuisine reduit en pratique.* Paris: Veuve Pissot-Didot-Brunet Fils, 1742.

[Massialot, F.]. *Le Cuisinier roïal & Bourgeois.* Paris: C. Prudhomme, 1705 [1691].

[M.C.D., pseudonym of Briand]. *Dictionnaire des alimens, vins et liqueurs, leurs qualités, leurs effets, relativement aux différens âges, & aux différens tempéramens; avec la maniere de les apprêter, ancienne et moderne, suivant la méthode des plus habiles Chefs-d'Office & Chefs de Cuisine, de la Cour & de la Ville,* 3 vols. Paris: Gissey-Bordelet, 1750.

[Menon]. *La Cuisinière Bourgeoise, suivie de l'office, À l'usage de tous ceux qui se mêlent de dépenses de Maisons. Contenant la maniére de disséquer, connoître & servir toutes sortes de Viandes.* Brussels: F. Foppens, 1753 [1746].

[Menon]. *La Nouvelle Cuisine, avec de nouveaux menus pour chaque Saison de l'année, Qui explique la façon de travailler toutes sortes de Mets, qui se servent aujourd'hui, en gras & en maigre; très-utile aux personnes qui veulent diversifier une Table par des Ragoûts nouveaux. Pour servir de continuation au nouveau Traité de cuisine.* Paris: J. Saugrain, 1742.

[Menon]. *La Science du Maître d'Hôtel Confiseur, à l'usage des Officiers, avec des Observations sur la connoissance & les propriétés des Fruits. Enrichie de Desseins [sic] en Décoration et Parterres pour les Desserts. Suite du Maître d'Hôtel Cuisinier.* Paris: Paulus-du-Mesnil, 1750.

[Menon]. *La Science du Maître d'Hôtel Cuisinier, avec des Observations sur la connoissance & propriétés des Alimens.* Paris: Paulus-du-Mesnil, 1749.

[Menon]. *Nouveau Traité de la Cuisine.* Paris: M.-É. David, 1739.

[Méré, A. G., Chevalier de]. *Maximes et sentences, et reflexions morales et politiques.* Paris: E. Du Castin, 1687.

[Meusnier de Querlon, A.-G.]. "Apologie des Modernes ou Reponse du Cuisinier françois auteur des Dons de Comus, à un patissier anglois" (1st ed. 1740), in S. Mennell, *Lettre d'un pâtissier anglois.*

Mme Dacier. *Des causes de la corruption du gout.* Amsterdam: P. Humbert, 1715.

Mme Dacier. *Homere défendu contre l'Apologie du R. P. Hardouin, ou Suite des causes de la Corruption du Goust.* Paris: J.-B. Coignard, 1716.

Montaigne, M. de. *Essais*, ed. P. Coste. The Hague: P. Gosse and J. Neaulme, 1727 [1580].

Montesquieu. Ch.-L. de Secondat (Baron de). *Essai sur le goût, précédé de Éloge de la sincérité.* Paris: Armand Colin, 1993 [1757].

Morvan de Bellegarde, J.-B. *Lettres curieuses de littérature et de morale.* Paris: J. and M. Guignard, 1702.

Muret, M. *Traité des Festins.* Paris: G. Desprez, 1682.

Nicole, P. "La Civilité chrétienne," in *Essais de morale, contenus en divers traitez sur plusieurs devoirs importans*, vol. 2. Luxembourg: A. Chevalier, 1737 [1670].

Nodé, P. *Déclamation contre l'erreur execrable des Maleficiers, Sorciers, Enchanteurs, Magiciens, Devins, & semblables observateurs des superstitions: lesquelz pullulent maintenant couvertement en France: à ce que recherche, et punition d'iceux soit faicte, sur peine de rentrer en plus grands troubles que jamais.* Paris: J. de Carroy, 1578.

Pascal, B. *Pensées*, ed. P. Sellier. Paris: Pocket, 2003 [1670].

[Patin, G.]. *Traité de la conservation de santé, par un bon regime et legitime usage des choses requises pour bien et sainement vivre.* Paris: J. Jost, 1632.

Perrault, Cl. *Du bruit et de la musique des Anciens.* Leiden: P. Vander, 1721.

Perrault, Cl. *Essais de physique ou Recueil de plusieurs traitez touchant les choses naturelles*, 4 vols. Paris: J.-B. Coignard, 1680.

Piles, R. de. *Conversations sur la connoissance de la peinture et sur les jugements qu'on doit faire des tableaux*, vol. 1. Paris: N. Langlois, 1677.

Platine (B. Sacchi). *Le Platine en François, d'après l'édition de 1505*, preface by S. Serventi and J.-L. Flandrin, trans. M. Ribot. Houilles: Manucius, 2003 [1505].

Plato. *Gorgias*, rev. ed., ed. M. Canto-Sperber. Paris: Garnier/Flammarion, 2007.

Plato. *Le Banquet*, ed. L. Brisson. Paris: Flammarion, 2005.

Plato. *The Republic of Plato*, ed. F. MacDonald Cornford. Oxford: Clarendon Press, 1948.

Plato. *Timée Critias*, ed. L. Brisson. Paris: Flammarion, 2001.

Pline l'Ancien. *Histoire naturelle*. Paris: Les Belles Lettres, 1947–.

Pline l'Ancien. *Histoire naturelle*, book 7, ed. R. Schilling. Paris: Les Belles Lettres, 1977

Pluche, A. *Le spectacle de la nature ou entretiens sur les particularités de l'histoire naturelle, qui ont paru les plus propres à rendre les Jeunes-Gens curieux, & à leur former l'esprit*, vol. 8 ("Contenant ce qui regarde l'homme en société avec Dieu"). Paris: Veuve Estienne, 1751–1752.

Pluche, A. *Le spectacle de la nature ou entretiens sur les particularités de l'histoire naturelle, qui ont paru les plus propres à rendre les Jeunes-Gens curieux, & à leur former l'esprit*, vol. 5 ("Contenant ce qui regarde l'Homme considéré en lui-même"). Paris: Veuve Estienne and Fils, 1746.

[Poncelet, P.]. *Chymie du gout et de l'odorat, ou principes pour composer facilement, & à peu de frais, les Liqueurs à boire, & les Eaux de senteurs*. Paris: Pissot, 1766 [1755].

[Poncelet, P.]. "Dissertation préliminaire sur la salubrité des Liqueurs, & l'harmonie des saveurs," in *Chymie du gout et de l'odorat, ou principes pour composer facilement, & à peu de frais, les Liqueurs à boire, & les Eaux de senteurs*, iii–xxvj. Paris: Pissot, 1766 [1755].

Poncelet P. *Nouvelle Chymie du gout et de l'odorat ou l'Art de composer facilement & à peu de frais les liqueurs à boire & les eaux de senteurs, nouvelle édition entièrement changée, considérablement augmentée & enrichie d'un procédé nouveau pour composer des liqueurs fines sans eau-de-vie, ni vin, ni esprit de vin, proprement dit; de plusieurs dissertations intéressantes, & d'une suite d'observations physiologiques sur l'usage immodéré des liqueurs fortes*. Paris: Pissot, 1774 [1755].

Porta, J.-B. de. *La magie naturelle ou les secrets et miracles de la nature. Edition conforme à celle de Rouen (1631)*. Rouvray: Editions du Prieuré, s.d. [1993].

Rabelais, F. *Œuvres complètes*, ed. M. Huchon. Paris: Gallimard, 1994.

Renaudot, Th. *Recueil général des questions traictees és Conferences du Bureau d'Adresse, sur toutes sortes de Matières; Par les plus beaux esprits de ce temps*, 5 vols. Paris: L. Chamoudry, 1655–1656.

Renaudot, Th. *Recueil général des questions traictees és Conferences du Bureau d'Adresse, sur toutes sortes de Matieres; Par les plus beaux esprits de ce temps*, vol. 1, 2nd ed. Paris: L. Chamhoudry, 1656.

Renaudot, Th. *Recueil général des questions traittées és Conferences du Bureau d'Adresse és années 1633–34–35 iusques à present, sur toutes sortes de matières, par les plus beaux esprits de ce temps*, vol. 2. Paris: L. Chamhoudry, 1655.

Restif de la Bretonne. *Sara ou la dernière aventure d'un homme de quarante-cinq ans*. Paris: Stock, 1984 [1783].

Richelet, P. *Dictionnaire de la langue françoise ancienne et moderne*, 2 vols. Amsterdam: Aux dépens de la Compagnie, 1732.

Ripa, C. *Iconologie ou, Explication nouvelle de plusieurs images, emblemes, et autres figures hyerogliphiques des vertus, des vices, des arts, des sciences, des causes naturelles, des humeurs differentes, & des passions humaines: oeuvre augmentée d'une seconde partie, necessaire a toute sorte d'esprits, et particulierement a ceux qui aspirent a estre, ou qui sont en effet orateurs, poetes, sculpteurs, peintres, ingenieurs, autheurs de medailles, de devises, de ballets, & de poëmes dramatiques / tirée des recherches et des figures de Cesar Ripa; moralisées par I. Baudoin.* Paris: M. Guillemot, 1643.

Ripa, C. *Iconologie ou les principales choses qui peuvent tomber dans la pensee touchant les Vices et les Vertus, sont representees soubs diverses figures, gravées en cuivre par Jacques de Bie, Et moralement explicquées par I. Baudoin.* Paris: J. de Bie, 1643 [1593].

Rochefort, C. de. *Dictionnaire general et curieux contenant les principaux mots, et les plus usitez en la langue françoise.* Lyon: P. Guillimin, 1685.

Rohault, J. *Traité de Physique,* 6th ed. Paris: G. Desprez, 1692 [1671].

Rousseau, J.-J. "Émile ou De l'éducation" (1st ed., 1762), in *Œuvres complètes,* ed. B. Gagnebin et al., vol. 4. Paris: Gallimard (La Pléiade), 1969.

Rousseau, J.-J. *Œuvres complètes,* 5 vols., ed. B. Gagnebin and M. Raymond. Paris: Gallimard (La Pléiade), 1959–1995.

Sade, D. A. F. *Œuvres,* 3 vols., ed. M. Delon. Paris: Gallimard (La Pléiade), 1990.

Saint-Evremond, Ch. de. *Entretiens sur toutes choses,* ed. D. Bensoussan. Paris: Desjonquères, 1998.

Saint-Evremond, Ch. de, "Quelques observations sur le goût & le discernement des François," in *Œuvres meslées,* vol. 7, 108–130. Paris: C. Barbin, 1684.

Sales, F. de (Saint). *Introduction to the Devout Life,* ed. Th. Barns. London: Methuen, 1906 [1609].

Sales, F. de (Saint). *Œuvres,* ed. A. Ravier, in the R. Devos collection. Paris: Gallimard (La Pléiade), 1969.

[Seran de La Tour]. *L'Art de sentir et de juger en matiere de gout,* 2 vols. Paris: Pissot, 1762.

Serres, O. de. *Le théâtre d'agriculture et ménage des champs.* Paris: Métayer, 1600.

[Surin, J.-J.]. *Les fondemens de la vie spirituelle, Tirez du Livre de l'Imitation de Iesus-Christ. Composé par J.D.S.F.P. et une lettre spirituelle à une Dame de qualité, traitant des moyens de conserver l'esprit de pauvreté, au milieu des richesses.* Lyon: R. Glaize, 1682.

[Tomkis, Th.]. *Lingua, or The Combat of the Tongue and the Five Senses for Superiority.* London: G. Eld for S. Waterson, 1607.

Traité de la civilité nouvellement dressé d'une maniere exacte & méthodique & suivant les regles de l'usage vivant. Lyon: J. Certe, 1681.

Viard, A. *Le cuisinier impérial, ou l'art de faire la cuisine et la patisserie pour toutes les fortunes, avec différentes Recettes d'Office et de Fruicts confits, et la manière de servir une Table depuis vingt jusqu'à soixante Couverts. Par A. Viard, Homme de bouche.* Paris: Barba, 1806.

Voltaire, F.-M. Arouet (known as), "Défense du Mondain, ou L'Apologie du Luxe," in *Les Œuvres complètes de Voltaire,* vol. 16, ed. N. Cronk, 304–309. Oxford: Alden Press, 2003 [1737].

Voltaire, F.-M. Arouet (known as). *Dictionnaire philosophique.* De l'imprimerie de la société littéraire-typographique, 1785 [London, 1764].

Voltaire, F.-M. Arouet (known as), "Le Mondain," in *Œuvres complètes,* vol. 16, ed. N. Cronk, 295–303. Oxford: Alden Press, 2003 [1736].

Voltaire, F.-M. Arouet (known as), "Le Temple du Goût," in *Œuvres diverses de Monsieur de Voltaire,* vol. 5, 207–246. London: J. Nourse, 1746.

Voltaire, F.-M. Arouet (known as). *Œuvres complètes*. Oxford: Voltaire Foundation, 1968–.

Wier, J. *De l'imposture et tromperie des diables, des enchantements et sorcelleries*. Paris: J. Du Puys, 1569 [1563].

Secondary Literature

Ackerman, D. *A Natural History of the Senses*. London: Phoenix, 2000 [1990].

Adam, R. "Précisions sur l'*Ouverture de cuisine* de Lancelot de Casteau, imprimée à Liège en 1604." *De Gulden Passer (Le compas d'or)*, no. 1 (2012): 89–96.

Adnès, P. *Dictionnaire de spiritualité ascétique et mystique*, vol. 6, s.v. "Goût spirituel," col. 626–644. Paris: Beauchesne, 1967.

Albala, K. (ed.). *A Cultural History of Food in the Renaissance*, vol. 3. London: Berg, 2012.

Albala, K. *Food in Early Modern Europe*. Westport, CT: Greenwood Press, 2003.

Albala, K. "Historical Background to Food and Christianity," in Albala and Eden, *Food and Faith in Christian Culture*, 7–19.

Albala, K. "The Ideology of Fasting in the Reformation Era," in Albala and Eden, *Food and Faith in Christian Culture*, 41–57.

Albala, K., and T. Eden (eds.). *Food and Faith in Christian Culture*. New York, Columbia University Press, 2011.

Alexandre-Bidon, D. "Trop gourmand ? Le corps obèse dans l'iconographie medievale," in Karila-Cohen and Quellier, *Le corps du gourmand*, 133–144.

Alexandre-Bidon, D. *Une Archéologie du goût: céramique et consommation: moyen âge-temps modernes*, preface by H. This. Paris: Picard, 2005.

Allen, G. Debus. "La médecine chimique," in Grmek, *Histoire de la pensée médicale en Occident*, vol. 2, 37–59.

Aries, Ph., and G. Duby (eds.). *Histoire de la vie privée*, 5 vols. Paris: Seuil, 1985–1987.

Aron, J.-P. *Essai sur la sensibilité alimentaire à Paris au XIXᵉ siècle*. Paris: Armand Colin, 1967.

Aron, J.-P. *Le mangeur du XIXᵉ siècle. Une folie bourgeoise: la nourriture*. Paris: Denoël/Gonthier, 1973.

Audidière, S., J.-Cl. Bourdin, J.-M. Lardic, F. Markovits, and Y. Ch. Zarka (eds.). *Matérialistes français du XVIIIᵉ siècle (La Mettrie, Helvétius, d'Holbach)*. Paris: Presses universitaires de France, 2006.

Audouin-Rouzeau, F., and F. Sabban (eds.). *Un aliment sain dans un corps sain*, Actes du Deuxième colloque de l'IEHCA. Tours: Presses Universitaires François-Rabelais, 2007.

Aziza-Shuster, E. *Le médecin de soi-même*. Paris: Presses universitaires de France, 1972.

Bajomée, D., J. Dor, and M.-É. Henneau (eds.). *Femmes et livres*. Paris: L'Harmattan, 2007.

Bakhtine, M. *L'œuvre de François Rabelais et la culture populaire au Moyen Âge et sous la Renaissance*, trans. A. Robel. Paris: Gallimard, 1970.

Barrère, J.-B. *L'idée de goût de Pascal à Valéry*. Paris: Klincksieck, 1972.

Barthes, R. "Pour une psychosociologie de l'alimentation." *Annales. Économies, sociétés, civilisations* 16, no. 2 (1961): 977–986.

Barthes, R. *Sade, Fourier, Loyola*. Paris: Seuil, 1971.

Becchi, E., and D. Julia (eds.). *Histoire de l'enfance en Occident*, 2 vols. Paris: Seuil, 1998.

Becker, K. (ed.). "Studia Alimentorum 2003–2013. Une décennie de recherche. A Decade of Research." *Food and History*, 10, no. 2 (2012): 9–25.

Bell, R. M. *Holy Anorexia*. Chicago: University of Chicago Press, 1987.

Bely, L. *La France moderne, 1498–1789*. Paris: Presses universitaires de France, 2003.

Bendiner, K. *Food in Painting from the Renaissance to the Present*. London: Reaktion Books, 2004.

Bensoussan, D. "Le goût selon Saint-Evremond," in Montandon, *Du Goût, de la Conversation et des Femmes*, 23–39

Bensoussan, M. *Les particules alimentaires. Naissance de la gastronomie au XVIᵉ siècle. De François Iᵉʳ à la colonisation de l'Amérique du Nord*, preface by A. Capati. Paris: Maisonneuve and Larose, 2002.

Berg, M., and E. Eger (eds.). *Luxury in the Eighteenth Century: Debates, Desires and Delectable Goods*. New York: Palgrave Macmillan, 2003.

Berry, C. *The Idea of Luxury: A Conceptual and Historical Investigation*. New York: Cambridge University Press, 1994.

Bessis, S. (ed.). *Mille et une bouches. Cuisines et identités culturelles*, special issue Mutations/Mangeurs series, no. 154 (March 1995).

Bierlaire, F. "Colloques scolaires et civilités puériles," in Becchi and Julia, *Histoire de l'enfance en Occident*, vol. 1, 255–285.

Bierlaire, F. "Érasme, la table et les manières de table," in Margolin and Sauzet, *Pratiques et Discours alimentaires*, 147–160.

Bierlaire, F. "Zoologie et rhétorique chez Érasme," in Kieffer, R. (ed.). *Parole sacrée, Parole profane . . . De la religion à l'éloquence*, presented at the international colloquium, Luxembourg, 1990, 179–188. Luxembourg: Courrier de l'éducation Nationale (numéro spécial), 1991.

Billaud, I., and M.-C. Laperrière (eds.). *Représentations du corps sous l'Ancien Régime. Discours et pratiques*. Laval: Presses de l'Université Laval, 2007.

Blanco, M. "Le goût des Espagnols: l'émergence d'un concept," in Montandon, *Dictionnaire raisonné de la politesse*, 1–22.

Bobis, L. *Une histoire du chat. De l'Antiquité à nos jours*. Paris: Fayard, 2006 [2000].

Boer, W. de, and C. Göttler (eds.). *Religion and the Senses in Early Modern Europe*. Leiden: Brill, 2013.

Bologne, J.-C. *Histoire de la pudeur*. Paris: Hachette, 1986.

Bonnet, J.-Cl. "La table dans les civilités." *La qualité de la vie au XVIIᵉ siècle, Marseille*, no. 109 (2nd trimester 1977): 99–104.

Bonnet, J.-Cl. "Le réseau culinaire dans l'Encyclopédie." *Annales. Économies, sociétés, civilisations* 31, no. 5 (1976): 891–914.

Bonnet, J.-Cl. "Le système de la cuisine et du repas chez Rousseau." *Poétique, revue de théorie et d'analyse littéraires*, no. 22 (1975): 244–267.

Bonnet, J.-Cl. "Les manuels de cuisine." *Aliments et cuisine: Dix-huitième siècle*, no. 15 (1983): 53–63.

Bord, A. *Jean de la Croix en France*. Paris: Beauchesne, 1993.

Boudier, V. *La cuisine du peintre. Scène de genre et nourriture au Cinquecento*. Tours: Presses universitaires François Rabelais, 2010.

Bourdieu, P. *La Distinction: critique sociale du jugement*. Paris: Minuit, 1979.

Bourdieu, P., and J.-Cl. Passeron. *La Reproduction. Éléments pour une théorie du système d'enseignement*. Paris: Ed. Minuit, 1970.

Boutaud, J.-J. *Le sens gourmand. De la commensalité–du goût–des aliments*. Paris: Jean-Paul Rocher, 2005.

Brugière, B. (ed.). *Les figures du corps dans la littérature et la peinture anglaises et américaines. De la Renaissance à nos jours*. Paris: Publications de la Sorbonne, 1991.

Brulotte, G. "Pour un imaginaire du goût," in *Le goût dans tous ses états*, edited by M. Erman, 21–32. Berne: Peter Lang, 2009.

Bury, E. *Littérature et politesse. L'invention de l'honnête homme 1580–1750*. Paris: Presses universitaires de France, 1996.

Bynum, C. W. "Fast, Feast and Flesh: The Religious Significance of Food to Medieval Woman," in *Food and Culture: A Reader*, 2nd ed., ed. C. Counihan and P. van Esterik, 121–140. New York: Routledge, 2008 [1997].

Bynum, C. W. *Holy Feast and Holy Fast: The Religious Significance of Food to Medieval Women*. Berkeley: University of California Press, 1987.

Bynum, W. F., and R. Porter (eds.). *Medicine and the Five Senses*. Cambridge: Cambridge University Press, 1993.

Camporesi, P. *Le Goût du chocolat. L'art de vivre au XVIIIe siècle*, trans. J. Bouzaher. Paris: Tallendier, 2008 [1992].

Camporesi, P. *L'officine des sens. Une anthropologie baroque*. Paris: Hachette, 1989.

Canévet, M., P. Adnès, W. Yeomans, and A. Derville. *Les sens spirituels*. Paris: Beauchesne, 1993.

Carter, T. "The Sound of Silence: Models for an Urban Musicology," in *Musik und Urbanität: Arbeitstagung der Fachgruppe Soziologie und Sozialgeschichte der Musik in Schmökwitz (Berlin, 26–28 novembre 1999)*, ed. Ch. Kaden and V. Kalisch, 13–23. Essen: Verlag Blaue Eule, 2002 (revised in *Urban History* 29 [2002]: 8–18).

Casagrande, C., and S. Vecchio. *Histoire des péchés capitaux au Moyen Âge*, trans. P.-E. Dauzat. Paris: Aubier, 2003.

Casagrande, C., and S. Vecchio. *Les péchés de la langue*, trans. Ph. Baillet, preface by J. Le Goff. Paris: Ed. du Cerf, 1991.

Cassirer, E. *La philosophie des Lumières*, trans. and comments P. Quillet. Paris: Fayard, 1970 [1932].

Certeau, M. *La Fable mystique (XVIe–XVIIe siècle)*. Paris: Gallimard, 2002 [1982].

Certeau, M. de, L. Giard, and P. Mayol. *L'invention du quotidien*, vol. 2, *Habiter, cuisiner*. Paris: Gallimard, 1994.

Champion, C. *Hors-d'oeuvre. Essai sur les relations entre arts et cuisine*. Gallardon: Menu-Fretin, 2010.

Chantalat, Cl. *À la recherche du goût classique*. Paris: Klincksieck, 1992.

Chantalat, Cl. "Deux monographies sur la notion de goût du début du XVIIIe siècle," in Montandon, *Du Goût, de la Conversation et des Femmes*, 41–54.

Charbonneau, F. *L'école de la gourmandise de Louis XIV à la Révolution*. Paris: Desjonquères, 2008.

Chartier, R. "Bibliothèque bleue," in *Dictionnaire encyclopédique du Livre*, ed. P. Fouche, D. Péchoin, and P. Schuwer, 294–295. Paris: Ed. Cercle de la Librairie, 2002.

Chartier, R. "Distinction et divulgation: la civilité et ses livres," in R. Chartier, *Lectures et lecteurs dans la France d'Ancien Régime*, 45–86. Paris: Seuil, 1987.

Chartier, R. "Le monde comme représentation," in *Annales. Économies, Sociétés, Civilisations* 44, no. 5 (1989): 1505–1520.

Chartier, R., G. Duby, L. Febvre, P. Francastel, and R. Mandrou. *La sensibilité dans l'histoire*. Brionne: G. Montfort, 1987.

Chiou, D.-L. *Homo gastronomicus: les régimes du goût et le plaisir alimentaire à l'âge moderne (1650–1850)*, thèse inédite en Histoire et civilisation. Paris: Ecole des Hautes Etudes en Sciences Sociales (EHESS), 2003.

Claflin, K. W. "Food among the Historians: Early Modern Europe," in Claflin and Scholliers, *Writing Food History*, 38–58.

Claflin, K.W., and P. Scholliers (eds.). *Writing Food History: A Global Perspective*. London: Berg, 2012.

Classen, C. (ed.). *A Cultural History of the Senses*, 6 vols. London: Bloomsbury, 2014.

Classen, C. (ed.). *The Book of Touch*. Oxford: Berg (Sensory Formations Series), 2005.

Classen, C. *The Color of Angels: Cosmology, Gender and the Aesthetic Imagination*. London: Routledge, 1998.

Classen, C. *The Deepest Sense: A Cultural History of Touch*. Chicago, University of Illinois Press, 2012.

Classen, C. "The Witch's Senses: Sensory Ideologies and Transgressive Feminities from the Renaissance to Modernity," in Howes, *Empire of the Senses*, 70–84.

Classen, C. *Worlds of Sense: Exploring the Senses in History and Across Cultures*. London: Routledge, 1993.

Classen, C., D. Howes, and A. Synnott. *Aroma: The Cultural History of Smell*. London: Routledge, 1994.

Cohen, E., and J. Csergo (eds.). *L'artification du culinaire. Sociétés et représentations*, no. 34 (2012).

Cohen, S. *Animals as Disguised Symbols in Renaissance Art*. Leiden: Brill, 2008.

Connor, S. "The Menagerie of the Senses." *Senses and Society* 1, no. 1 (2006): 9–26

Corbin, A. "Histoire et Anthropologie sensorielle. Anthropologie et Sociétés 14, no. 2, "Les cinq sens," ed. D. Howes (1990): 13–24.

Corbin, A. *Le Miasme et la Jonquille. L'odorat et l'imaginaire social XVIIIe-XIXe siècles*. Paris: Aubier, 2003 [1982].

Corbin, A. *Les Cloches de la Terre. Paysage sonore et culture sensible dans les campagnes au XIXe siècle*. Paris: Albin Michel, 2001 [1994].

Cottingham, J. "'A Brute to the Brutes?': Descartes' Treatment of Animals,' in *Philosophy* 53, no. 206 (October 1978): 551–559.

Coulon, C. *La table de Montaigne*. Paris: Arléa, 2009.

Counihan, C., and P. van Esterik (eds.). *Food and Culture: A Reader*, 2nd ed. New York: Routledge, 2008 [1997].

Courtine, J.-J., and C. Haroche. *Histoire du visage. Exprimer et taire ses émotions (XVIᵉ– début XIXᵉ siècle)*. Paris: Payot and Rivages, 1994 [1988].

Cowan, A., and J. Steward. *The City and the Senses: Urban Culture since 1500*. Aldershot-Burlington: Ashgate, 2008.

Csergo, J. "L'art culinaire ou l'insaisissable beauté d'un art qui se dérobe. Quelques jalons (XVIIIᵉ–XXIᵉ siècle)," in Cohen and Csergo, *L'artification du culinaire*, 13–36.

Darnton, R. *L'aventure de l'Encyclopédie. Un best-seller au siècle des Lumières*, preface by E. Le Roy Ladurie, trans. M.-A. Revellat. Paris: Perrin, 1979.

Dear, P. "A Mechanical Microcosm: Bodily Passions, Good Manners, and Cartesian Mechanism," in Lawrence and Shapin, *Science Incarnate*, 51–82.

Delahaye, E. "Les tapisseries de 'La Dame à la licorne,'" in Gélard and Sirost, "Langages des sens," 57–64.

Delfosse, A. "Exciter les sens pour bouleverser les cœurs: les processions post-tridentines dans les régions de culture baroque," in *Musiques et réformes religieuses aux XVIᵉ et XVIIᵉ siècles: statuts, fonctions, pratiques*, ed. Th. Psychoyou, 25–37. Paris: Université de Paris Sorbonne (Le Jardin de Musique V/2), 2008.

Delfosse, A. *La "Protectrice des Païs-Bas": stratégies politiques et figures de la Vierge dans les Pays-Bas espagnols*. Turnhout: Brepols, 2009.

Delfosse, A., and Th. Glesener (eds.). *Lire, écrire et éduquer à la Renaissance*. Brussels: Archives et Bibliothèques de Belgique, 2014.

Delon, M. *Le savoir-vivre libertin*. Paris: Hachette, 2002.

Delumeau, J. (ed.). *La mort des pays de cocagne. Comportements collectifs de la Renaissance à l'âge classique*. Paris: Publication de la Sorbonne, 1976.

Delumeau, J. *Le péché et la peur. La culpabilisation en Occident XIIIᵉ–XVIIIᵉ siècles*. Paris: Fayard, 1983.

Delumeau, J. *Une histoire du paradis. Le jardin des délices*. Paris: Fayard, 1992.

Delumeau, J., and M. Cottret. *Le catholicisme entre Luther et Voltaire*. Paris: Presses universitaires de France, 1996 [1971].

Delville, M. *Food, Poetry and the Aesthetics of Consumption: Eating the Avant-Garde*. London: Routledge, 2008.

Delville, M., A. Norris, and V. von Hoffmann (eds.). *Le Dégoût. Histoire, Langage, Ethique et Esthétique d'une émotion plurielle*. Liège: PULg ("Cultures sensibles"), 2015.

Denis, M., and N. Blayau. *Le XVIIIᵉ siècle*. Paris: Armand Colin, 2004.

Dens, J.-P. *L'honnête homme et la critique du goût: esthétique et société au XVIIᵉ siècle*. Lexington: French Forum, 1981.

Descola, Ph. *Par-delà nature et culture*. Paris: Gallimard, 2005.

Desjardins, L. *Le corps parlant. Savoirs et représentations des passions au XVIIᵉ siècle*. Laval: Presses de l'Université Laval, 2001.

Dictionnaire de Spiritualité Ascétique et Mystique. Paris: Beauchesne, 1937–1995.

Dictionnaire de Théologie Catholique, 15 vols. Paris: Letouzey et Ané, 1903–1972.

Dugan, H., *The Ephemeral History of Perfume. Scent and Sense in Early Modern England*, Baltimore: The Johns Hopkins University Press, 2011.

Dupont, F. "Grammar of Roman Dining," in Flandrin and Montanari, *Food: A Culinary History*, 113–127.

Durand, Y. *L'ordre du monde: idéal politique et valeurs sociales en France, XVIᵉ–XVIIIᵉ siècle*. Paris: SEDES, 2001.

Ebert-Schifferer, S. *Natures mortes*, trans. D.-A. Canal. Paris: Citadelles and Mazenod, 1999.

Ehrard, J. *L'Idée de Nature en France dans la première moitié du XVIIIe siècle*, 2 vols. Chambéry: Imprimeries Réunies, 1963.

Elias, N. *La Civilisation des mœurs*. Paris: Calmann-Lévy, 1973.

Elias, N. *La Dynamique de l'Occident*. Paris: Calmann-Lévy, 1975.

Elias, N. *La Société de Cour*. Paris: Calmann-Lévy, 1974.

Elias, N. *Über den Prozess der Zivilisation. Soziogenetische und psychogenetische Untersuchungen*. Basel: Verlag Haus zum Falken, 1939.

Erman, M. (ed.). *Le goût dans tous ses états*. Berne: Peter Lang, 2009.

European Institute for the History and Cultures of Food (IEHCA), Villa i Tatti of Florence (The Harvard University Center for Italian Renaissance Studies), Mellon Foundation, and the National Library of France. *Food Bibliography*. http://www.foodbibliography.eu.

Febvre, L. "La sensibilité et l'histoire: Comment reconstituer la vie affective d'autrefois?" *Annales d'histoire sociale (1939–1941)* 3, no. 1/2 (January–June 1941): 5–20.

Femmes et corps: chaire études femmes, études de genre 2002–2003, ed. J. Dor. Liège: Ferulg, 2003.

Ferguson, P. P. *Accounting for Taste: The Triumph of French Cuisine*. Chicago: University of Chicago Press, 2004.

Ferguson, P. P. "The Senses of Taste." *The Senses in History: American Historical Review* 116, no. 2, (April 2011): 371–384.

Ferino-Pagden, S. (ed.). *I cinque sensi nell'arte. Immagini del sentire*, Milano, Leonardo Arte, 1996. Catalogue of the exhibition, Cremona, Centro culturale "Città di Cremona," Santa Maria della Pietà (September 21, 1996–January 12, 1997).

Ferrières, M. *Nourritures canailles*. Paris: Seuil, 2007.

Ferrières M. *Sacred Cow, Mad Cow: A History of Food Fears*, trans. J. Gladding. New York: Columbia University Press, 2006.

Ferry, L. *Homo Aestheticus. L'Invention du goût à l'âge démocratique*. Paris: Grasset and Fasquelle, 1990.

Ferry, L. *Le Sens du Beau. Aux origines de la culture contemporaine*. Paris: Le Livre de Poche, 2005.

Figeac, M. "À la recherche du goût dans les sources littéraires du siècle des Lumières," in Meyzie, *La gourmandise entre péché et plaisir*, 13–28.

Figeac, M. (ed.). *L'ancienne France au quotidien. Vie et choses de la vie sous l'Ancien Régime*. Paris: Armand Colin, 2007.

Fink, B. *Les liaisons savoureuses. Réflexions et pratiques culinaires au dix-huitième Siècle*. Saint-Étienne: Publications de l'Université de Saint-Étienne, 1995.

Fink, B. "Manger du regard," in *Cycnos* 11, no. 1, 1994. http://revel.unice.fr/cycnos/?id=1351 (accessed April 10, 2016).

Fischler, Cl. "Editorial: Magie, charmes et aliments," in Fischler, *Manger Magique*, 10–19.

Fischler, Cl. *L'homnivore*. Paris: Odile Jacob, 2001.

Fischler, Cl. (ed.). *Manger Magique. Aliments sorciers, croyances comestibles*. Paris: Autrement (Série Mutations/Mangeurs, no. 149), 1994.

Flandrin, J.-L. *Chronique de Platine. Pour une Gastronomie historique*. Paris: Odile Jacob Histoire, 1992.

Flandrin, J.-L. "De la diététique à la gastronomie, ou la libération de la gourmandise," in Flandrin and Montanari, *Histoire de l'alimentation*, 683–703

Flandrin, J.-L. "Dietary Choices and Culinary Technique, 1500–1800," in Flandrin and Montanari, *Food: A Culinary History*, 403–417.

Flandrin, J.-L. "From Dietetics to Gastronomy: The Liberation of the Gourmet," in Flandrin and Montanari, *Food: A Culinary History*, 418–432.

Flandrin, J.-L. "Histoire du goût," in Centre national interprofessionnel de l'Économie Laitière (CNIEL). *Lemangeur-ocha.com* (Observatoire CNIEL des Habitudes Alimentaires). http://www.lemangeur-ocha.com/uploads/tx_sm ilecontenusocha/01_Histoire_du_gout.pdf (accessed June 30, 2009).

Flandrin, J.-L. "La distinction par le goût," in Aries and Duby, *Histoire de la vie privée*, vol. 3, 261–302.

Flandrin, J.-L. "La diversité des goûts et des pratiques alimentaires en Europe du XVIe au XVIIIe siècle." *Revue d'histoire moderne et contemporaine* 30 (1983): 66–83.

Flandrin, J.-L. "Le goût et la nécessité: sur l'usage des graisses dans les cuisines d'Europe occidentale (XIVe-XVIIIe siècle)." *Annales. Économies, sociétés, civilisations* 38, no. 2 (1983): 369–401.

Flandrin, J.-L. *L'ordre des mets*. Paris: Odile Jacob, 2002.

Flandrin, J.-L. "Médecine et habitudes alimentaires anciennes," in Margolin and Sauzet, *Pratiques et Discours alimentaires à la Renaissance*, 85–95.

Flandrin, J.-L. "Pour une histoire du goût," in *La cuisine et la table*, ed. J. Ferniot and J. Le Goff, 13–19. Paris: Seuil, 1986.

Flandrin, J.-L. "Seasoning, Cooking, and Dietetics in the Late Middle Ages," in Flandrin and Montanari, *Food: A Culinary History*, 313–327.

Flandrin, J.-L., and M. Montanari (eds.). *Food: A Culinary History from Antiquity to the Present*, trans. A. Sonnenfeld. New York: Columbia University Press, 1999.

Flandrin, J.-L., and M. Montanari (eds.). *Histoire de l'alimentation*. Paris: Fayard, 1996.

Fontenay, E. de. *Le silence des bêtes. La philosophie à l'épreuve de l'animalité*. Paris: Fayard, 1998.

Foucault, M. *Histoire de la sexualité*. Paris: Gallimard, 1976–1984.

Foucault, M. *Les mots et les choses. Une archéologie des sciences humaines*. Paris: Gallimard, 1966.

France, P. *Politeness and Its Discontents: Problems in French Classical Culture*. Cambridge: Cambridge University Press, 1992.

Franco Junior, H. *Cocagne. Histoire d'un pays imaginaire*. Paris: Arkhê, 2013.

Franssen, M. "The Ocular Harpsichord of Louis-Bertrand Castel: The Science and Aesthetics of an Eighteenth-Century Cause Célèbre." *Tractrix*, no. 3 (1991): 15–77.

Freedman, P. (ed.). *Food: The History of Taste*. Berkeley: University of California Press, 2007.

Fritz, J.-M. *Paysages sonores du Moyen Âge. Le versant épistémologique*. Paris: Champion (coll. "Sciences, Techniques et civilisations du Moyen Âge à l'aube des Lumières"), 2000.

Gallegos, D., and A. McHoul. "'It's Not about Good Taste. It's about Tastes Good': Bourdieu and Campbell's Soup . . . and Beyond." *Senses and Society* 1, no. 2 (2006): 165–182.

Gelard M.-L. (ed.). *Usages et langages des sens*. Nancy: Presses Universitaires de Nancy/ Editions Universitaires de Lorraine ("Epistemologies du corps," ed. Andrieu B.), 2013.

Gélard, M.-L., and O. Sirost (eds.). "Langages des sens." *Communications*, no. 86 (2010).

Gélis, J. "Le corps, l'Église et le sacré," in *Histoire du corps*, ed. G. Vigarello, vol. 1, *De la Renaissance aux Lumières*, 17–107. Paris: Seuil, 2005.

Gigante, D. *Taste: A Literary History*. New Haven, CT: Yale University Press, 2005.

Gillet, Ph. *Le Goût et les mots. Littérature et gastronomie (14ᵉ–20ᵉ siècles)*. Paris: Payot, 1987.

Ginzburg, C. *Le sabbat des sorcières*. Paris: Gallimard, 1992.

Ginzburg, C. *Les Batailles nocturnes: Sorcellerie et rituels agraires en Frioul: XVIᵉ–XVIIᵉ siècles*. Lagrasse: Verdier, 1980 [1966].

Ginzburg, C. *Mythes emblèmes traces. Morphologie et histoire*, trans. M. Aymard et al. Paris: Verdier/poche, 2010 [1986].

Ginzburg, C. "Représentation: le mot, l'idée, la chose." *Annales: Économies, sociétés, civilisations* 46, no. 6 (1991): 1219–1234.

Girard, A. "Du manuscrit à l'imprimé: le livre de cuisine en Europe aux 15ᵉ et 16ᵉ siècles," in Margolin and Sauzet, *Pratiques et Discours alimentaires à la Renaissance*, 107–117.

Girard, A. "Le triomphe de 'La Cuisinière bourgeoise': Livres culinaires, cuisine et société en France aux XVIIᵉ et XVIIIᵉ siècles." *Revue d'histoire moderne et contemporaine* 24 (1977): 497–523.

Goldgar, A. "The Absolutism of Taste: Journalists as Censors in 18th-Century Paris," in Myers and Harris, *Censorship and the Control of Print*, 87–110.

Gossiaux, P.-P. *L'homme et la nature. Genèses de l'anthropologie à l'âge classique 1580–1750. Anthologie*. Brussels: De Boeck Université, 1993.

Grant, M. *Galen on Food and Diet*. London: Routledge, 2000.

Grieco, A. J. "Food and Social Classes in Late Medieval and Renaissance Italy," in Flandrin and Montanari, *Food: A Culinary History*, 302–312.

Grieco, A. J., O. Redon, and L. Tongiorgi Tomasi (eds.). *Le monde végétal (XIIᵉ–XVIIᵉ siècles). Savoirs et usages sociaux*. Saint-Denis: Presses Universitaires de Vincennes, 1993.

Grmek, M. D. (ed., with B. Fantini). *Histoire de la pensée médicale en Occident*, vol. 2, *De la Renaissance aux Lumières*. Paris: Seuil, 1997.

Grmek, M. D., and R. Bernabeo "La machine du corps," in Grmek, *Histoire de la pensée médicale en Occident*, vol. 2, 7–36.

Guéroult, M. *Descartes selon l'ordre des raisons*, 2 vols. Paris: Aubier-Montaigne, 1968.

Gutton, J.-P. *Bruits et sons dans notre histoire. Essai sur la reconstitution du paysage sonore*. Paris: Presses universitaires de France, 2000.

Habermas, J. *L'espace public. Avec une préface inédite de l'auteur*, trans. M. B. de Launay. Millau: Payot et Rivages, 2008.

Haechler, J. *L'Encyclopédie de Diderot et de . . . Jaucourt. Essai biographique sur le chevalier Louis de Jaucourt*. Paris: Honoré Champion, 1995.

Harvey, E. D. (ed.). *Sensible Flesh: On Touch in Early Modern Culture.* Philadelphia: University of Pennsylvania Press, 2003.

Havelange, C. "Livres de recettes et auto-médication. Figures de la guérison au XVIIIe siècle." *La Vie Wallonne* 63 (Liège 1989): 5–26.

Havelange, C. "Manger au XVIIIe siècle. Quelques éléments d'interprétation d'un discours médical." *Anthropozoologica*, second numbered special issue (1988): 155–161.

Havelange, C. *De l'œil et du monde. Une histoire du regard au seuil de la modernité.* Paris: Fayard, 1998.

Havelange, I., and S. Le Men. *Le magasin des enfants. La littérature pour la jeunesse (1750–1830).* Montreal: Bibliothèque Robert-Desnos, 1988.

Henneau, M.-E. "A corps perdu sur les chemins de Dieu. Le corps dans la quête mystique des cisterciennes liégeoises XIIIe–XVIIe s.," in *Femmes et corps*, ed. J. Dor, 75–93.

Holtz, G., and Th. Maus de Rolley (eds.). *Voyager avec le diable. Voyages réels, voyages imaginaires et discours démonologiques (XVe–XVIIe siècles).* Paris: Paris-Sorbonne University Press, 2008.

Houdard, S. "Le secret de Jean-Joseph Surin ou l'expérience de l'impensable damnation," in *Les Dossiers du Grihl.* http://dossiersgrihl.revues. org/3675 (accessed November 30, 2011). DOI 10.4000/dossiersgrihl.3675.

Houdard, S. *Les invasions mystiques. Spiritualités, hétérodoxies et censures au début de l'époque moderne.* Paris: Les Belles Lettres, 2008.

Houdard, S. *Les sciences du diable. Quatre discours sur la sorcellerie.* Paris: Ed. du Cerf, 1992.

Howes, D. (ed.). *Empire of the Senses: The Sensual Culture Reader.* Oxford: Berg (Sensory Formations Series), 2005.

Howes, D. "Charting the Sensorial Revolution." *Senses and Society* 1, no. 1 (2006): 113–126.

Howes, D. "Cross-talk between the Senses." *Senses and Society* 1, no. 3 (2006): 381–390.

Howes, D. "Présentation. Les sensations discrètes de la bourgeoisie." *Anthropologie et sociétés* 14, no. 2 (1990): 5–12.

Howes, D. *Sensual Relations: Engaging the Senses in Culture and Social Theory.* Ann Arbor: University of Michigan Press, 2003.

Howes, D., and C. Classen. *Ways of Sensing: Understanding the Senses in Society.* London: Routledge, 2014.

Howes, D., and M. Lalonde. "The History of Sensibilities: of the Standard of Taste in Mid-Eighteenth Century England and the Circulation of Smells in Post-Revolutionary France." *Dialectical Anthropology* 16, no. 2 (June 1991): 125–135.

Hyman, Ph., and M. Hyman. "La Chapelle and Massialot: An Eighteenth Century Feud." *Petits Propos Culinaires*, no. 2 (1979): 44–45; no. 8 (1981): 35–40.

Hyman, Ph., and M. Hyman. "Printing the Kitchen: French Cookbooks, 1480–1800," in Flandrin and Montanari, *Food: A Culinary History*, 394–402.

Hyman, Ph., and M. Hyman (eds.). *The French Cook: Englished by I.D.G., 1653.* Sheffield: Equinox (Southover Press Historic Cookery and Housekeeping), 2001.

I cinque sensi/The Five Senses, Micrologus, (special issue) 10 (2002).

Jacobs, M., and P. Scholliers. *Eating Out in Europe: Picnics, Gourmet Dining and Snacks since the Late Eighteenth Century.* Oxford: Berg, 2003.

Jacques-Chaquin, N., and M. Preaud. *Le Sabbat des sorciers en Europe (XVᵉ–XVIIIᵉ siècles)*, presented at the international colloquium E.N.S. Fontenay-Saint-Cloud, November 4–7. Grenoble: Jérôme Millon, 1993.

Jahan, S. *Les renaissances du corps en Occident. 1450–1650.* Paris: Belin, 2004.

Janson, H. W. *Apes and Ape Lore in the Middle Ages and the Renaissance.* London: Warburg Institute, 1952.

Jaquet, C. *Philosophie de l'Odorat.* Paris: Presses Universitaires de France, 2010.

Joubaud, C. *Le Corps humain dans la philosophie platonicienne: étude à partir du Timée*, preface by L. Brisson. Paris: Vrin, 1991.

Julien, F. *Eloge de la Fadeur, à partir de la pensée et de l'esthétique de la Chine.* Paris: P. Picquier, 1991.

Jütte, R. *A History of the Senses: From Antiquity to Cyberspace*, trans. J. Lynn. Cambridge: Polity Press, 2005.

Kafker, F. A. *The Encylopedists as a Group: A Collective Biography of the Authors of the* Encyclopédie. Oxford: Voltaire Foundation, 1996.

Kafker, F. A., with S. L. Kafker. *The Encyclopedists as Individuals: A Biographical Dictionary of the Authors of the* Encyclopédie. Oxford: Voltaire Foundation, 1988.

Kalof, L., and W. Bynum. *A Cultural History of the Human Body in the Renaissance*, vol. 3. Oxford: Berg, 2010.

Kambouchner, D. *Descartes et la philosophie morale.* Paris: Hermann, 2008.

Kambouchner, D. *L'homme des passions*, 2 vols. Paris: Albin Michel, 1995.

Karila-Cohen, K., and F. Quellier (eds.). *Le corps du gourmand. D'Héraclès à Alexandre le Bienheureux.* Rennes: Presses Universitaires de Rennes ("Table des hommes"), 2012.

Kelly, D. *Yuck! The Nature and Moral Significance of Disgust.* Cambridge, MA: MIT Press, 2011.

Kermode, J. F. "The Banquet of Senses." *Bulletin of John Rylands Library Manchester* 44, no. 1 (September 1961): 68–99.

Kisby, F. "Introduction: Urban History, Musicology and Cities and Towns in Renaissance Europe," in *Music and Musicians in Renaissance Cities and Town*, ed. F. Kisby, 1–13. Cambridge: Cambridge University Press, 2001.

Knabe, P.-E. "Esthétique et art culinaire." *Aliments et cuisine. Dix-huitième siècle*, no. 15 (1983): 125–136.

Knowles, D., and J. Skorupski (eds.). *Virtue and Taste: Essays on Politics, Ethics and Aesthetics.* Oxford: Blackwell, 1993.

Kolnai, A. *On Disgust.* Chicago: Open Court, 2004 [1929].

Korsmeyer, C. *Making Sense of Taste: Food and Philosophy.* Ithaca, NY: Cornell University Press, 1999.

Korsmeyer, C. *Savoring Disgust: The Foul and the Fair in Aesthetics.* Oxford: Oxford University Press, 2011.

Korsmeyer, C. (ed.). *The Taste Culture Reader: Experiencing Food and Drink.* Oxford: Berg (Sensory Formations Series), 2005.

Krampl, U., R. Beck, and E. Retaillaud-Bajac (eds.). *Les cinq sens de la ville du Moyen Âge à nos jours.* Tours: Presses universitaires François-Rabelais, 2013.

Kulbrandstad Walker, S. T. "Appetites: Food, Eating and the Senses in Sixteenth-Century Italian Art," in Sanger and Kulbrandstad Walker, *Sense and the Senses in Early Modern Art*, 109–128.

Kümin, B. (ed.). *A Cultural History of Food in the Early Modern Age*, vol. 3. London: Berg, 2012.

La Varenne, F.-P. de. *Le Cuisinier françois. D'après l'édition de 1651*, preface by M. Hyman and Ph. Hyman. Houilles: Manucius, 2001.

Laplantine, F. *Le social et le sensible. Introduction à une anthropologie modale*. Paris: Téraèdre, 2005.

Laurendon, G. L. (ed.). *L'art de la cuisine française au XVIIe siècle (L.S.R., L'art de bien traiter; Pierre de Lune, Le cuisinier; Audiger, La maison réglée)*. Paris: Payot (Les grands classiques de la gastronomie), 1995.

Laurioux, B. (ed.). "Cuisine et médecine au Moyen Âge." *Cahiers de Recherches Médiévales*, special issue, no. 13 (2006): 223–266.

Laurioux, B. *Gastronomie, humanisme et société à Rome au milieu du XVe siècle. Autour du De honesta voluptate de Platina*. Florence: Sismel-Edizioni del Galluzzo (Micrologus Library), 2006.

Laurioux, B. *Manger au Moyen Âge*. Paris: Hachette Littératures, 2002.

Lawrence C., and S. Shapin (eds.). *Science Incarnate: Historical Embodiments of Natural Knowledge*. Chicago: University of Chicago Press, 1998.

Le Breton, D. "Du goût en bouche au goût de vivre," in *Le goût dans tous ses états*, edited by M. Erman, 5–19. Berne: Peter Lang, 2009.

Le Breton, D. *La Saveur du monde. Une anthropologie des sens*. Paris: Métailié, 2006.

Le Brun, J. "Mutations de la notion de martyr au XVIIe siècle d'après les biographies spirituelles féminines," in *Sainteté et martyre dans les religions du livre*, ed. J. Marx, 77–90. Brussels: Editions de l'ULB ("Problèmes d'histoire du christianisme," no. 19), 1989.

Le Cuisinier françois, ed. J.-L. Flandrin, Ph. Hyman, and M. Hyman. Paris: Montalba, 1983.

Le Guérer, A. "Le déclin de l'olfactif. Mythe ou réalité?" *Anthropologie et sociétés* 14, no. 2 (1990): 25–45.

Le Guérer, A. *Les Pouvoirs de l'Odeur*. Paris: Odile Jacob, 2002 [1988].

Le Ru, V. "La méthode des éléments de D'Alembert dans *l'Encyclopédie.*" *Recherches sur Diderot et sur l'Encyclopédie*, no. 21 (1996): 91–97.

Le siècle de Vatel, Dix-septième siècle, no. 217 (2002), no. 4 (special issue)

Lebrun, F. *Le XVIIe siècle*. Paris: Armand Colin, 2003.

Lebrun, Fr. *Se soigner autrefois: médecins, saints et sorciers aux 17e et 18e siècles*. Paris: Temps actuels/Messidor, 1983.

Lebrun, J. *La jouissance et le trouble. Recherches sur la littérature chrétienne de l'âge classique*. Geneva: Droz, 2004.

Leclercq, P. (ed.). *La joyeuse entrée du prince-évêque de Liège Robert de Berghes*. Brussels: Le Livre Timperman (Gastronomie historique), 2009.

Lecoq, A.-M. *La Querelle des Anciens et des Modernes XVIIe–XVIIIe siècles*, foreword by M. Fumaroli. Paris: Gallimard, 2001.

Lemke, H. *Ethik des Essens. Eine Einführung in die Gastrosophie*. Berlin: Akademie Verlag, 2007.

Lévi-Strauss, Cl. *Le cru et le cuit*. Paris: Plon, 2004 [1964].

Livres en bouche. Cinq siècles d'art culinaire français, catalog of the exposition presented at the Bibliothèque de l'Arsenal, November 21, 2001–February 17, 2001. Paris: Hermann, 2001.

Losfeld, C. *Politesse, morale et construction sociale. Pour une histoire des traités de comportements (1670–1788)*. Paris: Champion, 2011.

Magendie, M. *La politesse mondaine et les théories de l'honnêteté, en France, au 17ᵉ siècle, de 1600 à 1660*. Paris: Presses universitaires de France, 1925.

Mandrou, R. *Introduction à la France moderne (1500–1640). Essai de psychologie historique*. Paris: Albin Michel, 1998.

Mandrou, R. *La France aux XVIIᵉ et XVIIIᵉ siècles*, ed. M. Cottret. Paris: Presses universitaires de France, 1993.

Mandrou, R. *Magistrats et sorciers en France au XVIIᵉ siècle. Une analyse de psychologie historique*. Paris: Plon, 1968.

Mandrou, R. *Possession et sorcellerie au XVIIᵉ siècle. Textes inédits*. Paris: Fayard, 1979.

Marenco, Cl. *Manières de table, modèles de mœurs: 17ᵉ–20ᵉ siècle*. Cachan: E.N.S.-Cachan, 1992.

Margolin, J.-C., and R. Sauzet (eds.). *Pratiques et Discours alimentaires à la Renaissance*, Actes du colloque de Tours (1979). Paris: Maisonneuve et Larose, 1982.

Marty, F. *Sentir et goûter. Les sens dans les "Exercices spirituels" de saint Ignace*. Paris: Ed. du Cerf, 2005.

Marx, J. (ed.). *Sainteté et martyre dans les religions du livre*. Brussels: Ed. de l'ULB ("Problèmes d'histoire du christianisme," no. 19), 1989.

Maurice, K., and O. Mayr (eds.). *The Clockwork Universe: German Clocks and Automata, 1550–1650*. Washington, DC: Smithsonian Institution, 1980.

Mauzi, R. *L'idée du Bonheur dans la littérature et la pensée françaises au XVIIIᵉ siècle*. Paris: Armand Colin, 1960.

Mayr, O. *Authority, Liberty, and Automatic Machinery in Early Modern Europe*. Baltimore, MD: Johns Hopkins University Press, 1986.

Mazauric, S. *Savoirs et Philosophie à Paris dans la première moitié du XVIIᵉ siècle. Les Conférences du bureau d'adresse de Théophraste Renaudot (1633–1642)*. Paris: Publication de la Sorbonne, 1997.

Mazauric, S. *Théophraste Renaudot. De la petite fille velue et autres conférences du Bureau d'Adresse (1632–1642)*. Langres: Klincksieck, 2004.

Mennell, S. *All Manners of Food: Eating and Taste in England and France from the Middle Ages to the Present*. Oxford: Basil Blackwell, 1985.

Mennell, S. *Lettre d'un pâtissier anglais, et autres contributions à une polémique gastronomique du XVIIIᵉ siècle*. Exeter: University of Exeter Printing Unit, 1981.

Menninghaus, W. *Disgust: Theory and History of a Strong Sensation*, trans. H. Eiland and J. Golb. Albany: State University of New York Press, 2003.

Mervaud, Ch. *Voltaire à table. Plaisir du corps, plaisir de l'esprit*. Paris: Desjonquères, 1998.

Meuret, I. *L'anorexie créatrice*. Paris: Klincksieck, 2006.

Meyzie, Ph. (ed.). "La gourmandise entre péché et plaisir." *Lumières*, no. 11 (1st semester 2008).

Meyzie, Ph. *La Table du Sud-Ouest et l'émergence des cuisines régionales (1700–1850)*. Rennes: Presses Universitaires de Rennes, 2007.

Meyzie, Ph. *L'alimentation en Europe à l'époque moderne. Manger et boire XVIe s.–XIXe s.* Paris: Armand Colin, 2010.

Michel, D. *Vatel et la naissance de la gastronomie*. Paris: Fayard, 2000.

Miller, W. I. *The Anatomy of Disgust*. Cambridge, MA: Harvard University Press, 1997.

Mintz, S. W. *Sweetness and Power: The Place of Sugar in Modern History*. New York: Penguin Books, 1985.

Montanari, M. *Entre la poire et le fromage ou comment un proverbe peut raconter l'histoire*. Paris: Agnès Viénot, 2009.

Montanari, M. *La faim et l'abondance. Histoire de l'alimentation en Europe*, trans. M. Aymard. Paris: Seuil, 1995.

Montanari, M., and I. Prosperi. "Entre le ventre et la gueule, dans la culture médiéval," in Karila-Cohen and Quellier, *Le corps du gourmand*, 37–55.

Montandon A. (ed.). *Bibliographie des traités de savoir-vivre en Europe du Moyen Âge à nos jours*. Clermont-Ferrand: Association des publications de la faculté des lettres et sciences humaines de Clermont-Ferrand (Université Blaise Pascal), 1995.

Montandon, A. (ed.). *Dictionnaire raisonné de la politesse et du savoir-vivre du Moyen Âge à nos jours*. Paris. Seuil, 1995.

Montandon, A. (ed.). *Du Goût, de la Conversation et des Femmes* Clermont-Ferrand: Association des Publications de la Faculté des Lettres et Sciences Humaines de Clermont-Ferrand (Université Blaise-Pascal), 1994.

Montandon, A. (ed.). *Pour une histoire des traités de savoir-vivre en Europe*. Clermont-Ferrand: Association des Publications de la Faculté des Lettres et Sciences humaines de Clermont-Ferrand (Université Blaise-Pascal), 1994.

Montandon, A. (ed.). *Traités de savoir-vivre italiens (I Trattati di saper-vivere in Italia)*, Clermont-Ferrand, Association des Publications de la Faculté des Lettres et Sciences humaines de Clermont-Ferrand (Université Blaise-Pascal), 1993.

Mortier, R., and H. Hasquin (eds.). *Autour du Père Castel et du clavecin oculaire*. Brussels: Ed. de l'ULB, 1995.

Moshenska, J. *Feeling Pleasures: The Sense of Touch in Renaissance England*. Oxford: Oxford University Press, 2014.

Moulin, L. *Les liturgies de la table. Une histoire culturelle du manger et du boire*. Anvers: Fonds Mercator, 1988.

Muchembled, R. *La Sorcière au Village (XVe–XVIIIe siècle)*. Paris: Julliard/Gallimard, 1979.

Muchembled, R. *Le roi et la sorcière. L'Europe des bûchers (XVe–XVIIIe siècle)*. Paris: Desclée, 1993.

Muchembled, R. *Les derniers bûchers. Un village de Flandre et ses sorcières sous Louis XIV*. Paris: Ramsay, 1981.

Muchembled, R. *Société, cultures et mentalités dans la France moderne XVIe–XVIIIe siècle*, 3rd ed. Paris: Armand Colin, 2003 [1990].

Muchembled, R. *Une histoire du diable, XIIe–XXe siècles*. Paris: Seuil, 2000.

Murray Schaffer, R. *The Tuning of the World.* New York: Knopf, 1977.

Myers, R., and M. Harris (eds.). *Censorship and the Control of Print in England and France 1600–1910.* Winchester: St Paul's Bibliographies, 1992.

N'Diaye, C. (ed.). *La Gourmandise. Délices d'un péché.* Paris: Autrement (Série Mutations/Mangeurs), no. 140 (1993).

Nordenfalk, C. "The Five Senses in Late Medieval and Renaissance Art," *Journal of the Warburg and Courtauld Institutes* 48 (1985): 1–22.

North, M. *Material Delight and the Joy of Living: Cultural Consumption in the Age of Enlightenment in Germany,* trans. P. Selwyn. Aldershot: Ashgate, 2008 [2003].

O'Rourke Boyle, M. *Senses of Touch: Human Dignity and Deformity from Michelangelo to Calvin,* Leiden: Brill, 1998.

Onfray, M. *La raison gourmande.* Paris: Grasset, 1995.

Onfray, M. *Le ventre des philosophes: critique de la raison diététique.* Paris: Grasset, 1989.

Parasecoli, F., and P. Scholliers (eds.). *A Cultural History of Food,* 6 vols. London: Berg, 2012.

Paresys, I. (ed.). *Paraître et apparences en Europe occidentale. Du Moyen Âge à nos jours.* Villeneuve d'Ascq: Presses universitaires du Septentrion, 2008.

Parmentier, B. *Le siècle des moralistes. De Montaigne à La Bruyère.* Paris: Seuil, 2000.

Pastoureau, M. *Bleu. Histoire d'une couleur.* Paris: Seuil, 2006 [2000].

Pastoureau, M. *Le cochon. Histoire d'un cousin mal-aimé.* Paris: Gallimard, 2009.

Pastoureau, M. *L'ours: histoire d'un roi déchu.* Paris: Seuil, 2007.

Peterson, S. T. *Acquired Taste: The French Origins of Modern Cooking.* Ithaca, NY: Cornell University Press, 1994.

Peterson, S. T. *The Cookbook That Changed the World: The Origins of Modern Cuisine.* London: NPI Media Group, 2006.

Pilcher, J. M. (ed.). *The Oxford Handbook of Food History.* Oxford: Oxford University Press, 2012.

Pinkard, S. *A Revolution in Taste: The Rise of French Cuisine, 1650–1800.* Cambridge: Cambridge University Press, 2009.

Poirier, J. (ed.). *Histoire des mœurs,* 3 vols. Paris: Gallimard (La Pléiade), 1990–1991.

Poirrier, Ph. *Les enjeux de l'histoire culturelle.* Paris: Seuil, 2004.

Poirrier, Ph. (ed.). *L'histoire culturelle: un "tournant mondial" dans l'historiographie?,* afterword by R. Chartier. Dijon: Éditions Universitaires de Dijon, 2008.

Poutrin, I. *Le voile et la plume. Autobiographie et sainteté féminine dans l'Espagne moderne.* Madrid: Casa de Velázquez/Ciudad Universitaria, 1995.

Quellier, F. *Des fruits et des hommes. L'arboriculture fruitière en Île-de-France (vers 1600– vers 1800).* Rennes: Presses Universitaires de Rennes, 2003.

Quellier, F. *Gourmandise. Histoire d'un péché capital,* Paris: Armand Colin, 2010.

Quellier, F. *La Table des Français. Une histoire culturelle (XVᵉ–début XIXᵉ siècle).* Rennes: Presses Universitaires de Rennes, 2007.

Quiviger, F. *The Sensory World of Italian Renaissance Art.* London: Reaktion Books, 2010.

Raga, E. "Bon mangeur, mauvais mangeur. Pratiques alimentaires et critique sociale dans l'oeuvre de Sidoine Apollinaire et ses contemporains." *Revue belge de philologie et d'histoire* 87 (2009): 165–196.

Rancière, J. *Le partage du sensible. Esthétique et politique.* Paris: La fabrique, 2000.

Redon, O., and B. Laurioux. "Histoire de l'alimentation entre Moyen Âge et Temps modernes. Regards sur trente ans de recherches," in Redon, Sallmann, and Steinberg, *Le Désir et le Goût*, 53–96.

Redon, O., L. Sallmann, and S. Steinberg (eds.). *Le Désir et le Goût. Une autre histoire (XIIIe–XVIIIe siècles).* Saint-Denis: Presses Universitaires de Vincennes, 2005.

Revel, J. "Les usages de la civilité," in Aries and Duby, *Histoire de la vie privée*, vol. 3, 167–208.

Revel, J.-F. *Un festin en paroles. Histoire littéraire de la sensibilité gastronomique de l'Antiquité à nos jours.* Paris: Plon, 1995 [1978].

Rey, A. *Antoine Furetière. Un précurseur des Lumières sous Louis XIV.* Paris: Fayard, 2006.

Rey, A. (ed.). *Dictionnaire culturel en langue française.* Paris: Le Robert, 2005.

Rey, R. *Histoire de la douleur.* Paris: La Découverte/Poche, 2000 [1993].

Roche, D. *La culture des apparences. Une histoire du vêtement XVIIe–XVIIIe siècle.* Paris: Fayard, 1989.

Roche, D. *La France des Lumières.* Paris: Fayard, 1993.

Romagnoli, D. "La courtoisie dans la ville: un modèle complexe," in Romagnoli, *La Ville et la Cour*, 25–88.

Romagnoli, D. (ed.). *La Ville et la Cour. Des bonnes et des mauvaises manières.* Paris: Fayard, 1995 [1991].

Romagnoli, D. "'Mind Your Manners': Etiquette at the Table," in Flandrin and Montanari, *Food: A Culinary History*, 328–338.

Romeyer Dherbey, G. (ed.). *Corps et âme. Sur le De Anima d'Aristote* études réunies par Ch. Viano. Paris: Vrin, 1996.

Romeyer Dherbey, G. "La construction de la théorie aristotélicienne du sentir," in Romeyer Dherbey, *Corps et âme*, 127–147.

Rosé, I. "Le moine glouton et son corps dans les discours cénobitiques réformateurs (début du IXe siècle–début du XIIIe siècle)," in Karila-Cohen and Quellier, *Le corps du gourmand*, 191–219.

Rosenfeld, S. *A Revolution in Language: The Problem of Signs in Late 18th-Century France.* Palo Alto, CA: Stanford University Press, 2001.

Rosenfeld, S. *Common Sense: A Political History.* Cambridge, MA: Harvard University Press, 2011.

Rosenfeld, S. "Deaf Men on Trial: Language and Deviancy in Late Eighteenth-Century France," in *Faces of Monstrosity in Enlightenment Thought, Eighteenth-Century Life* 21, no. 2 (May 1997): 157–175.

Rouby, C., B. Schaal, D. Dubois, R. Gervais, and A. Holley (eds.). *Olfaction, Taste and Cognition.* Cambridge: Cambridge University Press, 2002.

Roy-Garibal, M. *Le Parnasse et le Palais. L'œuvre de Furetière et la genèse du premier dictionnaire encyclopédique en langue française (1649–1690).* Paris: Honoré Champion, 2006.

Sabban, F., and S. Serventi. *La Gastronomie au Grand Siècle. 100 recettes de France et d'Italie.* Paris: Stock, 1998.

Sanger, A. E., and S. T. Kulbrandstad Walker. "Introduction: Making Sense of the Senses," in Sanger and Kulbrandstad Walker, *Sense and the Senses in Early Modern Art*, 1–16.

Sanger, A. E., and S. T. Kulbrandstad Walker (eds.). *Sense and the Senses in Early Modern Art and Cultural Practice*. Farnham-Burlington: Ashgate, 2012.

Schlanger, J. E. *Les métaphores de l'organisme*. Paris: Vrin, 1971.

Scholar, R. *The Je-Ne-Sais-Quoi in Early Modern Europe: Encounters with a Certain Something*. Oxford: Oxford University Press, 2006.

Scholliers, P. (ed.). *Food, Drink and Identity: Cooking, Eating and Drinking in Europe since the Middle Ages*. Oxford: Berg, 2001.

Scholliers, P. "The Many Rooms in the House: Research on Past Foodways in Modern Europe," in Claflin and Scholliers, *Writing Food History*, 59–71.

Scholliers, P. "Twenty-five Years of Studying un Phénomène Social Total: Food History Writing on Europe in the Nineteenth and Twentieth Centuries." *Food, Culture and Society* 10, no. 3 (2007): 449–471.

Schuster Cordone, C. *Le crépuscule du corps. Images de la vieillesse féminine*. Paris: Infolio, 2009.

Seguin, M. S. *Science et religion dans la pensée française du XVIIIᵉ siècle: le mythe du Déluge universel*. Paris: Honoré Champion, 2001.

Serres, M. *Les cinq sens*. Paris: Grasset, 1985.

Shapin, S. "The Philosopher and the Chicken. On the Dietetics of Disembodied Knowledge," in Lawrence and Shapin, *Science Incarnate*, 21–50.

Silver, S. R. "Locke's Pineapple and the History of Taste: (John Locke) (Critical Essay)." *Eighteenth Century: Theory and Interpretation* 49, no. 1 (2008): 43–65. http://www.highbeam.com/doc/1G1-179348621.html (accessed February 17, 2010).

Smith, M. "Producing Sense, Consuming Sense, Making Sense: Perils and Prospects for Sensory History," *Journal of Social History*, 40/4 (Summer 2007): 841–858.

Smith, M. *Sensing the Past: Seeing, Hearing, Smelling, Tasting, and Touching in History*. Berkeley: University of California Press. 2007.

Smith, Woodruff D. *Consumption and the Making of Respectability, 1600–1800*. New York: Routledge, 2002.

Spang, R. *The Invention of the Restaurant: Paris and Modern Gastronomic Culture*. Cambridge, MA: Harvard University Press, 2000.

Spary, E. "Making a Science of Taste: The Revolution, the Learned Life, and the Invention of Gastronomie," in *Consumers and Luxury: Consumer Culture in Europe, 1650–1850*, ed. M. Berg and H. Clifford, 170–182, Manchester: ManchesterUniversity Press, 1999.

Spary, E. "Ways with Food." *Journal of Contemporary History* 40, no. 4 (2005): 763–771.

Spary, E., and U. Klein (eds.). *Between Market and Laboratory: Materials and Expertise in Early Modern Europe*. Chicago: University of Chicago Press, 2009.

Spary, E. *Eating the Enlightenment: Food and the Sciences in Paris, 1670–1760*. Chicago: University of Chicago Press, 2012.

Spary, E. *Feeding France: New Sciences of Food, 1760–1815*. Cambridge: Cambridge University Press, 2014.

Spary, E. *Utopia's Garden: French Natural History from Old Regime to Revolution*. Chicago: University of Chicago Press, 2000.

Staum, M. *Cabanis: Enlightenment and Medical Philosophy in the French Revolution*. Princeton, NJ: Princeton University Press, 1980.

Steinmetz, R. "Conceptions du corps à travers l'acte alimentaire aux XVIIᵉ et XVIIIᵉ siècles." *Revue d'histoire moderne et contemporaine* 35 (1988): 3–35.

Stiénon, V. *La Littérature des Physiologies. Sociopoétique d'un genre panoramique (1830–1845).* Paris: Classiques Garnier, 2012.

Stiénon, V. "Lectures littéraires du document physiologique. Méthodes et perspectives." *MethIS—Méthodes et Interdisciplinarité en Sciences humaines*, no. 2 (2009): 71–85.

Strivay, L. *Enfants sauvages. Approches anthropologiques.* Paris: Gallimard, 2006.

Summers, D. *The Judgment of Sense: Renaissance Naturalism and the Rise of Aesthetics.* Cambridge: Cambridge University Press, 1990.

Takats, S. *The Expert Cook in Enlightenment France.* Baltimore, MD: Johns Hopkins University Press, 2011.

Tarot, C. "De l'Antiquité au monde Moderne: Le sel du baptême. Avatar d'un rite, complexité d'un symbole." *Le Sucre et le Sel, Journal d'agriculture traditionnelle et de botanique appliquée* 35, no. 35 (1988): 281–302.

Telfer, E. *Food for Thought: Philosophy and Food.* London: Routledge, 1996.

Tervarent, G. de. *Attributs et symboles dans l'art profane: dictionnaire d'un langage perdu (1450–1600).* Geneva: Droz, 1997.

"The Senses in History." *American Historical Review* 116, no. 2 (April 2011).

Thomas, K. *Man and the Natural World: Changing Attitudes in England 1500–1800.* London: Allen Lane, 1983.

Tomasik, T. J., and J. M. Vitullo (eds.). *At the Table: Metaphorical and Material Cultures of Food in Medieval and Early Modern Europe.* Turnhout: Brepols, 2007.

Vaquero, S. *Baltasar Graciàn, la civilité ou l'art de vivre en société.* Paris: Presses universitaires de France, 2009.

Varela, F., E. Thomson, and E. Rosch. *The Embodied Mind: Cognitive Science and Human Experience.* Cambridge, MA: MIT Press, 1991.

Viala, A. *La France galante. Essai historique sur une catégorie culturelle, de ses origines jusqu'à la Révolution.* Paris: Presses universitaires de France, 2008.

Viallon-Schoneveld, M. (ed.). *Le boire et le manger au XVIᵉ siècle. Actes du Colloque du Puy-en-Velay.* Saint-Étienne: Publications de l'Université de Saint-Étienne, 2004.

Vicaire, G. *Bibliographie Gastronomique.* Paris: P. Rouquette et Fils, 1890.

Vigarello, G. (ed.). *Histoire du corps*, vol. 1, *De la Renaissance aux Lumières.* Paris: Seuil, 2005.

Vigarello, G. *Histoire de la beauté. Le corps et l'art d'embellir de la Renaissance à nos jours.* Paris: Seuil, 2004.

Vigarello, G. *Le propre et le sale. L'hygiène du corps depuis le Moyen Âge.* Paris: Seuil, 1985.

Vigarello, G. *Le sain et le malsain: santé et mieux-être depuis le Moyen Âge.* Paris: Seuil, 1993.

Vigliano, T. *Humanisme et juste milieu au siècle de Rabelais. Essai de critique illusoire.* Paris: Les Belles Lettres, 2009.

Vinge, L. *The Five Senses: Studies in a Literary Tradition*, Acta regiae societatis humanorum litterarum Ludensis, vol. 72. Lund: Gleerup, 1975.

Von Hoffmann, V. *Goûter le monde. Une histoire culturelle du goût aux temps modernes.* Brussels: P.I.E. Peter Lang ("L'Europe alimentaire"), 2013.

Von Hoffmann, V. "Le goût et le toucher de la ville. La perception sensible de la ville par les 'sensorialités basses': l'exemple des *Mémoires* de Casanova," in Krampl, Beck, and Retaillaud-Bajac, *Les cinq sens de la ville*, 131–138.

Von Hoffmann, V. "Le Sensible et le Culinaire. Les Prémisses d'une artification au XVIIIe siècle," in *L'Oeuvre culinaire. Art de cuisiner et cuisines d'artistes, 18ᵉ–21ᵉ siècle*, edited by J. Csergo and F. Desbuissons. Paris: Le Manuscrit (coll. Gastronomica—Food Library), 2016.

Weiss, A. S. *Comment cuisiner un phénix*. Paris: Mercure de France, 2004.

Weiss, A. S. *Feast and Folly: Cuisine, Intoxication, and the Poetics of the Sublime*. Albany: State University of New York Press, 2002.

West-Sooby, J. (ed.). *Consuming Culture: The Arts of the French Table*. Newark: University of Delaware Press, 2004.

Wheaton, Barbara Ketcham. *Savoring the Past: The French Kitchen and Table from 1300 to 1789*, Philadelphia: University of Pennsylvania Press, 1983.

Wilgaux, J. "Gourmands et gloutons dans les sources physiognomoniques antiques," in Karila-Cohen and Quellier, *Le corps du gourmand*, 23–36.

Wintroub, M. *A Savage Mirror: Power, Identity, and Knowledge in Early Modern France*. Stanford, CA: Stanford University Press, 2006.

Yeomans, W., and A. Derville. "Gourmandise et gourmandise spirituelle," in *Dictionnaire de spiritualité ascétique et mystique*, vol. 6., 616–626. Paris: Beauchesne, 1967.

Zarka, Y. Ch. "Préface. Les deux voies du materialism," in Audidière et al., *Matérialistes français*, vii–xv.

Index

Page numbers in *italics* indicate illustrations.

VIKTORIA VON HOFFMANN is a postdoctoral researcher at the University of Liège.

Studies in Sensory History

The University of Illinois Press
is a founding member of the
Association of American University Presses.

———————————————————————

University of Illinois Press
1325 South Oak Street
Champaign, IL 61820-6903
www.press.uillinois.edu